BRITISH ACADEMY

LIBRARY

CATHARINE MACAULAY AND MERCY OTIS WARREN

Catharine Macaulay and Mercy Otis Warren

The Revolutionary Atlantic and the Politics of Gender

KATE DAVIES

OXFORD
UNIVERSITY PRESS

OXFORD
UNIVERSITY PRESS

Great Clarendon Street, Oxford OX2 6DP

Oxford University Press is a department of the University of Oxford.
It furthers the University's objective of excellence in research, scholarship,
and education by publishing worldwide in

Oxford New York

Auckland Cape Town Dar es Salaam Hong Kong Karachi
Kuala Lumpur Madrid Melbourne Mexico City Nairobi
New Delhi Shanghai Taipei Toronto

With offices in

Argentina Austria Brazil Chile Czech Republic France Greece
Guatemala Hungary Italy Japan Poland Portugal Singapore
South Korea Switzerland Thailand Turkey Ukraine Vietnam

Oxford is a registered trade mark of Oxford University Press
in the UK and in certain other countries

Published in the United States
by Oxford University Press Inc., New York

© Kate Davies 2005

The moral rights of the author have been asserted
Database right Oxford University Press (maker)

First published 2005

All rights reserved. No part of this publication may be reproduced,
stored in a retrieval system, or transmitted, in any form or by any means,
without the prior permission in writing of Oxford University Press,
or as expressly permitted by law, or under terms agreed with the appropriate
reprographics rights organization. Enquiries concerning reproduction
outside the scope of the above should be sent to the Rights Department,
Oxford University Press, at the address above

You must not circulate this book in any other binding or cover
and you must impose the same condition on any acquirer

British Library Cataloguing in Publication Data
Data available

Library of Congress Cataloging in Publication Data
Davies, Kate, 1973–
Catharine Macaulay and Mercy Otis Warren : the revolutionary Atlantic and the
politics of gender / Kate Davies.
p. cm.
Includes index.
ISBN 0–19–928110–6 (acid-free paper)
1. Macaulay, Catharine, 1731–1791. 2. Warren, Mercy (Otis) 1728–1814.
3. Historiography—English-speaking countries—History—18th century.
4. United States–History–Revolution, 1775–1783—Historiography. 5. Women—
English-speaking countries—Intellectual life. 6. Historians—United States—Biography.
7. Historians—Great Britain—Biography. I. Title.
DA3.M25D38 2005   941.07'3082–dc22   2005024337

Typeset by Newgen Imaging Systems (P) Ltd., Chennai, India
Printed in Great Britain
on acid-free paper by
Biddles Ltd., King's Lynn, Norfolk

ISBN 0–19–928110–6   978–0–19–928110–7

1 3 5 7 9 10 8 6 4 2

Acknowledgements

To quote from the Thomas Hollis Diary; Thomas Hollis marginalia; correspondence between Catharine Macaulay and Thomas Hollis; Catharine Macaulay and Edward Dilly; Thomas Hollis and Timothy Hollis, and the Samuel Stockton letters, I am grateful to the Houghton Library, Harvard. To cite the correspondence of Elizabeth Montagu, Mercy Otis Warren, and Elbridge Gerry, I am grateful to the Huntington Library. For quotations from Catharine Macaulay Papers, I am grateful to the Gilder Lehrman Collection, New York Historical Society. For quotations from the manuscripts of Catharine Macaulay's *History of England from the Accession of James I to that of the Brunswick Line* and *The History of England from the Revolution to the Present Time in a Series of Letters to a Friend* and letters between Catharine Macaulay and Lord Buchan, I am grateful to the New York Historical Society. To quote from letters between Catharine Macaulay and Samuel Adams, I am grateful to the Lenox Foundation, New York Public Library. To quote from the Mercy Warren Papers; the Warren–Adams Papers; the Winslow–Warren Papers; Josiah Quincy's Journal; the Thomas Hollis Papers, and the Hannah Winthrop–Mercy Warren correspondence, I am grateful to the Massachusetts Historical Society. For quotations from the Matthew Ridley Papers, I am grateful to the Boston Public Library. To cite the journal of Henry Marchant, I am grateful to the Rhode Island Historical Society. To quote from the correspondence of Catharine Macaulay and Benjamin Franklin, I am grateful to the American Philosophical Society. To quote from the correspondence of Hesther Thrale and Elizabeth Montagu, I am grateful to the John Rylands University Library, Manchester. To cite the correspondence of John Wilkes, I am grateful to the British Library.

For permission to reproduce Figures 16, 17, 18, 19, 20, 21, 22, 23, and 24, I am grateful to the Library of Congress department of prints and photographs. For permission to reproduce Figures 15 and 25, I am grateful to the Lewis Walpole Library. For permission to reproduce Figures 5 and 6, I am grateful to the National Portrait Gallery, London. For permission to reproduce Figure 3, I am grateful to the John Rylands

University Library, Manchester. For permission to reproduce Figure 4, I am grateful to the Houghton Library, Harvard. For permission to reproduce Figure 8, I am grateful to the Metropolitan Museum of Art, New York. For permission to reproduce Figure 10, I am grateful to Dickinson College Library, Pennsylvania. For permission to reproduce Figure 11, I am grateful to the Winterthur Museum. For permission to reproduce Figure 13, I am grateful to the Virginia Museum of Fine Arts. For permission to reproduce Figure 14, I am grateful to the Tate Gallery, London.

A Clark Library Fellowship and a Massachusetts Historical Society Fellowship made international research in the book's early stages possible. I am grateful to the boards of trustees of both institutions. For monies and grants that enabled me to travel to other libraries, I am grateful to the American Society for Eighteenth Century Studies; the Huntington Library; the Arts and Humanities Research Board, and the University of York F. R. Leavis fund. I am grateful to Louis Cataldo of the Barnstable County Archives for answering some of my queries about the Otises. For helpful information about the Brownlow Street Lying-in Hospital I am grateful to the Library of the Royal College of Midwives.

Research for this book was conducted in a number of different libraries and has benefited from the support and interest of many curators and librarians. I would particularly like to thank the staff of the Houghton Library, the Massachusetts Historical Society, the John Rylands University Library, Manchester, and the National Library of Scotland. Thanks to Sophie Goldsworthy at Oxford University Press for first taking interest in the project, and to Elizabeth Prochaska, Andrew McNeillie, Tom Perridge, and Jacqueline Baker for seeing the book through its later stages. Particular thanks to Hilary Walford and Frances Grant for their work with the typescript.

I have worked on this book within the supportive interdisciplinary environment of the University of York's Centre for Eighteenth-Century Studies. I am grateful to all students and staff of the Centre and particularly Clare Bond. Many people have shared their ideas and read or commented on chapters. Among these are John Arnold, John Barrell, Natasha Glaysier, Harriet Guest, Ben Harker, Matthew Hilton, Jackie Labbé, Anthony Leyland, Claire Lockwood, Devoney Looser, Emma Major, Marcus Nevitt, Richard Steadman-Jones, Mary Peace,

Acknowledgements

Jane Rendall, and Eve Tavor-Bannet. Thanks to Matthew Mackenzie and Bill Leavenworth for generous hospitality and good times in 2002. I am also grateful to those who have supported this project with their wit and friendship. These include Sue and Wal Davies, Emily Weygang, and particularly Tom Barr, who has shared with me the seasons, rooms, and (latterly) cupboards in which this book was written.

Contents

List of Illustrations x
Abbreviations xii

Introduction: Catharine Macaulay and
Mercy Otis Warren: Women, Writing, and the
Anglo-American Public Sphere 1

1. Catharine Macaulay, Thomas Hollis,
 and the London Opposition 34
2. 'Out-Cornelia-izing Cornelia': Portraits, Profession,
 and the Gendered Character of Learning 73
3. *Belle Sauvage*: Catharine Macaulay and
 the American War in Britain 122
4. Mercy Otis Warren's Revolutionary Letters 180
5. *Free and Easy*: Boston's Fashionable Dilemma 220
6. Mercy Otis Warren's Independence 248
 Conclusion: Public Voices 304

Index 311

List of Illustrations

1. G. B. Cipriani, *Catharina Macaulay* (1764). Engraving.   62
2. Marcus Junius Brutus, Denarius (54 BC). Head of Liberty and Consul L. Junius Brutus between two lictors, preceded by accensus.   64
3. G. B. Cipriani, *O Fair Britannia Hail!* (1760). Engraving. Reproduced by courtesy of the John Rylands Library, Manchester.   64
4. G. B. Cipriani, *Sketch for the Robe of Britannia* (c.1760). Drawing, with suggestions in the hand of Thomas Hollis. Reproduced by permission of the Houghton Library, Harvard.   65
5. Robert Edge Pine, *Catharine Macaulay* (c.1778). Oil on canvas. Reproduced by courtesy of the National Portrait Gallery, London.   66
6. J. F. Moore, *Catharine Macaulay, History* (1778). Statue. Reproduced by courtesy of the National Portrait Gallery, London, with the permission of Warrington Library.   69
7. Page after Richard Samuel, *The Nine Living Muses of Great Britain* (1778). Engraving. Reproduced in *Johnson's Ladies' New and Polite Pocket Memorandum for 1778*.   77
8. *Catharine Macaulay* (c.1778). Derby porcelain statuette. Reproduced by permission of the Metropolitan Museum of Art, New York.   83
9. After Catherine Read, *Catharine Macaulay* (c.1765). Engraving.   89
10. *Catharine Macaulay* (c.1775). Derby porcelain statuette. Reproduced by permission of Dickinson College Library, Pennsylvania.   96
11. Catharine Macaulay (c.1777–80). Derby porcelain statuette. Reproduced courtesy of the Winterthur Museum.   97
12. After Catherine Read, *Catharine Macaulay as a Roman Matron Lamenting the Lost Liberties of Rome* (1770). Reproduced in the *London Magazine* (1770).   110
13. Angelica Kauffman, *Cornelia, Mother of the Gracchi, Displaying her Children as her Treasures* (1785). Oil on canvas. Reproduced by permission of the Virginia Museum of Fine Arts, Richmond, Wilkins Fund.   111

List of Illustrations   xi

14. Gavin Hamilton, *Agrippina Landing at Brundisium with the Ashes of Germanicus* (1778). Oil on canvas. Reproduced by permission of the Tate Gallery, London.   116
15. *The Female Combatants, or Who Shall* (1776). Engraving. Reproduced by courtesy of the Lewis Walpole Library, LWLPR04040.   123
16. *The Association Meeting at York* (1780). Engraving. Published by Robert Laurie. Reproduced by courtesy of Library of Congress Prints and Photographs, LC-USZ62-45446.   145
17. *The Parricide, or, A Sketch of Modern Patriotism* (1776). Engraving. Published in the *Westminster Magazine* (1776). Reproduced by courtesy of Library of Congress Prints and Photographs, LC-USZC4-5290.   152
18. *The European Diligence* (1779). Engraving. Published by W. Humphrey. Reproduced by courtesy of Library of Congress Prints and Photographs, LC-USZ62-45438.   156
19. *Britannia's Ruin* (1779). Engraving. Published by Mary Darly. Reproduced by courtesy of Library of Congress Prints and Photographs, LC-USZ62-58615.   157
20. *Mr Trade and Family, or, the State of ye Nation* (1779). Engraving. Reproduced by courtesy of Library of Congress Prints and Photographs, LC-USZ62-1520.   166
21. *The Auspicious Marriage* (1778). Engraving. Published in the *Town and Country Magazine*, 10 (1778), 623.   168
22. Matthew Darly, *Miss Carolina Sulivan, one of the Obstinate Daughters of America* (1776). Engraving. Reproduced by courtesy of Library of Congress Prints and Photographs, LC-USZ62-5284.   168
23. Matthew Darly, *Noddle Island, or, HOW we are Deceived* (1776). Engraving. Reproduced by courtesy of Library of Congress Prints and Photographs, LC-USZ62-5323.   169
24. Matthew Darly, *Bunker's Hill, or, America's Head-Dress* (1776). Engraving. Reproduced by courtesy of Library of Congress Prints and Photographs, LC-USZ62-54.   169
25. Matthew Darly, *A Speedy & Effectual Preparation for the Next World* (1778). Engraving. Reproduced by courtesy of Lewis Walpole Library, LWLPR, 04194.   170

Abbreviations

AA	Abigail Adams
AFC	L. H. Butterfield, (ed.), *Adams Family Correspondence*, 6 vols. (Cambridge, Mass.: Harvard University Press, 1963)
CM	Catharine Macaulay
EG	Elbridge Gerry
EL	Ellen Lothrop
GLC	Gilder Lehrman Collection, New York Historical Society
GW	George Warren
HE MS	*History of England from the Accession of James I to that of the Brunswick Line*, manuscript copy, New York Historical Society
HL	Houghton Library, Harvard
HW	Hannah Winthrop
JA	John Adams
JW	James Warren
MHS	Massachusetts Historical Society
MOW	Mercy Otis Warren
MOWP1	Mercy Otis Warren Papers (1), Massachusetts Historical Society
MOWP2	Mercy Otis Warren Papers (2), Massachusetts Historical Society
NYHS	New York Historical Society
TH	Thomas Hollis
WAP	Warren–Adams Papers, Massachusetts Historical Society
WW	Winslow Warren
WWC	Winthrop–Warren Correspondence, Massachusetts Historical Society

Introduction

Catharine Macaulay and Mercy Otis Warren: Women, Writing, and the Anglo-American Public Sphere

> You see madam, I disregard the opinion that women make but indifferent politicians.... When the observations are just and do honor to the heart and character, I think it very immaterial whether they flow from a female lip in the soft whispers of private friendship or whether thundered in the senate in the bolder language of the other sex.
>
>   (Mercy Otis Warren to Catharine Macaulay, December 1774)

> My friends and fellow citizens... if a civil war commences between Great Britain and her colonies, either the mother country, by one great exertion, may ruin both herself and America, or the Americans, by a lingering contest, will gain an independency; and in this case, all those advantages, which you for some time have enjoyed by your colonies, and advantages which have hitherto preserved you from a national bankruptcy, must for ever have an end; whilst a new, a flourishing, and an extensive empire of freemen is established on the other side of the Atlantic, you, with the loss of all those blessings you have received by the unrivalled state of your commerce, will be left to the bare possession of your foggy islands; and this under the sway of a domestic despot.
>
>   (Catharine Macaulay, *An Address to the People of England, Scotland and Ireland on the Present Important Crisis of Affairs*, December 1774)

My two epigraphs introduce two writers and close friends. Both epigraphs were written at the turn of the year in which a colonial crisis became a civil war and both intimate how their authors saw themselves as participants in national and international debates. The first argues for the political significance of women's friendship and correspondence. In the second, a woman claims the language of citizenship and public exhortation. Both are suggestive of the ways in which eighteenth-century women might regard themselves as 'politicians' in an Anglo-American context.

Catharine Macaulay and Mercy Otis Warren exchanged letters and ideas with one another for almost twenty years. From cosmopolitan London and Bath and provincial Massachusetts they sustained a close friendship that was almost entirely epistolary and dependent on unreliable transatlantic crossings. Their friendship and its important correspondence framed their literary and political careers. Drawn to each other by mutual admiration of their republican principles and intellectual abilities, Macaulay and Warren began writing to each other in 1773. Macaulay had already been fêted in Britain and the American colonies for her historical and political writing, while Warren was producing verse dramas which commemorated the ideals of the New England patriots she counted herself among. Both professed a thorough knowledge of classical history and commonwealth theory; both saw its application to contemporary political crises, and the republican writings of both were celebrated in different ways on each side of the Atlantic for the patriotism and learning they displayed. Their friendship was a crucible of the ideas through which both women figured in the literary public sphere. Whether sharing vital information on public matters or sympathizing with personal losses and misfortunes, each regarded the other as 'my valuable friend', who 'nor time nor distance nor the accidents of life will lead me to view with an indifferent eye'.[1]

As Macaulay's and Warren's epistolary friendship framed their writing lives, so their experience of the separation of Britain from its North American colonies also shaped and formed their literary careers. 'We live', as Warren put it to Macaulay, 'in an age of Revolution'.[2] The colonial disputes, war, and its political and economic aftermath in the United States and Britain stimulated their public interests and changed their private lives. Both women saw Britain and America irrevocably altered by the effects of intra-national conflict and its attendant debates on constitutional reform, popular sovereignty, the moral and commercial

[1] MOW to CM, July 1789, MOWP1.   [2] Ibid.

dimensions of imperialism, and the meanings of national character. Macaulay and Warren felt that as women of learning they had a particular role to play in such debates. They were confident in the political acumen that meant they might intervene, writing letters and pamphlets, treatises and poems, which achieved different kinds of public circulation and acclaim. They also argued that their gender itself qualified them to produce what both described (with characteristic self-assurance) as the definitive republican histories of their respective nations. In their different ways, using a language of sentiment or affection, of learning or profession, both argued, in an era when public history was regarded as a definitively 'masculine' genre, that women made the best historians. Warren and Macaulay saw themselves, as women and as writers, at the intellectual heart of Atlantic political culture.

This book looks at why this was the case. The second part of my introduction sets out the critical and theoretical bases of this project in some detail. I shall begin, though, with a short biography of the revolutionary friendship of Catharine Macaulay and Mercy Otis Warren.

I Friends and Republicans

The third of thirteen children, Mercy Warren was born on 14 September 1728 into one of Massachusetts' most prominent, wealthy families.[3] Catharine Macaulay was born three years later to a family no less prominent in England's south-east.[4] Warren's grandfather, John Otis, had

---

[3] Only seven of Warren's brothers and sisters survived their childhoods. My account of Warren's life draws on Rosemarie Zagarri's short biography, *A Woman's Dilemma: Mercy Otis Warren and the American Revolution* (Wheeling, Ill.: Harlan Davidson, 1995), and Jean Fritz, *Cast for a Revolution: Some American Friends and Enemies* (Boston: Houghton Mifflin, 1972). On Warren's writing, the best and most comprehensive account is Jeffrey Richards, *Mercy Otis Warren* (New York: Twayne, 1995). Other useful accounts of Warren in this context include: Katharine Anthony, *First Lady of the Revolution: The Life of Mercy Otis Warren* (New York: Doubleday, 1958); Maud McDonald Hutcheson, 'Mercy Warren, 1728–1814', *William and Mary Quarterly*, 10 (1953), 378–402; Marianne B. Geiger, 'Catharine Sawbridge Macaulay and Mercy Otis Warren: Historians in the Transatlantic Republican Tradition', Ph.D. Diss. (New York University, 1986), Mary Elizabeth Regan, 'Pundit and Prophet of the Old Republic: The Life and Times of Mercy Otis Warren, 1728–1814', Ph.D. Diss. (American University, 1951).

[4] My account of Macaulay's life owes much to the ground-breaking scholarship of Bridget Hill, *The Republican Virago: The Life and Times of Catharine Macaulay* (Oxford: Clarendon Press, 1992). Other useful accounts of Macaulay in this context include: Mildred Chaffee Beckwith, 'Catharine Macaulay: Eighteenth-Century Rebel', Ph.D.

been an agent for the New England Company and a key member of the Massachusetts House of Representatives in the early eighteenth century. He was Barnstable's leading merchant and, in his lifetime, tripled his family's assets through his canny management of the trade in herring, whale oil, and box iron, as well as more luxury colonial commodities like mohair and plate.[5] As John Otis rose to economic eminence in provincial Massachusetts, Catharine Macaulay's grandfather, Jacob Sawbridge, became embroiled as an MP and director in the disastrous collapse of the South Sea scheme. His expropriated assets did remarkably little damage to the estate that enabled his family to figure large in the political life of the Kentish countryside and the City of London.[6] The family fortunes of both women were rooted firmly in the imperial commercial mechanisms of which their writing later offered such important critiques.

While Mercy Warren's biographers have stressed the rigorous gravity of her parents and the industry to which she was encouraged as a child, it would be hard to miss the sense of entitlement as well.[7] The household in which Warren lived until her marriage included a black slave and a host of indentured Indian servants whose debts and labour maintained the fortunes of colonial merchant families like hers.[8] Less the stable 'little

Diss. (Ohio State University, 1953); Florence and William Boos, 'Catharine Macaulay: Historian and Political Reformer', *International Journal of Women's Studies*, 3 (1980), 49–65; Lucy-Martin Donnelly, 'The Celebrated Mrs Macaulay', *William and Mary Quarterly*, 6 (1949), 172–207; Geiger, 'Catharine Sawbridge Macaulay and Mercy Otis Warren' Carla Hay, 'Catharine Macaulay and the American Revolution', *The Historian*, 56 (1994), 301–16; Bridget Hill, 'Daughter and Mother: Some New Light on Catharine Macaulay and her Family', *British Journal for Eighteenth-Century Studies*, 22 (1999), 35–49; Barbara Brandon Schnorrenberg, ' "The Brood-Hen of Faction": Mrs Macaulay and Radical Politics, 1765–75', *Albion*, 11 (1979), 33–45; Susan Staves, ' "The Liberty of a She-Subject of England": Rights Rhetoric and the Female Thucydides', *Cardazo Studies in Law and Literature*, 1 (1989), 161–83.

[5] On John Otis, see John Waters, *The Otis Family in Provincial and Revolutionary Massachusetts* (Chapel Hill, NC: University of North Carolina Press, 1968), 59. See also David Hackett Fischer, *Albion's Seed: Four British Folkways in America* (Oxford: Oxford University Press, 1989), and Gary Nash, *Urban Crucible: The Northern Seaports and the Origins of the American Revolution* Cambridge, Mass.: Harvard University Press, 1979).

[6] On Jacob Sawbridge and the South Sea Bubble, see Hill, *Republican Virago*, 5; Geiger, 'Catharine Sawbridge Macaulay and Mercy Otis Warren', 21–6 and John Carswell, *The South Sea Bubble* (London: Cresset Press, 1960), 34–6, 110–17.

[7] See, for example, Zagarri, *A Woman's Dilemma*; Anthony, *First Lady of the Revolution*; Fritz, *Cast for a Revolution*.

[8] James Otis (senior's) legal duties notoriously included the 'guardianship' of the Wampanoag, against the inequities of which Mashpee was established as an autonomous

commonwealth' than a family unit defined by the disputes between the native and colonial populations which her father and uncle oversaw, it was perhaps inevitable that Warren would later adopt a critique of Indian affairs that differed from that of her male relatives.[9] Always close to her brother James, Warren was educated alongside him in the home of her uncle, Jonathan Russell. Though she was not introduced to the classical languages that would qualify the male Otises for their Harvard educations, Warren read very widely, was encouraged to write creatively, and developed there that interest in republican political theory and history that would remain a lifelong preoccupation.

Unlike Warren's, Catharine Macaulay's education was often described as a matter more of accident than design. At their impressive home at Olantigh, the daughters of John Sawbridge received little formal instruction. Macaulay and her sister were left to the care of a governess, and it was later said that they were never encouraged in any activity beyond the narrow expectations of their rank and sex.[10] Her dedicated and solitary pursuit of her own interests in classical history and politics from the volumes of her father's extensive library (and, no doubt, from the rectory at nearby Godersham from where she also borrowed books) has very often been mythologized (and not least by herself), yet

---

district in 1763. On the Wampanoag's petition against James Otis and Sylvanus Bourne, see Francis G. Hutchins, *Mashpee: The Story of Cape Cod's Indian Town* (Tilton: Amarta Press, 1979), 72–3. See also Amelia Bingham, *Mashpee: Land of the Wampanoags* (Mashpee, Mass.: Mashpee Historical Commission, 1970), 39, Marion Vuilleumeir, *Indians on Olde Cape Cod* (Taunton: Sullwold Publishing, 1970), 58. On Indian indenture in eighteenth-century Cape Cod, see David Silverman, 'The Impact of Indentured Servitude on the Society and Culture of Southern New England Indians, 1680–1810', *New England Quarterly*, 74 (2001), 623–66, and ' "We Chuse to be Bounded": Native American Animal Husbandry in Colonial New England', *William and Mary Quarterly*, 60 (2003), 511–49. As Silverman writes, 'the best way to press Indians into service was to allow them to run up debts with English merchants, then demand the balance and bring them to court when they could not pay . . . Indians became increasingly dependent on store credit for clothing and sustenance.' One of these stores was Otis's in Barnstable. Silverman, 'Indians and Indentured Servitude', 625. The female servant whose death Mercy Warren mourned in 1771 (after her marriage and her move to Plymouth) was evidently Indian.

[9] Zagarri, *A Woman's Dilemma*, 8. Zagarri is citing John Demos, *A Little Commonwealth: Family Life in Plymouth Colony* (Oxford: Oxford University Press, 1970). See my discussion of Warren's account of, and interest in, American Indians in her *History* in Chapter 6.

[10] Mary Hays, *Female Biography, or, Memoirs of Illustrious Women, Alphabetically Arranged*, 6 vols. (London: Richard Philips, 1803), v. 289.

Macaulay's struggle to acquire the intellectual independence she coveted and claimed is undoubted.[11] In later life, she criticized the deep inequalities of male and female education; denounced 'those to whose care my infancy was committed', and wrote with understandable resentment of 'the unremitting industry... necessary to the task of cultivating ones own mind and the pursuing and undertaking science in a girl's place without a guide'.[12]

Macaulay's 'natural love of freedom' and the analogous appeal she found in 'the annals of the Roman and Greek republicks' may well have been represented as spontaneous and unintentional, yet her intellectual interests were clearly influenced by a shared familial identity.[13] The attraction of particular kinds of political and historical writing to the young Macaulay and Warren was self-consciously bound up with the brands of oppositional Whiggism their families had espoused by mid-century. As the Otises pitted themselves against Thomas Hutchinson's embattled loyalism, so the Sawbridges maintained the virtue of distance from the disappointing capitulations of a Pulteney or a Chatham.[14] If family meant that both women associated themselves with the legacy of the commonwealthmen, then marriage afforded both an environment in which such political identifications flourished.[15] As I suggest in discussions of George Macaulay and James Warren later in this book, part of the evident assurance Macaulay and Warren felt as political writers in the 1760s and 1770s was derived from partners who were so thoroughly

[11] See, for example [unattrib.], 'Account of the Life of Mrs Catharine Macaulay Graham', *European Magazine and London Review*, 4 (1783), 330, and Hays, *Female Biography*. See also Hill, Republican Virago, 10. An intriguing later representation of Macaulay's self-directed education is found in Joseph Johnson, *Clever Girls of our Time and how they Became Famous Women* (London: Gall and Inglis, 1888). I discuss Macaulay's account of her own education in the 'Introduction' to her *History* in Chapter 2.
[12] Science here carries the broader eighteenth-century sense of knowledge in general. CM, *Letters on Education with Observations on Religious and Metaphysical Subjects* (London: E. & C. Dilly, 1790), 30; CM to Ralph Griffith, Nov. 1790, GLC. There is a useful account of Macaulay's and Griffith's exchange by Devoney Looser, ' "Those Historical Laurels which Once Graced My Brow are Now in their Wane": Catharine Macaulay's Last Years and Legacy', *Studies in Romanticism*, 42 (2003), 203–25.
[13] CM, *HE* MS, vol. i, introduction.
[14] On the Otises and Hutchinson, see Fritz, *Cast for a Revolution*, and Bernard Baylin, *The Ordeal of Thomas Hutchinson* (Cambridge, Mass.: Harvard University Press, 1974). On the Sawbridges and William Pultney, see Hill, *Republican Virago*, 7.
[15] Caroline Robbins, *The Eighteenth-Century Commonwealthman* [1959] (New York: Athenaeum Press, 1968).

supportive of their intellectual endeavours.[16] Familial and marital connections also brought both women into the informal, extra-parliamentary milieux of radical London and Massachusetts. At the Macaulays' dinners, Wilkite radicals and old Whigs, baronets and middle-rank professionals, and moderate Anglican and dissenting churchmen met to discuss parliamentary reform and the American situation. After Macaulay published the first volume of her *History of England from the Accession of James I to that of the Brunswick Line* to such great acclaim in the autumn of 1763, invitations to these dinners and conversations with the historian were much sought after.[17] Macaulay continued to host a regular evening after her first husband's death and out of the participatory debate of these occasions produced important pamphlets and circular letters.[18] Mercy Warren's Plymouth home, meanwhile, had been a focal point of local politics during the 1760s and by the 1770s became a hub of those at state level as well. It was here that Warren met the circle of prominent Massachusetts men and women with whom she regularly corresponded and here that she was encouraged to produce those animating letters and admonitory plays that starkly

[16] For discussion of George Macaulay, see Chapter 2. I discuss James and Mercy Warren's relationship in Chapters 4 and 6.

[17] See, for example, Sylas Neville, Diary, 9 July 1767 and 15 July 1767, in *The Diary of Sylas Neville, 1767–1788*, ed. Basic Cozens Hardy (Oxford: Oxford University Press, 1950). The research and production of Macaulay's eight-volume *History of England from the Accession of James I to that of the Brunswick Line* dominated her life after her first marriage, appearing over a twenty-year period: vol. i (London: E. & C. Dilly, 1763); vol. ii (London: E. & C. Dilly, 1765); vol. iii (London: E. & C. Dilly, 1767), vol. iv (London: E. & C. Dilly, 1768); vol. v (London: E. & C. Dilly, 1771); vol. vi (London: A. Hamilton, 1781); vol. vii (London: A. Hamilton, 1781); vol. viii (London: A. Hamilton, 1783).

[18] Macaulay published a number of political pamphlets in the 1760s and 1770s: *Loose Remarks on Certain Positions to be Found in Mr Hobbes' Philosophical Rudiments of Government and Society with a Short Sketch of a Democratical form of Government, in a Letter to Signor Paoli* (London: T. Davies, 1767) (and a second edition, including Macaulay's letter to Benjamin Rush, 1769); *Observations on a Pamphlet Entitled Thoughts on the Cause of the Present Discontents* (London: E. & C. Dilly, 1770); *An Address to the People of England, Scotland and Ireland on the Present Important Crisis of Affairs* (London: E. & C. Dilly, 1775) (and a second edition, 1779). Macaulay's circular letters included the 'letter which was written...to a friend upon the necessary qualifications for a representative of parliament...distributed upon the eve of the general election', which Edward Dilly sent to John Adams to circulate in America. Edward Dilly to JA, 4 Mar. 1774, in *Papers of John Adams*, ed. Robert J. Taylor, 8 vols. (Cambridge, Mass.: Harvard University Press, 1977), ii., 18. The letter was to Macaulay's friend John Collett Ryland. I discuss it in Chapter 1.

dramatized her favoured contrast between virtuous colonial resistance and British imperial-ministerial corruption.[19] Well-established transatlantic networks of commercial and political connection meant that Macaulay and Warren's circles often converged. The flourishing exchange of British and American oppositionist publications facilitated by Thomas Hollis, John Almon, and the Dilly brothers, and a more informal (perhaps more 'private') culture of sharing and circulating personal-political letters at social gatherings, enabled the groups who met in the homes of both women to think of themselves as proximate, connected, and engaged with the same concerns. While visiting the British friends of America at the turn of 1775, Josiah Quincy might share letters from Mercy Warren as well as intelligence of colonial preparations for the coming war.[20] Macaulay's many letters to Massachusetts were seen by the men of the Boston committee and by the women of the South Church, and were also circulated among a wide circle of political friends of both sexes.[21] As Eve Tavor-Bannet writes of transatlantic cultures of correspondence (in an echo of Alison Gilbert-Olson's suggestive phrase), 'letters made the empire work'.[22] It was correspondence that had allowed the British Atlantic to imagine itself as a community; correspondence that forged the political bonds between Boston's and London's cultures of reform; and correspondence that enabled these cultures to picture the meanings of Atlantic conflict, conciliation, or separation.[23] During the war, oppositional debate was

[19] MOW, *The Adulateur* (1772); *The Defeat* (1773); *The Group* (1775). On Warren's home in the 1760s and 1770s, see Chapter 4.
[20] Warren had given Quincy a package to take to Britain in 1774. She later got into trouble with her friend Hannah Lincoln (Quincy's sister) for writing openly about his mission to Britain as an agent for the congress. See MOW to Hannah Lincoln, 3 Sept. 1774, MOWP1, and 6 Dec. 1774, MOWP2: 'When I hinted to you my friendly wishes for the welfare of a friend by nature closely connected with you I had no suspicion that I was therein guilty of a breach of trust . . . had I not supposed you must be well acquainted with every material circumstance with regard to that gentleman's transactions . . . '. These letters also suggest how far Warren was an insider in such affairs.
[21] For further discussion of this issue, see Chapter 3.
[22] Eve Tavor-Bannet, 'Prologue', Empire of Letters: Epistolary Manuals and Transatlantic Correspondence, unpublished MS. Alison Gilbert-Olson, *Making the Empire Work: London and American Interest Groups 1690–1790* (Cambridge, MA: Harvard University Press, 1992).
[23] On women's networks and letter writing, see, for example, Sarah Richardson, ' "Well Neighboured Houses": The Political Networks of Elite Women, 1780–1860', in Kathryn Gleadle and Sarah Richardson (eds.), *Women in British Politics, 1760–1860: The*

often dependent on private transactions and exchanges rather than official institutions and publications.[24] Macaulay and Warren's epistolary friendship was one of very many in which an associative Anglo-American culture was defined.[25]

Of the two women, Macaulay's role was emphatically the more public. For many republicans in Britain and America, the 'female patriot', whose virtues were substantiated in her writing and commemorated in prints and Derby figurines, did not just articulate but also

Power of the Petticoat (Basingstoke, Macmillan, 2000), 56–73, and Edith Gelles, *Abigail Adams: A Writing Life* (London: Routledge, 2002). On letters and commerce, see Toby Dietz, 'Formative Ventures: Eighteenth-Century Commercial Letters and the Articulation of Experience', in Rebecca Earle (ed.), *Epistolary Selves: Letters and Letter Writers 1600–1945* (Aldershot: Ashgate, 1999), 59–78. Other general accounts of eighteenth-century epistolary culture include: Keith Stewart, 'Towards Defining an Aesthetic for the Familiar Letter in Eighteenth-Century England', *Prose Studies* (1982), 179–92; Bruce Redford, *The Converse of the Pen: Acts of Intimacy in the Eighteenth-Century Familiar Letter* (Chicago: University of Chicago Press, 1986); William Merrill Decker, *Epistolary Practices: Letter Writing in America before Telecommunications* (Chapel Hill, NC: University of North Carolina Press, 1998).

[24] See Richard Brown, *Knowledge is Power: The Diffusion of Information in Early America 1700–1865* (Oxford: Oxford University Press, 1989), and *Revolutionary Politics in Massachusetts: The Boston Committee of Correspondence and the Towns, 1772–1774.* (New York: Norton, 1970).

[25] Such associative cultures of course ranged across the political spectrum. On Atlantic political and commercial cultures, see, for example, Harry Dickinson (ed.), *Britain and the American Revolution* (London: Longman, 1998); Eliga Gould, *The Persistence of Empire: British Political Culture in the Age of the American Revolution* (Chapel Hill, NC: University of North Carolina Press, 2000); Peter Linebaugh and Marcus Rediker, *The Many-Headed Hydra: The Hidden History of the Revolutionary Atlantic* (London: Verso, 2000); Kathleen Wilson, *The Sense of the People: Politics, Culture and Imperialism in England, 1715–1785* (Cambridge: Cambridge University Press, 1995), and *The Island Race: Englishness, Empire and Gender in the Eighteenth Century* (London: Routledge, 2003); John Sainsbury, *Disaffected Patriots: London Supporters of Revolutionary America, 1769–1782* (Kingston and Montreal: McGill-Queens University Press, 1987); Stephen Conway, *The British Isles and the War of American Independence* (Oxford: Oxford University Press, 2000); Bernard Bailyn, *The Ideological Origins of the American Revolution* (Cambridge, Mass.: Harvard University Press, 1967); Alison Gilbert-Olson, *Making Empire Work*, and 'The London Mercantile Lobby and the Coming of the American Revolution', *Journal of American History*, 69 (1982), 21–41; Colin Bonwick, *English Radicals and the American Revolution* (Chapel Hill, NC: University of North Carolina Press, 1977); Isaac Kramnick, *Republicanism and Bourgeois Radicalism: Political Ideology in Late Eighteenth-Century England and America* (Ithaca, NY: Cornell University Press, 1990); J. G. A. Pocock, *The Machiavellian Moment: Florentine Political Thought and the Atlantic Republican Tradition* (Princeton: Princeton University Press, 1975), David Hancock, *Citizens of the World: London Merchants and the Integration of the British Atlantic Community 1735–1785* (Cambridge: Cambridge University Press, 1995).

visibly embodied their political objectives. In Massachusetts, Warren was well known as the sister of the charismatic James Otis and held a real literary cachet in her own right as a woman of learning and a daughter of liberty. But, while her patriotic poems were admired and her letters were awaited and prized, between Plymouth and Boston Warren's politics and femininity did not draw that very distinctive kind of publicity that Macaulay attracted. Warren's biographers often emphasize her veneration of 'the celebrated female historian', but Macaulay was perhaps equally flattered by their personal and political connection. 'I must thank you, dear sir,' Macaulay wrote to their mutual friend, John Adams, 'for the pleasure you have given me in introducing to me so agreeable a correspondent as Mrs Warren.'[26] As Macaulay said in her first letter to Warren, her correspondence was particularly welcome because, as the sister of the celebrated James Otis and a notable republican in her own right, Warren promised contact with the kind of patriotic heroism that Macaulay had celebrated in her *History* and which now seemed so distant in a Britain whose political cultures were dominated by corruption and expediency. 'To be distinguished in such a manner by a woman of your sentiments and so nearly connected to the greatest patriots of the age gives me', Macaulay told Warren, 'the most pleasing ideas of importance. But I should be little deserving of that distinction if I did not entirely simpathise with you for the public weal of America.'[27] Macaulay's first letters to Warren are characterized by her acute awareness of the public status she had by then attained as well as by a language of sympathy, which is used here to confirm the irrefutable authenticity of her politics. Warren similarly represented women's affectionate personal attachment as analogous to the sincerity of their political feeling. 'The feelings of sympathy in your benevolent heart', Warren wrote to Macaulay, simultaneously commending her friend's political and sentimental characters, 'have been discovered on several occasions when you have surveyed the system of oppression formed against the injured Americans'.[28]

In the winter of 1774, the women agreed about the 'fatal infatuation' of the intolerable acts which, Warren told Macaulay, were 'threatening to involve this growing continent in the same thraldom that awaits the

[26] CM to JA, 11 Sept. 1774, in *The Papers of John Adams*, ed. Taylor, ii. 164.
[27] MOW to CM, 7 June 1773, MOWP1; CM to MOW, 11 Sept. 1774, WAP.
[28] MOW to CM, 7 June 1773, MOWP1.

miserable Asiatic'.[29] Both felt that the colonial conflict would prove the making or breaking of Britain. Macaulay might have 'flattered [her]self', that the Americans 'would be the saviours and liberators of the whole British Empire' but by the turn of the year had sent a pamphlet to Massachusetts in which she saw the end of the 'fatal infatuation' in probable and painful civil war.[30] Her radical *Address to the People* called on 'the large body of my countrymen unjustly debarred the privilege of election', to 'Rouse! and unite in one general effort... till you draw the attention of every part of the government to their own interests, and to the dangerous state of the British empire'.[31] Warren saw something more affirming and nationalistic in the difficult prospect of American and British conflict: 'if the British ministry would continue their absurd and unjust measures till the sceptre trembles in the hand of royalty and the mistress of the isles sits solitary and alone', she wrote in typically energetic terms to Macaulay, 'yet the oppressed colonies will rise to glory and grandeur, and perhaps behold the tottering empire from whence they sprang become the contempt of its enemies and the derision of nations'.[32]

In the early years of the war, maintaining a transatlantic friendship was problematic and tricky. 'The circumstances of the times render every conveyance uncertain,' Warren wrote to Macaulay in 1777, 'except one cloathed with royal authority.'[33] The correspondence of Warren's Massachusetts circle was often intercepted by the colonial administration, and she and her female friends sometimes wrote partially in code or left their letters unsigned for fear of their seizure.[34] In London, meanwhile, a letter from Macaulay found in Stephen Sayre's apartments was

[29] MOW to CM, 4 Dec. 1774, MOWP1.
[30] CM to MOW, 11 Sept. 1774, WAP.   [31] CM, *An Address to the People*, 29.
[32] MOW to CM, Aug. 1775, MOWP1.
[33] MOW to CM, 15 Feb. 1777, MOWP1.
[34] Intercepts of the Warren–Adams circle appear in the list included in K. G. Davies, *Documents of the American Revolution, 1770–1783*. Colonial Office Series: 10 (Dublin: Irish University Press, 1976), 64. There is also a short account here of government intercepts of private correspondence in 1775–6. For further discussion of this, see Julie Flavell, 'Government Intercepts of Letters from America and the Quest for Colonial Opinion in 1775', *William and Mary Quarterly*, 58 (2001), 403–31. See also Harry Dickinson, 'Introduction', and John Derry, 'Government Policy and the American Crisis, 1760–1776', both in Dickinson (ed.), *Britain and the American Revolution*. On Abigail Adams and interception, see Edith Gelles, *Abigail Adams: A Writing Life* and *Portia: The World of Abigail Adams* (Bloomington, Ind.: Indiana University Press, 1992).

thought evidence of a supposed American plot to kidnap George III on his way to open parliament.[35] As an outspoken and radical pro-American, Macaulay felt increasingly persecuted. She was accused of spying and often felt she was being spied upon. While Warren began to test her abilities as a historian in the detailed accounts of the war that reached her friend via Paris and Rotterdam, Macaulay turned her epistolary hand to her *History in a Series of Letters*, which veiled its critique of North's ministry and the American war in a stinging account of the 1720s. This unpopular text was condemned as inflammatory and unpatriotic by a loyalist Britain anxious at the prospect of French invasion.[36] And for Warren, as intra-national conflict turned into an ever-more monstrous world war, so it appeared to her that American patriots had lost their political direction. For both women, the revolutionary flame burned far less brightly by the turn of 1779.[37]

By 1779 Warren and Macaulay were both thought to be planning republican histories of the American war. Macaulay had discussed writing a history of America with her colonial friends in the 1760s and received many packages of information and offers of hospitality from the continent with this in mind.[38] William Gordon was willing, James Bowdoin told her in 1777, 'to furnish you with some papers... which may facilitate your plan you told me of, of continuing your history, if God spared your life to the end of the present war (which by the way I pray God may shortly terminate)'.[39] Macaulay appears to have had the

---

[35] On Macaulay's letter and the Sayre affair, see *London Evening Post*, 26–28 Oct. 1775. I discuss the rumours of Sayre's plot at greater length in Chapter 3.

[36] This was pointed out in the *History*'s unfavourable reviews. See, for example, *Gentleman's Magazine* (1778), 528: 'Nothing can more strongly mark the partiality and defects of this writer, than her mentioning the "advantage which the French fleet obtained at Beachy Head".'

[37] On 5 Oct. 1778, Warren published a poem in the *Boston Gazette* entitled 'The Genius of America Lamenting the Absurd Follies of the Day' which suggested how far she felt the revolution had failed. It was also in 1778–9 that Macaulay's friendship with Thomas Wilson and marriage to James Graham were loudly vilified and satirized in Britain. See Chapters 3 and 6.

[38] See, for example, 'Sophronia' (Sarah Prince-Gill) to CM, 8 Dec. 1769, and James Bowdoin, Samuel Pemberton, and Joseph Warren to CM (on behalf of the town of Boston), 23 Mar. 1770, GLC.

[39] James Bowdoin to CM, 25 Mar. 1777, GLC. Included with Bowdoin's letter was one from William Gordon, with a request that he and Macaulay share the documents and information they had gathered about the war. William Gordon to CM, 25 Mar. 1777, GLC. I have found no record of Gordon and Macaulay pooling material, but, as is well

definite intention of expanding what was already a magisterial historical project to accommodate the current crisis.[40] In Massachusetts, meanwhile, Warren's friends knew from the war's outset that she was carefully copying letters and gathering materials for what she called her 'annals'. 'I hope the historick page increases to a volume,' Abigail Adams wrote encouragingly in the winter of 1775.[41] At the close of the war, Warren reworked what she had written to Macaulay over the past decade and integrated her letters into a polished historical narrative, which she gave to her son Winslow to read. And Macaulay decided to further her American historical projects by visiting the continent in person.[42]

In the spring of 1784, British papers carried the news that 'the celebrated Mrs Macaulay Graham and her husband embarked on board a ship in the Downs, bound to North America. Whether she is gone to frame a code of laws for that continent', the *Gentleman's Magazine* ruminated, 'we have not heard'.[43] Macaulay and Warren had often expressed the desire to meet and were finally able to do so that year. 'I suppose that Mrs Macaulay and Mrs Warren have compared notes on the history of liberty on both sides the Atlantic,' John Adams wrote from London.[44] Personal acquaintance increased the women's mutual affection and respect. 'I think her not only a learned but a virtuous worthy character,' Warren told her son Winslow, 'possessed of much sensibility of heart'.[45] Warren clearly understood Macaulay's personal and physical 'delicacy' and knew how much she had 'suffered . . . by the spirit of party', but could not stop their friendship being temporarily injured from the same cause.[46] In a post-war Massachusetts whose factional volatility matched only its perceived economic instability, the

---

known, Gordon later produced a history of the war: William Gordon, *History of the Rise, Progress and Establishment of the Independence of the United States* (New York: Campbell, 1789).

[40] See also Hays, *Female Biography*, 303, and Hay, 'Catharine Macaulay and the American Revolution'.   [41] AA to MOW, Nov., 1775, WAP.

[42] Warren's early draft of her *History*, which she gave to Winslow, is included in MOWP2, 'Letters Containing Many of the Most Remarkable Events for the Memorable Era of the Stamp Act, 1765, to the Commencement of Hostilities between Great Britain and the American Colonies, 1775'. Part of the purpose of Macaulay's trip was to encourage subscriptions for a planned American edition of her *History of England*. See the publication proposal she published in the *American Herald*, 1 and 15 Nov. 1784.

[43] *Gentleman's Magazine* (1784), 378.   [44] JA to JW, 26 Apr. 1785, WAP.
[45] MOW to WW, Dec. 1784, MOWP1.
[46] MOW to WW, Dec. 1784, MOWP1.

two women quarrelled over their position as 'old republicans' in the *Sans Souci* debate. In the Boston papers, Warren was vilified as a figure whose politics had unsexed her against the apparently more appropriately feminine Macaulay. 'Let the features of your sex be traced in the compositions of your pen,' Warren was admonished by a rabid writer in the *Boston Gazette*, 'and thus shall you receive the applause which is due to *real* genius'.[47]

Macaulay's plans to republish her *History of England* by subscription in America foundered, and during her quiet retirement with William Graham she 'employed [her] thoughts on education' and decided not to pursue producing an account of the recent war.[48] But Warren and Macaulay's friendship proved more cheering and enduring than either found the political scene on each side of the Atlantic ('the having seen and conversed in person with the author', Macaulay told Warren warmly of one of her letters, 'gave an additional pleasure to the renewal of our old correspondence').[49] Writing to her friend of the interminable absurdity and 'pompous shew' of Warren Hastings's trial, Macaulay concluded dryly that 'we have gained no virtue by the loss of America'.[50] And for the Anti-Federal Warren, appalled at a plan of government in which she saw many of the political faults of British constitutional monarchy, the United States' gains of sovereignty had entailed the loss of republicanism. 'It ill becomes an infant government', she told Macaulay,

whose foreign and domestic advantages are large, and whose resources are small, to begin in the splendour of Royalty; to shackle its commerce, to check the manufactures; to damp the spirit of agriculture by imposts and excises and instead to deprive the people of the means of subsistence; to amass sums for the augment of exorbitant salaries; to support the regalia of office; and to puff up the ostentatious pomp for which the ambitious have sighed and desired.[51]

In their different ways in their later years, Warren and Macaulay developed personal aesthetics and political ideas based profoundly on a sense of loss.[52]

---

[47] 'Guess Who', *Boston Gazette and Country Journal*, 14 Feb. 1785. For further discussion on the *Sans Souci* controversy, see Chapter 5.
[48] CM to MOW, 6 Mar. 1787, WAP.   [49] CM to MOW, 6 Mar. 1787, WAP.
[50] CM to MOW, Mar. 1788, WAP.   [51] MOW to CM, July 1789, MOWP1.
[52] This is apparent in the later letters of both women as well as Warren's *History of the Rise, Progress and Termination of the American Revolution* [1805], ed. Lester Cohen, (Indianapolis: Liberty Classics, 1989), and her *Observations on the New Constitution and*

But, at the turn of the 1790s, both women found they had more to hope for from the political debate surrounding revolutionary France than from that on Federalist America. Though Macaulay was reported to have said of the American Constitution in 1787 that it 'would do, for the foundation of it was democracy', in 1790 she certainly appeared to have concurred with Warren's republican critique of Washington's administration: 'history furnishes *no example* of any government in a large empire which, in the strictest sense of the word, has secured to the citizen the full enjoyment of his rights'.[53] As Warren facilitated the publication of a Boston edition of Macaulay's 'ingenious and just' *Observations on the Reflections of the Right Honourable Edmund Burke on the Revolution in France*, she felt that she was opening a new transatlantic dialogue 'productive of good both to Europe and America. It appears to me that it will lead to the discussion of questions that have for some time lain dormant, and to the universal vindication of opinions that have of late been too unfashionable to voice.'[54] But Macaulay died at home in Berkshire before seeing the effects of this transatlantic discussion and before reading the two volumes of Warren's *Poems Dramatic and Miscellaneous* that her friend had sent her proudly from Massachusetts (which celebrated classical political women in ways in which she would have certainly approved). Her death also meant she was unable to appreciate the impact of her *Letters on Education* on an admiring Mary Wollstonecraft.[55]

For Mercy Warren, the death of 'a woman of superior genius and ability', 'my learned and worthy friend, Mrs Macaulay', was a loss in a

on the Federal and State Conventions (Boston, 1788). On Macaulay's and Warren's sense of loss, see also Looser, 'Those Historical Laurels,' Hill, *Republican Virago*; Zagarri, *A Woman's Dilemma*, and my discussion in Chapter 6.

[53] John Adams told Warren in 1807 that this was his understanding of Macaulay's view of the constitution. JA to MOW, 11 July 1807, WAP. CM, *Observations on the Reflections of the Right Honourable Edmund Burke on the Revolution in France in a Letter to the Right Honourable Earl of Stanhope* (London: E. & C. Dilly, 1790), 88.

[54] MOW to CM, 21 May 1791. Warren's edition of Macaulay's *Observations* included a short preface echoing the same sentiments and was printed by I. Thomas and E. Andrews, who had recently published the edition of her *Poems, Dramatic and Miscellaneous*, 2 vols. (1790).

[55] On Wollstonecraft's and Macaulay's connection, see Wendy Gunther Canada, 'The Politics of Sense and Sensibility: Mary Wollstonecraft and Catharine Macaulay Graham on Edmund Burke's *Reflections on the Revolution in France*', in Hilda Smith (ed.), *Women Writers and the Early Modern British Political Tradition* (Cambridge: Cambridge University Press, 1998), and Bridget Hill, 'The Links between Catharine Macaulay and Mary Wollstonecraft: New Evidence', *Women's History Review*, 4 (1995), 177–92.

decade marked by many painful bereavements.[56] From the house she loved at Plymouth, she wrote admonitory letters on the conduct of state and national politics and lively educational epistles for the young people of her family circle. She urged the study of history and politics to her nieces and granddaughters, dismissing as prejudice the gendered and cultural preconceptions that might have discouraged them. 'Who can say', Warren enquired rhetorically of her niece Sally Sever, 'how far the conduct even of a single female may operate on the manners, the character and the happiness of society?'[57] She received respectful letters from Judith Sargent Murray, who acknowledged how Warren's politics appeared to alienate her literary character from public appreciation in Federalist America.[58] And, after welcoming Jefferson's election as the nineteenth century turned, Warren finally brought out the assured *History of the Rise, Progress and Termination of the American Revolution*, which she had first begun to write in her epistolary exchanges with Macaulay. This definitively 'old' republican work, loud in its critique of America's first two administrations and the men who controlled them, was at the time of its publication the focus of more controversy than acclaim.[59]

Catharine Macaulay and Mercy Warren's political and personal exchanges during the years that surrounded colonial conflict and the constitutional formation of the new United States underpin the narrative of this book. My account of the shape of their friendship is indebted to Bridget Hill's and Rosemarie Zagarri's useful biographies and has also been enriched by working with the manuscripts of both women. The collections of Warren's correspondence and papers in Boston are perhaps already well known, but less familiar are Macaulay's letters in the Houghton Library; the recently acquired papers of the Gilder Lehrman collection; and her letters and manuscripts at the

---

[56] MOW to GW, n.d., 1794, MOWP1, and MOW to WW, n.d., 1791, MOWP1.
[57] MOW to Sally Sever, n.d., 1784, MOWP1.
[58] Murray wrote that perceptions of Warren's politics were preventing the development of the subscription list to her *History*: 'very many urge the political principles attributed to the otherwise admired writer as a reason for withholding their signatures.' Judith Sargent Murray to MOW, 1 June 1805, WAP. See also Murray to MOW, 4 Mar. 1796. On Warren's political alienation in Federalist Massachusetts, see Chapter 6.
[59] See, for example, *The Panoplist, or, The Christian's Armory*, 2 (1807), 380–4, 429–32. Jeffrey Richards discusses reviews of Warren's *History* in the final chapter of *Mercy Otis Warren*.

New York Historical Society and elsewhere.[60] These collections not only enlarge our critical understanding of Warren and Macaulay's Anglo-American dialogue but tell also of the instructive dissimilarity of two women who are often described as being so much alike. There was a world of differences between Plymouth and London, and these, as well as the Atlantic Ocean, divided them. There was certainly (as I have stressed) a loose equivalence to the ways in which their grandfathers' capitalist adventures allowed Warren and Macaulay later to dissociate the patriotic interests of their families from those of commerce, court, and political corruption, but the cultures which enabled this to occur were, of course, poles apart. While Warren might well picture herself as a virtuous farmer in provincial Massachusetts, Macaulay's notion of virtue was bound up with the particularly modern Whiggish turn of the city of London.[61] As I later show, Warren conceived of sociability as an extension of rural retirement and domesticity.[62] She would have baulked at the culture of metropolitan politeness in which Macaulay exercised her republicanism and certainly lived in horror of the contemporary European *ton*. Macaulay's urban lifestyle not only involved fashionable commodities that she clearly enjoyed, but also meant that she might think of her learning more in terms of its professional character. Her canny publishing deals and her 1774 defence of authors shows an evident awareness of writing as an enabling source of women's financial independence.[63] As she bequeathed the copyright of her *Poems, Dramatic and Miscellaneous* to her son Winslow as 'the only thing I can properly call my own', Warren certainly acknowledged the benefits of

[60] There are holdings of Warren's manuscripts and letters in the Massachusetts Historical Society; the Boston Public Library; the Houghton Library, Harvard; the Library of Congress and the Huntington Library. Many of Macaulay's letters in the Gilder Lehrman Collection are drafts (written on the reverse of letters received) not fair copies, and Macaulay's correspondence was evidently much wider than the letters that are currently extant in the Massachusetts Historical Society, Houghton Library, American Philosophical Society, Boston Public Library, New York Public Library, New York Historical Society Library, Pierpoint Morgan Library, and Rhode Island Historical Society Library. Warren occasionally refers to, or quotes from, letters she has received from Macaulay that have not been located.
[61] Though it is important to remember the ways in which both women might also be seen in opposite terms. Warren's family background was (as I have said) solidly commercial, and Macaulay proposed a classical agrarian foundation to her political utopia in her *Sketch on a Democratical form of Government*. [62] See Chapter 4.
[63] I discuss Macaulay's publishing deals in Chapter 2. See CM, *A Modest Plea for the Property of Copyright* (London: E. & C. Dilly, 1774).

literary property to married women.[64] But, though she often defended the public and political status of her writing, she did not often regard her figuring in the literary marketplace in terms of its *professional* character. Religion also marked important distinctions between Warren and Macaulay. While both espoused the virtue of tolerance of most protestant modes and forms, their liberality was very different in tenor and in substance. Mary Hays's anxious defence of Macaulay's faith in her *Female Biography* suggests how often the woman who described 'liberty as an object of secondary worship' was associated with and attacked for an assumed scepticism.[65] Macaulay's sense of her class perhaps itself entailed a need to remain within the Church of England, but throughout her adult life she was surrounded by liberal middle-rank professionals of many different sects.[66] Macaulay shared close sentimental friendships with Quaker women; she was influenced in her reading by those whose Anglicanism, like Augustus Toplady's, had taken an evangelical turn, and she was certainly sympathetic to the dissent of her good friends Theophilus Lindsey, Thomas Hollis, and James Burgh.[67] Perhaps most tellingly, she was drawn to the benefaction of Thomas Wilson, whose loyalty to the Church did not stop him being a founder member of the Wilkite Society for the Supporters of the Bill of Rights. In her 1783 *Treatise on the Immutability of Moral Truth* (which she later reworked into her important *Letters on Education*) an enlightened Christianity is the cornerstone of that just equality and benevolence which represented to her the moral best that a society might attain.[68] So there was certainly, as Lynne Withey has argued, a perfectionist element to her religious thinking, but she did not see the millennium, as Mercy Warren clearly did, bound up with Empire's westward course.[69] Macaulay disliked any shade of religion that represented God as 'partial in the distribution of reward and punishment', and Warren's prophetic discourse of

[64] MOW to WW, 10 June 1791.   [65] Hays, *Female Biography*, 298–9.
[66] On Macaulay's religion, see Hill, *Republican Virago*, 149–64, and Susan Staves, 'Church of England Clergy and Women Writers', in Nicole Pohl and Betty Schellenberg (eds.), *Reconsidering the Bluestockings* (San Marino: Huntington Library, 2003), 81–105.
[67] I discuss Macaulay's sentimental friendship with Quaker women in Chapter 2.
[68] CM, *A Treatise on the Immutability of Moral Truth* (London: A. Hamilton, 1783).
[69] See Lynne Withey, 'Catharine Macaulay and the Uses of History: Ancient Rights, Perfectionism and Propaganda', *Journal of British Studies*, 16 (1976), 59–83. On religion and republicanism in colonial and revolutionary America, see, for example, Ruth Bloch, *Visionary Republic: Millennial Themes in American Thought, 1756–1800* (Cambridge: Cambridge University Press, 1985).

New England's providential calling definitely was not hers.[70] Nor did Macaulay find, like Warren, the same useful and authoritative juncture between a language of patriotic resolution and that of Christian resignation. Warren's letters and private poems show just how closely her politics were bound up with a faith that demanded submission to God's will as one condition of the privilege it granted to speak for the providential plan.[71] An enemy to infidelity as she was to superstition, and persistently anxious that her sons' spiritual lives would suffer from reading Gibbon and Priestley (though she admired the latter's politics and of course loved the technical panache of the *Decline and Fall*), Warren kept up a steady stream of counsel against deism's appeal. With typical brusqueness she described Paine's *Age of Reason* to her son George as 'jejune trumpery'.[72]

Both women also had a very strong sense of their contrasting personalities and could play up to each other's awareness of their differences. In conversation, Macaulay was said to be notoriously declamatory, and Warren was happy to let her know that her long sentences did not always please the ear.[73] Macaulay, in her turn, sometimes found her friend's style relentless and uncompromising and told Warren that her 'animated severity' had wounded her own 'delicacy of sentiment'.[74] A language of sentiment or of feeling was, as will be seen, crucial to both women's accounts of their personal and political characters, yet their take on this language might also differ radically. Macaulay often expressed irritation that her childhood had not been physically Spartan enough to help her sustain the demands she made of her body and mind. The visceral language of sensation and injury she used in reference to her own ill health and her public's neglect in her later years comes from a different (though certainly related) register from Warren's sentimental account of American women's 'immutable' affections and attachments.[75]

---

[70] CM, *Letters on Education*, 4.
[71] See Edmund Hayes, 'The Private Poems of Mercy Otis Warren', *New England Quarterly*, 54 (1981), 199–224.   [72] MOW to GW, July 1795, MOWP1.
[73] See, for example, MOW to JA, 27 Apr. 1785, WAP.
[74] CM to MOW, 15 July 1785, WAP.
[75] See, for example, CM to Ralph Griffith, November 1790, GLC, and MOW to CM, July 1789, MOWP1. On sentiment and sensibility in this context, see: Jay Fliegelman, *Prodigals and Pilgrims: The American Revolution against Patriarchal Authority* (Cambridge: Cambridge University Press, 1982); Sarah Knott, 'A Cultural History of

But what connects Macaulay and Warren's use of languages of feeling, and indeed what particularly distinguishes their correspondence, is the continuity both women perceived between sentiment or sensibility and the political characters they claimed as republican women. 'Can patriotism', Macaulay enquired of Warren, as if to corroborate their shared affection, 'dwell in a heart where friendship has no place?'[76] Warren also saw women's love of country as peculiarly bound up with the 'social and benevolent feelings' that had their root where 'the parental, the filial and the family affections operat[e] strongly and pervad[e] every faculty of the soul'.[77] Ideas of privacy and affection, of sentiment and sociability, afforded Macaulay and Warren (this book suggests) powerful confirmation of the political authority they often claimed. Such ideas were central to the ways in which they might imagine a public role for themselves or link the predominantly civic discourses they espoused to their own position as women. With this in mind, I now want to move on to consider some recent historical and critical approaches to eighteenth-century British and American women and writers.

II Republicanism and the 'Problem of Gender'

John Pocock perceives an incongruity between Macaulay and Warren's femininity and their adoption, articulation, and critique of republican ideals of citizenship. This 'problem of gender' (to which he returns on a number of occasions in an article in Hilda Smith's useful collection of essays as well as in his *Barbarism and Religion*) suggests that the identification of these two historians with republicanism should have somehow precluded their identification of themselves as women.[78] 'What was a woman', he asks of Macaulay, 'doing adopting so unreservedly an ideology based wholly on ancient civic virtue, on a reading of the Greek and Roman classics?'[79] Similarly, in a brief discussion of

---

Sensibility in the Era of the American Revolution', Ph.D. Diss. (Oxford University, 1999); Bruce Burgett, *Sentimental Bodies: Sex, Gender and Citizenship in the Early Republic* (Princeton: Princeton University Press, 1998); Julie Ellison, *Cato's Tears and the Making of Anglo-American Emotion* (Chicago: Chicago University Press, 1999).

[76] CM to MOW, 15 July 1785, WAP.
[77] MOW to GW, 4 July 1785, MOWP1.
[78] J. G. A Pocock, 'Catharine Macaulay, Patriot Historian', in Hilda Smith (ed.), *Women Writers and the Early Modern British Political Tradition*, 243–59, at 249.
[79] Ibid. 248.

Macaulay's American tour and Warren's Anti-Federalist *History*, he writes: 'we might ask... why these powerful female intellects adopted so primarily masculine a central value as that of classical citizenship.'[80] Pocock also argues here that modern feminism does not find its roots in classical republicanism, but is rather the heir to the other of the two discourses he often suggests divide the eighteenth century to which he gives the shorthand of 'commerce' rather than 'virtue'.[81] For him, Warren and Macaulay are disallowed a feminist perspective because they were republicans and logically excluded from republicanism because they were women.

There are a few points suggested by his reading with which this book takes issue. Macaulay and Warren's use of a republican discourse should be considered not simply in terms of the ways in which their sex disqualified them from citizenship under the conditions of that discourse (a fact of which both women were certainly aware, as we shall see), but rather as a question of the identifications they were capable of making. As Whigs of a particular commonwealth hue, it was inevitable that Warren and Macaulay would find the 'masculine' classical ideal of liberty appealing. They might also describe the affirming qualities of their political intellects as 'manly' in ways that were clearly related to this ideal. Warren's friends and husband were commending her political intellect and patriotic tenacity when they spoke of her 'masculine genius', and Macaulay explained that 'when we compliment the appearance of a more than ordinary energy in the female mind we call it masculine'.[82] As Macaulay's iconographic association with Marcus Junius Brutus might suggest, the masculinity these women claimed for their writing was intimately bound up with a politics that was particularly civic, definitively republican.[83] Yet, even as Macaulay and Warren associated the values of a generically 'public' masculinity with their own

---

[80] J. G. A. Pocock, *Barbarism and Religion II: Narratives of Civil Government* (Cambridge: Cambridge University Press, 1999), 257.

[81] 'Modern feminism... might seem to derive more from the other side of the great Eighteenth Century debate, that which asserted the primacy of commerce over virtue' (Pocock, 'Catharine Macaulay', 251). Pocock is of course suggesting that the discourse of modern feminism is liberal in a way that would exclude Macaulay and Warren, but, as this book reveals, their republicanism (and feminism) certainly possessed recognizably liberal elements.

[82] CM, *Letters on Education*, 204. JW to MOW, 6 June 1776, MOWP2.

[83] I discuss Macaulay's association with Brutus in Chapters 1 and 3.

literary characters, so they might also regard ideas of the feminine as lending value to the authority they claimed. 'The Greco-Roman ideal of citizenship', writes Pocock, 'was above all patriarchal and assumed a rigid separation between the public and private spheres'.[84] If classical republicanism relegated the feminine to a private sphere whose associations with intimacy and propinquity meant it was utterly, inevitably devalued, then this was not the case with the eighteenth-century version of that discourse that Warren and Macaulay articulated nor, indeed, with the cultural milieux in which they more generally wrote and lived. In metropolitan London and provincial Massachusetts the conception of the separation of the private from the public spheres was certainly not as rigid as the classical Athenian division between *oikos* and *polis* to which Pocock here refers. Privacy might define a culture of associational, oppositionist republicanism, such as that espoused by the Boston Committee of Correspondence (which was founded in Warren's home) or the London radical clubs and societies whose members met and conversed at Macaulay's table. It could imply the importance of the ideas conveyed by correspondence, or denote the positive social virtues of women's transatlantic converse. Or it might, when the *polis* was seen as marked by a corruption believed to be endemic, suggest the irrefutable and opposing value of the language of the heart.

The gendered associations of eighteenth-century discourses and their attendant distinctions between ideas of publicity and privacy were perhaps more diverse and flexible than Pocock in his account of Macaulay and Warren's political identifications might allow. As I later suggest, Warren and Macaulay really did not see anything weird about writing as republicans while writing as women, but might use a varied range of gendered characteristics to explain or legitimate that connection, or to render the identity of a 'female patriot historian' that bit more publicly persuasive and rhetorically powerful. Equally, the republicanism of a Massachusetts' Anti-Federalist or a London 'disaffected patriot' was not at all times self-identical, invariable, or consistent, and it was not always emphatically classical either. As Barbara Taylor rightly notes of Pocock's account of Macaulay: 'he ignores all aspects of her thought that do not tally with his portrait of her as a quintessentially republican thinker, including her theology, her natural rights philosophy and her

[84] Pocock, 'Catharine Macaulay', 249.

feminism.'[85] Some of the 'aspects of thought' that Pocock neglects to consider are, I think, precisely those through which Warren and Macaulay might connect their experience of their gender—their awareness of their own status as women—to the political and economic discourses of which they proved such adept public exponents. In different ways for Warren and Macaulay, then, ideas concerning the 'natural' affections, feminine privacy, religion, learning, profession, sensibility and sociability inflected, and were imbricated with, the republicanism they espoused. Rather than seeing an intractable discontinuity between their gender and their politics, it is through their synthesis of these ideas, the variety of their identifications, and their particular use of the political discourses that both found so appealing that a feminist reading of these important republican women might emerge.

Feminist approaches to eighteenth-century British women's history and writing have been influenced by a reinvigorated debate on the public, the private, and the social. Often engaging with Hannah Arendt's and Jurgen Habermas's now familiar models of public space, such approaches have enabled the broad reconsideration of the particular modernity of eighteenth-century women's social networks, their participation in the literary marketplace, and their reading and writing practices.[86] For example, in an influential study, Anne Mellor has

---

[85] Barbara Taylor, *Mary Wollstonecraft and the Feminist Imagination* (Cambridge: Cambridge University Press, 2003), 297.

[86] Examples are numerous and include: Elizabeth Eger *et al.* (eds.), *Women, Writing and the Public Sphere 1700–1830* (Cambridge: Cambridge University Press, 2000); Hannah Barker and Elaine Chalus (eds.), *Gender in Eighteenth Century England: Roles, Representations and Responsibilities* (London; Longman, 1997); Kathryn Gleadle and Sarah Richardson (eds.), *Women in British Politics, 1760–1860*; Vivien Jones (ed.), *Women and Literature in Britain, 1700–1800* (Cambridge: Cambridge University Press, 2000); Harriet Guest, *Small Change: Women, Learning, Patriotism, 1750–1810* (Chicago: Chicago University Press, 2000); Lawrence Klein, 'Gender and the Public/Private Distinction in the Eighteenth Century: Some Questions about Evidence and Analytic Procedure', *Eighteenth-Century Studies*, 29 (1995); Paula Backsheider and Timothy Dykstal (eds.), *The Intersection of the Public and Private Spheres in Early Modern England* (London: Cassell, 1996); Naomi Tadmor, ' "In the Even my Wife Read to Me": Women, Reading and Household Life in the Eighteenth Century', in James Raven, Naomi Tadmor, and Helen Small (eds.), *The Practice and Representation of Reading in England* (Cambridge: Cambridge University Press, 1996); Deborah Heller, 'Bluestocking Salons and the Public Sphere', *Eighteenth-Century Life*, 22 (1998), 59–82; in a French context Dena Goodman, *The Republic of Letters: A Cultural History of the French Enlightenment* (Ithaca, NY: Cornell University Press, 1994), and 'Public Sphere and Private Life: Toward a Synthesis of Current Historiographical Approaches to the Old Regime', *History*

argued that 'women participated fully in the discursive public sphere as Habermas defined it'.[87] Yet, in a book where, as Devoney Looser notes, Catharine Macaulay is 'curiously omi[tted]', Mellor makes such participation the exclusive privilege of those women whose literary projects she reads as laudably loyalist and moral: who were more oblique, perhaps, in their account of the link between the conservative political and economic discourses that energized their writing and their own position as women.[88]

A more complex account of conservative British women's relationship to interrelated public, private, and social 'spheres' emerges from the collected essays of Nicole Pohl's and Betty Schellenberg's excellent *Reconsidering the Bluestockings*.[89] Betty Rizzo's, Elizabeth Child's, and Susan Staves's contributions all suggest how women's social networks might have licensed their 'intellectual autonomy' or enabled them to think of their learning, philanthropy, or commercial–industrial activities in terms of their (ambivalently) public significance.[90] In an important essay, Emma Major reads the bluestocking 'politics of sociability' and the very specifically Anglican national identity to which these women saw themselves connected as 'the inverse of Hannah Arendt's concept of society as that 'curiously hybrid realm where private interests assume national importance'.[91] And (in marked contrast to

and Theory, 3 (1992), 1–20, and in a German one, Hannah Arendt, *Rahel Varhnhagaen, The Life of a Jewess*, ed. Liliane Weissberg (Baltimore: Johns Hopkins University Press, 1997).

[87] Anne Mellor, *Mothers of the Nation: Women's Political Writing in England, 1780–1830* (Bloomington, Ind.: Indiana University Press, 2000), 2.

[88] Looser, 'Those Historical Laurels', 224. Mellor's account of More's conservatism seems to take the rectitude of her project of the moralizing of commerce as read.

[89] Nicole Pohl and Betty Schellenberg (eds.), *Reconsidering the Bluestockings* (San Marino: Huntington Library, 2003).

[90] Betty Rizzo, 'Two Versions of Community: Montagu and Scott', 193–215 (looks at Sarah Scott's and Elizabeth Montagu's competing models of community); Elizabeth Child, 'Elizabeth Montagu, Bluestocking Businesswoman', 153–75 (investigates the public dimensions of Elizabeth Montagu's personae as industrialist, philanthropist, and salonnière); Susan Staves, 'Church of England Clergy and Women Writers', 81–105 (explores the many different ways in which the Anglican clergy supported and promoted a culture of women's learning). All in Pohl and Schellenberg (eds.), *Reconsidering the Bluestockings*. Quote from Staves at 103.

[91] Emma Major, 'The Politics of Sociability: Public Dimensions of the Bluestocking Millennium', in Pohl and Schellenberg (eds.), *Reconsidering the Bluestockings*, 175–193, at 182 and quoting Hannah Arendt, *The Human Condition* (Chicago: Chicago University Press, 1958), 35.

Mellor) Harriet Guest stresses the importance of picturing the continuity between the feminisms of Catharine Macaulay and the bluestockings in terms of the space Habermas's *Structural Transformation* can be read as implying for women's participation in a literary public sphere.[92] As this book makes clear, an easily perceived ideological gulf often divided the republican Macaulay and Warren from these British women whose accounts of nationhood were so predominantly loyalist or liberal. And yet, in both Britain and America, ideas about the advantages of women's learning; about the socially beneficial effects of their intellects and conversation; and about the moral character of femininity itself meant that it was often useful for these women to think of themselves as connected rather than opposed. Macaulay wrote of herself and Elizabeth Montagu as members of a 'sisterhood' of writers. She considered her learning in terms of its polite function in ways that were clearly related to those of Montagn's assemblies.[93] Warren (who was equally familiar with the term 'sisterhood' as it was applied to New England's women of learning) admired bluestocking intellects where she could not approve of their politics, read a wide range of seventeenth- and eighteenth-century British women's writing, and encouraged her friends and her five sons to do the same.[94] When she came to choose an authoritative cultural figure to whom to dedicate her 1790 *Poems, Dramatic and Miscellaneous*, Warren selected Elizabeth Montagu, with whom she subsequently corresponded. The volume's opening piece celebrated herself and Montagu as 'sister pen[s]' and called for an appreciation of women's writing beyond the 'local fondness' of national distinction.[95]

---

[92] Harriet Guest, 'Bluestocking Feminism', in Pohl and Schellenberg (eds.), *Reconsidering the Bluestockings*, 59–81.
[93] CM to Edward Dilly, 22 Apr. 1774, HL. See my discussion of these issues in Chapter 2.
[94] Warren had read works by, for example, Elizabeth Singer Rowe, Hesther Chapone (she preferred the poems of Phillis Wheatley, which she read around the same time), Elizabeth Carter, Elizabeth Montagu, and Anna Laetitia Barbauld. On her sons' reading British women's writing, see, for example, MOW to GW, n.d., 1794, MOWP1.
[95] Abigail Adams and Warren both admired Montagu's *Essay*. 'I should have wished to have formed an acquaintance with her', Adams wrote to Warren from London 'had I not learnt that she was a violent anti-American' (AA to MOW, 14 May 1787, WAP). Warren was still keen to have Montagu's endorsement of her poems despite evident political (and national) differences. MOW, 'To Mrs Montagu, Author of "Observations on the Genius and Writings of Shakespeare"', *Poems, Dramatic and Miscellaneous* (Boston: I. Thomas and E. T. Andrews, 1790), ll. 12, 23.

The Anglo-American milieux in which Macaulay and Warren wrote and lived might describe themselves as polite as well as political, as civil as much as potentially civic in tone. One feature of these cultures was the encouragement of women's intellectual sociability and their writing. This meant that Mercy Warren and Catharine Macaulay might productively think of themselves together with other women of learning in terms of what Pohl and Schellenberg describe in their introduction to *Reconsidering the Bluestockings* as a 'collectively articulated and recognizable, if informal, sense of identity'.[96]

Yet particular national and political differences might also be important to the ways in which Warren and Macaulay understood their identities as women and as authors. These could be understood in terms of a different but related critical strand in women's history. In the 1980s, the ground-breaking work of Linda Kerber, Mary-Beth Norton, and Jane Rendall suggested various reinterpretations of women's roles in revolutionary and early republican America.[97] What Kerber influentially called 'republican motherhood' described a model of femininity that associated women's domestic virtues with national civic morality. Linking classical notions of female patriotism with eighteenth-century ideals of sentimental femininity, the figure of the 'republican mother' might exemplify the interrelationship of the private and the public even as she herself confirmed (by her embodiment of intimate and domestic virtues which remained normatively defined) women's exclusion from the 'masculine' realm of politics. Yet such models of femininity might offer American women a means of imagining their political characters and suggest ways, as Jane Rendall put it, of 'uniting public and private responsibilities for women'.[98] More recently, scholars have re-examined Kerber's model in specific American contexts and locales. Jan Lewis looks at the relationship of ideas of republican femininity to those of conjugal affection, Eyal Rabinovitch traces an influence on nineteenth-century women's associations, and Rosemarie Zagarri has explored the

[96] Nicole Pohl and Betty Schellenberg, 'Introduction: A Bluestocking Historiography', in Pohl and Schellenberg (eds.), *Reconsidering the Bluestockings*, 15.

[97] Linda Kerber, *Women of the Republic: Intellect and Ideology in Revolutionary America* (New York: Norton, 1980); Mary-Beth Norton, *Liberty's Daughters: The Revolutionary Experience of American Women, 1750–1800* (London: Little, Brown and Co, 1980); Jane Rendall, *The Origins of Modern Feminism: Women in Britain, France and the United States, 1780–1860* (Chicago: Lyceum Books, 1985).

[98] Rendall, *The Origins of Modern Feminism*, 34.

European dimensions of these ideas and their links to different Federalist and Democratic–Republican accounts of gender.[99] Linda Kerber has also redefined her account of women, domesticity, and citizenship in a peculiarly restrictive High Federalist context.[100] The important essays of Ruth Bloch, meanwhile, explore a variety of the 'gendered meanings of virtue'. In some persuasive readings of the overlapping discourses of eighteenth-century Anglo-America (religious, political, and literary-sentimental) Bloch stresses the breadth of the private and social roles which under a banner of republican femininity (broadly defined) might facilitate women's relationship to a sense of the public.[101]

Macaulay and Warren saw their republicanism and their gender as related in ways that suggest that range of meanings that Bloch argues underpinned eighteenth-century America's models of patriotic femininity. They often described themselves as Roman matrons, figures whose patriotism and public status were bound up with their personal affections, familial attachments, and an apparently indubitable moral privacy. Warren celebrated Roman women in her revolutionary poems and her *Sack of Rome*, and her choice of epistolary pseudonym (Marcia) suggests a political identification beyond the familiar conventions of eighteenth-century women's correspondence. Equally, as Philip Hicks

---

[99] Jan Lewis, 'The Republican Wife: Virtue and Seduction in the Early Republic', *William and Mary Quarterly*, 44 (1987), 689–721; Rosemarie Zagarri, 'Morals, Manners and the Republican Mother', *American Quarterly*, 44 (1992), 192–215, and 'The Rights of Man and Woman in Post-Revolutionary America', *William and Mary Quarterly*, 55 (1998), 203–30; Eyal Rabinovitch, 'Gender and the Public Sphere: Alternative Forms of Integration in Nineteenth-Century America', *Sociological Theory*, 19 (2001), 344–70. See also Paula Baker, 'The Domestication of Politics: Women and American Political Society, 1780–1920', *American Historical Review*, 89 (1984), 620–47; Carole Pateman, 'Equality, Difference, Subordination: The Politics of Motherhood and Women's Citizenship', in Gisela Bock and Susan James (eds.), *Beyond Equality and Difference: Citizenship, Feminist Politics and Female Subjectivity* (London: Routledge, 1992), 19–20; Peter Messer, 'Writing Women into History: Defining Gender and Citizenship in Post Revolutionary America', *Studies in Eighteenth Century Culture*, 28 (1999), 341–60; Mary P. Ryan, *Women in Public: Between Banners and Ballots* (Baltimore: Johns Hopkins University Press, 1990).

[100] Linda Kerber, 'The Paradox of Women's Citizenship in the Early Republic: The Case of *Martin vs. Massachusetts*, 1805', *American Historical Review*, 97 (1992), 349–78.

[101] Ruth Bloch, 'The Gendered Meanings of Virtue in Revolutionary America' (1987), 'Religion, Literary Sentimentalism and Popular Revolutionary Ideology' (1994), and 'Gender and the Public/Private Dichotomy in American Revolutionary Thought' (2001), all reprinted in *Gender and Morality in Anglo-American Culture, 1650–1800* (Berkeley and Los Angeles: University of California Press, 2003).

has shown in an important essay, Roman women also figure prominently in Macaulay's historical writing.[102] She was represented 'lamenting the lost liberties of Rome' in a popularly reproduced portrait by Catherine Read, and the figure of the *Matrona* was one of her favourite ways of staging her reputation in the 1760s and 1770s.[103] The patriotic *Matrona* united the sentimental elements of classical republicanism with perhaps more modern ideas of properly 'feminine' feeling. Thus, for two women who were certainly aware of how ideas of gender difference provided powerful sources of authority for their political arguments and identities, the *Matrona* clearly possessed a real appeal. While she represented the link of 'feminine' privacy to patriotism, she was also associated with ideas of learning or cultural acquisition. Her role could be seen as public in the sense that it was admonitory and inspirational: in that her rational exhortations might themselves increase the nation's stock of virtue. Though notions of maternity were certainly important to the ideal of the *Matrona*, as Macaulay and Warren defined it, they were also, as I later suggest, only part of a wide range of sentimental identifications (both unconscious and strategic) through which these women pictured the correlation between the civic political discourses of which they were such articulate exponents and their own gendered position.

It is important to bear in mind that the ideal of the *Matrona* was related to an international eighteenth-century tradition of representing female intellectuals familiar, for example, to the women of the blue-stocking circle. It was in these terms that Catherine Read wanted to paint a series of portraits of British learned women as Roman matrons or that the women of France or Spain might be celebrated for their classical knowledge.[104] Yet, while the *Matrona*'s generic sentimental, civic, and

[102] See Philip Hicks, 'Catharine Macaulay's Civil War: Gender, History and Republicanism in Georgian Britain', *Journal of British Studies*, 41 (2002), 170–98. See also Sue Wiseman, 'Catharine Macaulay: History, Republicanism and the Public Sphere', in Eger *et al.* (eds.), *Women, Writing and the Public Sphere*, 181–99, and Claire Gilbride-Fox, 'Catharine Macaulay: An Eighteenth-Century Clio', *Winturthur Portfolio*, 4 (1968), 129–42.

[103] As I suggest in Chapter 2. According to the *London Magazine* in its account of Macaulay's life (illustrated by Read's portrait of her lamenting Rome's lost liberties), the characters of historian and Roman matron were synonymous: 'It was only a short time after her marriage that she gave herself to the world, as prefixed to this months magazine, the impartial historian, and the Roman Matron', *London Magazine* (July 1770), 331.

[104] On eighteenth-century Spanish learned women, see Monica Bolufer, 'On Women's Reason, Education and Love: Women and Men of the Enlightenment in Spain and

scholarly connotations might suggest the international community of eighteenth-century women of learning, there was also perhaps something markedly different about her appearance as a figure for the politics of Atlantic republicanism. And this difference was bound up with the very particular kinds of patriotism the culture of the American colonies were believed to foster and engender in their elite women of learning. When Catharine Macaulay wrote to Sarah Prince-Gill that she was often disappointed to find that 'just sentiments on the rights of nature and society with generous feelings for public liberty are so uncommon in our sex', Prince-Gill was happy to inform her this was not the case in Massachusetts.[105] She knew many women, she told Macaulay, 'who are warm ascribers and steady friends of liberty' and who cultivated their patriotism alongside their intellects. 'What more rational than to employ the powers of genius and of eloquence in... defending the rights of humanity?' she asked her. 'Yes, my dear madam, there are among us... women not a few animated with this philanthropy!'[106] As Alfred Young notes, Prince-Gill's 'animated' patriotic philanthropy drew its energy from the particular associational culture of Boston's South Church.[107] 'I glory in my country!' Prince-Gill wrote to Macaulay, celebrating the writing and actions of their mutual friend James Otis. 'I glory in Boston my native town.... Our ancestors wisely took care to instil the principles of liberty into the minds of their children and to their provident care it is owing that America hath made such a noble stand against the inroads of despotism and produces such noble

France', *Gender and History*, 10 (1998), 183–216, and 'Los Intelectuales Valencianos y la Cultura Británica del Siglo XVIII', *Estudis*, 12 (2001), 237–40. On Read's portrait of Elizabeth Carter as a Roman matron, see Guest, 'Bluestocking Feminism'. On Read's portraits, see Victoria Manners, 'Catherine Read: The English Rosalba', *The Connoisseur* (Dec. 1931), 376–6; (Jan. 1932), 35–40; (Mar. 1932), 171–8.

[105] CM to Sophronia (Sarah Prince-Gill), n.d., 1769, GLC. For the factual background of the Macaulay–Gill correspondence, see Monica Letzring, 'Sarah Price Gill and the John Adams–Catharine Macaulay Correspondence', *Proceedings of the Massachussets Historical Society*, 53 (1977), 107–15. On Gill, see also Laurie Crumpacker and Carol F. Karlsen, Introduction, *The Journal of Esther Edwards Burr, 1754–1757*, ed. Crumpactes and Karlsen (New Haven: Yale University Press, 1984).

[106] Sarah Prince-Gill to CM, 8 Dec. 1769, GLC.

[107] Alfred F. Young, 'The Women of Boston, "Persons of Consequence" in the Making of the American Revolution, 1765–76', in Harriet Applewhite and Darlene B. Levy (eds.), *Women and Politics in the Age of the Democratic Revolution* (Ann Arbor: University of Michigan Press, 1990), 181–226.

defenders of her rights.'[108] Macaulay's American correspondents and friends told her that she would feel particularly at home in New England because of the women of its prominent political and religious families who, like her, were well read in history and politics and saw themselves as the heirs of particularly classical republican virtues.[109] This was one reason why Macaulay was so interested in Boston women like Elizabeth Mayhew and Sarah Prince-Gill and why she found the friendship of Mercy Otis Warren so welcome and gratifying.[110] It was to an already-established and distinctive Atlantic tradition of representing the republican politics of gender that Warren and Macaulay were writing when they began corresponding in 1773.

In the second half of the eighteenth century, ideas of gender difference shaped the cultural understanding of what Anglo-American conflict and nationhood might mean. As Kathleen Wilson, Dror Wahrman, and Linda Colley have all persuasively argued, in an era of imperial conflict and national redefinition, gender lent persuasive clusters of ideas to bolster often anxious accounts of the 'imagined communities' which the Atlantic connected and divided.[111] As Wahrman writes of the representation of the American war in Britain, notions of masculinity and femininity fulfilled a 'broader function... in providing a convenient way of talking about the bigger issues of identity... raised by this

[108] Sarah Prince-Gill to CM, 8 Dec. 1769, GLC.
[109] It was in these terms that James Otis praised the virtues of both the women of Massachusetts and Macaulay. Macaulay's *History* was, he wrote, 'proof of the truth of an old observation which I shall express in my own way: God and Nature... in point of genius have been equally kind to both sexes: and were it not for the tyranny of custom... every age and nation would furnish more frequent instances of ladies rivalling the gentlemen in the arts and sciences' (James Otis to CM, 27 July 1769, GLC). Otis also famously alluded to women's intellectual and political equality in his *Rights of the British Colonies Asserted and Proved* (1764).
[110] See, for example, CM to JA, 11 Sept. 1774 on Warren's correspondence: 'there is no circumstance can flatter me more than the being a favorite... of women of equal sentiment to your fair friend' (*The Papers of John Adams*, ed. Taylor).
[111] Benedict Anderson, *Imagined Communities: Reflections on the Origin and Spread of Nationalism* (London: Verso, 1991); Wilson, *The Island Race*; Linda Colley, *Britons: Forging the Nation, 1707–1837* (London: Pimlico, 1992); Dror Wahrman, 'The English Problem of Identity in the American Revolution', *American Historical Review*, 106 (2001), 1236–62. See also Felicity Nussbaum, *Torrid Zones: Maternity, Sexuality and Empire in Eighteenth-Century English Narratives* (Baltimore: Johns Hopkins University Press, 1995); Laura Brown, *The Ends of Empire: Women and Ideology in Early Eighteenth-Century England* (Ithaca, NY: Cornell University Press, 1993); Bloch, 'The Gendered Meanings of Virtue in Revolutionary America' (1987).

crisis'.[112] Such notions were integral to British and American cultures and the discourses that defined the relationship between them. They were written into the debate on transatlantic association and difference, on unity and separation, and played an insistent role in this debate's redefinition in the 1780s and 1790s. Particular feminine or masculine models might serve as shorthand for legitimation or censure, for avid patriotic celebration or bitter national reproach. They were also crucial to Macaulay and Warren's self-conception and representation as women and (as Warren said) as 'politicians'. I have already suggested some of the ways in which these women might connect ideas of gender difference to the public voice they claimed, and this book looks at how such ideas might emerge in response to particular Anglo-American debates or specific moments in the political culture of the eighteenth-century Atlantic. Thus, while both women often (importantly) wrote to the premiss that the mind had no sex, they might also claim a distinction of gender to secure their literary authority or qualify the indubitable nature of their politics in an era when the truths of patriotism and nationhood were never wholly self-evident but hotly contested.

Each chapter of this book explores a different way in which they might do so. I do not offer comprehensive biographical readings of Warren and Macaulay's lives or provide fully detailed accounts of the content and ideas of their expansive historical writing (though their histories and their lives of course feature importantly throughout).[113] The intention

---

[112] Wahrman, 'The English Problem of Identity in the American Revolution', 1251.

[113] Philip Hicks is writing a book on Macaulay's historical and political theory. Useful accounts of Macaulay's historical writing to date include Devoney Looser, ' "Deep-Immersed in the Historic Mine": Catharine Macaulay's "History in Letters" ', in Looser, *British Women Writers and the Writing of History, 1670–1820* (Baltimore: Johns Hopkins University Press, 2000), 119–50; Bridget and Christopher Hill, 'Catharine Macaulay and the Seventeenth Century', *Welsh History Review*, 3 (1967), 381–402, and 'Catharine Macaulay's "History" and her "Catalogue of Tracts" ', *Seventeenth-Century History*, 8 (1003), 269–85; Barbara Brandon Schnorrenberg, 'An Opportunity Missed: Catharine Macaulay on the Revolution of 1688', *Studies in Eighteenth-Century Culture*, 20 (1990), 231–40; Wiseman, 'Catharine Macaulay'. On Warren's *History* the best work is that of Lester Cohen. See his 'Explaining the Revolution: Ideology and Ethics in Mercy Otis Warren's Historical Theory', *William and Mary Quarterly*, 37 (1980), 200–18, and *The Revolutionary Histories: Contemporary Narratives of the American Revolution* (Ithaca, NY: Cornell University Press, 1980. See also Nina Baym, 'Mercy Otis Warren's Gendered Melodrama of Revolution', *South Atlantic Quarterly*, 90 (1991), 531–54; Richards, *Mercy Otis Warren*; William Raymond Smith, *History as Argument: Three Patriot Historians of the American Revolution* (The Hague: Mouton, 1966).

here has been rather to select some moments between the colonial crises of the 1760s and the first administrations of the United States, suggesting how Macaulay and Warren contributed to and participated in Anglo-American political debate and exploring the cultural (and gendered) significance that might be seen to be attached to this participation. I begin by examining Macaulay's relationship to the models of masculine virtue which defined British opposition politics in the 1760s and early 1770s. I suggest here just how persuasively Macaulay embodied a patriotism apparently unavailable to men in public office, and how her gender might have granted her, as a writer and republican, a certain political advantage. In Chapter 2 I turn to consider (from the opposite gendered perspective) how Macaulay's transatlantic fame was also crucially bound up with those ideas of learning, profession, and domesticity which were celebrated as particularly feminine in Britain during the years immediately prior to the American war. In the third chapter I look more closely at Britain's shifting gender politics between 1769 and 1783. It is only in the context of an anxiously loyalist nation undergoing complex and urgent redefinitions of patriotism under the shadow of war, I argue, that Catharine Macaulay's association with ideas of savage and sexual excess at the turn of the 1780s can be fully understood. The perspective then moves across the Atlantic, to colonies coming to terms with the dissolution of the imperial-sentimental family of which they saw themselves a part. Here I suggest that Mercy Otis Warren's revolutionary correspondence with women reveals how conservative and normative ideas of privacy and feeling might be bound up with a sense of the public thought in the 1770s to be distinctively American. Chapter 5 examines a rather different Anglo-American conflict in the debate on national and cultural identity with which Macaulay and Warren were involved, as republicans and women of learning, in Boston during 1784–5. Competing notions of corrupt and virtuous femininity had come to be (I suggest here) peculiarly essential to America's early nationalist sense of itself. The book's long final chapter, written in a series of nine, accretive readings, might be read as an extended example (or perhaps culmination) of my methods of research and writing throughout. Closely tracing Warren's perspective on political debate in the 'critical period' (from Shays's rebellion to Jefferson's election), I suggest how the gendered aesthetics of her Anti-Federalism (based on a profound sense of republican displacement and disenchantment) lent her a particularly powerful means of articulating the link between her femininity and her politics. By the turn of the 1790s, Macaulay and Warren's transatlantic friendship—what the latter described as their 'immutable attachment'—came to represent, for both, a source of powerful consolation in an era they saw characterized by personal losses and political disappointments. Warren and Macaulay felt increasingly marginal to the transatlantic political culture in which they had both, two decades earlier, figured so significantly. Yet paradoxically, as I suggest in conclusion, it was precisely this sense of loss and displacement that engendered Macaulay and Warren's newly confident, perhaps indignant, sense of themselves as female and republican political subjects. Republicanism certainly enabled Warren and Macaulay's feminism in so far as their perceptions of the failure of the former in the project of the revolutionary Atlantic allowed the latter to emerge.

1

Catharine Macaulay, Thomas Hollis, and the London Opposition

On 7 June 1773, Mercy Otis Warren wrote to Catharine Macaulay enquiring:

Has the Genius of Liberty which once pervaded the bosom of each British hero animating them to the worthiest deeds forsaken that devoted island, or has she only concealed her lovely form until some more happy period shall bid her lift her avenging hand to the terror of every arbitrary despot and to the confusion of their impious minions on each side the Atlantic?[1]

This question began Macaulay and Warren's correspondence and a friendship that was to last almost twenty years. To Warren's question Macaulay replied:

You ask me, dear Madam, whether the Genius of Liberty has entirely forsaken our devoted isle. The acts of parliament which have passed this session and to which we have tamely submitted will be a compleat answer to that question. But that the Goddess of Liberty has left in the minds of individuals some traces of her former residence will, I hope, appear plainly to you in the conduct of myself...[2]

The movement here from a genius (whose loss is discovered in the behaviour of a corrupt parliament and a supine populace) to a goddess (who still resides in her mind) suggests just how far Catharine Macaulay might have regarded herself as Liberty's last English representative.[3] Her

---

[1] MOW to CM, 7 June 1773, MOWP1.
[2] CM to MOW, 11 Sept. 1774, WAP. Over a year elapsed between Warren's question and Macaulay's response, due, as Macaulay put it herself in this letter, to 'a long period of uninterrupted sickness'.
[3] In this letter Macaulay also mentions her brother, John Sawbridge's, parliamentary efforts in the American cause, so perhaps British Liberty here has a familial rather than an individual identity.

claim here is entirely characteristic of her self-representation of this era more generally as well as of the way in which she was portrayed by many of her contemporaries. To the British and American Whigs and radicals of the 1770s opposition, Liberty's genius did indeed seem to have expired, and Catharine Macaulay, England's 'incomparable female patriot', represented one last hope of its revival.[4]

The year that elapsed between Mercy Warren's question and Catharine Macaulay's response had given these two republican women real reason to lament. Following the Boston Tea Party, the British government passed the four coercive acts to which Macaulay refers. Resistance to the ministry's repressive measures in both Houses of Parliament was slight, and support for American liberties from London's corporations was unusually unforthcoming.[5] While the House of Commons appeared to fall under the thrall of the ministry, public spirit out of doors seemed suddenly subsumed by private mercantile concerns. It was a year in which the *Annual Register* might describe the voice of Whig and radical dissent as 'weak and unavailing', a year in which 'opposition seemed reduced to little more than a name'.[6] During 1773–4, oppositional politics became fractured and confused; corruption and private interests seemed to have engulfed the public sphere, and political antagonists like Samuel Johnson and James Burgh might agree that the term 'patriot' had become unmeaning and outmoded.[7]

The traditional values of masculine virtue and public spirit, which republicans like Catharine Macaulay and Mercy Warren so much admired, were, in 1773–4, perhaps least apparent in the political spaces where they were supposed to be preserved and perpetuated. From British political institutions and public men there was, the two women agreed, little to hope. 'The constitution and government' were, as Macaulay put it, completely 'vitiated', and according to Warren the 'national

---

[4] MOW to CM, 7 June 1773, MOWP1.

[5] On the dissociation between the American cause and London's formerly sympathetic corporations and merchants, see John Sainsbury's definitive account, *Disaffected Patriots: London Supporters of Revolutionary America, 1769–1782* (Quebec: McGill Queens University Press, 1987), Chs. 2, 3. [6] *Annual Register* (1773), 62.

[7] The argument that ideas of patriotism were confused or meaningless was made from opposite political perspectives by Samuel Johnson, *The Patriot* (1774), in *The Works of Samuel Johnson, X. Political Writings*, ed. Donald J. Greene (New Haven: Yale University Press, 1977), and James Burgh, *Political Disquisitions* (London: E. C. Dilly, 1774–5).

legislature' was now simply 'the dupe of venality and corruption'.[8] Far from being the principle which animated the British Constitution, its institutions and elected representatives, Liberty seemed, to Macaulay and Warren, an alien concept in a political culture characterized by corruption and expediency. If Liberty was to be found anywhere in 1774, then it was perhaps in Boston, where, Mercy Warren wrote, 'the genius which once animated Hampdens', Harringtons' and Pyms' has taken up . . . residence', or in Bath, where the woman whose writings had done so much to revive the virtues of the commonwealthmen was there being celebrated as their living embodiment.[9]

By 1774 Catharine Macaulay was regarded as the figurehead and public voice of British and American republicanism. During the decade that preceded the American war, Old and City Whigs, Wilkite radicals, colonial agents, and churchmen from the full spectrum of Anglican and nonconformist backgrounds celebrated her politics, promoted her writing, gathered at her salon, or struggled to acquire an introduction. Regarded as the exemplar of a 'patriotic virtue . . . the most heroic', the early volumes of her *History of England* were said by John Adams to 'strip off the gilding and false lustre from worthless princes and nobles, and bestow the reward of virtue, praise, upon the generous and worthy only'.[10] For Americans she was a 'patroness of liberties' whose writing proved, as Mercy Warren's brother James Otis told her after reading the early volumes of her *History*, 'that God and Nature . . . in point of Genius have been equally kind to both sexes'.[11] New-born New England babies were named in her honour, and colonial leaders promised that the continent would 'raise monuments' to her 'memory and fame'.[12] To her political contemporaries in the London opposition, meanwhile, Catharine Macaulay—salonnière, pamphleteer, historian, patriot—had come to represent the renewed hope of the good old cause.

This chapter explores Catharine Macaulay's fame in the 1760s in the context of the disaffection among the London opposition with British political culture and the masculine identities associated with it.

---

[8] CM, *Observations on a Pamphlet Entitled Thoughts on the Cause of the Present Discontents* (London: E. C. Dilly, 1770), 7 (hereafter cited as *Observations*); MOW to CM, 4 Dec. 1774, MOWP1. [9] MOW to CM, 7 June 1773, MOWP1.
[10] JA to CM, 9 Aug. 1770, *The Diary of John Adams*, ed. L. H. Butterfield, 4 vols. (Cambridge, Mass.: Harvard University Press, 1961), i. 360.
[11] James Otis to CM, 27 July 1769, GLC.
[12] James Bowdoin to CM, 25 Mar. 1777, GLC.

I examine how her patriotic self-confidence and her notoriety might be associated with shifts in the values republicanism attached to notions of gender difference. Looking at Macaulay's pamphlets and letters, the political writing of her contemporaries, and the career of her friend Thomas Hollis, I suggest how in Britain during the years immediately preceding the American war the fall of public man, in his traditional civic republican sense, might precipitate, in the figure of Catharine Macaulay, the rise of female patriotism.[13]

I Patriotic Fame

The Gilder Lehrman collection of Catharine Macaulay's papers includes a short anonymous verse from 1763, 'On Mrs Macaulay's *History of England*'. The verse celebrates the virtues of Macaulay and her writing and is copied in her own hand:

> Born without souls, born for man's delight,
> To charm the sensual touch and wandering sight,
> This the sole use of woman?—impious Turk!
> Profane reviler of heaven's fairest work!
> Shall bolts and bars their noble fire restrain
> By genius as by beauty formed to reign?
> To empire here one far superior see
> Who bids ev'n lordly man himself be free.
> No priestly gorgon cramps her native flame,
> No party nonsense warps her generous aim;
> To man she points the paths his sires have trod;
> Burst his fond chains and snaps the statesman's rod—
> And while, by pay or prejudice misled,
> S——t's and H——e's enshrine the guilty dead
> She from the pedant's hearse and tyrant's grave
> Strips the false plumes that slave historians gave
> And soaring free, where man has checked the flight
> Shows woman fitter both to rule and write.[14]

This verse is typical of representations of Macaulay throughout the 1760s and 1770s, and the fact that she copied and retained it suggests she was happy to be described in this manner. The figure of the learned

---

[13] I am echoing the title of Richard Sennet's *Fall of Public Man: On the Social Psychology of Capitalism* (New York: Vintage, 1977).

[14] [Unattrib.], 'On Mrs Macaulay's *History of England*, 30th November, 1763', GLC.

woman as a kind of erudite empress would perhaps have been familiar to her from earlier texts such as John Duncombe's *Feminiad* (1754) or Thomas Seward's 'Female Right to Literature' (1748).[15] Like these more overtly nationalist poems, the first eight lines of this verse use the language of slavery and imperialism to produce a fairly standard account of the relationship between women's learning and civilized society. The substitution of the empire of beauty for one of genius simply allows Macaulay's intellect to be regarded with the same sort of gallant deference as the enslaved woman whose physical charms inspire desire. As focuses of masculine idolatry, both figures are objectified in the same way. But the verse's second half claims something further for Macaulay's learning in its specifically patriotic and republican nature. As Turkish despotism is linked with Stuart tyranny, Macaulay is seen to effect liberation from a particularly British kind of slavery—namely, that which bound men to a corrupt political system and allowed them to forget the virtuous example of their commonwealth forebears. This verse suggests that Macaulay is the 'fair superior' because her patriotism is not threatened by religious tests, party prejudice, or the pay of the Crown. Unlike that of men, whose principles might be compromised by faction or the pressures of institutional compliance, Macaulay's republicanism remains 'native'—remains pure and untainted. In other words, since she is beyond the system, her patriotism is beyond reproach. It is this position of political exteriority which seems unavailable to her male contemporaries (and particularly to those 'slave' historians which the verse condemns) that renders her 'fitter both to rule and write'.

It is Macaulay's gender, then, that accords her the objectivity that the men in this verse seem to lack. The language of flight in the verse's final lines suggests her escape not only from the obvious prejudice that might be levelled at women of learning but also from the narrative of Britain's political decline and fall which her *History* was praised for describing. Her femininity excludes her from the political order yet her patriotism surpasses it. Since she is, in effect, denied office and its demands, she offers her historical and political critique from a position of disinterested

---

[15] John Duncombe, *The Feminiad: A Poem* (London: M. Cooper, 1754); Thomas Seward, 'The Female Right to Literature, in a Letter to a Young Lady from Florence', in R. Dodsley (ed), *Poems by Several Hands* (London: R. Dodsley, 1748), 296. Both these poems play on a language of imperialism or perhaps orientalism in their accounts of the social benefits of women's learning.

exteriority—a position that is clearly gendered and that this verse represents as both powerful and authoritative.

Here, as in the many other contemporary texts in which she was lionized, Macaulay embodies the values of political independence and public virtue that lay at the heart of British and American republicanism throughout the eighteenth century. Her role is public not only in the sense that she seems in this verse an iconic figure, but because she is represented as possessing the rationality and generality of perspective that enables her to speak for the nation's political interests. Macaulay clearly thought of herself in these terms. In a letter of 1769 she writes to Thomas Hollis thanking him for one of his many gifts of the pamphlets and tracts that formed the raw research material of the later volumes of her *History*. 'I see', says Macaulay in that portentous tone so characteristic of her letters and published writings, 'there are no ages of mankind so degenerate but that disinterested virtue meets with additional reward to the mere consciousness of doing well'.[16] It is typical of Macaulay to be able to turn an expression of thanks into both a slur on the degeneracy of the times and the suggestion of her own superiority. That same year, after receiving the present of a 'magnificent' French snuffbox from her friend Lord Nuneham, she wrote: 'we have yet one nobleman who dispising the senseless dissipation of a worthless age makes it his business to distinguish public virtue.'[17] Macaulay's claim to disinterest in these letters is, of course, mere polite conceit, yet it also suggests how quickly, how easily, she might associate herself with an idea of public virtue.

Much of the argumentative power of Macaulay's response to Burke's *Thoughts on the Cause of the Present Discontents* comes from the force of contrast between her authorial identity (which she describes as being founded on rational disinterest) and his (which she represents as a sort of diseased manifestation of his desire for personal emolument).[18] Similarly, in the manuscript draft of the introduction to her *History's* first volume, Macaulay suggests that her disinterestedness might actually serve to compensate for modernity's unfortunate political shortcomings. 'The societys of the modern ages of the world', she writes, 'are not constituted with powers to bring to an impartial tribunal men trusted in the higher officers of the state. An historian', she confidently asserts, 'is

[16] CM to TH, 9 Jan. 1769, HL.
[17] CM to Lord Nuneham, 5 June 1769, GLC.
[18] CM, *Observations*.

the only person that can preside at such a tribunal'.[19] Later volumes of her *History* are peppered with references to the 'illustrious example' she herself provides of republican independence and impartiality compared with the Tory bias represented by the figure of David Hume, her favourite 'slave historian'.[20] In terms of republicanism's American dimensions, Macaulay's belief in her public role was profound and unambiguous. Writing to Mercy Warren of her hopes that 'the Americans will be the saviours and liberators of the whole British Empire', she expresses her regret that she cannot cross the ocean in order to provide the 'animating example' that might assist the people of Massachusetts 'to support a proper spirit'.[21] It's as if America cannot fulfil its republican promise without her emancipatory presence.

During the 1760s and early 1770s, Macaulay quite evidently considered herself to supply the public standard of patriotic inspiration on both sides of the Atlantic. And she was not that far wrong. The critical reception of the early volumes of her *History* and the scale and nature of the adulation that followed was, in both Britain and America, entirely unprecedented.[22] Macaulay's fame was, as I suggest in a later chapter, quite clearly bound up with that polite and nationalistic celebration of learned women which was so central to British and American literary culture during these decades. Yet her acclaim was unprecedented because of the politics with which she was associated—because of the particular senses in which she might be regarded as a public voice, a public figure. If during this decade Macaulay spoke of herself with such extraordinary self-confidence as republicanism's modern embodiment, it was because this is how she was regarded and promoted by her contemporaries on both sides of the Atlantic.

A real sense of cultural excitement surrounded Macaulay and her publications in the 1760s and 1770s. Her *History* was so warmly

---

[19] CM, This *HE* MS, vol. i, introduction, first draft. This sentence was deleted from later drafts.

[20] See, for example, CM, *History of England from the Accession of James I to that of the Brunswick Line*, vol. vi. (London: A. Hamilton, 1781), p. xiii.

[21] CM to MOW, 11 Sept. 1774, WAP.

[22] For further discussion on Macaulay's fame in the 1760s and the early reception of the *History*, see Bridget Hill, *The Republican Virago: The Life and Times of Catharine Macaulay* (Oxford: Clarendon Press, 1992), and Susan Staves ' "The Liberty of a She-Subject of England": Rights Rhetoric and the Female Thucydides', *Cardazo Studies in Law and Literature*, 1 (1989), 161–83.

welcomed because it was so significantly different from those that had preceded it, in terms of both its explicitly republican content and its careful use of sources, its scholarly nature.[23] The *History* was regarded as a patriotic corrective to the national historical record and was praised as such by Pitt on the floor of the House of Lords. 'Your excellent history [has] been much admired here from its first publication,' James Otis wrote to Macaulay from Boston; 'it is every day sought after and read with great avidity... you have displayed greater talent for history than those who at any period have attempted the British annals,' he concluded warmly.[24] Her account of the Commonwealth and Stuart era was enough, William Livingston enthused from New York, 'to inspire even a court minion with the love of liberty and render the most zealous advocate for despotism, like Milton's Satan on beholding the happiness of Eve, at least for a moment, stupidly good'.[25]

Macaulay's pamphlet publications were equally well regarded. Her *Loose Thoughts* on Hobbes and her utopian *Sketch of a Democratic Form of Government* went through a number of editions and were highly sought after. Her dismissal of Edmund Burke's *Thoughts on the Causes of the Present Discontents* was widely read. These interventions into contemporary political debate were commended for their seriousness and perspicuity and her writing admired for its rational, masculine, and 'nervous' qualities.[26] When Burke made the often cited remark on the responses to his *Thoughts*—'the virago is the best among them'—he captured the way in which Macaulay might be regarded as the opposition's iconic representative.[27] Even the backhanded compliments of Macaulay's political opponents acknowledged her status as republican spokesperson and patriot.

Macaulay's Massachusetts' friends believed firmly in her authority and influence. In effect, they treated her as a mediator between the London opposition and the political establishment. In 1770 a committee was established in Boston to produce a narrative of the events

[23] I discuss the 'scholarly' appeal of Macaulay's *History* in Chapter 2.
[24] James Otis to CM, 27 July 1769, GLC.
[25] William Livingston to CM, 22 Sept. 1769, GLC.
[26] See, for example, *Gentleman's Magazine*, 36 (1766), 439. 'Nervous' here carries the eighteenth-century meaning of 'vigorous, forcible, free from insipidity and confusion'. See *The Oxford English Dictionary*.
[27] Thomas W. Copeland *et al.*, *The Correspondence of Edmund Burke*, 10 vols. (Cambridge: Cambridge University Press, 1958–78), ii. 150.

surrounding the infamous 'massacre', which the town voted to transmit to Macaulay with a request for her 'interposition and influence'.[28] In subsequent years, as a result of further decisions made at town meetings, Macaulay continued to receive packages of intelligence and copies of legal proceedings from William Cooper, Boston's then town clerk.[29] Macaulay's American correspondents clearly felt that their information would be useful to her in her historical project, clearly thought of her as *their* national historian. Indeed, until the late 1780s it was expected among Macaulay's American readers that she would soon produce a history of the recently concluded war precisely because of the amount of material she was known to have gathered from political institutions and individuals in Massachusetts, Rhode Island, New York, and Virginia throughout the 1760s and 1770s.[30] While Americans became increasingly disillusioned with Britain, its parliament, its political men, and each 'fresh instance of venality' the public sphere displayed, Catharine Macaulay seemed to them to retain the virtuous patriotism they associated with their own opposition to government.[31] As a later chapter explores at greater length, Macaulay was clearly regarded as the chronicler and the 'patroness' of the political interests of America's north and middle colonies.

In an era of profound political disaffection among the Atlantic republican community, then, Macaulay's position as a writer of highly regarded works of political history and interventionist pamphlets in which she made no bones about her radical opinions meant she was regarded as possessing a crucial public role. In a range of popular writing during this decade, Macaulay is frequently spoken of as if she were about to be elected to parliament. Claims for her political candidacy often followed satiric accounts of the general effeminacy of modern Britain and its political life in particular. In 1766, for example, Macaulay

[28] James Bowdoin, Samuel Pemberton, and Joseph Warren to CM, 23 Mar. 1770, GLC. See also CM to the town of Boston, 9 May 1770, Matthew Ridley Papers, MHS, in which she commends Bostonians 'for exhibiting a rare and admirable instance of patriotic sentiment tempered with forbearance and the warmth of courage with discretion' and promises 'every service which it is in my power to perform, the town of Boston may command and may depend upon a faithful and ardent execution'.
[29] See, for example, William Cooper to CM, 8 Dec. 1772, GLC.
[30] Macaulay discussed writing a history of the American conflict with many of her friends and correspondents. See further discussions in this book's Introduction and Chapter 3.   [31] MOW to CM, 7 June 1773, WAP.

formed a key member of the 'female ministry' which was proposed in that year's *Annual Register*. The author of the *Proposal* argued that government ministers were so effeminate, corrupt, and ineffectual that patriotic women should legitimately step into their shoes.[32] Similarly, in an essay in which George Coleman claimed to have heard 'that Mrs Macaulay will certainly be the Middlesex member', he also complained about that fashionable aberration, 'a thing of the neuter gender... called a macaroni'.[33] In an era when ideas of masculine deviance were shorthand for national moral and political decline, Macaulay, as a patriot and a woman, might represent something particularly powerful and persuasive. She was fêted so avidly and wrote with such extraordinary confidence during the 1760s and 1770s, because, I suggest, she was regarded as possessing that independent and disinterested perspective that now seemed for modern public man impossible to attain. For Whigs and radicals, who saw the actions of the ministry as merely the tip of the iceberg of an iniquitous and emasculated political culture, Catharine Macaulay might represent the ideal of public virtue which Britain, in the years preceding the war with America, seemed so obviously to lack.

II The Fall of Public Man

Throughout the decade when Catharine Macaulay reached the height of her patriotic fame, the Whig critique of the corruption of government and civil society rose to a new pitch. In their tracts, treatises, and letters to the press, Macaulay and her contemporaries professed their hostility to parliamentary corruption, taxation, and public credit in a language very similar to that of their Tory and Country predecessors. Yet, unlike the opponents of Walpole's administrations whose energies were directed towards the change of political institutions from within, oppositional writing of the 1760s and 1770s was characterized by its glum insistence that parliament had become vitiated to the extent that it was incapable of its own reform. For Whigs and radicals on both sides of the Atlantic, George III's government had come to signify the source of a corrupt and corrupting power isolated from those whose collective

[32] [unattrib.], 'Proposal for a Female Ministry', *Annual Register* (1766), 209–12.
[33] George Coleman, *Prose on Several Occasions* (London: T. Cadell, 1787), ii. 87, 91. The essay was originally written and published in 1770. Middlesex was, of course, Wilkes's disputed seat.

interests it was supposed to represent. The insular and inaccessible state organism—its legislative and judicial assemblies peopled with ministerial hirelings and its shadowy, powerful administrative machine controlling the army and the national debt—was regarded by opposition writers as the master spring of cultural degeneration. Civil society, they argued, displayed the same signs of depravity that characterized the political public sphere; independent identities were betrayed and subsumed by the addictive pleasures that fashionable culture afforded and those who might once have been virtuous citizens were bound in a web of desire and gratification, of acquisition and expenditure. The decline in the standards of private manners and morals, lamented by a host of commentators during these years, seemed to have its inception in the dissolution of the stable values of public life.[34]

This account of the progressive deterioration of public virtue, of which Macaulay herself was a vocal exponent, expressed its opposition to government and society in terms of their effects on contemporary masculine identities. According to John 'Estimate' Brown's anxious prognosis, the defining characteristic of the age was 'a vain, luxurious and selfish *effeminacy*' as men had apparently deviated from the even path of public resolve and lost themselves in the bewildering byways of

[34] On the political culture of the London opposition in the 1760s and 1770s, see, for example, Stephen Maccoby, *English Radicalism 1762–1785: The Origins* (London: George Allen and Unwin, 1955); Ian R. Christie, *Wilkes, Wyvill and Reform: The Parliamentary Reform Movement in British Politics* (London: Macmillan, 1962); Colin Bonwick, *English Radicals and the American Revolution* (Chapel Hill, NC: University of North Carolina Press, 1977); Eugene Black, *The Association: British Extra-Parliamentary Political Organization 1769–1793* (Cambridge, Mass.: Harvard University Press, 1963); John Brewer, *Party Ideology and Popular Politics at the Accession of George III* (Cambridge: Cambridge University Press, 1976); John Cannon, *Parliamentary Reform 1640–1832* (Cambridge: Cambridge University Press, 1973); George Guttridge, *English Whiggism and the American Revolution* (Berkeley and Los Angeles: University of California Press, 1966); Solomon Lutnick, *The American Revolution and the British Press* (Columbia: University of Missouri Press, 1967); Harry Dickinson, *Liberty and Property: Political Ideology in Eighteenth-Century Britain* (London: Methuen, 1977); Peter N. Miller, *Defining the Common Good: Empire, Religion and Philosophy in Eighteenth-Century Britain* (Cambridge: Cambridge University Press, 1994); George Rudé, *Wilkes and Liberty: A Social Study of 1763 to 1774* (Oxford: Clarendon Press, 1962); Kathleen Wilson, *The Sense of the People: Politics, Culture and Imperialism in England, 1715–85* (Cambridge: Cambridge University Press, 1995); Sainsbury, *Disaffected Patriots*. The classic account of oppositional Whig politics is Caroline Robbins, *The Eighteenth-Century Commonwealthman: Studies in the Transmission, Development and Circumstance of English liberal Thought from the Restoration of Charles II until the War with the Thirteen Colonies [1959]* (New York: Athenaeum Press, 1968).

private influence.[35] Instead of providing the arena in which virtue might realize itself, political culture was now perceived to generate a range of emasculating dependencies. While the writers of the opposition still regarded a patriotic identity, realized through participation and attained in public office, as their political ideal, a troublesome question mark hung over the larger issue of whether masculine virtue, in the republican terms that had been used to define it, might still represent a viable goal in itself. The grounds upon which the alignment between public virtue and masculinity was founded were, during the years Catharine Macaulay was acclaimed, by no means clear. Masculine patriotism seemed an outmoded ideal, 'public virtue' had, as James Thomson had warned thirty years earlier, 'become the public scoff', and the ideal of office ceased to represent an unambiguously honourable political objective.[36] Public masculinity seemed under threat: not from those foreign influences which Old Whigs traditionally berated as triggers of modernity's moral decline, but from within the very national institutional spaces where it was supposed to be preserved. Throughout the late 1760s and early 1770s, Whigs and radicals wrote texts which attested to their concern that masculine virtue and independence, in their received republican senses, might become remote and alienated ideals in a political culture dominated by the forces of the private sphere.

'That there was and is much effeminacy of spirit in England is readily admitted,' Thomas Hollis remarked in the margins of his copy of John Brown's *Estimate of the Manners and Principles of the Times*, '[and] the grand occasioners of it were and are the ministry'.[37] The source of the national 'effeminacy of spirit' might easily be traced to government and its officials. To republicans like Hollis it seemed that that Britain had written its own moral decline into its constitutional settlements, its institutions, and their representatives. A number of opposition Whigs, Macaulay included, argued that the process of national political emasculation was exacerbated rather than eradicated by the Glorious Revolution. 'The flaws in the revolution system', she wrote in her

---

[35] John Brown, *Estimate of the Manners and Principles of the Times* (London: L. Davis and C. Reymers, 1757), 29.

[36] James Thomson, *Liberty* [1735], in *The Complete Poetical Works of James Thomson*, ed. J. Logie Robertson (London & New York: Oxford University Press, 1908), part 5, l. 327.

[37] TH, annotation to p. 91 of John Brown's *Estimate of the Manners and Principles of the Times*, Hollis copy, HL.

Observations on Burke's *Thoughts on . . . the Present Discontents*, 'left full opportunity for private interests to exclude the public good'. The most admired parts of the constitution were, she wrote, no more than theatrical façades disguising internal political decay: 'Parliament, the great barrier of our much boasted constitution, while it preserved its forms, annihilated its spirit.' With the revolution, Macaulay argued, 'a system of corruption began' and 'was the policy of every succeeding administration'. The consequences were the manifest present discontents that Whigs like herself opposed:

> the destructive grievance of a debt of one hundred and forty millions, a grievance which operates powerfully and variously against public freedom and independence; a strong military standing force, contrary to the very existence of real liberty; an army of placemen and pensioners, whose private interest is repugnant to the welfare of the public weal; septennial parliaments, in violation of the firmest principle in the constitution; and heavy taxes imposed for the advantage and emolument of individuals, a grievance never submitted to by any people not essentially enslaved.[38]

Macaulay's Old-Whiggish oppositions between firmness and submission, between independence and enslavement, display a traditional sense of the public defined by the values of masculine virility. To be active in government was, to a Whig of Macaulay's stamp by 1770, to be effeminized by default, since any involvement in administration might betray a complicity with the corruption and expediency which the constitution itself legitimated. Government ministers had necessarily sacrificed their capacity to act independently let alone for the good of the public. They were merely, Macaulay wrote, 'under the specious pretensions of public zeal . . . planning schemes of private emolument and private ambition'. In accepting the pay or the titles of the Crown, she wrote, a minister experienced 'the humiliating, the dependent, invidious, and mortifying state of [an] immediate slave to an absolute monarch'.[39] In Macaulay's typically uncompromising terms, ministerial office was in effect an admission of political impotence.[40]

---

[38] CM, *Observations*, 15.   [39] Ibid. 20.

[40] On Macaulay's account of the Glorious Revolution, see Barbara Brandon Schnorrenberg, 'The Brood-Hen of Faction: Mrs Macaulay and Radical Politics, 1765–1775', *Albion*, 11 (1979), 33–45, and, ' "An Opportunity Missed": Catharine Macaulay on the Revolution of 1688', *Studies in Eighteenth-Century Culture*, 20 (1990), 231–40; Staves, 'The Liberty of a She-Subject of England'; Lynne Withey, 'Catharine Macaulay

To Macaulay and her political contemporaries, the examples of Pultney and Chatham—independent patriots turned servile ministers—had proved that republican virtue was impossible to retain in office. William Pitt's capitulation of patriotism to a peerage had proved to them that something was rotten at the nation's political core. Shocked by what he termed Pitt's 'unparalleled prostitution and apostacy', Thomas Hollis was disconsolate.[41] 'Alas the patriot!', he wrote, 'the great commoner! the defender of America! May the medals of the lost Pitt be now flattened, like his virtues!'[42] Macaulay was perhaps even more scathing. In conversation with Henry Marchant, she is reported to have said that:

> Pitt by his inconsistencies and fondness of a title &c has sullied his glories and has barred the publick from giving him those crowns of laurels his successful administration would otherwise have justly claimed...he acts rather from sudden motives and impressions than from any fixed plan or principles.[43]

In swapping his laurels for a title Pitt is said to have exchanged the rewards of virtue for the insubstantial pleasures of aristocratic appearance. Macaulay's Lord Chatham is apparently unable to deal in generalities, appreciate solid value, or see the bigger picture. Her account of him as driven by 'sudden motives and impressions' suggests an attachment to the private and the particular inimical to that public objectivity thought the ruling characteristic of the ideal republican statesman.

Through its focus on political emasculation, the writing of the extra-parliamentary opposition discovered a crisis in masculinity whose effects reached further than the placemen and pensioners who suffered the brunt of their derision. Just as the state's dependence on mutable financial structures and the caprices of the executive had sapped the lifeblood of the body politic, so they argued, private dependencies and interests had depleted masculine political autonomy in its widest sense. The motives of any candidate for office might be regarded as matter for

and the Uses of History: Ancient Rights, Perfectionism and Propaganda', *Journal of British Studies*, 16 (1976), 59–83. See also my discussion of Macaulay's representation of William III in Chapter 3.

[41] TH to Edmund Quincy, Jr., 1 Oct. 1766, Hollis Papers, MHS.
[42] TH to Elizabeth Mayhew, 4 Oct. 1766, Hollis Papers, MHS.
[43] Macaulay, reported in conversation with Henry Marchant. Marchant, *Journal*, 29 Apr. 1772, Rhode Island Historical Society. On Marchant's trip to Britain, see David S. Lovejoy, 'Henry Marchant and the "Mistress of the World"'' *William and Mary Quarterly*, 12 (1955), 375–98.

suspicion. 'I will not deny the possibility of your having a patriot minister,' wrote Richard Price, 'but I do not myself conceive how such a man is to arrive at such a station'.[44] Joseph Priestley was similarly convinced that bribes, patronage, and the political process itself invariably corrupted even the most virtuous of candidates: 'though your members be sent to parliament in the most uncorrupt and honourable manner, they will not long continue uncorrupt. It is too much to be expected of human nature in this luxurious and expensive age.'[45] Patriotism and public spirit seemed exhausted and outmoded. The political system engendered and perpetuated masculine corruption, since, as Macaulay argued, parliamentarians were 'men whom the very nature of their trust must render corrupt': men whose political characters, in other words, would invariably be destroyed by the nature of public office itself.[46] 'Whether indeed', enquired John Cartwright, 'the house of commons be in a great measure filled with idle school boys, insignificant coxcombs, led-captains and toad-eaters, profligates, gamblers, bankrupts, beggars, contractors, commissaries, public plunderers, ministerial dependents, hirelings and wretches that would sell their country or deny their God for a guinea, let every man judge for himself'.[47]

In August 1773 Macaulay wrote a letter to John Collett Ryland in response to his request for her opinion on the question of 'what kind of man will it be proper to elect to the representative office in the ensuing parliament'. This letter achieved a much broader circulation than its immediate addressee among London's radical groups and was included by her publishers, the Dillys, in the packages of pamphlets they sent that year to Massachusetts.[48] Her answer to Ryland is intriguing for the categorical nature of its response as well as for its style, which treads that line between intimate exchange and public proclamation that was later

[44] Richard Price, *Additional Observations on the Nature and Value of Civil Liberty* (London: T. Cadell, 1777), 43.
[45] Joseph Priestley, *An Address to Protestant Dissenters of All Denominations on the Approaching Election of Members of Parliament with Respect to the State of Public Liberty in General and American Affairs in Particular* (London: J. Johnson, 1774), 7.
[46] CM, *Observations*, 28.
[47] John Cartwright, *Take Your Choice! Representation and Respect, Imposition and Contempt, Annual Parliaments and Liberty, Long Parliaments and Slavery*... (London: John Almon), p. x.
[48] See, for example, Edward Dilly to JA, 4 Mar. 1774, in *Papers of John Adams*, ed. Robert J. Taylor, 8 vols. (Cambridge, Mass.: Harvard University Press, 1977), ii. 18. See also my discussion of Macaulay's transatlantic correspondence in Chapter 3.

to characterize her *History in a Series of Letters*. In essence, Macaulay argues that the conditions of modern England render the election of a virtuous man to an uncorrupted position impossible. England, she writes to Ryland, 'from the earliest period of its empire to the present moment never was in so perilous, so desperate a state'. Her account of the perilous nature of this state is worth quoting:

> We live in times when the Empire of corruption has no bounds. To the parliament, the court and the army, we may add every corporation through the whole dominion; to every corporation we may add all the inhabitants ... the dire infection hath spread from rank to rank. It has tainted the vitals of the commonwealth and from thence extended its putrid influence to all its members.... Self-interest, which destroys every good tendency in the human character, was never known from the dawn of man to exert with more malignant force than in the breasts of our contemporary countrymen. The merciless statesman, the [illegible] placeman, the opulent landholder, the rapacious monopoliser, the extortionate retailer feel alike its influence.[49]

Corruption and self-interest have here spread from their source at the heart of the nation through the social ranks till the scale of the malady seems pandemic. It is crucial to Macaulay's account that there is no retreat or escape from the empire of corruption, for, by this point in the 1770s, it was felt among the administration's Whig opponents that a space for independent critique was extremely hard to find. From the embattled minority who supported place and rotation bills in the House of Commons there was little to hope. The oppositional voice that had been provided by London's corporations was increasingly being silenced through their reliance on government contracts, and it seemed that anyone's patriotic allegiances might be sold for trade, for a title, or for a promise. Corruption, in Macaulay's letter to Ryland, characterizes political activity within and without parliamentary doors, irrespective of differences of wealth and social status. Parliament and corporations, retailers and landholders, are equally willing to forfeit probity to self-interest. Macaulay's narrative of the effects of the empire of corruption leaves no difference between inside and outside, between defiled and untainted: no political space free from infection.

It is perhaps unsurprising, then, that in answer to Ryland's question Macaulay replied that 'it is not a common character, my friend, to whom

[49] CM to John Collett Ryland, Aug. 1773, GLC.

I would give my vote on the ensuing election'. 'The man capable of performing his duty in such a trust,' she writes, 'is I am afraid much easier to be described than found'.[50] Macaulay typically has more faith in the integrity of her own critique than in the patriotic characters of any candidate for public office. Though she suggests to Ryland that the conditions of modern England render the appearance, let alone the election, of the virtuous man highly improbable, she remains secure in her conviction of her own political identity, her just claim to call the elected to account. So, while she herself might be said to embody a 'patriotic virtue... the most heroic', it seemed hard to imagine how a republican man in England could retain his independence while seeking office or election.

It is worth saying a few brief words here about the eighteenth century Whig opposition and its traditional perception of public masculinity. Despite the uncompromising terms of earlier commonwealthmen, the ideal of public man had, from the turn of the century, perhaps always been subject to a somewhat uncertain definition. For Molesworth, for Shaftesbury, for Trenchard and Gordon, masculine virtue excels in the past and, because for a true Whig modernity is inevitably faulty, is always in the present defined by its anxious resistance to the many forms of the private which threatened it.[51] In eighteenth-century republicanism, masculinity is perhaps forever on the brink of a crisis. But there is a particular urgency about the oppositional critique of government, public life, and public men in the late 1760s and 1770s that, I think, goes some way towards explaining later shifts in the representation of republican political identities in Britain, as well as accounting for the noisy celebration of Catharine Macaulay's patriotic virtue (as this chapter is suggesting). The insistence with which Whigs and radicals described the process of the nation's political emasculation at the turn of the 1770s concerned the perceived fatuity of *any* British opposition to

[50] CM to John Collett Ryland, Aug. 1773, GLC.
[51] See Robbins, *Commonwealthman*; Bernard Bailyn, *The Ideological Origins of the American Revolution* (Cambridge, Mass.: Harvard University Press, 1967), J. G. A. Pocock, *The Machiavellian Moment: Florentine Political Thought and the Atlantic Republican Tradition* (Princeton: Princeton University Press, 1975). See also Isaac Kramnick, *Republicanism and Bourgeois Radicalism: Political Ideology in Late Eighteenth-Century England and America* (Ithaca, NY: Cornell University Press, 1990), and John Brewer, *Party Ideology and Popular Politics at the Accession of George III* (Cambridge: Cambridge University Press, 1976).

the direction of the state's powerful fiscal–military machine and, as the dispute with the American colonies turned towards war, the meanings and valence of patriotism itself.

Kathleen Wilson and Eliga Gould have written persuasively about how the meanings of British patriotism shifted from the mid- to late 1770s during the war for American independence. When the links between republicanism, rebellion, and enmity were undeniable, loyalists laid strong claim to notions of patriotism and Britain's discourses of nationhood and empire.[52] The mid 1770s evidently witnessed confusion over ideas of the love of country, which Samuel Johnson's *Patriot*, with its description of patriotism as a coin emptied of solid value and contemporary currency, makes very clear.[53] But in the years immediately preceding the American war and the growth of domestic loyalism it precipitated, the traditional commonwealth notion of a patriot, associated with public men and politicized masculinity, was eroded in part by the very republicans for whom it served such a high ideal. While an American son of liberty, united in virtuous opposition to a regime perceived as tyrannical might, in 1773, easily style himself a patriot, for a disaffected London Whig who perceived his efforts towards parliamentary reform as ever more futile, who was increasingly suspicious of the motives of his friends and contemporaries, and who saw the finger of the administration in every political pie, it was far otherwise. In such a political culture, as James Burgh suggested in his dystopian *Crito* of 1767, notions of patriotism and public masculinity might seem obsolete, even imaginary. Public spirit, his gloomy narrator remarks, was now an 'antiquated virtue . . . in our times, reckoned so romantic that there are not wanting among us some who will dispute that it ever existed'.[54] In the radical and sceptical *Letters on England* published by John Almon in 1772, the idea of patriotism has been reclaimed and refuted to the point of meaningless absurdity:

all the explanations, harangues and flights of imagination which have been jumbled together to form that imaginary monster of perfection called a patriot,

---

[52] Kathleen Wilson, *The Sense of the People: Politics, Culture and Imperialism in England 1715–1785* (Cambridge: Cambridge University Press, 1995), and Eliga Gould, *The Persistence of Empire: British Political Culture in the Age of the American Revolution* (Chapel Hill, NC: University of North Carolina Press, 2000). See my discussion of loyalist patriotism in Chapter 3.

[53] Samuel Johnson, *The Patriot* (1774), in *The Works of Samuel Johnson, x. Political Writings*, ed. Donald J. Greene (New Haven: Yale University Press, 1977), 390.

[54] James Burgh, *Crito* (London: Dodsley, 1767), 60.

are but an unintelligible jargon...a pretence to the famed virtue [i.e. patriotism] is the road to corruption and marks a man as one who wants only a bidder who will rise to his price.[55]

For a political culture that had, like Macaulay in her letter to Ryland, begun to see extra-parliamentary and parliamentary political cultures in much the same light, *any* invocation of patriotism could be regarded as matter for immediate suspicion. As Richard Price put it, his contemporaries 'have been led to a conviction that all patriotism is imposture and all opposition to the measures of government nothing but a struggle for power and its emoluments'.[56] In other words, Whigs and radicals now saw patriotism as a mask for personal aggrandisement; independent opposition disguising private ambition and the ideal of public masculinity itself as unsustainable. For the London opposition, as 'Junius' wrote in 1769, 'professions of patriotism are become stale and ridiculous'.[57] By the turn of the 1770s, then, any claim to the name of patriot might seem cynical at best.

In their polemic against the corrupt, privatized roles of ministers, office-holders, political candidates, and finally, the very idea of patriotism itself, the Whig and radical opposition was addressing those broader issues of political and constitutional reform that were coming to a head in the American crisis. However, such attacks inevitably affected oppositional claims to political legitimacy because a denial of the possibility of active virtue was, in republican terms, a denial of the basic premiss of masculinity itself. While within their clubs and societies oppositionists were developing those forms of association politics which are now regarded as the prototypes of a Habermasian bourgeois public, when writing about the corruptions of office and the failure of patriotic ideals they still deployed the patrician modes of address that characterized the commonwealth tradition they admired.[58] Thus the political subject whose virtuous resistance to tyranny was coupled with an agonal display of eloquence in the public sphere remained the ideal of most of the writers

---

[55] [Unattrib.], *Letters Concerning the Present State of England, Particularly Respecting the Politics, Arts, Manners and Literature of the Times* (London: John Almon, 1772), 26.
[56] Price, *Additional Observations*, 42.   [57] *London Chronicle*, 8 Aug. 1769.
[58] Jurgen Habermas, *The Structural Transformation of the Public Sphere: An Inquiry into a Category of Bourgeois Society* [1966], trans. Thomas Burger (Cambridge: Polity Press, 1989).

of the Whig and radical opposition. The problem was that, in a political culture where the public sphere seemed so debased and corruption so endemic, this form of public masculinity would remain an ideal and nothing more. Political Britain had now become, according to James Burgh, 'a nation of women and children': a polity of privately bound disenfranchised dependants rather than independent publicly oriented beings.[59] Modern political identities seem corrupted and feminised almost by definition and the loss of a masculinity characterised by its virile 'athletic labours,' ever ready to 'lay the axe to the root of corruption' could only be lamented.[60]

Macaulay and her contemporaries struggled to define a modern, virtuous, and politicized masculinity. What the defining characteristics of such an identity might be seemed unclear. A notable feature of many novels written during this period is the failure of the male hero to demonstrate the virtue accorded to his gender and social status by taking on the responsibilities of office and becoming a representative of the public good. For example, the benevolent baronets of Samuel Richardson's and Sarah Scott's mid-century fiction regard office as a deviation from, rather than a realization of, virtue. Neither Richardson's Sir Charles Grandison nor Scott's Sir George Ellison view political independence, verified through property and personality and substantiated in office, as an attainable or even desirable goal.[61] Similarly, Tobias Smollet's Matthew Bramble considers all modern public men to be 'such a pack of venal and corrupted rascals, so lost to all sense of honesty... that in a little time, I am fully persuaded, nothing will be infamous but virtue and public spirit'. Bramble refuses to participate in the electoral process, believing that the two candidates he must choose between are characterized by the same manifest degeneracy: 'I should think myself a traitor to my country if I voted for either.'[62] Bramble remains committed to a notion of country, retains a patriotic ideal ratified by a public and a nation, but believes modern elections and institutions

[59] James Burgh, *Political Disquisitions, or, An Enquiry into Public Errors, Defects and Abuses*... 3 vols. (London: E. & C. Dilly, 1774–5), iii. 59.
[60] Burgh, *Crito*, 52–3.
[61] Samuel Richardson, *The History of Sir Charles Grandison* [1753] (Oxford: Oxford University Press, 1986), and Sarah Scott, *The History of Sir George Ellison* (London: A. Millar, 1766).
[62] Tobias Smollett, *The Expedition of Humphry Clinker* [1771] (Oxford: Oxford University Press, 1984), 77.

signify an organized betrayal of that ideal. He declines to engage with contemporary politics because he considers the roles of those who represent the public interest to be so privatized by corruption that they are insufficiently masculine. Yet he is also a character who seems feminized by that very refusal to participate; by his failure to claim his mark of citizenship through suffrage, by his eremeticism, his misanthropy.

Bramble's disaffection with political institutions and processes was characteristic of many of his real-life contemporaries. John Brewer has described the unwillingness of 'the writers of some of the most inspired political pamphlets and newspaper letters of the period... to involve themselves in the every day cut and thrust of politics' as 'fastidiousness'.[63] This word captures the double bind which Matthew Bramble and his like represented: that, while participation was perceived to have a tainting effect on masculine political identity, a refusal to participate might be interpreted as similarly emasculating. By the Whigs and radicals of the London opposition, the problem of participation or retreat might be understood as a Hobson's Choice between two private identities. Either one displayed and destroyed one's political identity by engaging in a process regarded as necessarily corrupt, or one distanced oneself from that corruption, in effect denying that identity. This dilemma is typified by Catharine Macaulay's good friend Thomas Hollis, the Old-Whig ideologue whom Bernard Bailyn memorably describes as 'that one-man propaganda machine in the cause of liberty', whose career I discuss in the following section.[64]

III A Private Man

Thomas Hollis, a man of sizeable independent fortune who owned property in Bedfordshire and Dorset, spent his adult life quietly campaigning for political reform. Throughout the 1760s, he worked closely with printmakers and publishers like John Almon, acquiring the canonical texts of the Commonwealth tradition and distributing them on both sides of the Atlantic. Hollis dispersed the works of Milton, Harrington, Sydney, and Molesworth in libraries in Berne and Zurich as well as making (often anonymous) donations of seventeenth-century

---

[63] John Brewer, 'English Radicalism in the Age of George III', in J. G. A. Pocock (ed.), *Three British Revolutions* (Princeton: Princeton University Press, 1980), 343.
[64] Bailyn, *The Ideological Origins of the American Revolution*, 40.

tracts and prints to the British Museum or to contemporary republican authors, like Macaulay, who he knew would make good use of them. 'Purchased last night,' Hollis recorded in his diary on 10 April 1765:

one hundred and forty five volumes and tracts relating to the history of England, chiefly during the civil wars; with the intention of bringing them NOBLY into use, by presenting them anonymously to the ingenuous Mrs Catharine Sawbridge Macaulay who is now writing that most important period of our history.[65]

A committed Old Whig and fanatic collector of republican artefacts, Hollis financed and edited reprints of a number of the works of his political forebears and contemporaries, often designing their elaborate frontispieces and binding seals himself.[66] He had what he described as 'a propensity, an affection' for the people of North America, 'those of Massachusetts and Boston in particular', who were, he wrote, 'the most sensible and worthy of them all and best affectioned to Revolution principles'.[67] He spent a substantial part of his income donating texts which espoused those principles to the new library at Harvard and he was regarded by the prominent radicals of Boston's West and South churches as their political ally and benefactor.[68]

While Hollis was impressed by Boston's republicanism, British politics were to him a source of despair. He was urged to stand for the Dorchester constituency in 1760 and 1763 and that of Westminster in 1769, but flatly refused.[69] He baulked at the prospect of tests and electioneering, and deplored the corruption of the House of Commons. In reply to his friend Jonathan Mayhew, who enquired why he had never taken the opportunity of furthering the public good by standing for office, Hollis wrote: 'I have served my country faithfully eleven years

[65] TH, *Diary*, 10 Apr. 1765, HL.
[66] For detailed discussion of Hollis's title pages, cover designs, and commissions, see W. H. Bond, *Thomas Hollis of Lincoln's Inn: A Whig and his Books* (Cambridge: Cambridge University Press, 1991). See also Caroline Robbins, ' "The Strenuous Whig": Thomas Hollis of Lincoln's Inn', *William and Mary Quarterly*, 7 (1950), 406–53.
[67] TH to Edmund Quincy Jr., 1 Oct. 1766, Hollis Papers, MHS, and TH, Diary, 24 July 1768.
[68] Hollis was a very close friend of Jonathan Mayhew and Andrew Elliot. He was also, as Sarah Prince-Gill's correspondence with Catharine Macaulay testifies, well known and highly regarded by Thomas Prince of Boston's South Church. See 'Sophronia' (Sarah Prince Gill) to CM, 25 April 1769, GLC.
[69] See Francis Blackburne, *Memoirs of Thomas Hollis esq.*, 2 vols. (London: n.p., 1780), i. 153.

past, though in silence and in small matters.'[70] To his relative, and radical associate, Timothy Hollis, he spoke in plainer terms: 'I had leif never go into H——l as into a present H of C.'[71] Hollis found the entire political process acutely depressing: he did not vote, and is reputed to have wept at scenes of electioneering in 1768.[72] 'The times seek corruption!' he remarked in his diary, after having turned down the offer of a parliamentary seat. 'I can live contented without glory, but cannot suffer shame.'[73] Highlighting a passage in his copy of John Brown's *Estimate of the Manners and Principles of the Times* ('at a time when capacity, courage, honour, public spirit are rare, the remaining few who possess those virtues will often be shut out from the stations which they would fill with honour'), Hollis acknowledged that the preservation of public virtue in Britain perversely demanded exclusion from the public sphere itself. 'It is so and has been so for many years,' he remarked beside the passage in the margin.[74]

Describing his collecting and distributing activities as a 'plan of private patriotic action', Hollis pursued his 'unremitting campaign' quietly, idiosyncratically, and, as far as was possible, anonymously.[75] Though he actively supported the causes of the London radicals and the American colonists through personal donations and by financing a variety of oppositionist publications, he distanced himself from the noisy culture of the Wilkites, declined to discuss politics in public, terminated his friendships with Pitt and other politicians, withdrew into his study, and refused to admit visitors, describing himself as 'extremely shy of new acquaintance.'[76] He insisted that his American correspondents destroy his letters and instructed them never to mention his aid in publishing their political texts, his donations of books to their libraries, or himself by name in their newspapers. 'I must request *in earnest*', he wrote to Mayhew, that you do not . . . take notice in any shape of my name. I will serve,' he

[70] TH to Jonathan Mayhew, 22 Nov. 1764, Hollis Papers, MHS. See also Blackburne, *Memoirs*, i. 229.
[71] i.e. 'hell' and 'house of commons'. TH to Timothy Hollis, 23–25 Feb. 1771, HL.
[72] See Blackburne, *Memoirs*, i. 103, 206; ii. 419.   [73] TH, Diary, 29 June 1769.
[74] TH, annotation to John Brown's *Estimate*, 119, HL.
[75] TH, letter to Timothy Hollis, 29 May 1771, HL.
[76] TH, letter to unnamed correspondent in Rome, July 1762, cited in Blackburne, *Memoirs*, i. 175. Blackburne comments that by the late 1760s 'Mr Hollis . . . seems not only to have declined public station, but to have withdrawn himself from associating with select parties composed of persons otherwise not exceptionable to him' (Blackburne, *Memoirs*, i. 419).

continued, 'tho' by ways unknown to anyone'.[77] With increasing frequency he contributed anonymous squibs and blind emblems to the *London Chronicle*, and began to annotate the books and tracts he sent to Harvard with his own minatory comments. On a copy of a collection of political essays he wrote: 'People of Massachusetts! When your country shall be cultivated, adorned like this country, and ye shall become elegant, refined in civil life—then, if not before, 'ware your liberties!' Another annotation, on the flyleaf of a handsomely bound blank book, read: 'this book was bound, long since, to have served a noble purpose. It may still have some noble purpose at Cambridge, in New England.'[78]

Hollis maintained that his eremetic retreat from active political life enabled him to sustain his virtue and integrity in a manner impossible for his more public contemporaries who were, he perceived, under constant pressure to capitulate to the system they despised. As the times were degenerate, he argued, so the ruling characteristic of those in the public eye must invariably be degeneracy: 'When the morals of a nation are so corrupted that all virtue is laughed at as an extreme folly what remedy is there?' he enquired of Edmund Quincy; 'our salvation shall not be effected by politicians, nor by any men, I fear, at this day in England.'[79] Hollis himself had no pretensions to the status of a man who might effect this process of national salvation. His overriding personal concern, as expressed in the diary he kept throughout the 1760s, was to maintain what he variously termed 'innocence', 'ingenuousness', or 'decorum' in opposition to and in spite of the corrupting influences of the fashionable world and the political public sphere. Hollis had a favourite description of himself, which, he repeated, in various forms, to more than one correspondent: 'Through all the changes of the times, I remain a true, unfeigned old Whig, almost a unic.'[80] Hollis believed that

[77] TH to Jonathan Mayhew, 6 Dec. 1763, Hollis Papers, MHS, emphasis in original.
[78] The first annotation is written in Hollis's handwriting on the flyleaf of the gift copy of [unattrib.], *A Collection of Letters and Essays in Favour of Public Liberty First Published in the Newspapers in the Years 1764, 1765, 1766, 1767, 1768, 1769 and 70* (London: J. Wilkie), held in the Houghton Library. The second annotation is taken from a blank book, bound in red Russia, which Hollis donated to the Houghton Library in 1765, shelfmark A 1455.5*. See also [Houghton Library], *Thomas Hollis and the Friends of American Liberty* (Cambridge, Mass.: Houghton Library Publications, 1972).
[79] See Blackburne, *Memoirs*, ii. 339.
[80] TH to Theophilus Lindsey, 12 Dec. 1771, in Thomas Belsham (ed.), *Memoirs of the Late Revd. Theophilus Lindsey, M.A* (London: J. Johnson, 1812), 507. See also TH to Andrew Elliot, 5 Dec. 1769, Hollis Papers, MHS.

his silence, his anonymity, enabled him to maintain his republicanism in an 'unfeigned' and virtuous fashion, yet he also acknowledged that it privatized his political identity. In 1767, he sent to the recently widowed Elizabeth Mayhew a package of 332 prints he had commissioned and designed. Of these 300 were portraits of Jonathan Mayhew, 'a good and great public man'. The remaining 32 were of Hollis himself, 'his friend and your friend,' he wrote, 'the mere effigy of a plain, private man'.[81] In a gesture that was itself, in the level of its visibility and self-promotion, highly unusual for Hollis, he expresses his desire to be commemorated alongside the undoubtedly more public and politically outspoken Mayhew as a man whose privacy was the sole source of his virtue.

While respecting his principles, Hollis's friends considered that his seclusion from public life had affected his political personality, tainting him with signs of domesticity and feminine detail. A number of his associates remarked on his 'preciseness' of manners, his fussiness, his habit of constantly updating inventories of his possessions, and his obsession with housekeeping.[82] His frequent complaints about the negligence of his servants and his lengthy and detailed descriptions of the contents of his cabinet made him notorious in the coffee houses he frequented during the early 1760s.[83] Samuel Johnson described Hollis as 'a dull, poor creature as ever lived', and, according to the sniping pen of Horace Walpole, he was nothing more than 'an old woman who goes to the mercers to buy a bombazine with etchings of the death of Brutus and Cassius'.[84] Hollis's obsession with republican history, which was displayed in his collections of coins and tracts; his purchase of the bed John Milton was reputed to have died on; the cryptic maxims he published anonymously; his naming of the fields of his Dorset estate after commonwealth writers and his custom of signing bankers' cheques with the names of classical heroes and orators seemed for many, like Walpole, to be private and eccentric rather than public and political.[85] With no arena save that of his study, Hollis's grand 'plan' for the preservation of liberty

[81] TH to Elizabeth Mayhew, 18 Aug. 1767, Hollis Papers, MHS.
[82] See Blackburne's account of contemporary views of Hollis's lifestyle in *Memoirs*, ii. 221 30. [83] Blackburne, *Memoirs*, i. 125.
[84] G. B. Hill and L. F. Powell, *Boswell's Life of Johnson* (Oxford: Oxford University Press, 1934), 97. *Letters of Horace Walpole*, ed. Arnold Toynbee (Oxford: Oxford University Press, 1904), li. 157. In return, Hollis thought Johnson a 'selfish reptile' (TH, Diary, 21 July 1760). [85] See TH, Diary, 12 June 1761.

and the public good was regarded by many of his contemporaries as a curious, preterite, and feminine interest.

For Hollis and his contemporaries, then, a private retreat from the public sphere might seem the only way of preserving one's integrity under the conditions of political modernity. This retreat appeared virtuous, but was also, as I have suggested, understood to be incompatible with the republican ideal of an active, participatory, political masculinity. If, for Thomas Hollis, public man was fallen and effeminized and a man of private virtue seemed insufficiently masculine, then patriotic femininity might still embody a republican ideal. It was as the public face of his private politics that Hollis promoted and praised Catharine Macaulay.

IV A Public Woman

In Hollis's diary, Catharine Macaulay's conduct and personality are repeatedly singled out for praise. Unlike the MPs and London radicals of whose motives he was invariably suspicious, Macaulay seemed to him to signal the possibility of a form of republican commitment that remained untainted by the age's endemic corruption. Macaulay became an important figure in Hollis's 'plan' precisely because her exclusion from the degenerate sphere of the public rendered the purity of her political sentiments unquestionable. Hollis was one of her *History*'s first readers. He received a copy on the day it was published and immediately informed Macaulay how impressed he was with her 'spirited and magnanimous' introduction.[86] On completing the first volume some weeks later, he recorded in his diary that it was 'full of the freest and noblest sentiments of Liberty'.[87] After reading the second volume, Hollis wrote to Macaulay:

Madam,
I have read the second volume of your *History*, and admire unfeignedly the industry, judgement, energy, elegance, faithfulness and magnanimity that is in it. I shall preserve it choicely, a monument of a noble lady, noble above all parchment.[88]

---

[86] TH to CM, 5 Nov. 1763, HL. On the title page of the manuscript draft of her *History*, Macaulay recorded: 'this work was begun the beginning of October 1762 and published the 5th day of November 1763.' Hollis must have read her introduction and written to her to commend it that same day. *HE* MS.

[87] TH, Diary, 30 Nov. 1763.

[88] TH to CM, 15 Jan. 1765, HL. This letter is also cited, with slightly different wording, in Blackburne, *Memoirs*, i. 264.

Aside from the 'elegance' Hollis ascribes to Macaulay's writing, the noble virtues he associates her with would certainly be thought of as masculine or public. To Whigs like Hollis, energy, judgement, and magnanimity would seem terms more appropriate to the description of Roman oratory than the accomplished production of a modern learned woman. The early volumes of Macaulay's *History* were often praised for their 'nervous' qualities, for that 'more than ordinary energy' which, as she put it herself in her *Letters on Education*, was understood to render 'a female mind... masculine'.[89] By Whig friends and associates, such as Richard Baron and Sylas Neville, Macaulay's personality was described as 'abstract' and devoid of the desires and passions which were understood in the discourse of classical republicanism to feminize character.[90] For Hollis, then, the masculine attributes associated with Macaulay and her writing were indicative of the unambiguously public function of her *History* and patriotic character.

Almost as if they were discussing the preservation of a public monument, Hollis wrote to his friend Theophilus Lindsey that Macaulay must be 'maintained... for her many extraordinary qualities and the cause's sake'.[91] Hollis 'maintained' Macaulay's part in the cause through his library and private connections with printmakers, publishers, and personal correspondents. He supplied her with rare interregnum tracts in his possession and visited her frequently, before and after the death of her first husband, to discuss the progress of her work. He arranged the publication, design, and distribution of the pamphlets she wrote in the 1760s and vigorously promoted her *History* on both sides of the Atlantic. American admirers of Macaulay and her *History*, shy of corresponding with a woman of her fame and status unintroduced, first approached her through Hollis, as her conduit and confidant.[92] When one looks behind the network of Boston and London

[89] *Gentleman's Magazine*, 36 (1766), 439; CM, *Letters on Education with Observation on Religious and Metaphysical Subjects* (London: E. C. Dilly, 1790), 204–5.
[90] See the report of Baron's and Neville's account of Macaulay as a 'woman without passion' and 'abstract' features. Sylas Neville, Diary, 15 July 1767, in *The Diary of Sylas Neville, 1767–1788*, ed. Basil Cozens Hardy (Oxford: Oxford University Press, 1950).
[91] TH to Theophilus Lindsey, n.d., *Memoirs of the Late Revd. Theophilus Lindsey, M.A.*, ed. Thomas Belsham (London: J. Johnson, 1812), 509.
[92] See Elizabeth Mayhew to TH, 13 May 1769, Hollis Papers, MHS: 'It is at the desire of a lady, with whom I have the pleasure of some acquaintance, that the inclosed comes to you, begging the favor that you would forward it to Mrs Macaulay.' The 'lady' is Sarah Prince-Gill.

radicals corresponding with each other during the 1760s and early 1770s, it is apparent (as indeed his contemporaries pointed out) that Hollis played no small part in facilitating the Atlantic exchange of republican ideas.[93] While Macaulay confidently provided the monumental history and the patriotic persona to go with it that English republicanism so evidently needed in the 1760s, Hollis furnished some private means and connections through which both she and her *History* were invisibly supported and promoted. Regarded as masculine for her eloquence and visibility as he was feminized by his silence and retreat, Catharine Macaulay became the public face of Thomas Hollis's private politics: the exponent of the cause, of his 'plan', the surrogate for the virtue he felt himself unable actively to practise.

After discussions with Catharine and George Macaulay prior to the publication of the *History*'s third volume, Hollis designed and commissioned the Cipriani print which formed its frontispiece (Fig. 1). Hollis particularly liked this addition to his series of 'liberty prints', describing it in his diary as 'very fine', and was unusually forthcoming about his hand in its design. He wrote to Elizabeth Mayhew that the idea for the print had been suggested to the Macaulays by 'a friend of theirs and Mrs Mayhews'—that is, himself.[94] 'Felicity is Freedom and Freedom is magnanimity!', he exclaimed opposite the print inside the handsomely bound quarto edition of the *History* that he deposited in Harvard Library. 'The author', he explained to Macaulay's American readers, 'is represented in the print in the character of the *Libertas* on the Roman denarius stricken by Brutus and Cassius after the exit of Julius Caesar, the tyrant, and the reverse of that denarius sheweth those heroes, attended by their lictors, going to sacrifice to Liberty. T.H.[95] This image of Macaulay as the Roman *Libertas* was famous in its own time, frequently reproduced and probably that which Lyttleton had in mind when he remarked that Macaulay's face was to be found 'on every printseller's counter'.[96] This print is

---

[93] See Robbins, *Commonwealthman*, and Bailyn, *The Ideological Origins of the American Revolution*.

[94] Hollis records his discussions with Macaulay, her husband, and Cipriani in some detail. See TH, Diary, 1, 3, 4, 16, 20, and 23, Feb. 1764. TH to Elizabeth Mayhew, 28 July 1769, Hollis Papers, MHS.

[95] TH's annotation to CM, *The History of England from the Accession of James I to that of the Brusnwick Line*, 2nd edn. (London: J. Nourse, 1766), i, HL.

[96] Lyttleton, quoted in George Otto Trevelyan, *The American Revolution* (New York: Longman, Green & Co., 1905), ii. 275.

Fig. 1. G. B. Cipriani, *Catharina Macaulay* (1764). Engraving.

perhaps the exemplary representation of Macaulay as the public face of the London opposition and as such is worth discussing in some detail.

Hollis based Macaulay's portrait on a republican coin in his collection, which, as he observes in his annotation in the Houghton Library copy of the *History*, was minted by Marcus Junius Brutus following Caesar's execution (Fig. 2).[97] When Hollis arranged the commission

[97] G. B. Cipriani, Sketch for the Robe of Britannia (*c.*1760). Drawing, with suggestions in the hand of Thomas Hollis. 'Drawings and Etchings by G. B. Cipriani with annotations by Thomas Hollis', MSTyp, HL.

with Cipriani, he ensured the inclusion of both sides of the coin on the portrait. The head of *Libertas* together with the figures of Brutus and Cassius was a composite image of which Hollis was evidently fond, and he had used it in an earlier Cipriani commission, the title taken from Mark Akenside, 'O Fair Britannia Hail!' (Fig. 3).[98] Across the hem of Britannia's robe in Hollis's typically complex and idiosyncratic design march the figures of Brutus and Cassius towards an altar dedicated to Liberty. Cipriani's sketch for the robe of Britannia in the Houghton Library shows the heads of Brutus and Cassius, the four figures in procession, suggestions in Hollis's hand, and the same *Libertas* from the obverse of the coin which was used in Macaulay's portrait. (Fig. 4). For Hollis, the ideal of Liberty and the notoriously uncompromising republican virtue of the first Brutus were inseparable, and Macaulay was associated iconographically with both.

Macaulay was evidently pleased with the print and later chose it as the frontispiece for the new Nourse and Dilly editions of her *History*. Her portrait seems only slightly modified from that of the *Libertas* on which she is based: the hair and jewels (of which more in a moment) are almost identical; the face has the same passionless abstraction attributed her by Richard Baron. Macaulay's facial features were often thought of as classically republican—by her sister-in-law, she was described as having 'a nose somewhere between the Grecian and the Roman', for example— and her republican physiognomy here matches that of later portraits of her in profile, such as those by Robert Edge Pine (Fig. 5).[99] Her head is garlanded with oak, associating her with a specifically British form of liberty and marking her as the heir of the Commonwealth heroes she celebrated in her *History*. Assimilating British patriotism to Roman republican virtue, then, the print suggests Macaulay's desired identity as a historian working in forms of heroic commemoration as well as endorsing her status as a woman who should herself be heroically commemorated. She gazes steadily ahead with imperturbable detachment, her portrait perhaps a similar rebuff to the tyranny of the Stuarts as Marcus Brutus's coin was meant to that of Caesar. Indeed, following her *History*'s fourth volume, which covered the reign of Charles I, this

---

[98] Hollis was fond of Akenside's poetry and anonymously donated to him (ostensibly as a source of inspiration) the bed in which John Milton was reputed to have died.

[99] Mrs Arnold cited in Mary Hays, *Female Biography, or, Memoirs of Illustrious Women, Alphabetically Arranged*, 6 vols. (London: Richard Phillips, 1803), v. 293.

Fig. 2. Marcus Junius Brutus, Denarius (54 BC). Head of Liberty and Consul L. Junius Brutus between two lictors, preceded by accensus.

Fig. 3. G. B. Cipriani, *O Fair Britannia Hail!* (1760). Engraving. Reproduced by courtesy of the John Rylands University Library, Manchester.

Fig. 4. G. B. Cipriani, *Sketch for the Robe of Britannia* (c.1760). Drawing, with suggestions in the hand of Thomas Hollis. Reproduced by permission of the Houghton Library, Harvard.

link was made explicit and Macaulay said to possess, as she put it herself, 'the stoicism of the first Brutus' for her account of his trial and death.[100] Macaulay's portrait connected her with the republican virtues of Marcus Brutus: virtues which were heroic, implacable, and, to her *History*'s eighteenth-century audience, undeniably masculine.

Shortly after he finalized the details of the engraving of Macaulay's portrait with James Basire, Hollis recorded in his diary that he was planning a similar design representing William Pitt, 'the face in profile that of Marcus Brutus'.[101] Hollis abandoned the design following Pitt's political capitulation, abandoning his associations with the republican who had eradicated Caesar and his tyranny as well. Lord Chatham might no longer be attributed the virtues of a latter-day Brutus, but Macaulay

[100] CM, *The History of England from the Accession of James I to that of the Brunswick Line*, vi, p. xii, Preface.   [101] TH, Diary, 18 Nov. 1765.

Fig. 5. Robert Edge Pine, *Catharine Macaulay* (*c.*1778). Oil on canvas. Reproduced by courtesy of the National Portrait Gallery, London.

was different. To the Whigs and radicals of the London opposition, Pitt's patriotic persona was eroded by the system in which he participated, yet Macaulay, positioned by virtue of her gender beyond political institutions and the corruption that seemed endemic to them, might still represent the republican ideal of masculine virtue. As I have already suggested, Macaulay herself regarded her political and historical critique as that bit more salient and authoritative because of the position of disinterested exteriority she could be said to occupy. She wrote of this position in terms akin to a classical republican notion of retirement. In her *Observations* she argued that, while Burke was bound up in the 'practical parts of administration' to the extent that he was unable to distance himself sufficiently to see in perspective, *her* leisured and exteriorized position as a 'speculative reasoner' enabled her to see government for what it was.[102] It was Macaulay's gendered position, a femininity defined by its exclusion from the political public sphere, which itself enabled her to represent a detached reason and retirement understood in republican terms as masculine. At a time when the ideal of patriotic masculinity seemed shattered by the effects of corruption and effeminacy, Catharine Macaulay's position of virtuous exteriority led her to be regarded and represented in the same terms as Marcus Brutus, a man who, in his notorious self-denial and magnanimity, was perhaps the archetype of republican political virility.

V Masculine/Feminine

In her suggestive study of British political cultures, *The Sense of the People*, Kathleen Wilson argues that, during the years preceding the war with America, the London opposition discovered a 'a newly charged hostility to the feminine in politics'. In an illuminating discussion of the 'phallic adventuring' of Wilkes and his associates, she explores how Whigs and radicals defined the 'true patriot' as the 'austere, forceful and independent masculine subject' and 'made explicit an intolerance for the feminine and effeminate'.[103] It was the urgency of these definitions of masculine political subjectivity, coupled with their discomfited and somewhat haunted quality, which intrigued me when I began to look at Catharine Macaulay's patriotic fame in the 1760s. At a time when the class bases of political subjectivity were undoubtedly shifting and when (on Macaulay's and Hollis's side of the Atlantic at least) the fall of public man in his traditional civic humanist sense seemed inevitable, the London opposition became more insistent and uncompromising in their definitions of masculine virtue, more classically republican, perhaps, in

[102] CM, *Observations*, 9.   [103] Wilson, *Sense of the People*, 221.

their attachment to the ideal. Yet, as the corrupt hand of government reached out to the City and its corporations, as the executive continued to flaunt its powers in the face of American resistance, and as, in London, the patriotic clamour grew louder and louder, the more patriotism itself appeared redundant. The opposition's noisy professions of political virility might thus be read more as signs of crisis than of self-confidence. So what Wilson fails to address, I think, is the prevailing note of gloom behind the bravado: the sense that, for many British Whigs and radicals, things could only get worse. And, while it is evidently true that the opposition described political corruption in terms of emasculation, Wilson's argument concerning its 'hostility' towards the feminine depends to some extent on the conflation of the idea of effeminacy with femininity *per se*. While effeminacy is, one might say, a feminine-associated quality that undoubtedly carried negative connotations for the London opposition, other models of femininity might be markers of positive value within republican discussions of political subjectivity. Femininity might point to the benefits of modernity within a civil culture of conversational exchange not entirely at odds with the Whig and radical understanding of the formation of political opinion within their own clubs and associations. Femininity could also be linked with notions of virtuous privacy or republican ideas of learning or retirement— with the very conditions, in other words, which might secure the emergence of a new English Cato. And at moments of political disaffection, when virtuous masculinity seemed a remote ideal, the minatory voice of the public sphere might well be understood as feminine.

It is in the context of these differences in eighteenth-century republicanism's gendered values that I have wished to situate Catharine Macaulay and her political writing in this chapter. The London opposition regarded her as representative of an ideal of public virtue, and, as such, she was frequently celebrated in terms that rendered her masculine in character. In prints and poems, in periodical reviews and personal correspondence, reputedly in Patience Wright's waxwork figure, and, later, in Thomas Wilson's notorious effigy, Macaulay embodies a patriotism that is bellicose and Minervan in stature (Fig. 6).[104] And,

[104] On Wright's waxwork effigy of Macaulay, see Charles Coleman Sellars, *Patience Wright: American Artist and Spy in George III's London* (Middletown, Conn.: Wesleyan

Fig. 6. J. F. Moore, *Catharine Macaulay, History* (1778). Statue. Reproduced by courtesy of the National Portrait Gallery, London, with the permission of Warrington Library.

throughout the early volumes of her *History,* her political pamphlets, and the letters she wrote to her British and American friends during the 1760s and 1770s, she speaks confidently from a position that both she and her audience acknowledged as masculine. In these years, her authorial voice lays assured claim to the detached rationality, the probity, and resolution which distinguished the eighteenth-century republican ideal of the independent political subject. Like that of Brutus, whose uncompromising virtue led him to regard the good of the public before the lives of his own sons, Macaulay's patriotism could be seen as the signature of a character that was savage, unfeeling, and definitively unfeminine.[105] In so far as she appeared to place what her patriotism demanded before those normative and, in eighteenth-century republican terms, properly feminine concerns of sentimental propinquity, she could have been said to have transgressed the bounds of her gender. Yet it is important to remember, I think, that Macaulay was so avidly celebrated by the London opposition and remained so confident and secure in the conviction of her own political identity precisely *because* of her gender. While, for Hollis and his contemporaries, her patriotism filled the space vacated by their lost ideal of public masculinity, she remained, unquestionably, a woman and was still regarded by them in some crucial senses as feminine. Macaulay's gender meant her role might be portrayed as iconic, that she might represent Liberty *her*self.[106] Equally, Macaulay's social status as London's republican salonnière, and, most importantly, her learning and her reputation *as* a woman of learning, meant that she was clearly associated with the ideals of modern femininity and refinement.

When Thomas Hollis sent Elizabeth Mayhew, who had expressed a quiet admiration for Macaulay as a modern female 'worthy', a copy of

University Press, 1976). On Wilson's statue, see Claire Gilbride Fox, 'Catharine Macaulay: An Eighteenth Century Clio', *Winturthur Portfolio*, 4 (1968), 129–42, and Hill, *Republican Virago*. See also Robert Pierpoint, *Catharine Macaulay, 'History': The Statue in the Warrington Town Hall* (Warrington: printed for the Author, 1910).

[105] For two intriguing contemporary discussions of Marcus Junius Brutus as a figure quintessentially opposed to modern sentiment and sensibility, see William Young, *The History of Athens Politically and Philosophically Considered with the View to an Investigation of the Immediate Causes of Elevation and Decline Operative in a Free and Commercial State*, 2nd edn. (London: J. Robson, 1786), 7, and Adam Smith, *The Theory of Moral Sentiments* [1759] (Oxford: Clarendon Press, 1976), 192.

[106] See Natalie Zemon Davis, 'History's Two Bodies', *American History Review*, 93 (1988), 1–30. See also Marina Warner, *Monuments and Maidens: The Allegory of the Female Form* (London: Picador, 1985).

her *History*, he made the following explanatory remarks on the *Libertas* portrait that formed its frontispiece: 'The necklace in the print, as on the antient medal, denotes that liberty, admits, seeks, possesses, every refinement of civil life; nor indeed can those refinements exist, for any time, without her.'[107]

As Hollis regarded the feminine elegance of Macaulay's writing as coexistent with the masculine magnanimity of its content, so he suggests here that republican liberty might be connected to a modern liberal idea of progress. Hollis evidently felt it was important to tell Elizabeth Mayhew of the meanings he had drawn into the necklace, and one might only speculate as to why. Perhaps to Hollis, a man who regarded Boston as republicanism's last hope in modernity, the progress of refinement signalled by the necklace was linked to liberty's westward course. Perhaps into his explanation was written a veiled assurance to Elizabeth Mayhew, a woman well known for her accomplished elegance, that Macaulay (of whose patriotic character she appeared nervous) was, just like herself, a modern woman of refinement and possibly fashion.[108] In any case, what his account of the necklace conveys is that, just as liberty and modern refinement were inseparable, so Macaulay's patriotism was linked to her femininity—*her* refined, modern character. The *Libertas* portrait that Hollis designed associated Macaulay with Marcus Brutus and a republican virtue which was understood as implacable, masculine, and even savage, the very antithesis of a modern sentimental identity. Yet the necklace adds a gloss to its subject's character as well as to the portrait's meaning. Just as Hollis suggests that the ideal of republican liberty is enhanced by the liberal polish of civil society, so Macaulay's tough republican profile is moderated by its feminine accoutrements. As *Libertas*, Macaulay successfully united those gendered values which republicans in the 1760s and 1770s (and Americans in particular) thought of as defining political promise: the perfect combination of patriotic masculinity and feminine progress.

[107] TH to Elizabeth Mayhew, 28 July 1769, Hollis Papers, MHS.
[108] The letters of Hollis's and Mayhew's Atlantic circle include a number of accounts of Elizabeth Mayhew's reputed elegance and accomplishment. See, for example, Andrew Elliot to TH, 4 Sept. 1766, Hollis Papers, MHS. Though Mayhew was one of the most prominent of Boston's women intellectuals, she clearly felt deferential in the face of Macaulay's learning. See, for example, her letter to TH of 10 Mar. 1770.

In the following chapter I turn to look at gender and republicanism in eighteenth-century Britain from the opposite perspective. Exploring Catharine Macaulay's association with ideas of domesticity, scholarly professionalism, and sentimentality, I suggest how her femininity and her learning might have been extolled in entirely conventional terms, even as she was, as this chapter has argued, celebrated by the transatlantic culture of opposition as the exemplar of an exceptional patriotic masculinity.

2

'Out-Cornelia-izing Cornelia': Portraits, Profession, and the Gendered Character of Learning

Assessing the merits of the first volume of Catharine Macaulay's *History of England*, the *Monthly Review* wrote:

> The great numbers among the fair sex who have figured in the republic of letters have given frequent checks to the vanity of such as presume that the privilege of thinking is confined to those who wear beards. Not to speak of the learned ladies of antiquity, how many among the moderns, from the French Dacier to the English Carter have distinguished themselves in the several branches of literature. But it was reserved for the fair Macaulay to tread the path of History and undergo the laborious task of collecting and digesting the political fragments which have escaped the researches of so many learned and ingenious men.[1]

Like Elizabeth Carter and her other contemporaries, Macaulay is commended for the addition she makes to the ranks of learned women in the republic of letters. Indicating the capacity of women to write in 'all branches of literature' as well as the progressive nature of the national culture that enables them to do so, her *History* attests to the advanced state of women's learning and British politeness. Macaulay's learning is read here as a sign of cultural continuity with the classical past as well as of Britain's national (and nationalist) claims to a distinctively modern civility. But does the 'fair Macaulay' exceed the gallant terms of the reviewer's critique? More than just a name to add to a national catalogue

---

[1] [Unattrib.], Review of CM, 'History of England from the Accession of James I to that of the Brunswick Line', *Monthly Review*, 29 (1763), 372.

of learned women, she stands for something singular, perhaps exceptional. Carter and Dacier might enhance the feminine gloss of their national republics of letters, yet Macaulay's learning is distinguished by the labour and original discovery here associated with it. While the status of her *History* is unambiguously public and political, that of her learning seems more nearly professional (her research skills surpassing those of male scholars). Though the reviewer suggests that the first function of women's learning is to admonish masculine vanity, there is also the sense that Macaulay's historical work might compensate for other shortcomings. While she is allied here to the figure of the professional male scholar as much as to that of the learned female luminary, for the *Monthly Review* Macaulay ultimately treads the path of history alone. Her learning occupies a culturally liminal position, a space that is 'reserved', specialized, isolated: that mediates between accomplishment and profession; aptitude and acquisition; between masculine and feminine in Britain's gendered division of knowledge.

What follows explores the cultural significance of that space. In the previous chapter I suggested how Macaulay's role might be regarded as both masculine and public. For opposition Whigs on both sides of the Atlantic she came to represent the promise of republican virility in a world of modern political emasculation. Yet, beyond the cultures of radicalism and reform, Macaulay was renowned to bluestocking hostesses and British MPs; to the wealthy women of Massachusetts and New York; to French philosophes and salonnières, all of whom commended her patriotism *and* her polite elegance, her republican principles *and* her sympathetic heart. Here, then, I am interested in approaching republicanism from the opposite direction, as it were: through the category of the feminine and through ideas of the gendered character of learning. I am interested in how Macaulay's femininity and her learning (by which I mean the association of her identity with a cluster of eighteenth-century notions of gender and culture) might be seen to license or enable her political appeal. In what ways could writing as, or indeed looking *like*, a woman of learning facilitate radical republican interventions? Why might femininity sanction the widespread cultural acceptability of a figure who professed and espoused a politics more commonly regarded by the British establishment as singularly divisive?

Recent research has foregrounded the figures of learned women and explored the centrality of notions of women's learning to the national and cosmopolitan cultures of the mid- to late eighteenth century.[2] The social significance of women's learning was varied and wide-ranging. Learning might contribute to that moral superiority commonly attributed to women in the cultures of religion, sentiment, and philanthropy which characterized the mid-century on both sides of the Atlantic. Equally, in Enlightenment debates on national progress and international competition, women's learning might be regarded as both agent and effect of that refinement the age demanded.[3] In works on conduct and education (as well as those of fiction) learning was promoted as the curiously private conduit through which a woman could connect herself to an idea of nation, of empire, or of other publicly 'imagined community'.[4] Learning might be represented as that freakish gift that allowed a labouring-class woman to outstrip her origins, as the appropriate expression of the gentry's leisure and sociability, or indeed as decorative aristocratic ornament.[5] Or it might, in an era of increasing social and occupational specialization, signal the financial

---

[2] Examples are numerous, but see Harriet Guest, *Small Change: Women, Learning, Patriotism 1750–1810* (Chicago: University of Chicago Press, 2000); Gary Kelly, 'Bluestocking Feminism', in Elizabeth Eger *et al.* (eds.), *Women, Writing and the Public Sphere 1700–1830* (Cambridge: Cambridge University Press, 2000); Vivien Jones (ed.), *Women and Literature in Britain, 1700–1800* (Cambridge University Press, 2000); Nicole Pohl and Betty Schellenberg (eds.), *Reconsidering the Bluestockings* (San Marino: Huntington Library, 2003); Paula Backsheider (ed.), *Revising Women: Eighteenth Century 'Women's Fiction' and Social Engagement* (Baltimore: Johns Hopkins University Press, 2000); Anne Mellor, *Mothers of the Nation: Women's Political Writing in England, 1780–1830* (Bloomington, Ind.: Indiana University Press, 2000); Sylvia Harstark Myers, *The Bluestocking Circle: Women, Friendship and the Life of the Mind in Eighteenth Century England* (Oxford: Clarendon Press, 1990). See also my discussion of recent bluestocking scholarship in the Introduction to this book.

[3] See Jane Rendall, *The Origins of Modern Feminism: Women in Britain, France and the United States, 1780–1860* (Basingstoke: Macmillan, 1985); Jane Rendall, 'Introduction', to William Alexander, *The History of Women from The Earliest Antiquity to the Present Time* [1779] (Bristol: Thoemmes Press, 1995); Sylvana Tomaselli, 'The Enlightenment Debate on Women', *History Workshop Journal*, 20 (1985); Susan Staves, ' "The Liberty of a She-Subject of England": Rights Rhetoric, and the Female Thucydides', *Cardazo Studies in Law and Literature*, 1 (1989), 161–83.

[4] See Benedict Anderson, *Imagined Communities: Reflections on the Origin and Spread of Nationalism* (London: Verso, 1991). Among other characters and figures in this context, Jane Austen's Fanny Price, whose historical and geographical learning sublimates her affection for her brother, himself a modest representative of Austen's moral and domesticated British Empire, springs to mind.

[5] In very different contexts, learning was represented as the freakish gift of, for example, Ann Yearsley and Phillis Wheatley.

independence associated with the professional status of the woman writer.[6]

This chapter looks at some of these ideas and associations in relation to Catharine Macaulay's femininity and her republican politics. My discussion is structured around a series of portraits in a variety of media: the popular engraving; the statuette; the exhibited painting; the obituary notice; the autobiographical preface; the miniature that might be privately passed from hand to hand, while alternately allowing a public intimate access to its subject through its reproduction in the pages of a magazine. Together these portraits represent a range of proscriptions and possibilities associated with women's learning in the mid- to late century, illuminating that liminal position Macaulay was described as occupying by the *Monthly Review*.

I Collectives and Exceptions

In the 1760s and 1770s Catharine Macaulay was frequently represented and considered alongside those other women for whose existence and learning Britain loudly applauded itself. In the words of one congratulatory critic: 'at no preceding period has there ever been in England, at the same time so many female authors as at present and possessed of such indisputable merit.'[7] In the years Macaulay was publishing the early volumes of her *History of England* to such widespread acclaim, that peculiarly English genre of group biography, which defined a narrative of progress in terms of the cumulative achievements of the women of the past, had been transformed into nationalist panegyric on the women of the present. Together with other women writers, patrons, and artists with diverse (and divergent) class, political, and religious affiliations, Macaulay featured in numerous celebratory groupings. These included Mary Scott's *Female Advocate* (in which she is asked to excuse the narrator's 'fond presumption') and Hannah More's *Search after Happiness* (where she is cited as evidence of the woman of learning's conventional

---

[6] See, for example, Mary Poovey, *The Proper Lady and the Woman Writer: Ideology as Style in the Works of Mary Wollstonecraft and Jane Austen* (Chicago: University of Chicago Press, 1984).

[7] [Unattrib.], *Dialogues Concerning the Ladies to Which is Added an Essay on the Antient Amazons* (London: T. Cadell, 1785), 152.

The NINE LIVING MUSES of GREAT BRITAIN.

Miss Carter, Mrs Barbauld, Mrs Angelica Kauffman, on the Right hand; Mrs Sheridan, in the Middle; Mrs Lenox, Mrs Macaulay, Miss More, Mrs Montague, and Mrs Griffith, on the Left hand.

Fig. 7. Page after Richard Samuel, *The Nine Living Muses of Great Britain* (1778). Engraving. Reproduced in *Johnson's Ladies' New and Polite Pocket Memorandum for 1778.*

moral and feminine virtues).[8] Perhaps the most famous of these groupings is Richard Samuel's painting of *The Nine Living Muses of Great Britain*, which began life in 1777 as the engraved frontispiece to *Johnson's Ladies, New and Polite Pocket Memorandum* (Fig. 7). Under Britannia's statue and backed by a wreath of oak, a keen and girlish Macaulay sits in the centre of the print, unfurling the scroll of history for the attention of Elizabeth Montagu and her fellow British 'muses'.

Elizabeth Carter was pleased by the print and wrote of the engraved figures as 'pretty', but, as she remarked to Elizabeth Montagu, 'I cannot very exactly tell which is you, which is I and which is anybody else'.[9]

---

[8] Mary Scott, *The Female Advocate: A Poem Occasioned by Reading Mr Duncombe's Feminead* (London: J. Johnson, 1774); Hannah More, *The Search After Happiness: A Pastoral Drama*, 3rd edn. (Bristol: S. Forley, 1774), 44.

[9] Elizabeth Carter to Elizabeth Montagu, 23 Nov. 1777, in Revd. Montagu Pennington (ed.), *Letters from Mrs Elizabeth Carter to Mrs Montagu between the Years 1755*

Recent discussions of Samuel's *Living Muses* perhaps hint at its subjects' perplexing interchangeability. For Elizabeth Eger, the image 'provides evidence of literary women as a collective class', while for Marcia Pointon the image is 'highly conventionalized', perhaps hardly a portrait at all in its indistinguishable and unidentifiable figures.[10] John Brewer wonders 'why Samuel chose these particular women. They were not', he notes, 'a coherent group'.[11] It could certainly seem curious that City Whig Macaulay is represented conversing happily with Tory Elizabeth Montagu, but part of the *The Nine Living Muses* force and function (perhaps indeed the continued interest it arouses) comes from the absorption of women's singular achievements into the celebratory collective identity with which the image endows them. There is no space here for the representation of individual distinction, let alone the kind of exceptionality the *Monthly Review* associated with Macaulay's learning, and it is important that the image's sole signs of differentiation are those it loosely associates with discipline or occupation (Hannah More's goblet; Angelica Kauffman's easel).[12] *The Nine Living Muses* might be read as the representation of one indeterminate classical female figure divided into nine cultural activities. Opposition, singularity, and difference are engrossed by the muses' graceful, monotonous unanimity.

Richard Samuel promoted the standard liberal view of the progress of Britain's polite arts and its national identity:

The encouragement of the polite arts is the striking characteristic that distinguishes a civilised people from a nation of Barbarians; they soften the

and 1800, 3 vols. (London: F. C. and J. Rivington, 1817), iii. 47–8. Pennington often made free with the dates of Carter's letters, and that attributed to this letter certainly seems inaccurate.

[10] Elizabeth Eger, 'Representing Culture: The Nine Living Muses of Great Britain', in Eger *et al.* (eds.), *Women, Writing and the Public Sphere*, 107. Marcia Pointon, *Strategies for Showing: Women, Possession and Representation in English Visual Culture, 1665–1800* (Oxford: Oxford University Press, 1997), n. 165. Miriam Leranbaum makes a similar point to Eger, writing that the painting 'captures the moment when English women as a group first gained acceptance as natural and important contributors to the cultural and artistic world' (Miriam Lerenbaum, 'The Nine Living Muses of Great Britain', in *Proceedings of the American Society for Eighteenth Century Studies* [1977] (Carbondale and Edwardsville, Ill.: Southern Illinois Univeristy Press, 1979), 23.

[11] John Brewer, *The Pleasures of the Imagination: English Culture in the Eighteenth Century* (London: Harper Collins, 1997), 78.

[12] Hannah More's goblet makes her a dramatist and Melpomene, the muse of tragedy. Kauffman's easel is certainly the sign of her occupation as a painter rather than an iconographical attribute: there was no muse of painting.

manners, humanise the mind and give birth to attention and civility which are the basis of politeness and render society truly amiable and engaging.[13]

As earlier suggested, women's learning might be regarded as equivalently representative of that modern liberal polish thought to make Britain characteristically British. By the 1760s it had become a commonplace to regard their polite achievements in an iconic or ornamental relation to national civility. In Samuel's *Nine Living Muses*, the characters of learned women fuse with those of the polite arts they collectively embody in a composite celebration of national progress. Of her inclusion in Samuel's *Nine Living Muses* Montagu wrote: 'unless we could all be put into a popular ballad, set to a favourite old English tune, I do not see how we could become more universally celebrated.'[14] Montagu's contented sense of her own celebration clearly displays her self-identification as properly patriotic, as well as her perception of women of learning as collectively emblematic of Britain's blue-water nationhood.

It was not uncommon to represent Catharine Macaulay as a British icon in Montagu's terms. Part of the *Annual Register*'s take on the administration's inefficacy in 1766 was its 'proposal for a female ministry', 'a salutary and patriotic scheme', bound to restore Britain to the propitious national condition of the golden ages of Anne and Elizabeth. The court, it was suggested, would be transformed by the civilizing presence of women of learning and talent, by the distinguished 'females of... abilities' the author declared himself at no loss to find: 'I only wish they may be fairly compared with the men who at present enjoy those places.' Up for appointment were:

Poet Laureate	Miss Carter
Royal Historiographer	Mrs Macaulay
King's Painter	Miss Read.[15]

It might well appear incredible that the republican Macaulay, for whom a royal place and pension would be completely anathema, is recommended as the court's historiographer. In other ways, too, Elizabeth Carter

---

[13] Richard Samuel, *Remarks on the Utility of Drawing and Painting* (London: Thomas Wilkins, 1786), 3. Samuel's Remarks were first delivered as a lecture to the Society of Arts on the occasion of his winning the gold medal for the best historical drawing in 1786.
[14] Elizabeth Montagu to Elizabeth Carter, Montagu to Carter, 24 Nov. 1777. Montagu Correspondence, Huntington Library, MO3435.
[15] [Unattrib.], 'Proposal for a Female Ministry', *Annual Register* (1766), 212.

could seem singularly unsuitable for the position for which she is proposed.[16] But the point here, as in Samuel's *Nine Living Muses*, is less the reality of these women's productions and activities, their personalities and politics. It is rather that in Britain such women of literary and artistic achievement exist, or might be named at all: that as signs of cultural progress they are available to become the group icon for that form of feminized national power earlier represented by queens Elizabeth and Anne.

In these and other celebratory groupings Macaulay's identity as woman of learning seems at odds with her politics. After all, Macaulay's position in the 'collective class' Elizabeth Eger describes was gained by her public questioning of those institutions and ideals of nationhood images like Samuel's *Nine Living Muses* seem complacently to applaud. In the decade his print and painting were produced, the terms most often used to describe the fame and cultural acceptability of women of learning were those of the conservative nationalism and polite sociability with which the women of the bluestocking circle are most usually associated. In celebratory representations of Macaulay's learning, this vocabulary often coexists or overlaps with that of classical republicanism. This combination of terms and vocabularies is immediately apparent in the 'Irregular Ode' Edmund Rack composed for Macaulay's birthday in 1777:

> In her fair pages Spartan Virtue shines;
> With Roman valour glow her nervous lines,
> Her polish'd shafts shall bear relentless sway,
> And to expiring freedom give the day.
> Her virtues all the virtuous shall revere,
> And aw'd by her, shall tyrants learn to fear,
> Kings taught by her, may make contention cease;
> With wisdom rule, and wear their crowns in peace.
> Go on, my fair! Till low beneath thy feet
> Oppression bends and freedom reigns complete;
> Go on—while every tongue repeats thy name,
> And crowns thy temples with the wreath of Fame
> Whose swelling trump from sea to sea shall sound

---

[16] Carter, a writer of private meditative poems, was hardly a candidate for the production of public panegyric. Read, who had painted Queen Charlotte and many of her children, might feasibly have been regarded as 'King's painter'.

Macaulay's name the listening world around;
And Public Virtue to thy mem'ry raise
A column of imperishable praise.[17]

Rack assigns Macaulay a combination of polite (feminine) and republican (masculine) characteristics. Notwithstanding the Spartan and Roman attributes with which she is associated in the first two lines, the tenor of this passage initially seems comparable with that of other contemporary verses that praise the gendered qualities of women's writing. Rack describes Macaulay's pages as 'fair', gesturing towards her femininity and suggesting that her gender is indelibly written into her prose. Similarly, in Anna Laetitia Barbauld's 'On Lady's Writing', 'polish'd lines' are seen as direct referents of the feminine virtues of modesty and chastity, as well as pointing to the writer's polite social skills: 'the same graces o'er her pen preside/As form her manners and her footsteps guide.'[18] Macaulay's writing is equally 'polish'd', a word often used in reference to the refining effects of feminine virtues on masculine social mores. Yet her 'polish'd shafts' seem ambiguously polite, and might be understood as the honed arrows of discursive attack as much as they seem the rays of feminine inspiration or illumination. The associations of the word 'nervous' are similarly ambiguous, carrying the mid-eighteenth-century masculine meaning of 'vigorous and forcible' as well as hinting at the feminine connotations of the word as 'feeling' and 'sensitivity' in the language of sensibility.[19] In Rack's ode, the refined qualities of feminine writing are rather uncomfortably juxtaposed with those of classical republican pugnacity—Spartan virtues are not usually thought of as of the shining kind. Indeed, the function of Macaulay's learning seems comparable to that of independent masculine militarism, as she is seen to crush corruption, restoring the breath of 'expiring freedom', as she writes. Rewarded not simply with the laurels symbolically offered to learned women in verses of this nature, but with a form

---

[17] Edmund Rack, 'An Irregular Ode', in *Six Odes Presented to that Justly Celebrated Historian, Mrs Catharine Macaulay on her Birthday and Publicly Read to a Polite and Brilliant Audience Assembled April 2nd at Alfred House, Bath, to Congratulate that Lady on the Happy Occasion* (London: E. C. Dilly, 1777), 26.

[18] Anna Laetitia Barbauld, 'On a Lady's Writing', in William McCarthy and Elizabeth Kraft (eds.) *The Poems of Anna Laetitia Barbauld* (Athens, Ga.: University of Georgia Press, 1994), 70.

[19] See my discussion of the 'masculine' meanings of 'nervous' in Chapter 1.

of public commemoration more usually reserved for military heroes, Rack's bellicose Minerva is no living muse. She would seem more at home leading the field of battle than engaging in polite conversation in the salon or at the tea table.

Yet Rack retains a certain measure of gallantry in his appeal to the 'fair' Macaulay, a mode of address perhaps inappropriate for one whose role seems something akin to a classical hero. This combination of 'masculine' republican and polite 'feminine' qualities is clearly visible in one of the versions of a Derby figurine, produced around 1778 (Fig. 8). Macaulay's right arm leans on four volumes of her *History*, set atop a column inscribed with the names of heroes of the interregnum, contemporary British radicals and American revolutionaries, who together indicate a continuity of republican values through a century's political struggle. In her left hand she holds a personal letter addressed to Dr Thomas Wilson, her friend and host in Bath during the mid-1770s, to whom she dedicated her controversial history of 1778. While one profile displays a polite and private Macaulay, the other celebrates her status as republicanism's modern embodiment. This small statuette takes politics into the drawing room, perhaps privatizing and feminizing its subject's patriotism through association with the sphere of leisure and hospitality, of polite interaction and display. Necessarily viewed by a small circle, who might examine the figure from either direction, republicanism here is as decorative as it is commemorative: the heroism of a Hampden alternating with the letter's suggestion of proximity, intimacy, and exchange. As the quill in Macaulay's right hand hovers between her volumes of national history and the single, personal epistle, so her learning is represented here as something that might shift between the production of public narrative and the expression of polite convention.

Macaulay's radical friends spoke of her as if she were a bluestocking hostess who exemplified these conventions of sociability and politeness. According to the *London Magazine* in 1770, her 'manner of living' was notable for the way in which it 'unite[d] elegance with hospitality'.[20] Her social circle enjoyed the evenings she held at Berners Street and later in Bath, describing them in terms bluestocking women would have found familiar. In the effusive letter he addressed to Macaulay (later reprinted

---

[20] [Unattrib], 'Memoirs of Mrs Catharine Macaulay', *London Magazine* (July 1770), 332.

Fig. 8. *Catharine Macaulay (c.1778).* Derby porcelain statuette. Reproduced by permission of the Metropolitan Museum of Art, New York.

with her reply as appendices to the second edition of her *Sketch of a Democratical Form of Government*), a young and aspirant Benjamin Rush complimented Macaulay's skills as a hostess. Her conversation augmented both the pleasure and the polish of her company: 'the highest honor to which a generous mind can arrive is to be capable of communicating happiness to its fellow creatures', he enthused.[21] In the same vein of sociable flattery, Macaulay replied that 'the pleasure I received from your elegant and polite letter was much alloyed by the hint it conveyed that I was not to expect any more of your conversation'.[22] A later account of Macaulay's hospitality commended her ability to increase the 'happiness' of her guests, enabling conversational exchanges in her smooth manoeuvres between groups of people and different rooms, displaying that 'ease, and true politeness, for which she is so eminently distinguished'.[23] Here Macaulay almost takes on the character attributed to Elizabeth Vesey, who epitomized the feminine ideal of bluestocking sociability in her 'magical' ability to create and sustain disparate circles of polite conversation.[24]

But, as in Samuel's *Nine Living Muses*, here the terms of Macaulay's representation appear almost too obvious, too generic, or conventional. Perhaps this vocabulary of elegant ease and polite circulation is merely that which is most easily available, being the discursive register through which ideas of the sociable benefits of women's learning and politeness gained such widespread currency and legitimacy in the 1760s and 1770s. As her exchange with Benjamin Rush reveals, Macaulay certainly regarded her sociable role in the generic terms of the feminine ideal of bluestocking civility, but she also described herself rather differently. In her letters, one of the phrases she uses in reference to herself is 'animating example' or 'animating influence', and this is precisely how she is represented in conversation in numerous personal accounts: less

---

[21] Benjamin Rush to CM, in CM, *Loose Remarks on Certain Positions to be Found in Mr Hobbes' Philosophical Rudiments of Government and Society with a Short Sketch of a Democratical Form of Government in a Letter to Signor Paoli. The Second Edition, with Two Letters; One from an American Gentleman to the Author which Contains some Comments on her Sketch of the Democratical Form of Government and the Author's Answer* (London: E. & C. Dilly, 1769), 29. [22] CM to Benjamin Rush, in CM, *Loose Remarks*, 32.
[23] [Unattrib], 'Introduction', to *Six Odes*, p. vii.
[24] Vesey's magical social skills were eulogized in Hannah More, *Bas Bleu* (1787). On Bluestocking conversation, see Emma Major 'The Politics of Sociability: Public Dimensions of the Bluestocking Millennium', in Pohl and Schellenberg (eds.), *Reconsidering the Bluestockings*, 174–92 at 179.

the facilitator of harmonious conversational exchanges and more a sort of luminary or admonitory figure.[25] According to her sister-in-law Mrs Arnold, Macaulay had 'brilliant talents for conversation'.[26] From Henry Marchant, we get some sense of this 'brilliance': 'Her spirit rouses and flashes like lightning upon the subject of liberty and upon the reflexion of anything noble and generous. She speaks undaunted and freely and disdains a cowardly tongue or pen.'[27] This seems more Demosthenes than Elizabeth Vesey. By her friend Mercy Otis Warren, Macaulay's eloquence was described as equally sublime, displaying a 'commanding genius and brilliance of thought'.[28] But, as Warren remarked with characteristic frankness, this 'often outruns her capacity of expression, which is... a little too prolix'.[29] Macaulay talked too much, too animatedly perhaps, to promote the polite conversational exchanges of the bluestocking salon.

Time and again, contemporary descriptions of Macaulay's learning and conversation shift between the generic and the exceptional. For example, Josiah Quincy's journal account of meeting Macaulay begins with his receipt of 'a very polite billet' followed by 'an hours agreeable converse' and ends with his remarking that 'she is indeed a most extraordinary woman'.[30] Timothy Hollis similarly found Macaulay's conversation conventionally 'agreeable', but he also told Sylas Neville that, 'though she plays at cards and talks of different subjects', she much preferred to speak of politics: 'she always returns to that'. 'He thinks this an odd character for a lady,' Neville reported, 'but not unbecoming because uncommon'.[31] Hollis's account is coloured in Neville's retelling by its hesitant sense of Macaulay's sexual difference. The weight of cultural assumption about women's learning and conversation is registered in that 'not unbecoming', which itself signals the potential of politics to deform femininity. Macaulay's character is 'not unbecoming because uncommon'—that is, she retains her sex's and her learning's

---

[25] See, for example, CM to MOW, 11 Sept. 1774, WAP.
[26] Mrs Arnold quoted in Mary Hays, *Female Biography, or, Memoirs of Illustrious Women, Alphabetically Arranged*, 6 vols. (London: Richard Phillips, 1803), v. 298.
[27] Henry Marchant, *Journal*, May 1772, Rhode Island Historical Society.
[28] MOW to JA, 27 Apr. 1785, MOWP1.
[29] MOW to JA, 27 Apr. 1785, MOWP1.
[30] Josiah Quincy, Journal, 31 Dec. 1774, MS, MHS.
[31] Sylas Neville, Diary, 24 June 1767, in *The Diary of Sylas Neville, 1767–1788*, ed. Basil Cozens Hardy (Oxford: Oxford University Press, 1950), 13.

gendered features in her 'agreeable' ability to please conversationally, her feminine capacity to *be* becoming. Her 'odd' or 'uncommon' qualities—the republican politics and masculine style for which she was thought of as distinctive—are here the mark of an exceptionality capable of being contained by the generic 'becoming' characteristics of the woman of learning.

Catharine Macaulay might be seen, then, to stand in both a parallel and an inimical relation to contemporary representations of women of learning: parallel in that the terms of her representation often appear to celebrate that liberal politeness and blue-water nationhood for which such women had become conventionally metonymic; inimical since she was also regarded as a figure whose radical politics and public status made her uncommon or exceptional. As I have been suggesting, sometimes in the same image text or breath Macaulay might seem all these things at once. By the mid-1770s, Macaulay, a radical woman with pro-American sympathies and non-conformist leanings, did not socialize or associate with the Tory and Anglican women of Britain's bluestocking circles, but she also clearly found it useful to think of herself in terms of her allegiance rather than her opposition to them. In 1774 she wrote to Edward Dilly of herself and Elizabeth Montagu as members of a 'sisterhood' of writers.[32] For Macaulay, their character and status as women of learning certainly provided a positive point of unity, of personal and cultural identification.

The conventional representation of women's learning in the 1760s and 1770s bolstered and consolidated normative notions of femininity as moral and sociable, as modest and refining. Yet, in so doing, it also afforded the women whose manifest differences it absorbed a certain degree of cultural legitimacy and visibility. In Macaulay's case, the generic expectations of her polite, learned, and feminine character often partially disguised, merged with, or contained her radical exceptionality. Macaulay's incorporation into that narrative of liberal progress (to which members of the bluestocking circle seem more obviously appropriable) and her representation as a woman of learning (a figure with a normative, positive cultural currency) contributed in part, I think, to her fame, her initial success, and her acceptability.

---

[32] CM to Edward Dilly, 2 Apr. 1774, HL. As I discuss in Chapter 3, by the late 1770s Montagu did not regard Macaulay in the same terms.

II 'More than Female Tenderness'

Like so many other metropolitan women who moved in polite literary circles, or indeed those of the provincial gentry who gathered in London for the season in the 1760s, Macaulay sat to the artist Catherine Read. As is evident from the suggestion of her appointment as court painter which I quoted from the *Annual Register* of 1766, Read had gained a widespread popular reputation as an artist, and her pastel portraits were commended for the particular grace and dignity they conferred on their female subjects. A disaffected Scot who undertook artistic training in Rome after the '45, Read later enjoyed extensive patronage from Britain's bluestocking women.[33] In June 1765 she was completing a portrait of Elizabeth Carter in oils at Elizabeth Montagu's request. Hinting at how Read had managed to capture the meanings of Carter's femininity and her learning in her 'penserosa style', Catherine Talbot described this painting as 'mild, unaffected... quite unlike the common run of staring portraits'.[34] The quality of unassuming mildness Read managed to impart to her sitters was frequently remarked upon. William Hayley described her style as 'soft' and 'graceful', and, for Frances Burney, 'nothing can be so soft, so delicate, or so blooming' as Read's pastels.[35] The terms used in reference to Read's portraits clearly resonate with those of Edmund Burke's 1757 *Treatise*. As one account of her art put it: 'This lady's crayons are filled with grace and elegance, her expression of mildness, youthful chearfulness, smiles and natural ease is uncommonly beautiful and renders her works truly pleasing. Her attitudes have great merit and the general effect of all her pieces agreeable.'[36] The aesthetic vocabulary applied here to Read's style is that of softness and delicacy, of smoothness and diminution. Her portraits are said to

---

[33] There is little contemporary research on Read, but see Harriet Guest, 'Bluestocking Feminism', in Pohl and Schellenberg (eds.), *Reconsidering the Bluestockings*, 59–81, and Victoria Manners, 'Catherine Read: The English Rosalba', *The Connoisseur*, Dec. (1931), 376–6; Jan. (1932), 35–40, and March (1932), 171–8.

[34] Catherine Talbot to Elizabeth Carter, 25 June 1765, in Montagu Pennington (ed.), *A Series of Letters between Mrs Elizabeth Carter and Miss Catherine Talbot, from the year 1741 to 1770*, 3 vols. (London: F. C and J. Rivington, 1819), ii. 20.

[35] Cited in Mildred Archer, *India and British Portraiture, 1770–1825* (London: Philip Wilson, 1979), 118, 119.

[36] [Unattrib.], *Letters Concerning the Present State of England, Particularly Respecting the Politics, Arts, Manners and Literature of the Times* (London: John Almon, 1772), 257.

encapsulate those graceful, pleasing qualities associated, in Burke's account of the beautiful, with 'agreeable' femininity.[37]

These qualities, this gendered aesthetic, is certainly apparent in Read's portrait of Macaulay, from 1765 (Fig. 9). The original no longer exists, but the portrait became the basis of two popular reproductions, one of which is illustrated here (the other, a mezzotint by Jonathan Spilsbury, is held in various versions by the National Portrait Gallery). The previous year, Macaulay had been associated with the Republican hero Marcus Junius Brutus in the *Libertas* portrait designed by Thomas Hollis (see Fig. 1). If, in Burke's terms, the *Libertas* portrait might be read in terms of sublime self-sacrifice and masculine impassivity, that of Read could be regarded as beautiful in its openness of countenance, in its variety of movement and texture, in the turn and sweep of hair and neck. While Macaulay's gaze and the historical scroll she grasps certainly suggest self-possession, determination, and self-confidence, her learning is also associated here with that pleasing grace and delicacy, that youthful mildness, thought so characteristic of Read's portraits.

Read's portrait and its reproductions coincided with a particular shift in Macaulay's popular cultural representation. In its review of the first volume of her *History* in 1763, the *Monthly Review* declared that it was 'not at liberty to suppose Mrs Macaulay married', since her independence of spirit seemed to the reviewer to preclude a vow of marital obedience.[38] While it declared itself entirely impressed with the style and content of her *History*, the *Monthly Review* felt that the nature, the public genre, of Macaulay's learning unsexed her. 'We would not recommend such a laborious composition to the practice of our lovely countrywomen,' the reviewer cautioned, a hint of anxiety behind his commonplace unpleasant gallantry, 'intense thought spoils a lady's features'.[39] By 1765, following Read's portrait and Macaulay's second volume, the *Monthly Review* had completely reversed its opinion of Macaulay's topsy-turvy sexual character. The reviewer had discovered her marriage to Dr George Macaulay: 'We are glad to find that the woman is not lost in the historian, and we are disposed to envy the happy husband, who enjoys an amiable companion, such as Lyttleton describes: "Who to the

[37] Edmund Burke, *A Philosophical Enquiry into the Origin of Our Ideas of the Sublime and the Beautiful* [1757] (London: Routledge and Kegan Paul, 1958).
[38] [Unattrib.], Review of Catharine Macaulay, 'History of England', *Monthly Review*, 29 (1763), 372.   [39] *Monthly Review*, 29 (1763), 373.

Fig. 9. After Catherine Read, *Catharine Macaulay (c.*1765). Engraving.

force of more than manly sense/Can join the softening influence/of more than female tenderness." '[40] From the figure of autonomous self-sufficiency, deformed and defeminized by her learning, Macaulay is transformed into something sentimental, desirable, even vaguely

[40] [Unattrib.], Review of Catharine Macaulay, 'History of England', *Monthly Review*, 32 (1765), 275. The lines (slightly misquoted by the reviewer) are from Lyttleton's *Monody to...a Lady* [1747], in *Poems* (Edinburgh: A. Donaldson, 1772), ll. 145–7.

eroticized as marriage is seen to restore that true balance of gendered characteristics that learned independence threatened to put out of kilter. The sexual unity of the lines from Lyttleton's *Monody* signal Dr Macaulay's double gain (in their original context, a doubled loss): the elevated and sentimental domesticity here attributed to feminine selfhood, and a sort of harmonious abstraction of the marriage itself. Marriage is seen to have a mutually 'softening' effect: just as the husband is able to enjoy Macaulay's 'softening influence', so the 'spoiled' features the *Monthly Review* earlier derided as the effect of her learning seem smoothed out and refeminized through heterosexual companionship (the woman is not lost in the historian). Marriage, sentiment, and sexual desire render the 'historian' amiable and agreeable, granting her, in the *Monthly Review*'s terms, an appropriately feminine character.

Until his death in 1766, Dr George Macaulay was physician and treasurer to the British Lying-In Hospital for Married Women in Brownlow Street, an institution for which Catharine Macaulay was listed as a prominent 'perpetual' benefactor.[41] As Donna Andrew has pointed out, like other mid-century philanthropic civic endeavours, lying-in hospitals drew largely from the discourse of sentiment for their charitable appeal.[42] *An Account of the British Lying-In Hospital* solicited public support in sentimental terms, appealing to men of sensibility who would be affected by 'motions of humanity and affection for the sex' and women of feeling 'naturally prompted by tenderness and compassion', to alleviate suffering maternity. Such people might congratulate themselves for their charitable efforts, 'evidence of the public spirit and humanity of the times'.[43] The Brownlow Street Hospital, an institution which appealed to British sympathies and claimed through its care of indigent mothers to protect the national population, described its role as both civic and sentimental.

This combination of public and private, civic and sentimental, is apparent in an account of the Macaulay's marriage that appeared in the *London Magazine*:

Dr Macaulay, who, if he was not the first born son of Apollo, was the twin brother of benevolence, from having an opportunity of becoming acquainted

---

[41] See the list of governors in [unattrib.], *An Account of the British Lying-In Hospital for Married Women in Brownlow Street, Long Acre* (London: C. Say, 1771), 37.

[42] Donna Andrew, *Philanthropy and Police: London Charity in the Eighteenth Century* (Princeton: Princeton University Press, 1989), 67.

[43] *An Account of the British Lying-In Hospital*, 3, 4, 5.

with her [Catharine Macaulay's] merits, soon became ambitious to be allied to them. Friendship . . . shone fair in such hearts as theirs. . . . Dr Macaulay, while his wife was establishing her claims to reputation with the literati, was far from idle, where, though in a sphere less distinguished, never will his name, never will his generous attention be forgotten by any of those who obtained admittance in the Brownlow Street hospital during his period of presiding there; and as he lived universally beloved by the best judges of the gentler passions, so he died universally lamented.[44]

The shifts in what one might describe as a gendered division of role or profession within the Macaulays' marriage deserve attention here. The account begins with the suggestion of a near parity of aptitude and activity: the literary and medical endeavours of husband and wife are marked by a clear sense of difference, but appear of equivalent value. A further sense of marital equality is reinforced by the idea of sentimental friendship at the centre of the passage, by the pair's companionate mutuality. But the description of Dr Macaulay's professional activities as belonging to a 'sphere less distinguished' than those of his wife perhaps shift the balance: less the image of the medical professional, these are terms one would more usually expect to be applied to the position of domestic privacy a wife appropriately occupied. Catharine Macaulay shines in the republic of letters, establishing her just claim to public reputation, while her husband's professional activities seem privatized perhaps because in their opposition to idleness they are also represented as something more akin to industry or labour. Dr Macaulay's professional status seems curiously attenuated. His humane generosity appears almost instinctual, while his masculinity is softened by its sympathetic character; by its sentimental association with and proximity to the maternal body; perhaps even by the affection in which he is said to be held by his grateful female patients, 'the best judges of the gentler passions'.

The traditionally gendered roles of husband and wife in the marriage are complicated by the positive models of sentimental masculinity and learned femininity that the Macaulays represent. The *London Magazine*

---

[44] [Unattrib.], 'Memoirs of Mrs Catharine Macaulay', *London Magazine*, July (1770), 331. For another idealized account of the Macaulays' marriage produced around the same time, see *Town and Country Magazine*, 1 (1769), 91–2. Here Macaulay is celebrated as a model of appropriate feminine domesticity: 'Mrs Macaulay is as remarkable for her discharge of the parental . . . as of the conjugal duties.'

concluded by representing their roles in what seem more conventional terms:

> it is greatly to be wished that as in her private character she is exemplary to her own sex, so the amiable conduct of her husband in his public one might be adopted for a rule of action where tenderness, attention and humanity are so particularly essential to soften the great miseries of our nature, sickness and poverty.[45]

The terms private and public seem too inflexible, too orthodox, to contain the gendered and professional positions the account earlier described. I do not think that the *London Magazine* is simply reversing what might be interpreted as the 'transgressive' roles it defined.[46] It is rather that its notion of the public, its models of gender, and its sense of the status of the Macaulays' marriage is coloured by that combination of the civic and the sentimental which Donna Andrew thinks characteristic of mid-century philanthropic British culture. George Macaulay clearly here represents a surfeit of sentiment, and perhaps the marriage is also distinguished by its abundance of the civic in its links to an institution that was also thought to protect the growth of national population; in Catharine Macaulay's political and historical productions as well as in the figure she cuts professionally in the republic of letters. Their marriage seems a microcosm of an ambiguously gendered intermediary public, where a woman's learning might be thought of in terms of its professional status as well as being seen as an extension of her exemplary private virtues; where the medical profession is represented alternately through ideas of industry and pure feeling; where masculinity might be defined by its maternal tenderness.

I will return to Catharine Macaulay's own persuasive embodiment of the civic and the sentimental at the end of this chapter. For the time being I want simply to reiterate that her marital status in the early 1760s might be seen, in the prints and periodical accounts through which she was publicized, to grant her learning, as it were, a particular femininity. This gendered character might, as in the *Monthly Review*, transform an

---

[45] 'Memoirs of Mrs Catharine Macaulay', 332.
[46] For a reading of the *London Magazine* account in these terms, see Stephen Howard's interesting article, '"A Bright Pattern to All Her Sex": Representations of Women in Periodical and Newspaper Biography', in Hannah Barker and Elaine Chalus (eds.), *Gender in Eighteenth Century England: Roles, Representations and Responsibilities* (London: Longman, 1997), 230–49, at 234.

unsexed independence into a desirable softness or, in the *London Magazine*, afford her an ambiguously public status within the civic and sentimental composite of her marriage. This softness and this sentiment are evident, I think, in the Read portrait of 1765, which also suggests a certain youthful ambition. It is important too to point out that George Macaulay took a great deal of pride in his wife's achievements and was a supportive and encouraging partner, promoting that image of learned independence and patriotism for which she was most famous. It was he who first suggested Thomas Hollis design the *Libertas* portrait and was enthusiastic about the result.[47] In the warm epitaph she wrote for him in 1766, Macaulay singled out his 'ineffable sweetness of temper' and his 'excellencies which flow from a good heart'.[48] Macaulay evidently regarded her husband in those affectionate and sentimental terms for which he in his professional role at Brownlow Street had become well known. Following his death, Macaulay's learning was, I think, more clearly associated with an idea of independence, less ambiguous, perhaps, in its professional status.

III The Business of a Historian

'How can you be so extravagant in these times', Catherine Talbot teased Elizabeth Carter, 'as to idle away your money in such a superfluity as a fine fancied mahogany case to figure in at the Museum? If you do not read newspapers you will think my head turned, but if you do, the article I mean will have caught your attention as it did ours. It must be you or Mrs Macaulay.'[49] Elizabeth Carter, whose sense of her own publicity was, as Harriet Guest has so cogently shown, both hesitant and complex, would be unlikely to purchase an expensive case for the display of her works and her own self-promotion.[50] Though I have been unable to find

---

[47] See TH, Diary, 1 Feb. 1764, HL: 'Dr Macaulay, at his last visit, having desired me to consider of a plan for a print of Mrs Macaulay, to be prefixed to the second volume of her History of England from the death of Queen Elizabeth to the accession of Geo I; the sketch of it was drawn this evening to my own intire satisfaction.' And 3 Feb.: 'Dr Macaulay with me from 7 to 12. Shewed him the sketch for the print of Mrs Macaulay, with many medals and books of medals in illustration and aid of the ideas contained in that sketch. The doctor was pleased to approve of the sketch intirely.'
[48] CM, draft epitaph for George Macaulay, Sept. 1766, GLC.
[49] Catherine Talbot to Elizabeth Carter, 26 Sept. 1766, in Montagu Pennington (ed.), *Letters between... Carter and Talbot*, ii. 40.
[50] Harriet Guest, 'The Independence of the Learned Lady', in *Small Change*, 111–33.

other references to this case, it is entirely plausible, I think, that Catharine Macaulay might well have acquired such an item. Macaulay was an author who evidently strove to control the process of her own publicity and who had a profound sense of the professional status of her learning. In 1774 she was planning her own exhibition in much the same terms as Talbot imagines. Edward Dilly had written asking her opinion of some details in one of her portraits that was in the early stages of production. 'The picture is not drawn for myself,' Macaulay told Dilly, explaining that she had no amendments to suggest. Rather, 'it is perhaps intended as a present to the British Museum'.[51] Macaulay clearly felt that by then she had developed the professional and scholarly reputation which would warrant such recognition.

Throughout the 1760s and 1770s Macaulay and her supporters used a variety of media to stage her reputation. Her sense of her own cultural visibility is evident in the letter to Dilly, and in the 1770s she seems to have sat for a portrait almost annually. In 1770 a miniature portrait of Macaulay by Catherine Read was popularly engraved, and in 1772 'a portrait of Mrs Macaulay' was listed in the exhibition of the *Society of Artists*.[52] The following year, Horace Walpole noted an 'indifferent' portrait of her by Richard Atkinson in the same exhibition.[53] In 1774 she sat for the portrait she mentions to Dilly, and at least two versions of Robert Edge Pine's portrait of Macaulay were painted in 1777 or 1778 (See Fig. 5). The Pine portraits seem to blend the conventions of the representation of women of the middling and upper ranks (who might be represented 'as' or in the character of a classical or sentimental heroine) with those commonly used in relation to professional men (whose masculinity was depicted in terms of what they did).[54] There is none of the feminine mildness of the Read portrait here. An impassive

[51] CM to Edward Dilly, 2 Apr. 1774, HL.
[52] See the review of the exhibition in the *Morning Chronicle*, 15 May 1772, 2.
[53] Walpole's full comment was that the portrait was 'indifferent and little like' (Horace Walpole's annotation to *A Catalogue of the Pictures, Sculptures, Models, Designs in Architecture, Drawings, Prints &c Exhibited by the Society of Artists of Great Britain* (London: Harriot Bunce, 1773), 88). I am grateful to Mark Hallett for this reference.
[54] See David Solkin, 'Great Pictures or Great Men? Reynolds, Male Portraiture and the Power of Art', *Oxford Art Journal*, 9 (1986), 42–9, and Gill Perry, 'Women in Disguise: Likeness, the Grand Style and the Conventions of Feminine Portraiture in the Work of Sir Joshua Reynolds', in Gill Perry and Michael Rossington (eds.), *Femininity and Masculinity in Eighteenth-Century Art and Culture* (Manchester: Manchester University Press, 1994), 18–41.

and imposing Macaulay stands with her quill, scroll, and the named and numbered volumes of her work. Is this Macaulay *as* History, or Macaulay the historian? Is the quill the sign of the business of her learning or an iconographical attribute?[55] Some of these portraits became available as prints, were engraved for British periodicals, and were even copied in woodcut in New England. In addition, various incarnations of the Derby statuette appeared during the mid- to late 1770s, produced from the same mould with different glazes, colours, details, and finishes (Figs. 10 and 11). All were porcelain, which suggests a certain exclusivity about their market (popular naval heroes, for example, might be reproduced from the same mould in cheaper pottery), though the range of finishes meant the cost of the figure might vary. Chelsea–Derby were obviously aware of a market among Britain's middling-rank Whigs for a range of Macaulays to suit different tastes and pockets. The unglazed version in Dickinson college Pennsylvania (Fig. 10) shows a more severe Macaulay holding a scroll inscribed 'magna carta' and 'bill of rights' in place of the letter to Thomas Wilson. Other examples are much more detailed and highly coloured, using more expensive techniques of enamelling and gilding. Once purchased, the statuette might also speak of its owner's pro-American sympathies (prominence is given in some versions to the association of the commonwealthmen with the 'American Congress' on the base of the pedestal).

Macaulay and her work had a distinctive place in the literary market. The scholarly nature of her *History* distinguished it in the early 1760s. In the words of one impressed reviewer, 'unless the public records of the kingdom shall be proved to have been vitiated and the handwriting of our princes and great men to have been forged, Mrs Macaulay's *History* must remain unsurpassed in point of fidelity'.[56] As is evident in the quotation from the *Monthly Review* with which I began this chapter, Macaulay's gender and the nature of her research and publications meant that she was regarded in terms of both her association with and her difference from the male professional scholars who were her contemporaries. Unlike David Hume, who thought of scholarship as 'the dark industry' and did not feel it had much to contribute to his *History* ('I have inserted no original papers and entered into no detail of minute,

---

[55] On the ways in which Macaulay's identity in representation veered between the iconographic and the real, see Natalie Zemon Davis, 'History's Two Bodies', *American History Review*, 93 (1988), 1–30.   [56] *Critical Review*, 16 (1763), 323.

Fig. 10. *Catharine Macaulay* (*c.*1775). Derby porcelain statuette. Reproduced by permission of Dickinson College Library, Pennsylvania.

Fig. 11. Catharine Macaulay (*c.*1777–80). Derby porcelain statuette. Reproduced courtesy of the Winterthur Museum.

uninteresting facts'), Macaulay thrived on historical research.[57] She spent long hours among the expanding collections of the British Library, and was constantly acquiring, borrowing, and loaning political tracts. For example, in 1773 James Burgh returned a bundle of tracts to her. 'These are valuable collections,' he wrote with approval and perhaps aspiration. 'I should have liked to have a set of my own.'[58] Macaulay regretted limiting the time of the loan, but was eager to familiarize herself again with the collection: 'it has become necessary to me in my present work.'[59] As Bridget Hill has carefully shown, Macaulay's own extensive collection of seventeenth- and eighteenth-century pamphlets and sermons included more than 5,000 items.[60]

Macaulay regarded her learning as her 'business':

> In this country where luxury has made a great progress, it is not to be supposed that the people of fortune will fathom the depth of politics, or examine the voluminous collections in which can only be found a faithful representation of the important transactions of past ages. It is the business of an historian to digest these and to give a true and accurate sense of them to the public.[61]

Her labour supplying the leisure of people of fortune, Macaulay's research is represented as a productive activity starkly opposed (as was her wont) to modern luxury and consumption. Her learning here is both a sign of occupational differentiation (a specialism marked by the particular tasks of assimilation and presentation) and a 'business' with a definite public function (perhaps comparable to that of other middle-class professions).

In her sense of herself as an author, Macaulay clearly identified with the class position of those Whigs and radicals to whom she explicitly addressed her writing. Despite the disclaimer of her *History*'s sixth volume that she writes for 'men of all conditions', it is ultimately the

---

[57] David Hume cited in E. C. Mossner, *The Life of David Hume* (Oxford: Oxford University Press, 1980), 316. Of Hume's attitude to the scholarship of Macaulay's *History* John Pocock writes 'Hume may well have recognised that her powers of research in libraries and manuscript collections exceeded his own' (J. G. A. Pocock, *Barbarism and Religion II: Narratives of Civil Government* (Cambridge: Cambridge University Press, 1999), 256).   [58] James Burgh to CM, 23 Nov. 1773, GLC.
[59] CM to James Burgh, 29 Nov. 1773, GLC.
[60] Bridget Hill and Christopher Hill, 'Catharine Macaulay's "History" and her "Catalogue of Tracts"', *The Seventeenth Century*, 8 (1993), 269–85.
[61] CM, *HE* MS, vol. i, introduction.

men of the professions who are most capable of reading her correctly: 'no moderate churchman or honest lawyer can, on cool reflection, be offended with the historian's free observations,' she announces.[62] The professional middling sort are granted moderation and cool reflection as a virtue of their class, enabling them to understand Macaulay's unwillingness to compromise in the face of the establishment's prerogative and privilege. Her introduction to her first volume might similarly be read in terms of her sense of middle-rank professionalism. 'Labour to attain truth, integrity to set it in its full light, are indispensable duties in an historian,' Macaulay writes, setting out her qualifications and licensing her claim to the position: 'I can affirm that I am not wanting in those duties.'[63] Macaulay's vocabulary of specialization, qualification, and profession (and perhaps, on occasion, her use of masculine nouns and pronouns) should be read, I think, in terms of her understanding of her own learning as equal in status and function to the 'business' of middle-rank masculinity. This equality is clearly something she has in mind in her recommendations of female industry and independence in her *Letters on Education*. Moreover, in the proposal she makes in her *Sketch of a Democratical Form of Government* that women should be granted autonomous annuities rather than the dower, there is, over and above her republican dislike of aristocratic women as the symbolic figures of the exchange and retention of excess value within their class, the suggestion or wish of a viable model of women's financial independence.[64]

Macaulay made no bones about her learning as a source of professional remuneration. The publication history of the *History* in the 1760s reveals her canny exploitation of its money-making potential. The early volumes were first produced as expensive and exclusive quarto volumes, significant numbers of which were given by Macaulay, her husband, and Thomas Hollis as gifts to prominent readers. By the mid-1760s, as she rose to prominence, Macaulay experimented with different lucrative formats: a more marketable octavo edition and a popular serialization of

---

[62] CM, *The History of England*, vi (London: A. Hamilton, 1781), p. xiii, preface.
[63] CM, *HE* MS, vol. i, introduction.
[64] CM, *Letters on Education with Observations on Religious and Metaphysical Subjects* (London: E. C. Dilly, 1790); CM, *Loose Remarks*. For another reading of Macaulay's arguments on female inheritance in this pamphlet, see Staves, 'The Liberty of a She-Subject'.

the first three volumes in weekly numbers at a shilling a piece.[65] As a widow in the late 1760s she was playing interested publishers off against each other, finally selling shares in all forthcoming volumes (much to the concern and chagrin of Cadell) to the Dilly brothers for a notoriously large sum.[66] Macaulay evidently felt that an independent income enhanced the public or patriotic function of scholarship as well. As she put it in her *Modest Plea for the Property of Copyright*, it was only the money made from learning which 'render[ed] it convenient to the circumstances of men of independent tempers to employ their literary abilities in the service of their country'.[67]

Macaulay's often-overlooked defence of authors and booksellers in the 1774 copyright debate is important because it displays her understanding of learning as the source of an independence that includes, but extends beyond, the pecuniary. Appealing to 'enlightened and generous individuals... who respect learned and ingenious persons', she pointed out that a realistic income from the sales of books and shares in copyright was the only way to free booksellers and authors from the double bind of patronage and dependency.[68] The buying and selling of books and shares prevented authors themselves being bought and sold in a world of wealthy sponsors and impoverished hacks: 'If literary property becomes common, we can have but two kinds of authors, men in opulence, and men in dependence.'[69] Clearly an argument which addresses her particular sense of class and social inequality, Macaulay's *Plea* ends with the remunerative autonomy of those of independent mind and middle rank who use their learning freely in the republic of letters for the 'the delight and instruction' of the public.[70] Her pamphlet might be read in Habermasian terms as a defence of the liberal and disinterested features

---

[65] An announcement of the serialization of *The History* appeared in the *London Chronicle*, 24 (1768), 13.

[66] See TH's account of Macaulay's canny wranglings: 'Mrs Macaulay has lately sold to Messrs Dilly, booksellers in the Poultry, the power of making an octavo edition of her works, she reserving her right afterward in those works, for 900l! Also the right of every future volume which she shall write, for one thousand pounds each volume!... the bargain seems to be a good one on her part.' (TH to Theophilus Lindsey, n.d, in *Memoirs of the Late Reverend Theophilus Lindsey*, ed. Thomas Belsham (London: J. Johnson, 1812), 508).

[67] CM, *A Modest Plea for the Property of Copyright* (London: E. & C. Dilly, 1774), 46. Macaulay clearly includes herself here in her use of the general masculine pronoun.

[68] Ibid. 37.   [69] Ibid. 32.   [70] Ibid. 41.

of a bourgeois public sphere arising from the private interests of the literary marketplace.[71]

Yet, while Macaulay might importantly describe her learning as a scholarly specialism or business, enabling her financial independence and granting her an equivalence of status with male middle-rank professionals, she might also legitimate her position as a woman of learning by claiming what seems to be the opposite. In Macaulay's own descriptions of her character and education, her sense of learning as a commodity, as a source of professional status and remuneration implicated in a modern division of labour, often clashes with an opposing idea of learning as the sign of her virtuous (and sentimental) exteriority to modern culture and the marketplace. Despite her clear sense of her own scholarliness and professionalism, Macaulay might also represent her learning as the product of pure feeling.

IV A Republican Education

In her *Treatise on the Immutability of Moral Truth* Macaulay remarked on that narrative of civil progress which linked the development of enlightened learning with the rise of commerce: 'Some consequences... are annexed to the more general use of letters and the extensiveness of commerce; but if civilisation is anything more than an alteration in the modes of vice and error, we have not yet attained to any laudable degree of civilisation.'[72] Macaulay writes that knowledge is a commodity equivalent to any other furnishing 'means to delude the imagination by an endless variety of fantastic objects of happiness'.[73] Among the few 'consequences' or gains of civilization, she mentions the softening of 'barbarous fierceness' in the humane treatment of prisoners of war ('men have agreed to spare one another, for the considerations of mutual security, when no interest tempts them to cut one another's throats').[74] But, though wars may be less barbarous, modern civilized humanity has not affected their frequency or injustice, and Macaulay evidently finds the 'fierceness' that enlightenment destroys appealing, since it represents an idea of civic unity untainted by dissipation. Macaulay appears to have the patriotic spirit of her favourite

---

[71] Jurgen Habermas, *The Structural Transformation of the Public Sphere: An Inquiry into a Category of Bourgeois Society* [1966], trans. Thomas Burger (Cambridge: Polity Press, 1989).

[72] CM, *A Treatise on the Immutability of Moral Truth* (London: A. Hamilton, 1783), 10.

[73] Ibid. 10.   [74] Ibid. 12.

early Romans in mind here, whose manners, as she puts it in her *Letters on Education*, 'partook of a savage rudeness', and among whom 'the fine arts were not practised... the sciences were not studied, nor commerce pursued'.[75] The early Romans were not tempted to exchange part of their patriotic identities for knowledge or any other commodity, with the consequence that 'the love of country... tinctured every part of their conduct and deportment'. 'Models of all that is sublime in the human character', the early Romans loved the republic precisely because they were unlearned, uncultured, and uncommercial.[76] Macaulay's terms resonate with those of her republican predecessors, the neo-Harringtonians. For the Old Whigs at the turn of the eighteenth century, as John Pocock writes, a properly patriotic citizen should 'desire nothing more than the public good to which he dedicated himself. Once he could exchange his freedom for some other commodity, the act became no less corrupting if that other commodity were knowledge itself.'[77]

For Macaulay, then, learning might signal that choice, substitution, or specialization which threatened the unity of the patriotic personality with dissolution. In this classical republican register, the advancement of civilized learning—which was itself represented in the mid- to late century by the iconic figures of learned women like herself—could also represent patriotism's irretrievable loss. Macaulay's account of learning as a distracting commodity might also usefully be considered alongside Anna Laetitia Barbauld's arguments in her *Of Inconsistency in our Expectations*, where the division of labour characteristic of commercial societies results in a world in which everything can be bought and sold:

We should consider this world as a great mart of commerce, where fortune exposes to our view various commodities, riches, ease, tranquillity, fame, integrity, knowledge. Every thing is marked at a settled price. Our time, our labour, our ingenuity, is so much ready money which we are to lay out to the best advantage.[78]

Taking modernity's narrative up where Macaulay left off, Barbauld suggests that the exchange of one's personality for a commodity in the

---

[75] CM, *Letters on Education*, 239.   [76] Ibid.
[77] J. G. A. Pocock, *The Machiavellian Moment: Florentine Republican Thought and the Atlantic Republican Tradition* (Princeton: Princeton University Press, 1975), 431.
[78] Anna Laetitia Barbauld, *Of Inconsistency in our Expectations* [1773], in *The Works of Anna Laetitia Barbauld*, ed. Lucy Aikin, 2 vols. (London: Longman, 1825), ii. 185.

marketplace does not corrupt but ultimately characterizes it, as the values of republican cohesion are replaced by private interests and specialisms. Her irony simulating the logic of the market where one man's deficiency is met by a surplus elsewhere, she contrasts the identities of two of the great mart's consumers who have chosen to purchase different commodities. One is rich and ignorant while the other is poor and learned: in exchanging their personalities for wealth or knowledge they have selected goods which seem of equivalent status. Yet Barbauld's account of what one gets for one's 'ready money' when purchasing the commodity or specialism of learning suggests qualities which transcend rather than characterize the great mart: 'A large comprehensive soul, well purged from vulgar fears, and perturbations, and prejudices; able to comprehend and interpret the works of man—of God. A rich, flourishing, cultivated mind, pregnant with inexhaustible stores of entertainment and reflection.'[79] Comprehensivity of soul and proximity to the divine are hardly worldy goods. Like the philosopher of Adam Smith's *Wealth of Nations*, Barbauld's man of learning feels himself 'lifted above the common bulk of mankind' and 'disqualifie[d] for the business of the world' through his 'turn for speculation'.[80] Knowledge buys one's way out of the great mart, enabling a disinterested perspective set beyond its competing interests, its atomization. It grants the independence necessary, in that classical republican discourse that certainly colours Barbauld's account, for the apprehension of the public good. And yet too, in its very disinterested exteriority, knowledge gives the character what Barbauld describes as 'oddities' or 'eccentricities'—the unsociable signs of a failure to participate. Two notions of knowledge or learning are in unresolved conflict here: first, the idea of learning as the professional choice, commodity, or specialism that enables one to take one's place among others in a bourgeois mart of competing interests. On the other hand, learning is the mark of an exclusion which enables independence and disinterest, but in its very autonomy also signals a non-participatory status that seems isolated, privatized, perhaps almost abject.

[79] Anna Laetitia Barbauld, *Of Inconsistency in our Expectations* [1773], ii. 189.
[80] Ibid. 190. On Smith's Philosopher, see Kathryn Sutherland, 'Adam Smith's Master Narrative: Women and the Wealth of Nations', in Stephen Copley and Kathryn Sutherland (eds.), *Adam Smith's Wealth of Nations: New Interdisciplinary Essays* (Manchester: Manchester University Press, 1995), 97–122, and John Barrell, 'Visualising the Division of Labour: William Pyne's "Microcosm"', in *The Birth of Pandora and the Division of Knowledge* (Basingstoke: Macmillan, 1992), 89–119.

These distinctions, these shifts between the values of an independent exclusion and, as it were, the business of learning, are particularly important to Macaulay's famous introduction to her *History*. In a passage she reworked a number of times in the manuscript she wrote:

> The general education of the English youth is not adapted to cherish those generous sentiments of independency which is the only characteristic of a real gentleman. The business of the public schools is nothing more than to teach the rudiments of grammar, and a certain degree of perfection in the Latin and Greek tongues. Whilst the languages of these once illustrious nations are the objects of attention, the divine precepts which they taught and practised are totally neglected. From the circle of these barren studies, the schoolboy is transplanted into the university. Here he is supposed to be initiated in every branch of knowledge which distinguishes the man of education from the ignorant herd; but here, as I am told and have great reason to believe, are taught doctrines little calculated to form patriots to support and defend the privileges of the subject in this limited monarchy.[81]

'Learning' here has its particular eighteenth-century sense of classical Greek and Latin and certainly appears a business which militates against republican independence. Macaulay often spoke of her lack of familiarity with classical languages: 'she told Mr F[lemming] that she has no learning', Sylas Neville reported in his diary.[82] In 1790 she wrote to Ralph Griffith that 'I am no classical scholar... my education in that respect has been more deficient than most of the finest writers in this country'. Macaulay's gender meant, as she pointed out to Griffith, that she was excluded from formal education and unable to learn Greek and Latin as a girl, writing with pride and perhaps some resentment of her own efforts at self-directed cultivation: 'the unremitting industry... of the task of cultivating one's own mind and the pursuing and undertaking science in a girl's place without a guide.'[83] But she also clearly felt, as is evident in introduction to her *History*, that a familiarity with classical languages might merely parody the form of what she regarded as a true republican education. In a sentence she reworked and then removed from the final draft of the introduction, Macaulay added: 'Greek and Latin languages are receptory vehicles to knowledge but they cannot be supposed without other assistance to infuse the principles of

---

[81] CM, *HE* MS, vol. i, introduction.   [82] Sylas Neville, Diary, 11 Mar. 1769.
[83] CM to Ralph Griffith, 24 Nov. 1790, GLC.

science.'[84] Macaulay's exclusion, her autonomous pursuit of science (knowledge), and her lack of 'learning' were perhaps signs of strength then, rather than deficiency, since the education of the youths she describes does not get beyond the container to the substance, simply substituting republican content with its empty forms.

Macaulay's language of forms and artifice here echoes that of John 'Estimate' Brown, who had earlier described the modern cultivation of English boys as a process of de-naturing.[85] For both writers there is the sense of a natural or innate civic virtue that is quashed and disguised in modern England behind a façade of culture and corruption. 'Having drudged through what is called a regular education,' Macaulay writes, youths are qualified only to become 'a magazine of other men's conceits', simulating the opinions of others as once they repeated their Greek and Latin. And the grand tour is

> the finishing stroke which renders them useless to all the good purposes of preserving the birthright of an Englishman. They grow charmed with every thing which is foreign, are caught with the gaudy tinsel of a superb court, the frolic levity of unreflecting slaves; and thus, deceived by appearances, are riveted in a taste for servitude.[86]

The grand tour might, in another republican register, function as that consummatory moment of a gentleman's education when he would, through the perfect alignment of taste and virtue, apprehend his own judiciousness in his response to European landscape and classical architecture.[87] But for Macaulay it can signal only the triumph of fashionable taste over civic virtue, since education has rendered men all polish and no patriotism. When men return to England and take up public office, they still seem struck by the gaudy, sensual appeal of Catholicism and monarchy, 'commen[cing] disciples of the first doctrine which accident flings in their way'.[88] The business of learning

---

[84] CM, *HE* MS, vol. i, introduction.

[85] Brown described boys as 'plants . . . exposed to the inclemencies of an unwholesome air without the intervention of a higher and more enlarged nursery' (John Brown, *An Estimate of the Manners and Principles of the Times* (London: L. Davis and C. Reymers, 1757), 30).   [86] CM, *HE* MS, vol. i, introduction.

[87] On the grand tour, see Robert Mayhew, *Enlightenment Geographies: The Political Languages of British Geography 1650–1850* (Basingstoke: Macmillan, 2000), and Chloe Chard, *Pleasure and Guilt on the Grand Tour: Travel Writing and Imaginative Geography* (Manchester: Manchester University Press, 1999).

[88] CM, *HE* MS, vol. i, introduction.

has effectively disqualified Englishmen from occupying that position of disinterested independence which she defines as their birthright. 'The form of the constitution may be preserved', she writes darkly, 'when the spirit of it is lost.'[89] The constitution has become all surface, all show. Englishmen have been effectively taught to sell their natural independence in exchange for the commodities of culture.

In her *Letters on Education* Macaulay similarly argued that virtuous characters are best retained by limiting children's contact with the world and its distracting commodities. She proposed that they should not study politics till the age of 19; may be introduced to the Bible only when they reach 21, and should be discouraged from reading Richardson altogether, or at the very least until 'an age when the judgement is sufficiently ripe to distinguish the wheat from the chaff'.[90] Students must, Macaulay writes, be kept 'in perfect ignorance that the vices of injustice and inhumanity have any existence'.[91] The implication is that any cultural influence may militate against the preservation of that innate virtue which might freely develop into a love of liberty. Macaulay's *Letters* are characterized by their insistence, also present in her *Introduction*, that all forms of human exchange necessarily pose a threat to natural independence. So, for example, if children are 'initiated into the circles of conversation', they risk the immediate sacrifice of their virtue to the pressures of sociability as 'the human character sinks into the gregarious animal' and 'every part of morals becomes fluctuating'.[92]

If the modern business of learning erodes virtue via contact with the world's commodities, then a truly patriotic identity should perhaps be situated in a space where the impulses of natural independence are not quashed by culture's artificial influences. This is a position Macaulay represents herself as occupying:

From my early youth I have read with delight those histories which exhibit Liberty in its most exalted state; the annals of the Roman and Greek republics.

[89] CM, *HE* MS, vol. i, introduction.
[90] CM, *Letters on Education*, 147. An interesting aside on this score is that, when Macaulay's daughter, Catharine Sophia, was herself in her early twenties, she felt compelled to apologize to her mother for including Richardson among her improving summer reading. Her list included 'Cook's last voyage to the South Seas; Coxe's Northern Tour, some travels through South America and many of Plutarch's lives and some of Plato's Dialogues to which list you must excuse me', she wrote to Macaulay, 'when I add Sir Charles Grandison' (Sophia Macaulay to CM, 1 Mar. 1785, GLC).
[91] CM, *Letters on Education*, 119.   [92] Ibid. 152.

Studies like these excite that natural love of Freedom which lies latent in the breast of every rational being, till stifled by prejudice, or extinguished by the sordid allurements of private interest. The effect which almost constantly attends such reading operated on my inclinations in the strongest manner, and Liberty became the object of a secondary worship in my delighted imagination. A mind thus disposed can never see through the medium held up by party writers; or incline to that extreme of candour, which, by coloring the enormous vices, and magnifying the petty virtues of wicked men, confound together in one undistinguished groupe, the exalted patriots who have illustriously figured in this country, with those time serving placemen who have sacrificed the most essential interests of the public to the baseness of their private affections.[93]

The difference between authentic and artificial political identities is expressed in the verbs which distinguish Macaulay's youthful reading from the stifling effects of prejudice (excite, delight). While the education of Englishmen was all form, hers is all substance. From its roots in childish curiosity and pleasure, her love of liberty becomes a sort of physical impulse abstracted into that reverence that so struck her *History*'s early reviewers, the 'object of secondary worship'.[94] Clearly identifying with the classical heroism she admires, Macaulay's republicanism (perhaps like that of Jean-Jacques Rousseau) seems at once passionate and philosophic.[95] Its origin is emotive, even bodily, yet it enables independent thought and a rationality or generality of perspective necessary to the apprehension of the public good. Indeed, it is precisely the spontaneous nature of Macaulay's love of liberty, inspired by her unmediated response to the histories of classical Greece and Rome, which licenses her exteriority to that world of competing private interests and party prejudice her *History* opposes. English history has become an affair of the heart: 'If the execution is deficient, the intention must be allowed to be meritorious, and if the goodness of my head may justly be questioned, my heart will stand the test of the most critical examination.'[96] This is no learned woman's diffident disclaimer. The heart is authoritative because it is the source of a conviction and authenticity that is not just unstylish but surpasses style. Indeed, style or

---

[93] CM, *HE* MS, vol. i, introduction.
[94] See, for example, *Monthly Review*, 29 (1763), 372.
[95] See, for example, Jean Starobinski, *Jean-Jacques Rousseau: Transparency and Obstruction* (Chicago: University of Chicago Press, 1988).
[96] CM, *HE* MS, vol. i, introduction.

execution may be the index of duplicity, as it is in Macaulay's first attack on Burke, whose eloquence itself signals 'that disgrace of human nature', the separation of 'an able head' from 'an honest heart'.[97] Wondering whether men of corrupt character could possibly be entrusted with public office, Macaulay asks impassionedly: 'Can there be such men? If I were to put the question to my own heart, it would answer that it was impossible there should be such.'[98] If the ignorance of the republican heart points to its naivety, it also signals its unquestionable purity of perspective. While writing from the head means that one is knowing, and hence open to suspicion, writing from the heart gives one's politics an indubitable quality whose source is their un-knowing. Macaulay's position of heartfelt ignorance carries clout because it is extrinsic to that cultured corruption she attributes to Burke, which, in the narrative of Britain's decline and imminent fall that her *History* relates, has become the ruling characteristic of the political public sphere. The ignorant heart may be the only place that virtue has left to go.

In the account I quoted earlier from the *London Magazine*, Macaulay is described as a woman of exemplary domestic character and private virtue. While her writing displayed, the *Magazine* conceded, a 'perspicuity' thought 'uncommon' in women, it also revealed the authentic (hence common) signs of her gender. This was apparently particularly evident in the pamphlet she had just published in reply to Burke's *Thoughts*:

To the honour of the female heart be it acknowledged that Mrs Macaulay knew nothing of that enthusiastic prejudice that so often misleads *the wiser sex*. Liberty was neither more nor less liberty in her estimation because under the management of a professed advocate; nay, more, she was doubly hurt to find it mangled by the hand that ought to have preserved it.[99]

Knowing nothing credits femininity. The female heart is honoured by Macaulay's naivety as a sign of her gendered character, and it is perhaps because she knows nothing of party prejudice that her 'uncommon' patriotism is able to be represented as expected, normative, naturalized.

---

[97] CM, *Observations on a Pamphlet entitled Thoughts on the Cause of the Present Discontents* (London: E. & C. Dilly, 1770), 5.
[98] CM, *HE* MS, vol. i, introduction.
[99] 'Memoirs of Catharine Macaulay', *London Magazine*, July (1770), 331. Emphasis in original.

But equally, Macaulay's gender here is the sign of an eccentricity or difference since, like Barbauld's man of learning, it is also the mark of her failure to participate in the public sphere. While prejudice and private interest characterize the participatory political endeavours of the *wiser sex*, Macaulay is granted autonomy and independence as a virtue of her exclusion and thus her femininity. As she is described as doubly hurt, so her position is doubly privatized, experiencing Burke's betrayal of Liberty at the level of the intimate as what seems like a keenly felt personal injury. In a way akin to Hannah Arendt's account of the classical *oikos*, what seems most politically marginal (the heart, feminine feeling) ends up exceeding the political through its authoritative combination of the civic and sentimental.[100] Macaulay's patriotic heart is qualified to know the public good precisely because it is un-knowing.

The *London Magazine*'s account of Macaulay's femininity and learning was accompanied by an illustration of her perfect combination of the civic and the sentimental: a portrait miniature by Catherine Read that showed her *In the Character of a Roman Matron Lamenting the Lost Liberties of Rome* (Fig. 12).

V Cornelia

After a visit to Macaulay at her new house in Berners Street, Thomas Hollis wrote to Theophilus Lindsey that she 'out-Cornelia-ized Cornelia'.[101] Hollis was comparing Macaulay to the famous widow of Tiberius and the mother of the Gracchi, who displayed both a remarkable devotion to the republic and an exemplary feminine privacy. In her familial and patriotic character Cornelia perhaps epitomized the ideal of the Roman *Matrona*, but she was also well known for her sociability, hospitality, and conversation; as Plutarch put it, 'she always had Greeks and other literary men about her'.[102] In the later eighteenth century, Cornelia was also represented as the perfect embodiment of

---

[100] Hannah Arendt, *The Human Condition* (Chicago: University of Chicago Press, 1958).

[101] TH to Theophilus Lindsey, n.d (but probably 1769), in *Memoirs of the Late Reverend Theophilus Lindsey*, ed. Thomas Belsham, 508.

[102] Plutarch, 'Life of Gaius Gracchus', in *Plutarch: Nine Lives*, ed. Ian Scott Kilvert (Harmondsworth: Penguin, 1965), 193. On Cornelia, see Mary R. Lefkowitz and Maureen B. Fan, *Women's Life in Greece and Rome* (Baltimore: Johns Hopkins University Press, 1992), and Richard Baumon, *Women and Politics in Ancient Rome* (London: Routledge, 1992).

Fig. 12. After Catherine Read, *Catharine Macaulay as a Roman Matron Lamenting the Lost Liberties of Rome* (1770). Reproduced in the *London Magazine* (1770).

republican magnanimity and feminine sentiment. In Angelica Kauffman's painting *Cornelia, Mother of the Gracchi, Displaying her Children as her Treasures*, for example, she turns away from the jewels displayed with evident delight by a corrupt courtesan, rejecting the luxury and desire symptomatic of Rome's imminent degeneracy (Fig. 13). Cornelia gestures instead towards her sons, future patriots, republican heroes, signs of superior value. Her role may be quintessentially sentimental in that it represents the emotional force of maternal attachment, but it is also patriotic in the sense that Cornelia regards the virtue that her sons may embody and exercise for the good of the public as being of greater worth

Fig. 13. Angelica Kauffman, *Cornelia, Mother of the Gracchi, Displaying her Children as her Treasures* (1785). Oil on canvas. Reproduced by permission of the Virginia Museum of Fine Arts, Richmond, Wilkins Fund.

than the private passions and desires aroused by fashionable commodities. Like Cornelia, then, Macaulay seemed to Hollis a figure of republican reproach: a private voice that when corruption reigned and virtue seemed untenable spoke publicly to remind men of the patriotic ties binding them to their country. 'The invidious censures which may ensure from striking into a path of literature rarely trodden by my sex', Macaulay announces in her introduction in a voice that seems more senatorial address than polite apologia, 'will not permit a selfish consideration to keep me mute in the cause of liberty and virtue'.[103]

In 1769 Macaulay had told John Wilkes:

The admiration of that patriotic virtue which... flourished in the glorious states of Greece and Rome and for a short period of time in this country always

[103] CM, *HE* MS, vol. i, introduction.

subsisted in my character. I have not like others stopt at admiration but endeavoured to regulate my own conduct by the most illustrious pattern of antiquity.[104]

As I suggested in my introduction, Macaulay clearly associated her political character with the republican and sentimental meanings of the figure of the Roman *Matrona*.[105] In much of her writing (and particularly in her *History*) there is an urgent and conscious sense of relationship between classical models of patriotism and her own authorial identity. In her *History*, too, as Bridget Hill, Sue Wiseman, and Philip Hicks have pointed out, heroic Roman women like Arria and Volumnia provide positive models of feminine and public virtue.[106] In much of her correspondence, Macaulay speaks as a Cornelia figure. For example, in 1771 John Dickinson sent proof of his 'sentiments of esteem' to Macaulay in a piece of American silk. More than a gift, the fabric would also be read as a sign of rebuke to the British, whose restrictions on American manufacturing he opposed in his *Farmer's Letters*.[107] Wearing Dickinson's silk, Macaulay would also be displaying her pro-American colours, becoming herself a sort of colonial mascot. But she responded to Dickinson's silk in a way that spun what it meant rather differently. 'It was with some difficulty that I could prevent my heart from the being somewhat elated with vanity on the reception of a present from a man of the most dignified character on the other side the Atlantic,' she writes, acknowledging the gift's address to fashionable hubris, 'nor can I ever wear the example of American industry and ingenuity without feeling a very sensible pleasure'.[108] But, though the gift appeared to please her as proof of America's productive capabilities and Dickinson's regard, she followed her thanks with admonition. Silk was a loaded gift for a

[104] Macaulay to John Wilkes, n.d (but included in Wilkes's correspondence for 1768–9), BL Add. MS 30, 866.
[105] See my discussion of classical republican femininity and the figure of the *Matrona* in the Introduction to this book.
[106] Philip Hicks, 'Catharine Macaulay's Civil War: Gender, History and Republicanism in Georgian Britain', *Journal of British Studies*, 41 (2002), 170–98; Bridget Hill, *The Republican Virago: The Life and Times of Catharine Macaulay* (Oxford: Clarendon Press, 1992); Sue Wiseman, 'Catharine Macaulay: History, Republicanism and the Public Sphere', in Eger *et al.* (eds.), *Women, Writing and the Public Sphere*, 181–99.
[107] John Dickinson to CM, 17. Dec 1771, GLC.
[108] CM to John Dickinson, n.d, 1771, GLC.

republican woman. It was the silkworm, after all, which had undone Rome:

> The best wish I can form for the Americans is that they would be always satisfied with the produce of their plentiful country that they would confine their ornaments to the limits of their own ingenuity and rather emulate that happy industrious simplicity and moderation which is to be found in the happy and virtuous periods of the Greek and Roman states than the vices and luxuries which afterwards prevailed in those illustrious republicks to their entire ruin.[109]

It is as if Macaulay cannot read silk (which she certainly wore) in terms other than the inevitable herald of luxury and imperial corruption. Of course, Dickinson's silk was *meant* to suggest that economic and industrial development which would remove America from the fixity of the much-applauded 'middle state', which so impressed British Whigs and radicals increasingly disturbed by their own country's commercial and imperial mobility.[110] It would perhaps have been uncharacteristic for Macaulay to respond in any other way. But there is something more behind the surface of their exchange, something that suggests a classical republican connection between the corruption of the feminine and the corruption of the empire. Dickinson intended his silk to flatter Macaulay's femininity at the same time as he wanted it to suggest the colonies' national progress and economic autonomy. Macaulay, who, like Cornelia and the courtesan, evidently recognized the gift's address to her sexual character and the fashionable desires assumed to characterize it, was perhaps also rejecting it as a sign of a particular kind of femininity as well as of America's potential decline and fall. In her cautionary remarks on the republic's proper interests of simplicity and moderation there speaks also the redress of her sexual and civic character.

Macaulay often expressed her affection for America and Americans in sentimental terms. In 1769–70 almost every letter she sent to an American correspondent includes a reference to her 'tender' feelings on their behalf. 'I do assure you madam,' she wrote to Sarah Prince-Gill in 1769, 'the patriots in this island simpathise very tenderly with our

---

[109] CM to John Dickinson, n.d, 1771, GLC.
[110] On America's 'middle state', see, for example, Richard Price, *Observations on the Nature of Civil Liberty, the Principles of Government and the Justice and Policy of the War with America* (London: T. Cadell, 1776).

American brethren'.[111] 'Every partisan of liberty simpathises with their American brethren,' she told James Otis that April 'and there is none among us in whom such a disposition is stronger than myself'.[112] 'The Americans', William Livingston wrote to Macaulay in September, 'have reasons to rejoice that... you have a tender feeling for their sufferings'.[113] It is as if the American colonies are the appropriate focus of her maternal solicitude. Indeed, she explicitly described them in these terms. In 1775, having read the resolutions of the American congress, Macaulay wrote of the 'sympathetic glow' she felt 'to hear our own children as the Americans are called breathing sentiments which would have done honour to our country in its most virtuous, its more vigorous days'.[114] In her conscious sense of pride, affection, and patriotic identification Macaulay is certainly here out-Cornelia-izing Cornelia.

In her correspondence with women Macaulay has a clearly developed sentimental character. This frequently emerges in representations of her friendships (she writes, for example, of how she and Mercy Warren speak 'the real language of the heart'), but her sentimentality is perhaps most apparent in her and her correspondents' mutual understanding of their patriotic and republican identities—their relationship to a sense of the public.[115] In 1774, having seen a draft copy of Macaulay's radical pro-American pamphlet, *An Address to the People*, her friend Mrs Knowles wrote of her concern of the precedent the British administration was setting with its American policy in terms of the erosion of civil liberties. She was afraid to express the full extent of her anxieties, 'lest I should affect a friend so tenderly sympathetic as is the gentle Catharine... My Catharine sees far... the very remotest consequences of maladministration escape not her view! My heart too draws many a deep sigh for the days that seem near at hand'.[116] Knowles is consolidating, perhaps defining, the terms of their friendship in this effusive sharing of republican sympathy. She represents her friend's politics as prophetic and also almost physical: Macaulay seems

[111] CM to 'Sophronia' (Sarah Prince-Gill), n.d, 1769, GLC.
[112] CM to James Otis, 27 Apr. 1769, HL.
[113] William Livingston to CM, 22 Sept. 1769, GLC.
[114] CM to Mr and Mrs Northcote, 20 Jan. 1775, GLC.
[115] CM to MOW, 15 July 1785, WAP.
[116] M. Knowles to CM, 27 Dec. 1774, GLC.

to possess a sensibility that enables her to register public faults, to feel encroachments on and losses of liberty. In some discussions of Macaulay, this physical sensibility, and its capacity to document political injury, manifests itself in tears. In the 1790s an anecdote was often repeated about the way she wept at the sight of the poverty and servitude of French peasants in the years before the Revolution.[117] But it is in Mercy Otis Warren's prose that this lachrymose Macaulay is perhaps most striking:

> Do you remember the pleasant morning when you came out from Boston and breakfasted with me at Milton? All nature looked gay and peace pervaded the land. You was delighted with the cheerful faces and independent countenances you met on your way; but I recollect you observed you could scarely forbear weeping over my country when you surveyed its present happiness and at the same time saw a disposition in many to trifle away its advantages so recently and so dearly purchased. If you was here now, my dear madam, perhaps the tear would be indulged.[118]

Warren's fantasy of Macaulay's tears is clearly bound up with her own profound sense of republican disaffection (discussed in this book's sixth chapter). But what is interesting here is that Macaulay's tears are evidently part of her private or feminine character (symptomatic of the propinquity and feeling of the *oikos*) yet themselves signal her capacity to understand the best interests of the new republic. Her tears—the signs of an authenticity of feeling more powerful because it seems inspired by liberty itself—register her republican identity. Like a Roman matron, her sentimental status is the index of her capacity for civic virtue as she experiences the public at the level of the emotive, the intimate, the bodily.

I now want to return, finally, to Catherine Read's portrait of Macaulay as a Roman matron, which appeared in the *London Magazine* (see Fig. 12). This image exemplifies, I think, the representation of Macaulay as a sentimental and admonitory Cornelia figure. Read depicts her grieving over an urn and holding a scroll on which is written 'the law of the people'. The urn presumably contains the remains of a conflagration of Roman liberties, but might just as easily represent a departed friend or lover. In a contemporaneous painting by Gavin Hamilton, for example, Agrippina weeps over the ashes of Germanicus in a comparable

---

[117] See, for example, Mary Hays, 'Catharine Macaulay', in *Female Biography*, v. 296.
[118] MOW to CM, July 1789, MOWP1.

Fig. 14. Gavin Hamilton, *Agrippina Landing at Brundisium with the Ashes of Germanicus* (1778). Oil on canvas. Reproduced by permission of the Tate Gallery, London.

manner (Fig. 14).[119] The obvious suggestion is that personal and patriotic attachments are interchangeable. Macaulay's love of the public—her grasp of the law of the people—thus seems in Read's miniature to be prompted by the same instinctual feminine feeling with which Agrippina regarded her patriot lover.[120] As the Roman matron, Macaulay could represent a love of liberty and virtue that seemed both civic and sentimental.

The layers of civic and sentimental meaning in Read's miniature are illuminated by the moment of its publication as an engraving. According

[119] On this painting, see Duncan Macmillan, 'Woman as Hero: Gavin Hamilton's Radical Alternative', in Gill Perry and Michael Rossington (eds.), *Femininity and Masculinity in Eighteenth-Century Art and Culture* (Manchester: Manchester University Press, 1994), 78–99.

[120] On Agrippina in the eighteenth century, see Jane Rendall's suggestive essay, 'Writing History for British Women: Elizabeth Hamilton and the Memoirs of Agrippina', in Clarissa Campbell-Orr (ed.), *Wollstonecraft's Daughters* (Manchester: Manchester University Press, 1996).

to the *London Magazine*, 'it was only a short time after her marriage that she gave herself to the world as prefixed to this month's magazine, the impartial historian and the Roman matron'.[121] By the time the print appeared in the July 1770 edition of the *Magazine*, Macaulay was, of course, a widow, who might certainly grieve like Agrippina for the loss of her partner. Indeed, the *Magazine* made this clear in its accompanying eulogy to George Macaulay's sentimental character, which I discussed earlier in this chapter. Macaulay's identity as a Roman matron was thus clearly bound up with actual bereavement—her status as the grieving wife of a much-missed man of singularly sympathetic (perhaps feminine) virtues. Moreover, as previously mentioned, in its account of her response to Burke's attack on British liberties Macaulay was described by the *Magazine* as writing from her heart and a position of un-knowing. Macaulay was, then, also grieving for lost British liberties—and indeed perhaps those of America as well. Two months before the print appeared, Macaulay had written to the Town of Boston in response to its request after the 'bloody massacre' for her 'interposition and influence' with the British government. Macaulay had been shocked by what had happened in Boston on 3 March that year. 'There is not a Bostonian though spectator of the bloody scene who feels more sensibly than myself the horrid transaction,' she wrote, again representing political indignation as emotive or bodily.[122] As the *London Magazine*'s Roman matron, then, Macaulay stages these connections between her own bereavement and the grief she feels on behalf of the public on both sides of the Atlantic: between personal loss, patriotic indignation, and internationalist republican feeling.

The object and its engraving seem particularly suited to this range of meanings. As Marcia Pointon writes in a suggestive article, the ambulant and tactile qualities of eighteenth-century portrait miniatures meant they were a conduit for the entry of privacy and intimacy into 'social and economic exchange systems, thereby participating in and contributing to public life'.[123] According to the *London Magazine*, the engraving was 'a faithful copy' of Read's 'genuine miniature'. The qualities of

[121] 'Memoirs of Catharine Macaulay', 331.
[122] CM to the Town of Boston, 9 May 1770, Mathew Ridley Papers, Boston Public Library.
[123] Marcia Pointon, 'Miniature Portraits in Eighteenth Century England', *Art Bulletin*, 78 (2001), 48–71, at 49.

authenticity the print encapsulated went, the *Magazine* said, beyond the reproductive: 'nor will the curious eye fail to discover, besides personal graces, the graces of intelligence that *speak* the soul accomplished'.[124] The genuine miniature seems to offer unmediated access to Macaulay's genuine intimacy. As the curious eye is invited to scrutinize the portrait for Macaulay's speaking features, it is said to gain admission to her intellectual and sentimental interiority. It is as if the promise of the *Magazine* to allow its readers 'the pleasure... of Mrs Macaulay's immediate acquaintance' is effected by means of this portrait: an affective object primarily intended as a keepsake or for private display.[125] The loss Macaulay embodies as a figure in grief is doubled at the level of the object, which in its duplication of sentimental interiority and self-hood itself signals their absence. First intended for personal possession or domestic exhibition, the figure of the Roman matron is intended to elicit sympathy and admiration for what she grieves (her personal and political loss) and for what she represents (her exemplary femininity). Through its engraving in the pages of a magazine, the miniature elicits this sympathy and admiration through sentimental circulation on a much broader scale. This scale itself is the signature of Macaulay's professional visibility, her public role as historian and possibly, via the miniature's commemorative function, her civic status.

Perhaps this miniature, more than any other portrait or representation of Macaulay I have looked at in this chapter, captures the ways in which she, as a woman of learning and radical patriotism in the 1760s and 1770s, might seem both so acceptable and so famous. The Roman matron was, in the decades Macaulay rose to fame, a persuasive figure of patriotism, private sentiment, and also, in Britain, ambiguous politeness. Catherine Read planned to represent a number of Britain's bluestocking women in a similar manner.[126] Clearly, the figure of the *Matrona* formed an appropriate frame of reference for eighteenth-century women's understanding of their own learning and their patriotism, perhaps like the civic-minded and widowed Cornelia with her salon of cultured Greek and Roman men. As Read's *Matrona* Macaulay represents a femininity whose 'uncommon' qualities are contained and

---

[124] 'Memoirs of Catharine Macaulay', 331. Emphasis in original.
[125] 'Memoirs of Catharine Macaulay', 331.
[126] See Manners, 'Catherine Read: The English Rosalba'.

valorized by their exemplary privacy or sentiment and a politics authorized by the claim the miniature makes of its experience at the level of the heart.

In 1790 Macaulay responded to the *Monthly Review*'s unfavourable account of the *Letters on Education* that had so impressed Mary Wollstonecraft.[127] Rather than merely condemning her ideas of women's intellectual equality, Macaulay wrote dryly, perhaps the reviewer had some alternative suggestions to 'encourage us in other laudable endeavours to fill up that void in the mind which has been made by prejudice and inattention'. 'It is under a full sense of the very inconveniences that I have my self struggled with', she wrote, 'that I recommend a learned education to women'.[128] Beneath her pride and understandable anger, Macaulay is here clearly and unambiguously articulating her personal sense of women's intellectual equality and the claims of her female contemporaries to the knowledge and the learning from which they, by virtue of their gender, were so often excluded.

In this chapter I have explored a variety of ways in which Macaulay's learning and her gender might be regarded in the 1760s and 1770s as ordinary—as culturally normative or acceptable—or indeed as singular or unusual. As a learned woman in Britain's polite 'sisterhood' of learned women, Macaulay's radicalism and her 'masculine' republican character might be sanctioned by the polite, 'feminine', or nationalistic conventions of representation that pertained to the group as a whole. Depictions of Macaulay as a married woman, meanwhile, attributed her a sexual character which obscured her troubling intellect and politics ('the woman is not lost in the historian') or contained her ambiguous public and private role within the sentimental compound of heterosexual companionship. While her status as a woman of learning might seem normative or acceptable, I argued, Macaulay's scholarly singularity itself allowed her a clearly defined professional space in Britain's republic of letters. The business of learning and the financial independence

---

[127] See Wollstonecraft's review of Macaulay's *Letters on Education* in the *Analytical Review*, 8 (1790), 241–54. See also Bridget Hill, 'The Links between Mary Wollstonecraft and Catharine Macaulay: New Evidence', *Women's History Review*, 4 (1995), 177–92.

[128] CM to Ralph Griffith, 24 Nov. 1790, GLC. Devoney Looser discusses Macaulay's response to the *Monthly Review*'s account of her *Letters* in ' "Those Historical Laurels which Once Graced My Brow are Now in their Wane": Catharine Macaulay's Last Years and Legacy', *Studies in Romanticism*, 42 (2003), 203–25.

it entailed were claimed by Macaulay in terms that reveal her class affiliations as a middle-rank professional. Though Macaulay saw learning as a private interest capable of abstraction into independence in the bourgeois public sphere, she also, I suggested, wrote of learning in classical republican terms as a distracting commodity. Rather than signalling her professional implication in a division of labour or knowledge, Macaulay's learning and her femininity might be seen to grant her sentimental exteriority to a masculine political public sphere that now disturbingly mimicked the getting and spending of modernity's great mart. Macaulay's informal and unmediated identification with patriotism through her youthful reading of classical history meant that she, unlike the dissipated Englishmen to whom she favourably compared herself, was able both to cultivate and to maintain her republican independence. While her privacy or femininity might be the mark of political marginality or eccentricity, they could also equally seem authoritative, I argued, precisely because of their exclusionary, non-participatory status. These shifts of affiliation between the private and the political, the masculine and the feminine, were encapsulated, I concluded, by the persuasive representation of Macaulay as Cornelia, the sentimental, civic, and ambiguously polite *Matrona*.

Macaulay clearly associated herself with what in today's terms might be seen as the conventions of eighteenth-century feminine sentiment and found the language of sensibility to carry a positive political resonance. This does not mean, as Greg Kucich would have it, that Macaulay's sexual character is somehow actually and materially inherent in her writing: that she always, inevitably, writes like a woman.[129] But neither does it mean that there is something inevitably calculated in her use of the language of feeling. As I have suggested, sentiment was not at odds with but profoundly bound up with Macaulay's sense of herself as republican and patriotic, and certainly contributed to what her contemporaries regarded as her virtuous 'masculine' political character. Ideas of femininity and learning were imbricated with broader eighteenth-century discourses (some of which this chapter has addressed), generating a range of identifications and associations, both proscriptive and enabling.

---

[129] Greg Kucich, ' "This Horrid Theatre of Human Suffering": Gendering the Stages of History in Catharine Macaulay and Percy Bysshe Shelley', in Thomas Pfau and Robert F. Gleckner (eds.), *Lessons of Romanticism: A Critical Companion* (Durham, NC: Duke University Press, 1998), 448–67.

If assumptions about Macaulay's gender concealed, contained, or indeed later condemned her radical politics, they certainly also, as I have argued in this chapter, licensed her to develop and express her abilities as a historian, her sense of women's intellectual equality, and their political relationship to a sense of the public.

3

Belle Sauvage: Catharine Macaulay and the American War in Britain

I will begin with a representation of femininity and patriotic or national identification, an image from 1776 entitled *The Female Combatants, or Who Shall* (Fig. 15). This print represents the war between Britain and America in the then familiar terms of familial conflict. In response to the mother country's attempts to force her rebellious daughter to obedience, a bare-breasted America plants a solid right fist in her face. Beneath the figure of Britannia, the withered tree of liberty and north-pointing compass provide comment on the administration, while America's cap and cockerel signal colonial determination and French sympathy. Here, America's representation as the figure of the savage conveys that idea of natural liberty with which the colonists' cause was often associated. By contrast, Britain's imperial corruption is suggested in the elaborate dress and extravagantly high head for which the fashions of the 1770s were notorious. The family quarrel is clearly one between the awkward possessions of empire and the exotic novelty of new nationhood: between the control or autonomy of parent and child. National opposition and identity are expressed as the difference between two femininities, each defined by its artificial or unmediated nature. But are mother and daughter really that dissimilar? As America's head is adorned with a ring of tall feathers, so the plumes of Britannia's wig exaggerate her height. As Britannia's face is coloured with modern cosmetics, so America's naked skin is decorated with an intricate and ornate pattern of tattoos. The bodies of both women are equally distorted by dress or ornament whose bright reds and blues (in the original print) echo and mirror each other. Both nations, in turn, are associated with a femininity similarly characterized by its aggression and spectacular display. In *The Female Combatants*, then, Britain, America, and the confused enmity of their

Fig. 15. *The Female Combatants, or Who Shall* (1776). Engraving. Reproduced by courtesy of the Lewis Walpole Library, LWLPR04040.

national positions are represented through the signs of a gendered excess, alterity, or disorder. This disorder—America's nude bellicosity, Britannia's fashionable extravagance, and the bodily deformity of both—manages simultaneously to suggest the opposition and resemblance between mother and daughter.

In this chapter I am interested in exploring these resemblances and oppositions. Why might Britannia's imperial modernity be signalled by her preposterous fashionable dress? What political claims could be expressed through the association of American republicanism with the figure of the Indian? How might the representation of aggressive or deviant femininities define the experience of what was, for Britain, a difficult civil war? Here I look at the cultural representation and understanding of the American war in Britain in terms of such images of femininity and nationality. While in North America the movement from colonies to independent states brought important redefinitions of nationhood, in Britain the experience of an initially unpopular and 'unnatural'; war prompted difficult reflections on the meanings of national identity and imperial endeavour. Part of that process of self-reflection involved changing representations of gender difference and a vigorous debate on British patriotism. Catharine Macaulay made significant interventions in that debate, and importantly became herself a subject of it. During the decade which saw the separation of Britain from its thirteen American colonies, Macaulay was notorious for her radical opposition to the war and North's ministry and that notoriety itself became part of the consideration of what the war might mean. She was the political figurehead of the Atlantic opposition as well as a woman whose personal relationships, fashionable tastes, and sense of independence were regarded as radical, unconventional, or excessive. As such, in a nation attempting to draw ranks around an embattled blue-water loyalism, she was regarded as some kind of affront both to feminine propriety and to a properly British patriotism. By the late 1770s Catharine Macaulay had become the focus of a scandal from which she never really ever escaped and which she clearly found deeply troubling. Her denunciation in Britain during the years of the American war set a precedent for the representation of republican women's intellects, sexuality, and politics over the decades that followed.

In two earlier chapters I explored the politics of Macaulay's celebrity in terms of the notions of patriotism and learning, sentiment and rationality, profession and domesticity, masculinity and femininity, and the exclusive independence and sociable exchange which contributed to it. Here I examine how, in a culture struggling with the terms of its own domestic and imperial self-definition, such notions might come to be associated with alterity rather than an acceptable exceptionality, with deviance rather than convention. I begin by looking at Macaulay's transatlantic friendships and correspondence; her pro-American pamphlet *An Address to the People* (1775; reissued 1779), and her controversial *History of England in a Series of Letters* (1778). This part of the chapter argues in some detail that these often overlooked parts of Macaulay's political *œuvre* (and in particular the *History*) should be read as important, perhaps definitive, accounts of the radical Atlantic opposition to North's ministry and the American war. The second part of the chapter looks in broader terms at the cultural context of the American war in Britain, suggesting how the radical Atlantic turn of Macaulay's republicanism meant she might be satirically represented as Brutus, as an Amazon, or as a North American Indian—figures whose violence and independence were read as threats to the sentimental cohesion of Britain's imperial family. Such feminine figures, I argue, had become the war's metaphoric stock in trade, affording a strong sense of national and political difference to a conflict whose notions of enmity could seem troublingly indistinct. I explore the resonance of such figures further in my reading of Samuel Jackson Pratt's *Emma Corbett* (a rarely considered but intriguing British fictional response to the American war) and look at how the Atlantic 'war of the affections' might be defined by the powerful contrast between ideas of savagery and of sentiment, between violent and violated femininity. Finally, with this pervasive cultural contrast in mind, I return to the increasingly unpleasant British condemnation of Macaulay, her marriage, and her fashionable tastes at the turn of the 1780s. I argue that it is under the conservative shadow that the American war cast across Britain that her denunciation as female grotesque or *belle sauvage* might be more fully understood.[1]

Part One

I Atlantic Correspondence

By the time the American conflict turned towards war, Catharine Macaulay was at the centre of a well-developed network of Atlantic

[1] Accounts of British culture and the American War of Independence I have found useful in writing this chapter include: Jay Fliegelman, *Prodigals and Pilgrims: The American Revolution against Patriarchal Authority* (Cambridge: Cambridge University Press, 1982); Harry Dickinson (ed.), *Britain and the American Revolution* (London: Longman, 1998); Kathleen Wilson, *The Sense of the People: Politics, Culture and*

correspondence. Among her many friends in the north and middle colonies, she counted Benjamin Franklin, John and Abigail Adams, James Otis and Mercy Otis Warren, Samuel Adams, John Dickinson, Ezra Stiles, the Lee brothers, William Livingston, James Bowdoin, and, later, George Washington—not an insignificant list. Her friendships were extended through transatlantic introductions, such as those with Benjamin Rush, Josiah Quincy, Henry Marchant, and Stephen Sayre, which themselves enabled new correspondences and connections.[2] As I suggested in this book's first chapter, colonial affairs and interests were at the heart of both the City of London and the 'real' Whig groups that formed her political milieu, and, as for many British radicals, she found America exerted a particular fascination. While in Westminster public virtue seemed to be gasping its last, Macaulay saw the thirteen colonies as the last British place where the Commonwealth 'spirit of Hampden and Pym' might be fruitfully revived.[3] She also clearly felt that her *History* provided the instruction and inspiration necessary to retain that spirit. As she wrote to James Otis, 'the principles on which I have written the History of the Stuart monarchs are, I flatter myself, in some measure correspondent to those of the great guardians of American Liberty'.[4] In similar terms, she told Benjamin Rush: 'I think that the general principles of the rights of mankind inculcated in my great work [are] of great advantage to them [the Americans].'[5] She frequently expressed a desire

Imperialism in England, 1715–1785 (Cambridge: Cambridge University Press, 1995); Stephen Conway, *The British Isles and the War of American Independence* (Oxford: Oxford University Press, 2000); Eliga Gould, *The Persistence of Empire: British Political Culture in the Age of the American Revolution* (Chapel Hill, NC: University of North Carolina Press, 2000); Bernard Bailyn, *The Ideological Origins of the American Revolution* (Cambridge, Mass.: Harvard University Press, 1967); Colin Bonwick, *English Radicals and the American Revolution* (Chapel Hill, NC: University of North Carolina Press, 1977); Linda Colley, *Britons: Forging the Nation 1707–1783* (London: Pimlico, 1992); John Sainsbury, *Disaffected Patriots: London Supporters of Revolutionary America, 1769–1782* (Kingston and Montreal: McGill-Queens University Press, 1987); Alison Gilbert-Olson, *Making the Empire Work: London and American Interest Groups 1690–1790* (Cambridge, Mass.: Harvard University Press, 1992), and 'The London Mercantile Lobby and the Coming of the American Revolution', *Journal of American History*, 69 (1982), 21–41.

[2] See, for example, Benjamin Rush's letter of introduction to Macaulay for Samuel Stockton, 'a young lawyer and . . . a firm advocate of the claims of America' (Benjamin Rush to CM, n.d., 1775, Samuel Stockton letters, HL).

[3] See MOW to CM, 7 June 1773, MOWP 1, and CM to MOW, 11 Sept. 1774, WAP.   [4] CM to James Otis, 27 Apr. 1769, HL.

[5] CM to Benjamin Rush, 20 Jan. 1769, in CM, *Loose Remarks on Certain Positions to be Found in Mr. Hobbes' Philosophical Rudiments of Government and Society with a Short*

to cross the Atlantic and had reputedly formed plans before Anglo-American hostilities commenced to emigrate to the Fairfax grant region of Virginia.[6]

Macaulay's controversial account of the reign and death of Charles I secured her Atlantic reputation. While Anglicans and Episcopalians might regard Charles I as a figure of national sentiment, guilt, and grief, for the Atlantic republican community he was the figurehead of that political tyranny that prompted the Commonwealth uprising to which they so often compared their own political endeavours. In her *History* Macaulay argued that Charles was 'necessarily excluded' from that 'compassion which is the constant attendant of liberal minds', because of the unparalleled turpitude of his administration and the 'dark parts of his character'.[7] By the time her fourth volume appeared, her readers were impatient for a republican corrective to David Hume and were more than familiar with the historical parallels thought to connect the reign of the present king with that of his Stuart predecessor.[8] 'It is truly amazing', William Livingston wrote in praise of her *History* from New York, 'that the nation, after so great a progress of science, should continue that solemn mockery of God whereby fools perpetuate what flatterers invented... the canonization of... tyrants'.[9] By its American readers, Macaulay's fourth volume was welcomed in terms of its opposition to that process of Charles I's mythic sentimentalization which was reinforced each 30 January and that David Hume had reinvented and perpetuated.[10] Like Jonathan Mayhew's famous republican anniversary

---

Sketch of a Democratic Form of Government in a Letter to Signor Paoli. The Second Edition, with Two Letters, One from an American Gentleman to the Author which Contains some Comments on her Sketch of the Democratical Form of Government and the Author's Answer (London: W. Johnson, E. & C. Dilly, 1769), 35. Thomas Hollis had a hand in the design of the title page of this edition and donated the copy of the pamphlet in the Houghton Library, Harvard.

[6] See Earl of Buchan to Arthur Lee, 5 Jan 1775, cited in *The Life of Arthur Lee*, 2 vols. (Boston, 1829), ii. 346.

[7] CM, *The History of England from the Accession of James I to the Elevation of the House of Hanover*, 3rd edn. (London: E. & C. Dilly, 1769), iv. 391.

[8] See, for example, the many implied comparisons between George III and Charles I in William Moore's *Whisperer* and Cuthbert Shaw's *Middlesex Journal* at the turn of the 1770s. These comparisons are discussed by Kathleen Wilson in her *The Sense of the People*.

[9] William Livingston to CM, 22 Sept. 1769, GLC.

[10] Macaulay's fourth volume cited 'nonsensical' and 'impious' anniversary sermons that compared the king to Christ and suggested that such turn of the century high-church excesses continued to taint Protestantism. CM, *History of England*, 3rd edn., iv. 399.

sermon in which Charles was described as a 'mock saint and a royal sinner', Macaulay's uncompromising account of his trial and death was extracted at timely moments of the colonial crisis in newspapers in Boston and New York.[11] By the turn of 1770 there was a contest over the meanings of the memory of the 1630s and 1640s being played out in the pages of Britain's new histories, periodicals, and pamphlets which preceded the American war. The story of Britain's regicide and republican experiment held a signal and salutary contemporary resonance in the worsening American crisis, and it was in this context that Macaulay's *History* was admired in the Atlantic political community.

During the 1770s Macaulay often spoke to her American friends of continuing her magisterial historical project through to the events of the colonial dispute and war.[12] To assist her endeavours, her correspondents sent her packages of manuscripts, pamphlets, histories, maps, summaries of colonial debates, and resolutions of which those extant are evidently only a small proportion. For example, Sarah Prince-Gill proudly sent Macaulay a copy of her father's (Thomas Prince) *History of New England* and expressed regret that Macaulay could not visit Massachusetts ('the land I glory in!') before writing its history. There, she told her, 'the love of liberty ... is in-wrought in the frame, transfuses every breath and beats in every babe'.[13] In her absence from America Macaulay could, Gill wrote, draw on her own well-connected sources of political information: 'the assistance of the noblest patriots in Boston (with whom I have the honor of a personal acquaintance) will not be wanting when ever you make the requisition.'[14] Macaulay was clearly impressed with Gill's patriotism and was to use Thomas Prince's *History* as a source in her account of the settling of America in her own *History*'s fifth volume. She

---

[11] Jonathan Mayhew, *A Discourse Concerning Unlimited Submission and Non-Resistance to the Higher Powers with Some Reflections on the Resistance Made to King Charles I* (Boston: D. Fowle, 1750), 41. See, for example, the *Pennsylvania Gazette*, 29 June 1769, and the *Boston Gazette*, 8 May 1769. Reprintings of Macaulay's account of the death of Charles I continued through the 1780s. See, for example, *Boston Gazette and Country Journal*, 28 Feb. 1785, and *American Herald* (4, 11, 18 Oct. 1784).

[12] See my discussions in Chapters 1 and 5. This was still thought to be the case in 1785 when Macaulay visited New England, but, as Macaulay told Mercy Warren in 1787, she had by then given up all thoughts of doing so. See, for example, The *Independent Ledger and American Advertiser*, Boston, 4 Apr. 1785, and CM to MOW, 6 Mar. 1787, WAP.

[13] 'Sophronia' (Sarah Prince-Gill) to CM, 25 Apr. 1769, GLC.

[14] Sarah Prince-Gill to CM, 25 Apr. 1769, GLC.

and Gill subsequently shared a warm, mutually admiring correspondence, which was cut short only by the latter's death.[15]

By 1774, as Anglo-American conflict began to seem unavoidable, Macaulay's network of Atlantic connections—which included colonial and expatriate American men and women, merchants and farmers, publishers and politicians—had become central to republicanism's cross-Atlantic continuity. One of her most intriguing sources of political intelligence was the Boston Committee of Correspondence, an organization linked to the London SSBR and from whom the Association Movement might be seen as later taking its cue. As Richard Brown's careful study has shown, the Committee enabled Massachusetts' oppositional culture through its sharing of information among diverse groups of freeholders.[16] Known to be at the centre of Britain's pro-Americanist groups and assumed to be directly connected to parliamentary business via her brother John Sawbridge, Macaulay was copied in on their proceedings—being treated, in effect, as a transatlantic outpost of New England's provincial political community.[17] After receiving a package from the Committee, she wrote to Sam Adams that 'every service which it is in my power to perform the town of Boston may command, and may depend upon a faithful and ardent execution'.[18]

One service Macaulay certainly performed was the circulation of the letters she received among the Whig and radical groups with whom she was associated.[19] Central to the political culture in which she participated was the semi-public sharing and discussion of such correspondence at her weekly salon and other forums.[20] The letter played a key role

[15] For a short, factual account of Sarah Prince-Gill's correspondence with Macaulay, see Monica Letzring, 'Sarah Prince-Gill and the John Adams–Catharine Macaulay Correspondence', *Proceedings of the Massachusetts Historical Society*, 53 (1977), 107–15.
[16] Richard D. Brown, *Revolutionary Politics in Massachusetts: The Boston Committee of Correspondence and the Towns, 1772–74* (Cambridge, Mass.: Harvard University Press, 1970).   [17] See, for example, CM to MOW, 11 Sept. 1774, WAP.
[18] See CM to the Town of Boston, 9 May 1770, Mathew Ridley Papers, MHS, and CM to Samuel Adams, 15 Apr. 1773, Samuel Adams Papers, Lennox Foundation, New York Public Library.
[19] For example, Macaulay's correspondence with Lord Buchan reveals the two friends copying and sharing information on Atlantic affairs as they jointly 'lament[ed] the state of America' (Lord Buchan to CM, 4 Sept 1768, GLC).
[20] This culture of debate and discussion around the sharing and reading aloud of political letters is implicit in, for example, Macaulay's correspondence with Benjamin Rush, reprinted in the second edition of her *Loose Remarks* (see. n. 5 above) and Macaulay's famous letter to John Collett Ryland, discussed in Chapter 1. See also n. 66 below.

in connecting and consolidating a dispersed Atlantic political community and was crucial to the exchange of radical ideas or information. Through copying, lending, and reading aloud, Anglo-American letters achieved informal circulations outside the 'public' sphere of print and publication.[21] In a political community that relied on correspondence for its unity and development, such exchanges were both commonplace and vital. The letter is sometimes perceived as a genre with which Macaulay was uncomfortable, or, indeed, unfamiliar. But it should be remembered that she was known among the Atlantic republican community not just as the author of the admired *History* but as a repository, circulator, and writer of political letters.[22] Her letters, in their turn, achieved a wider audience than their immediate addressees among the men and women of the colonies' political elite. For example, her correspondence with James Otis was familiar to others in Boston's South Church, while her letters to John Adams and Mercy Otis Warren achieved a broader Massachusetts readership through their circulation among the wide Warren–Adams circle.[23] The declamatory style of Macaulay's American correspondence is not simply a personal quirk, but a sign of her awareness of the semi-public status of her letters. As she advised John Dickinson on the maintenance of an appropriately republican national character, or warned John Adams after Thomas Hutchinson's resignation that, 'if American liberty is destroyed, the destruction will be effected by the vipers she nourishes in her own bosom', she is clearly aware that her comments will be more widely circulated and attended to; she knows she is addressing a political culture

---

[21] For a discussion of the importance of correspondence to British political culture, see, for example, C. A. Bayly, *Imperial Meridian: The British Empire and the World, 1780–1830* (London: Longman, 1989).

[22] I take issue here with Devoney Looser's assertion that 'Macaulay... did not easily take to the form she twice chose for publication'. This point of argument notwithstanding, Looser's account is very useful, as it situates Macaulay in the context of a tradition of women writing history in England, of which her book provides an excellent overview. Devoney Looser, *British Women Writers and the Writing of History, 1670–1820* (Baltimore: Johns Hopkins University Press, 2000), 136–7. See also Claire Gilbride-Fox, 'Catharine Macaulay: An Eighteenth Century Clio', *Winterthur Portfolio*, 4 (1768), 129–42, at 136.

[23] Sarah Prince-Gill, for example, had either read or heard Macaulay's letters to James Otis through her contact with the South Church's political community and Mercy Otis Warren copied and shared Macaulay's letters with Hannah Winthrop, Abigail Adams, and other Massachusetts' republicans.

as well as a personal friend.[24] Macaulay's American correspondence reveals the real significance of letters and their exchange to the culture of transatlantic radicalism from the late 1760s through the years of the American war.

Macaulay's most important correspondent was certainly Mercy Otis Warren. Their friendship, sustained almost entirely by correspondence over a twenty-year period, reveals, as I argued in this book's introduction, the centrality of elite women to Atlantic political culture as well as the importance of a language of sentiment to republicanism in its Anglo-American context. Despite their many differences (not least those, as I have suggested, of their familial and regional backgrounds and their religious affiliations), Warren and Macaulay shared a characteristic assurance in their knowledge of political theory, classical–republican precedent, and its application to contemporary Atlantic situations. So both women were able to write with real pleasure and utter conviction to each other of, for instance, the superiority of small over large republics, the importance of limiting executive power in government, and the deleterious effects of fashionable culture on political virtue. As Macaulay wrote to Warren in the character of an imperial counsellor ('the mortifications you have sustained on the article of commerce... will prove [more] advantageous in the event of things than otherwise'), so Warren wrote to Macaulay as a sort of sublime colonial visionary.[25] In 1774, for example, she told Macaulay of her fears for 'the lowering cloud which now darkens the American hemisphere'. American resistance to and conflict with Britain was, she wrote, beginning to seem inevitable:

> the seeds of empire are sown in this new world, the ball rolls westward fast... if the British ministry would continue their absurd and unjust measures till the sceptre trembles in the hand of royalty and the mistress of the isles sits solitary and alone; yet the oppressed colonies will rise to glory and grandeur, and perhaps behold the tottering empire from whence they sprang become the contempt of its enemies and the derision of nations.[26]

---

[24] CM to John Dickinson, n.d., 1771, GLC. CM to JA, Aug. 1773, in Robert J. Taylor (ed.), *Papers of John Adams*, 8 vols. (Cambridge, Mass.: Harvard University Press, 1977), i. 353.
[25] CM to MOW, 6 Mar. 1787, WAP. I discuss Warren's visionary republicanism, and her use of the language of sublimity, in Chapter 4.
[26] MOW to CM, 4 Dec. 1774, WAP.

Such shared portents of imperial separation, America's rise and Britain's fall became crucial to Macaulay's writings on American affairs, and particularly her important *Address to the People* of 1775.

II Addressing the People, 1774–1775

With her network of colonial correspondents and her London radical friends and contacts, Catharine Macaulay was ideally placed to interpret and capitalize upon the renewed debate on American affairs at the heart of British political life in 1774. The passing of the Quebec Act (which violated the sea-to-sea grants of colonial charters) and the Intolerable Acts (which ate away at Massachusetts' remaining political autonomy) was the source of much consternation and alarm among the Atlantic political community. Macaulay, who had been ill and out of action through the winter of 1773, had recovered sufficiently the following year to take an interest in the forthcoming election and the grim state of American affairs. By then in Bath, she received packages from America via the Dillys. From Massachusetts Abigail Adams wrote: 'Should I attempt to discribe to you the complicated miseries and distresses brought upon us by the late inhumane acts of the British Parliament my pen would fail me.'[27] Mercy Otis Warren provided her with more detail of the particular injustices of the new Mandamus council and 'the mad project of shutting up the port of Boston'. 'Though we are daily threatened with the depredations of Britain,' Warren wrote, 'yet each city from Nova Scotia to Georgia has her *Decci* and her *Sabi* ready to sacrifice their devoted lives to preserve inviolate and to convey to their children the inherent rights of men.'[28] As well as being inundated with anti-ministerial augury from Warren and her other correspondents, that winter Macaulay met and discussed American affairs with visiting friends from London and the colonies. In his journal, Josiah Quincy reports two meetings with Macaulay during the Christmas period, the second at her request to talk of political matters.[29]

There was a distinct air of urgency among British radical groups toward the end of 1774, arising from the feeling that the Intolerable Acts represented America's last straw, as well as the sense that, following such encroachments on and repressions of civil liberty in the colonies,

[27] AA to CM, 1774, in *AFC*, i. 177.   [28] MOW to CM, 4 Dec. 1774, WAP.
[29] Josiah Quincy, Journal, 31 Dec. 1774; 2 Jan. 1775; MS, MHS.

domestic political reform was now more necessary than ever. This urgency enhanced British radicals' commitment to unity with the Atlantic cause, but also highlighted the differences between London's disaffected patriots, and the determined, even optimistic colonists. Even as they articulated American claims in terms of their own political grievances, they seemed gloomy about any realistic prospect of a change at home. 'The people of this country are so dead to any generous principle in policy that they regard the quarrel of the government with the Americans only as it may affect their own interest,' Macaulay told John Adams in the autumn of 1774: 'I believe no evil short of the entire destruction of their property will produce an effectual opposition to the career of power.'[30] A surprised Quincy wrote in his London journal that winter that 'I have been every day more and more astonished to find what a strong hatred there is prevailing among the multitude of the kingdom against the ministry' and 'I find every day more reason to think that multitudes of fervent friends to America reside in this island'.[31] As the new year opened, Macaulay was receiving information about Massachusetts' appointment of its own governor ('as this is not confirmed to me by a second intelligence I doubt its authenticity') and reports of the first continental congress, whose resolutions and petitions were partly drafted by her (and Quincy's) friend and correspondent John Dickinson. In January she told her friends the Northcotes with some excitement that 'I have seen the manuscript of the petition of the... congress to the king'. 'It is a first-rate composition', she wrote, and 'full of noble sentiments':

In the declining, fallen state of England to hear our own children as the Americans are called breathing sentiments which would have done honour to our country in its most virtuous, its more vigorous days, must fill with great satisfactions every Englishman's breast untainted with the vices of the age.[32]

There is real anticipation here of America's republican promise, Britain's impending decline and fall, and the necessity of political action and opposition. Influenced by the grievances and resolve of her colonial correspondents and the reinvigorated anti-ministerial sentiment of the London opposition, Macaulay's energized pro-Americanism resulted

[30] CM to JA, 11 Sept. 1774, in Taylor (ed.), *The Papers of John Adams*, ii. 164.
[31] Josiah Quincy, Journal, 20, 24 Nov. 1774, MS, MHS.
[32] CM to Mr and Mrs Northcote, 20 Jan. 1775, GLC.

early in 1775 in the pamphlet that Paul Hunter Smith has called 'one of the most vigorous and inflammatory attacks on the government of George III penned during the 1770s'.[33]

Macaulay's *Address to the People* was certainly the most radical text that she had yet produced. The tone is characteristically that of a city Whig, but her arguments and intentions were both novel and provocative. She drew on some familiar classical republican dictums to which the intolerable acts had given a new, minatory spin. 'The conquests of foreign nations', she writes,

are dangerous triumphs, even to the liberty of republican states: but in limited monarchies, when on the conquered are imposed laws opposite and hostile to the limitations of power in these governments, it never fails of subjecting the conquerors to the same measure of slavery which they have imposed on the conquered.[34]

Such arguments not only brought to mind the proverbial example of Rome via Trenchard and Gordon, but also implied the lurking spectre of Catholicism, which Macaulay and her Americanist friends interpreted the Quebec Act as establishing and encouraging.[35] Her general argument here has two distinct purposes which co-exist (contradictorily, perhaps) in the *Address*. First, Britain's and America's mutual enslavement itself implies the unity of colonial and domestic political causes: empire binds country and colonies together to be equally affected, aggrieved, and indeed oppressed by the encroachments on civil liberty the intolerable and Quebec acts have now passed into law. But the bonds of mutual slavery also suggest an anti-imperial or anti-colonial argument *per se*, evoking that familiar republican idea of empire as progressive social disease or infection and perhaps hinting at the political reparation that conflict or separation might produce. The second strand of argument broods beneath the first in the *Address* in ways to which I shall shortly return.

The Intolerable and Quebec Acts should actually be welcomed, Macaulay remarked dryly, since they had finally forced America's hand

---

[33] Paul Hunter Smith, *English Defenders of American Freedoms 1774–8: Six Pamphlets Attacking British Policy* (Washington: Library of Congress Publications, 1972), 108.
[34] CM, *An Address to the People of England, Scotland and Ireland on the Present Important Crisis of Affairs* (London: E. & C. Dilly, 1775), 17.
[35] John Trenchard and Thomas Gordon, *Cato's Letters, or, Essays on Liberty Civil and Religious and Other Important Subjects*, 4 vols., 5th edn. (London: T. Woodward, 1748).

in opposition to a corrupt government:

> The ministry, by depriving them [the Americans] of every part of their rights which remained unviolated, have raised a spirit beyond the Atlantic which may either recover the opportunities we have lost of restoring the breaches which for near a century have been making in our constitution, or of sinking us in the lowest abyss of national misery.[36]

The present crisis should be regarded, Macaulay wrote, as an opportunity in Britain for active opposition to government and constitutional redress. Linking herself to the radical arguments of James Burgh (who called in his *Political Disquisitions* for the establishment of 'a grand national association for restoring the constitution') and highlighting the example of the colonists, whom the continental congress had shown to be 'convinced that their safety depends on their harmony' and 'united in one strong bond of union', Macaulay called on men whom class or religious difference excluded from the political process, 'unjustly debarred the privilege of election', to wake from the 'state of guilty dissipation in which you have too long remained' and to 'rouse and unite in one general effort!'[37] Going far beyond the commonplace opposition claims for rotation, tests, and shorter parliaments, Macaulay's *Address* used the colonial situation as the occasion to propose radical associationism, constitutional overhaul, and political reform.

Identifying herself as a citizen addressing fellow citizens, Macaulay argued that obvious 'ties of common interest' bound the taxed and unrepresented men of Britain and America together. 'They beg you', Macaulay wrote on the colonists' behalf, 'not to suffer your enemies to effect your slavery in their ruin.' Successful opposition meant the passions and interests of all must be drawn to the cause:

> Though men of true virtue, my fellow citizens (that is, men who have a just regard for the rights of nature, for the general happiness of the human species, and for the happiness of their countrymen in particular) will not willingly associate with those of loose principles, yet they will undoubtedly endeavour to stop the career of that government whose impolitic measures are every day adding numbers to the wretched mass of the ignorant, the needy and the profligate. To oppose government with success, such honest individuals must

---

[36] CM, *An Address to the People*, 8.
[37] Ibid. 5, 28–9. James Burgh, *Political Disquisitions, or, an Enquiry into Public Errors, Defects and Abuses*, 3 vols. (London: E. & C. Dilly, 1774–5), iii. 428.

make use of the assistance of the multitude, and consequently of good and bad citizens, of the rich and the poor, the learned and the unlearned, the wise and the foolish, that is, of every man who will co-operate with them in their designs whether he be led to such co-operation by the principle of justice, by interest, or by passion.[38]

Macaulay offered two bald choices to her readers: political enslavement and 'guilty dissipation', or, via the harnessing of the potentially unruly energies of all classes and citizens in the service of concerted anti-governmental opposition, what many of her contemporaries would have clearly interpreted as political revolution.

The purpose of Macaulay's *Address* is evidently to encourage the perception and reality of an anti-governmental Atlantic unity and to promote the redress of the colonial and constitutional grievances she had spent her political career thus far opposing. Such intentions were neither unusual nor, in the context of her republican milieu, particularly controversial. But there is a radical anti-British, anti-imperial undercurrent to the pamphlet which, for a writer of her nationality in 1775, was certainly uncommon.[39] Macaulay's minatory and prophetic voice in the *Address* appears to derive pleasure from the crisis: from the sense that both America and Britain had at last woken up and that the lingering colonial and constitutional troubles of the past decade were finally, dramatically, coming to a head. Like Mercy Otis Warren, she warned that 'a dark cloud hangs over the empire': 'if a civil war commences, either the mother country, by one great exertion, may ruin both herself and America, or the Americans, by a lingering contest will gain an independency'.[40] British writers rarely spoke of American independence before the war had even commenced. In the ensuing hostilities, Britain would, Macaulay predicted, 'become an easy prey to the courts of France and Spain', and, if sovereignty itself was not subsequently eroded, the very least that would happen was the total dereliction of Atlantic trade and commercial advantage, heralding an inevitable 'national bankruptcy'.[41] 'Whilst a new Empire of freemen is established on the other

---

[38] CM, *An Address to the People*, 14.
[39] In an excellent article, Carla Hay argues for the radicalism of Macaulay's address and suggests that it was one of the first British pamphlets to predict American independence. See Carla Hay, 'Catharine Macaulay and the American Revolution', *The Historian*, 56 (1994), 301–16, at 305.   [40] CM, *An Address to the People*, 26.
[41] Ibid. 26–7.

side of the Atlantic,' she wrote, 'you will be left to the bare possession of your foggy islands'.[42] These black imperial forecasts combine the discourse of decline and fall with that of empire's modern westward course.

Macaulay's presage of American independence and imperial downfall highlight, I think, that necessary contradiction in her *Address*. On the one hand, she strengthens the colonial cause by promoting Britons' connection to, and unanimity with, what she termed 'your American brethren'.[43] On the other, there is a boding energy and a certainty to her anti-British portents, suggestive of the desire or wish to bring on the inevitable (the image of the new Atlantic empire of freemen quite obviously appeals to her). Though the *Address*'s purpose is to prevent Anglo-American war through a reinvigorated Atlantic unity, there is, I think, an underlying acceptance of the necessity of concerted political (if not military) conflict, and indeed a prophetic optimism about America's future which recalls that of her friends and correspondents. Macaulay, like other British radicals in the mid-1770s, felt that the American crisis represented the last chance of the political reform and constitutional overhaul for which they had long been striving. As she wrote to Mercy Otis Warren, she did not 'doubt their [the Americans'] resolution. I flatter myself that they will be the saviours and liberators of the whole British Empire.'[44] To the Northcotes she wrote that she had composed the *Address* 'to shew my unabated zeal for the welfare of the poor and the liberties of the British empire more than from any prospect of success in this profligate state of public conduct'.[45] Macaulay clearly felt that the ministry's conduct had passed the point of no return and that conflict was, troublingly, therefore inevitable. 'Pray for those', Macaulay wrote archly to her Quaker friend Mrs Knowles at the turn of 1775, 'whose consciences permit them to defend the rights of nature'.[46] The *Address* was very well received by Americans and their sympathizers, though, as later parts of this chapter discuss, its particular radical turn played a significant part in the blanket condemnations of its author by an increasingly moderate or loyalist British population. As she circulated the pamphlet among her friends, so her publishers, the Dillys, included it in the packages they were sending to New England in the early months

[42] CM, *An Address to the People*, 27.   [43] Ibid. 11.
[44] CM to MOW, 11 Sept. 1774, WAP.
[45] CM to Mr and Mrs Northcote, 20 Jan. 1775, GLC.
[46] CM to Mrs Knowles, n.d., 1774, GLC.

of 1775.[47] It was subsequently reprinted in New York, and reproduced in Boston newspapers. 'We thank you, dear madam,' Ezra Stiles wrote from a tense Rhode Island that April, 'for interposing your kind offices, in your truly patriotic, pathetic and important *Address*'.[48]

The radical Atlantic turn of Macaulay's 1775 *Address* was clearly influenced by the political energy she drew from her new American contacts, friends, and correspondents. But her pro-Americanism was also bound up with the pessimism she felt as a republican about Britain's political future. Her historical writing of this period is distinguished by its wounded consternation at what she saw as a characteristically British failure to act in defence of political freedom, an 'unpardonable supineness on points in which the welfare of the constitution and the freedom and the opulence of their posterity were deeply interested'.[49] As she suggested to the Northcotes, the fact that Britain was irretrievably 'fallen' and 'profligate' meant there was now perhaps little hope of a change.[50] Thus there is in the *Address*, as in the later *History*, the glum, underlying assumption of the perpetuity of political corruption in the British government ('every act of administration . . . evidences a formed design to enslave the whole empire') and political apathy in the British people ('with the same guilty acquiescence, my countrymen, you have seen the last parliament finish their venal course').[51] It was this combination of political indignation and disappointment that characterized Macaulay's response to Atlantic affairs as the American colonies declared their independence and a grim civil war dragged on.

III A Disaffection, 1777–1779

In the autumn months of 1777, as John Burgoyne faced a decisive British defeat at Saratoga, Catharine Macaulay took a trip to France with her friend and future sister-in-law, Mrs Arnold. As Britain confronted the

---

[47] John Adams, for example, received four copies of the *Address* early in 1775 from the Dilly brothers in a packet that also contained a copy of James Burgh's recently completed *Political Disquisitions*. 'This lady, though in a very infirm state of health', Edward Dilly told Adams of Macaulay, 'could not refrain throwing in her mite into the public treasury' (Edward Dilly to JA, 13 Jan. 1775, WAP).
[48] Ezra Stiles to CM, 15 Apr. 1775, GLC.
[49] CM, *The History of England from the Revolution to the Present Time in a Series of Letters to a Friend* (Bath: R. Crutwell, 1778), 375. Hereafter cited as *History in a Series of Letters*.   [50] CM to Mr and Mrs Northcote, 20 Jan. 1775, GLC.
[51] CM, *An Address to the People*, 24, 6.

cultural pessimism fuelled by the war's deep unpopularity, so for Macaulay this was a time of particular anxiety, which she felt on two counts.

First, like Richard Price and her other radical friends, she was increasingly fearful for her own security following the suspension of habeas corpus in Britain. Her pro-American sympathies and contacts were all very well known, and increasingly more outlandish rumours of her treachery and espionage abounded in the British press (including the bizarre but perhaps not entirely unlikely suggestion that her waxwork effigy had been used by her friend, the American spy and sculptor Patience Wright, to transport intelligence of British troops and supplies to Philadelphia).[52] 'Though', as she put it, 'all freedom of intercourse is now cut off', Mercy Otis Warren still managed to smuggle Macaulay intelligence of Hessian atrocities and the treatment of American prisoners of war via 'a Mr S—P...a gentleman in whose honour I can confide'.[53] While William Gordon and James Bowdoin also found safe opportunities in 1777 to write to Macaulay, there is no record of any contact from Macaulay to her American correspondents that year.[54] When she finally replied to a 1777 letter from one of her expatriate American friends, Mrs Sowden, then in Rotterdam in the spring of 1778, she apologized for the belated nature of her response: 'I could not with any safety answer', Macaulay wrote, 'as all correspondence with the Americans is by act of parliament banned against the subjects of Great Britain.'[55] The Paris that Macaulay chose to visit in the closing months of 1777 was full of American expats, agents, and representatives, negotiating the terms of French support and celebrating the turn the war was taking in their favour. Watched by British agents and clearly afraid for her safety, Macaulay had to apologize to her friend Benjamin Franklin for her refusal to receive him at her apartments. She suffered the threat of 'imprisonment on any suspicion of my having held even a correspondence with your countrymen this side of the water'. If such a correspondence were discovered, she wrote, 'I would fall a sacrifice to the resentment of an administration, unpitied and unlamented as an

---

[52] See Thomas E. French, 'America's First Female International Spy', *Daughters of the American Revolution Magazine*, 99 (1965), 910–13, and C. H. Hart, 'Patience Wright, Modeller in Wax', *The Connoisseur*, 19 (1907), 18–22.

[53] MOW to CM, 1 Feb. 1777, MOWP1.

[54] James Bowdoin to CM, 25 Mar. 1777; William Gordon to CM, 25 Mar. 1777, GLC.

[55] CM to Mrs Sowden, 2 Feb. 1778, GLC.

impertinent individual'.[56] Though unwilling to sacrifice herself to the ministry's resentment, Macaulay reassured Franklin that 'the whole tenor of my conduct must have convinced you, Sir, that I should with pleasure sacrifice my life, could it be of any real service to the cause of public freedom'.[57] But she was currently serving the cause of freedom, she informed him, by 'nursing her constitution', in order that she might hope to complete a new historical project.

Macaulay's health was the other source of her anxiety in the autumn of 1777, and discussion of it went far beyond the commonplace exchange of information on physical well-being that is a feature of most eighteenth-century personal letters. Macauley was thought to be seriously ill. Letters from her American correspondents constantly refer to her endangered state; remarks on her recurrent illnesses appeared in British newspapers throughout that year, and her well-known expectation of her imminent death provided ballast to the satires on her femininity and sexuality (as later discussed).[58] In 1777 there were moments when Macaulay quite evidently believed death was at hand. She wrote to her close friend Lord Buchan of 1777 as the year when, with many occasions for alarm, she had managed to escape 'the grim tyrant'.[59] By 1777 Macaulay had not published anything for two years and appears to have written very few letters. She remained confined in Alfred House, attended by various doctors, of whom James Graham became that year the most notorious.[60] It should be remembered that much of the celebratory emphasis of her infamous forty-sixth birthday 'charade' in April 1777 was her apparently miraculous return to health under his care (she was to suffer a serious relapse the following year). Equally, an often omitted detail in discussions of Thomas Wilson's statue of Macaulay as *History* is that it was funerary as well as commemorative, placed in the chancel of St Stephen, Walbrook, in September 1777 in anticipation of

[56] CM to Benjamin Franklin, 8 Dec. 1777, Franklin Papers, American Philosophical Society, Philadelphia.
[57] Ibid. Mary Hays gave prominence to this letter in her account of Macaulay's life in her *Female Biography, or, Memoirs of Illustrious Women, Alphabetically Aranged*, 6 vols. (London: Richard Philips, 1803), v. 302.
[58] See, for example, James Bowdoin to CM, 25 Mar. 1777, GLC.
[59] CM to Lord Buchan, 23 Feb. 1778, Nytts.
[60] Bridget Hill and Devoney Looser discuss Macaulay's ill health in 1777: 'By the time she met James Graham, Macaulay must have been worried by her almost perpetual ill-health' (Hill, *The Republican Virago: The Life and Times of Catharine Macaulay* (Oxford: Clarendon Press, 1992), 94. Looser, *British Women Writers*, 137.

her death (see Fig. 6).⁶¹ Her illness that year had been, as she wrote to Lord Buchan, 'long and dangerous'. She had left Britain with the intention of travelling further south for the climate, but the international situation was such that she returned home prematurely. According to Mrs Arnold, Macaulay spoke often of death on this trip and 'anticipated ... her progress towards the grave'.⁶²

Macaulay's two fears—her concerns about the possibility of persecution for her pro-American sympathies, and her recurrent worries about the fragile state of her health—are key to understanding both the satiric backlash against her at the end of the 1770s and the particular nature of her response to Atlantic political affairs as the war dragged on. The tenor of her republicanism in 1777–9 had become equally fearful, displaying an anger and injury that seems simultaneously national and personal. This sense of deep injury is exemplified in her *History of England from the Revolution to the Present Time in a Series of Letters*, which should be read as an attack on North's administration and a strong statement in opposition to the continuing American war. No one was under any illusions about the purpose of its publication in the early months of 1778. As the *Monthly Review* noted, it was composed 'to shew us what treacherous ground we stand on'.⁶³ Other reviewers objected to Macaulay's designation of the term 'history' to a text that was so clearly narrating national failure in order to reflect on the present administration.⁶⁴ There was nothing new about Macaulay's use of the epistolary form, or the references to her eccentric patron Thomas Wilson as 'my friend': this combination of intimate with public address was common to the letters she had previously written for semi-public circulation (for example, her letter to John Collett Ryland, which had a transatlantic readership prior

---

⁶¹ The statue was often referred to as a tomb or mausoleum. See, for example, *Town and Country Magazine*, 10 Dec. 1778, 263. See also the bizarre third ode of the six published to celebrate Macaulay's forty-sixth birthday. The voice of the narrator recoils in horror from Macaulay's impending death, suggested by the statue and her tomb: 'Say not, these fears are mine in vain; | For ah! Behold in yonder fane [St Stephen Walbrook] | The marble tomb arise | Alas the monumental bust | And tribute to her fame, tho' just | Are horror to mine eyes! (*Six Odes Presented to that Justly Celebrated Historian, Mrs Catharine Macaulay on her Birthday and Publicly Read to a Polite and Brilliant Audience Assembled April 2nd at Alfred House, Bath, to Congratulate that Lady on the Happy Occasion* (London: C. Dilly, 1777), 29).

⁶² Mrs Arnold, reported in Mary Hays, *Female Biography*, v. 300.

⁶³ *Monthly Review*, 58/9 (1778), 112.

⁶⁴ See, for example, *Gentleman's Magazine* (1778), 530; *Critical Review*, 45 (1778), 130–4; *Westminster Magazine*, 6 (1778), 59–63.

to the 1774 election).[65] What was new about the *History . . . in a Series of Letters* was its combination of vitriol, disillusionment, and a utopianism both desperate and sisyphean.

With the copy of the *History* Macaulay sent to Lord Buchan, she observed that 'sentiments of liberty . . . are . . . entirely lost in these United Kingdoms.'[66] Her *History . . . in a Series of Letters* provided an expository account of that loss, of how 'our present state of danger and depravity' had become the terminus of political liberty and radical hope. 'I do not pretend to tell you novelties,' Macaulay informs Wilson/the reader, 'or to have any other end in this narration, but to revive your memory on the facts necessary to connect that train of events which have completed the overthrow of Whig principles'.[67] Macaulay managed to alienate some of her former supporters in her indictment of William III as an agent in that overthrow, whose succession began those 'wars and debts, which, as it has been often foreboded . . . must end in universal calamity'.[68] The history of the British eighteenth century was a grim tale of precipitous bellicosity, hastily agreed treaties, inadequate constitutional settlements, and the progressive exploitation of the nation's population and its property in the service of its aggression. 'It has ever been the bane of this country to rush into unnecessary and expensive wars,' she wrote. The British people were forced repeatedly to experience the 'horrors and distresses of war' and were 'beggared and fleeced' by government in the process.[69] The contemporary resonances of such remarks were, to a population currently experiencing the 'horrors and distresses' of a bloody, expensive, and then unpopular war, unmistakable.

'In . . . these times', Macaulay wrote, when 'pliant manners bend to exterior appearances without any regard to conduct or principles', the British had rendered themselves unable to comprehend public virtue or patriotic resistance, 'the people . . . were, as the people of Great Britain always are, half-stupid, half drunk, and half asleep'.[70] Britain had lost, she argued, all its political understanding along with its liberties. Since the nation was lost and struggle abandoned, what, then, was the point in

[65] I discuss the letter to Ryland in Chapter 1.
[66] CM to Lord Buchan, 23 Feb. 1778, NYHS.
[67] CM, *History in a Series of Letters*, 10
[68] Ibid. 202. This was the case with, for example, Macaulay's former friend Lord Harcourt. [69] CM, *History in a Series of Letters*, 200.
[70] Ibid. 371.

even narrating the story of its fall? Macaulay declared herself fatigued by arranging the 'annual revolution of the same unavailing arguments on the one side, and the same profligate venality on the other'.[71] Britain's national narrative of corrupt repetition inspired in her no political hope, no possibility of redress or reparation, but merely a tired and resigned desire to 'lay down my pen, and endeavour to refresh my wearied spirits with some work of imagination, where government answers its just end, where the princes are all wise and good, and the subjects happy and content'.[72] Macaulay's disconsolate wish for a political escape from the nightmare of British history became notorious in the book's reception: 'O may that genius live', an admiring Capel Lofft wrote in reference to Macaulay and her poor health in his *Observations* on her *History*, 'to see more than imaginary happiness of communities!'[73]

Macaulay's opposition to Britain's involvement in a grim civil war and the bleak outrage of her *History . . . in a Series of Letters* chimed with the national mood in 1778. As France joined America, the Rockingham Whigs turned against the government, and the parliamentary and extra-parliamentary opposition united in their take on the Keppel affair, there was, in John Sainsbury's words, 'an upsurge of national discontent', with its focus North's ministry.[74] I will say more about Britain's damaged sense of itself in 1778–9 in the second part of this chapter, but it is important to note here the particular feel of this discontent among the Whig and radical groups with whom Macaulay was associated. As Macaulay chose, in what was then an accusatory and repressive political climate, to veil her disgust at the war and the administration (albeit thinly) within a historical account of the 1720s, so there was a barely spoken distaste, even horror, at the continued British involvement in the war throughout the culture of opposition in 1778–9. The American war was, for Whigs and radicals across the political spectrum, by then the source of a fear and revulsion which run like a thread through the documents of the petitioning, correspondence, and association movements. With no prospect of reform, the empire seeming to consume

[71] CM, *History in a Series of Letters*, 367. [72] Ibid. 28.
[73] Capel Lofft, *Observations on Mrs Macaulay's History of England Lately Published from the Revolution to the Resignation of Sir Robert Walpole in a Letter to that Lady* (London: E. & C. Dilly, 1778), 13.
[74] John Sainsbury, *Disaffected Patriots: London Supporters of Revolutionary America, 1769–1782* (Kingston and Montreal: McGill-Queen's University Press, 1987), 144.

itself, an appalling loss of life, and tales of the war's horrors and atrocities, what hope was there? For example, if one looks at the correspondence of Yorkshire's Christopher Wyvill in 1779, it is remarkable how many men, of largely moderate Whig principles, use exactly the same language of political desperation, anxiety, or resignation as Macaulay's *History... in a Series of Letters*. 'Our governors [are] highly pleased with this general apathy in the body of the people,' John Lee observed, comparing the national mood to 'the mournful silence of a city... about to burn'.[75] William Anderson wrote in apocalyptic terms of the imminent 'downfall of empires', and William Constable of his deep desire to escape from a Britain now 'habitable only for merchants, nabobs, officers and dependents on the nod of a despot'.[76] 'We must all exert ourselves at this critical time, or God knows the fate of poor old England,' George Cary wrote to Wyvill. 'I *hope* we may live to see happier days.'[77] In the mezzotint commemorating the famous meeting of the Yorkshire Association on 30 December and its claims for peace and political reform, Macaulay's *History* is illustrated as one of the texts forming the principles of the delegates (Fig. 16).

Macaulay's *History... in a Series of Letters* is sometimes spoken of as a project she undertook ill-advisedly, misreading her audience, failing her historical project, and damaging her own reputation. Published between the 'charade' of the forty-sixth birthday and the scandal of the second marriage, it appeared in that period of her life and career that her biographer wished to ignore and to which her critics have nonetheless since paid the most attention.[78] Because it is read as symptomatic of a sort of personal inadvertency, the *History... in a Series of Letters* is also represented as a text over which its author exerted little control. But, as I have suggested, its political objectives are quite clear, and its manuscript evidences a hitherto overlooked personal intention. In introductory

[75] John Lee to Christopher Wyvill, 14 Dec. 1779, in Christopher Wyvill (ed.), *The Political Papers of Christopher Wyvill*, 6 vols. (York: Blanchard, n.d), ii. 167.

[76] William Anderson to Christopher Wyvill, 5 Dec. 1779; William Constable to Christopher Wyvill, 12 Dec. 1779; in *The Political Papers of Christopher Wyvill*, ii. 127, 144.

[77] George Cary to Christopher Wyvill, 30 Nov. 1779, in *The Political Papers of Christopher Wyvill*, ii. 2, 115.

[78] Of the Bath period, Hill writes, 'in an attempt to have Catharine Macaulay, her history, republicanism and radicalism taken seriously, why does she have to frustrate her biographer's designs by behaving in such a manner?' (Hill, *Republican Virago*, 121).

Fig. 16. *The Association Meeting at York* (1780). Engraving. Published by Robert Laurie. Reproduced by courtesy of Library of Congress Prints and Photographs, LC-USZ62-45446.

material which was removed prior to publication, Macaulay thanks Thomas Wilson for 'taking my daughter under your care and protection', perhaps signalling as she tendered that care the *History* as her final publication.[79] And it is with all its anxieties, its inward turn, its ire and despondency, that it remains one of the most important and characteristic anti-governmental texts of 1778. Macaulay's *History... in a Series of Letters* documents British opposition to the American war and to North's administration in an era typified by its profound sense

[79] CM, *History... in a Series of Letters*, MS copy, Nyhs. The manuscript is a fair copy in the hand of two amanuenses with deletions, additions, and corrections in Macaulay's hand. On Wilson's bequest to Macaulay's daughter, see Bridget Hill, 'Daughter and Mother: Some New Light on Catharine Macaulay and her Family', *British Journal for Eighteenth-Century Studies*, 22 (1999), 35–49. On Macaulay's relationship with Wilson, see Hill, *Republican Virago*, and, more recently, Susan Staves, 'Church of England Clergy and Women Writers', in Nicole Pohl and Betty Schellenberg (eds.), *Reconsidering the Bluestockings* (San Marino: Huntington Library, 2003), 94–6.

of political injury, its bleak utopian desires, its disaffection, and its discontents.

By the time Macaulay published her *History... in a Series of Letters* the predictions of American independence, French and Spanish intervention, and national misery she had made in her radical *Address* seemed to have been confirmed. As if to bear out their prescience, a new edition of the *Address* was published in 1779. But its reissue also followed North's Catholic Relief Act, and to many in the light of the events of 1780 the apparently rabble-rousing anti-papist spin of her republicanism seemed aggressive and disturbing. In the aftermath of the Gordon Riots, Macaulay never regained that position of cultural prominence and acceptability she had held in Britain through the 1760s and early 1770s. She was condemned as a figure of deviance, violence, and disorder—her culture's excluded projection of the excesses of the war she had herself so strongly opposed.

This part of the chapter has read Macaulay's *Address* and *History... in a series of Letters* as distinctive responses to the American war from a disaffected British republican at the centre of an important transatlantic political network. Before I move on to Part Two, I want to say a little more about the ways in which this period in Catharine Macaulay's personal and political life has figured in recent accounts. Some critics seem drawn to the years Macaulay spent in Bath through the anecdotal allure of the quack doctors, fashionable clothes, controversial statue, birthday *homage*, and the second marriage for which she was condemned by her contemporaries as freakish, deviant, and absurd. Her friendships and tastes are still discussed as inopportune or disastrous, while the *History... in a Series of Letters* is read, as I have said, as an unfortunate diversion from her more 'serious' historical writing. While accounts of these events as misjudged or inadvertent run the risk of re-enacting the prurience of the publicity Macaulay received at the time, she herself, it seems, must be repeatedly forgiven what are assumed to be her blunders by successive generations of historians and critics.[80] With the exception

---

[80] An early example of this is Lucy Martin Donnelly, 'The Celebrated Mrs Macaulay', *William and Mary Quarterly*, 6 (1949), 173–207. Later repetitions of this tendency include Cecile Mazuco-Than, '"As Easy as a Chimney Pot to Blacken": Catharine Macaulay, "The Celebrated Female Historian"', in Paula Backsheider and Timothy Dykstal (eds.), *The Intersection of the Public and Private Spheres in Early Modern England* (London: Cassell, 1996), 121–42.

of an incisive article by Carla Hay, Marianne Geiger's exploratory work, and some sections of Harriet Guest's important *Small Change*, the crucial cultural and political backdrop of Macaulay's (and, indeed, Britain's) experience of the American war is absent from such accounts.[81] What I am seeking to do here is to address and contextualize that absence. For 1775–80 was not only the period in which Macaulay's fashionable tastes and laudably independent choice of partner were nastily derided as the struggles of a woman of a certain age with her own mortality, but was also the period she became known as the unabashed exponent of a radical and articulate pro-American republicanism. In what follows I interpret these now familiar satiric appropriations and unpleasant representations of Catharine Macaulay in the late 1770s as particular responses to the cultural effects of a disturbing civil war and indeed to what she, as an intellectual woman, a republican, and a pro-American, might seem to signify to Britain at this moment.[82] Macaulay's politics, personality, and sexuality were represented as symptomatic of a cultural alterity and excess which was profoundly bound up with Britain's shifting sense of its national and imperial character in the years of Atlantic conflict.

Part Two

I Brutus

Catharine Macaulay had always had her critics. From the early volumes on, her *History* was condemned by British Tories for the radical gloss it gave to the constitutional history of the sixteenth and seventeenth centuries. There was a shift, however, in the tenor of such criticism after the publication of the fourth volume of her *History*—the volume that was so admired in North America. While colonists like William Livingston and James Otis might commend her account of the reign of

---

[81] See Hay, 'Catharine Macaulay and the American Revolution'; Harriet Guest, *Small Change: Women, Learning, Patriotism, 1750–1810* (Chicago: Chicago University Press, 2000), and Marianne B. Geiger, 'Catharine Sawbridge Macaulay and Mercy Otis Warren: Historians in the Transatlantic Republican Tradition', Ph.D. Diss. (New York University, 1986).

[82] Susan Staves's 1989 article remains one of the best accounts of these satires: ' "The Liberty of a She-Subject of England": Rights-Rhetoric and the Female Thucydides', *Cardazzo Studies in Law and Literature*, 1 (1989), 161–83. On Jodrell's satire, see Guest, *Small Change*.

Charles I as an exposure of that political and religious oppression which their ancestors had left Britain to escape, for many moderate Britons her narrative of the 1630s and 1640s appeared both unpatriotic and unfeeling. Macaulay had failed to represent Charles's death as a national tragedy and was twisting her knife in the back of the royal martyr. What really seemed to trouble British readers was not so much Macaulay's careful and exhaustive cataloguing of the successive constitutional abuses and faults of Charles's administration, nor even her defence of the rectitude of the signatories of his warrant, but her unsparing attack on his private character ('His chastity... were it allowed, was tainted with a degree of uxoriousness which gave it the consequences and properties of vice').[83] Macaulay's attack on Charles's then much-lauded sentimental persona was deemed indicative of a lack of feminine sensibility: 'Among all the hardships and cruelties inflicted upon Charles the First, I think it was by no means the least that ladies should rise up in this generation to... strip him of all his virtues.'[84] While Hume might be celebrated as the historian who 'shed a generous tear for the fate of Charles the First', Macaulay was castigated for her apparent inability to sentimentalize.[85] Such objections to Macaulay's demystification of Charles the Martyr came not just from moderate or conservative periodicals like the *Gentleman's Magazine* (which in 1774 published a series of short articles entitled 'gross misrepresentations in Mrs Macaulay's *History of England*') but from the very publications which had earlier applauded her politics and her cool 'masculine' narrative style.[86] In reviews of her fourth volume, republicanism is seen to effect the replacement of an admired feminine sensibility with a troubling feminine bellicosity. According to the *Monthly*

[83] CM, *History of England*, 3rd edn., v. 294–5.
[84] 'An Old Bachelor', *London Chronicle*, 25 (1769), 45.
[85] David Hume, 'My Own Life', in *Miscellanies for Sentimentalists* (Philadelphia: Robert Bell, 1778), 45. On Hume's *History of England* and sentimentality, see Mark Salber Phillips, ' "If Mrs Mure be not sorry for poor King Charles": History, the Novel and the Sentimental Reader', *History Workshop Journal*, 43 (1997), 111–31; Geoffrey Carnall, 'Historical Writing in the Later Eighteenth Century', in Craig Cairns (ed.), *The History of Scottish Literature 1660–1800* (Aberdeen: Aberdeen University Press, 1987); Laird Okie, 'Ideology and Partiality in David Hume's *History of England*', *Hume Studies*, 11 (1985), 1–32; J. C. Hilson, 'Hume: The Historian as Man of Feeling', in J. C. Hilson, M. Jones, and J. Watson (eds.), *Augustan Worlds: Essays in Honour of A. R. Humphreys* (Leicester: Leicester University Press, 1978), 205–22, Karen O'Brien, *Narratives of Enlightenment: Cosmopolitan History from Voltaire to Gibbon* (Cambridge: Cambridge University Press, 1997), 56–92.   [86] *Gentleman's Magazine* (1774), 303, 125, 557.

Review, her account suggested an irrational endorsement of regicide, 'an exuberance of zeal', and bloodthirsty 'enthusiasm'. 'She kindles as she proceeds,' the *Monthly Review* wrote, 'she has lost sight of that earlier candour we had with so much pleasure commended'.[87] For the *Monthly Review* it was just a short step from a commendable masculine candour to a regicidal aggression thought at odds with the writer's gender.

As critical reflections on the Commonwealth politics of Macaulay's *History* turned into indictments of her feminine character, she was made, in the 1770s, the matter of easy satiric appropriation. In the *Public Advertiser*'s 'humorous vision of an exhibition' of 1771, for example, Macaulay is linked to a female patriotism whose end result was violent assassination. Among the paintings listed were 'the Prodigal Son Returned, in Alto Relivo, by Mr Wilkes' and, by Edmund Burke, 'a Flower Piece from Fancy with Figures after the Antique'. Next to Burke, the *Advertiser* imagined a painting by Catharine Macaulay 'Judith, with the Head of Holofernes'.[88] While Burke's contribution suggests that preterite effeminacy with which he was so often later linked, Macaulay is associated with Judith, who decapitated a monarch of his imperial ambition along with his head, and who possessed a mythic, aggressive female agency, understood in terms of its savage excess.

Macaulay was evidently deeply troubled by representations of her as a woman of no sensibility and felt compelled to defend her much-reviled account of Charles I in her *History*'s sixth volume. 'I have been pursued with virulent invectives,' she wrote. 'I have been accused of a want of humanity and sympathy':

In this enquiry, I was so far from feeling myself the bloody-minded republican, as I have been termed by the butchery writers of these days, and so far even from possessing the stoicism of the first Brutus, that I shed many tears while I was writing his [Charles's] catastrophe and I have endeavoured to do justice to that part of his conduct which I thought truly great and worth the imitation of posterity.[89]

In dissociating herself from the republican hero who condemned his own issue to purify and renovate the *polis*, Macaulay concurred with her

---

[87] *Monthly Review*, 40 (1769), 363.
[88] *Public Advertiser*, Saturday 4 May 1771.
[89] CM, *The History of England from the Accession of James I to that of the Brunswick Line* (London: A. Hamilton, 1781), vi. 12.

own later account of Brutus as the primitive antithesis to modern sensibility: 'with a steadiness that appeared to border on insensibility [he] triumphed over the urgent calls of parental affection and... buried the characters of the man and the father.'[90] Yet Macaulay had herself earlier embraced the associations of her politics with Brutus's republican sublimity and masculine public spirit in the famous *Libertas* portrait designed by Thomas Hollis. Macaulay's patriotism was, as I argued in this book's second chapter, also imbricated in the 1760s and 1770s with a particular language of sentiment or of feeling. In the case of the royal martyr, it is important that she *might* (as she argues here) weep over his fate before rejecting that partiality which sympathy might induce. But, for many of her readers, Macaulay's exposure of 'the dark parts' of Charles's character and her apparently detached account of his death represented a rejection of sentiment *per se*. For a Britain still accustomed to regard Charles I as the shared focus of nationalist guilt and atonement, Macaulay's historical re-enactment of regicide might seem to ally her to the savage republican excesses of Brutus and the early Romans, whose virtues, as Macaulay herself put it, 'were often at enmity with their humanity'.[91]

The connection of Macaulay's politics and her gendered character to a masculine bellicosity and Brutus-like republican aggression was reinforced in many of the encomiums she received from her supporters in the 1760s and 1770s. In William Robertson's 'Eleutheria', for example, the classical spirit of liberty descends from Mount Olympus and is then embodied in Boudicca, the British warrior-queen and subsequently, Macaulay: 'Rouse! Rouse! My favourites, and prevent the yoke, | This is the time, and Liberty advises.'[92] Similarly, in Edmund Rack's 'Irregular Ode', Macaulay appears as a Boudicca-figure leading a patriotic onslaught:

> When my Britannia's noblest sons,
> Beneath oppression's iron hand
> All sad and bleeding lay;
> Then, arm'd with truth and reason's shield,
> She dauntless trod the doubtful field...[93]

---

[90] CM, *Letters on Education with Observations on Religious and Metaphysical Subjects* (London: R. & C. Dilly, 1790), 240. [91] Ibid. 240.

[92] [William Robertson], 'Eleutheria: A Poem Inscribed to Mrs Macaulay' (London: James Harrison, 1768), 7. This is Robertson the radical, not the enlightenment historian.

[93] Edmund Rack, 'An Irregular Ode Respectfully Inscribed to Mrs Macaulay', in *Six Odes*, 25.

In other celebratory representations of Macaulay she is displayed with the attributes of Minerva, who was, of course, a figure of war as well as of wisdom (and for Freud the quintessential 'phallic goddess'). This is most notably the case in Thomas Wilson's commemorative statue of 1777, which bears Minerva's insignia (see Fig. 6). The statue, with its classical impassivity and serene austerity, carries none of those associations of privacy or sentiment I have remarked upon as features of Macaulay's other portraits.

After 1775, the publication of her radical *Address*, and the commencement of Atlantic hostilities, Macaulay's pro-American politics were often understood in Britain as specifically anti-monarchical, anti-British, and aggressive. In 1775, for example, she was said to have encouraged and assisted Stephen Sayre's abortive plot to kidnap the King on his way to open parliament.[94] By January 1776 her reputed treachery had turned to anti-British action, as the *Morning Post* reported that she was about to embark for America, 'to take command of a large corps of American amazons'.[95] In representations of Macaulay in the early years of the war, the iconographical connotations of the British or classical-republican female warrior with which she had earlier been positively associated fused with the meanings of the figure of the Amazon or Indian princess, who, as Linda Colley notes, continued to symbolize the American colonies in the era's print culture.[96] So, a few months after the *Morning Post*'s announcement of her departure to lead the Amazonian colonial rebellion, a print appeared in the *Westminster Magazine* entitled *The Parricide, or, A Sketch of Modern Patriotism* (Fig. 17). The image depicted British radicals as the unnatural assassins of their mother country. As the figure of Discord holds aloft the blazing torches of war, familiar members of the parliamentary and extra-parliamentary opposition (Sawbridge, Chatham, Grafton, Fox, and an obvious boss-eyed Wilkes)

---

[94] Sayre was arrested and accused of spearheading a plot to kidnap the King on 26 Oct. 1775. His papers were seized, and among the 'evidence' kept against him was a letter from Catharine Macaulay. See *London Evening Post*, 26–28 Oct. 1775. For an amused account of the Sayre affair, see Horace Walpole to Horace Mann, 28 Oct. 1775, in W. S. Lewis (ed.), *The Correspondence of Horace Walpole*, 48 vols. (New Haven: Yale University Press, 1937–83), xxiv. 138.

[95] *Morning Post*, 19 Jan. 1776. In the early months of 1776, the populist *Morning Post* had changed its anti-ministerial views and had come out in full support of North's government. For a brief account of this see Solomon Lutnick, *The American Revolution and the British Press, 1775–1783* (Columbia, Miss.: University of Missouri Press, 1967), 24.

[96] Linda Colley, *Britons: Forging the Nation, 1707–1837* (London: Pimlico, 1992), 134.

Fig. 17. *The Parricide, or, A Sketch of Modern Patriotism* (1776). Engraving. Published in the *Westminster Magazine* (1776). Reproduced by courtesy of Library of Congress Prints and Photographs, LC-USZC4-5290.

encourage the stabbing of the exposed body of Britannia by their pro-American representative—Catharine Macaulay brandishing a dagger and tomahawk in the costume of an American Indian.

II Savagery and Sentiment, 1775–1776

In the wider context of the British representation of the American war, the figure of Macaulay as a weapon-wielding Indian contains three overlapping sets of meanings (generic, national or racial/cultural, and gendered) that I want briefly to unravel here. First, the figure calls up a certain generic association between *early* classical republicanisms (Sparta and Rome) and the arms-bearing independence thought in many British and French conjectural histories to be particularly characteristic of native societies. 'Mankind in their simplest state', as Adam Ferguson put it, 'are on the eve of erecting republics'.[97] Such connections between savagery

---

[97] Adam Ferguson, *An Essay on the History of Civil Society*, 4th edn. (London: T. Cadell, 1773), 165.

and republicanism were central to the era's stadial accounts of social progression, such as (most familiarly) Jean-Jacques Rousseau's *Discourse on the Origin of Inequality* (1754); Adam Smith's *Theory of Moral Sentiments* (1764); John Millar's *Origin of the Distinction of Ranks* (1771); and William Robertson's *History of America* (1778), to name but a few.[98] Drawing strands of anthropology, social fantasy, and classical history together in narratives of liberal modernity's losses and gains, North American 'Savages', Spartans, and early Romans might seem equally representative of that political liberty, masculine virtue, and independence sacrificed to the modern demands of the family, private property, and the state (the commercial marketplace, national fiscal/military institutions and mechanisms, and the division of labour).[99] In *The Parricide*, the Macaulay figure calls up such associations between savagery and republicanism, setting them in stark opposition to the sentimental/liberal ideal of modern nationhood that the helpless body of Britannia is clearly meant to represent.

Second, as the symbolic shorthand for North America, the Macaulay figure powerfully suggests national or cultural difference. Linda Colley sees such representations as entirely conventional, perhaps almost emptied of meaning, but it is important to bear in mind how much the figure of the Indian might be more specifically suggestive of liberty or anarchy and call up the then familiar colonial claims to 'natural' identities and political virtues assumed to set America in opposition to a cultured and corrupt modern Britain.[100] It was such associations of the figure of the Indian that Mercy Otis Warren drew on when she wrote to Catharine Macaulay of her vision of the coming war as a return to the

[98] On stadial social theory more generally, see: O'Brien, *Narratives of Enlightenment*; V. Hope, *Philosophers of the Scottish Enlightenment* (Edinburgh: Edinburgh University Press, 1984); David Spadafora, *The Idea of Progress in Eighteenth Century Britain* (New Haven: Yale University Press, 1990); J. G. A Pocock, *Barbarism and Religion, ii. Narratives of Civil Government* (Cambridge: Cambridge University Press, 1999).

[99] Such cultural comparisons are famously central to Frederick Engels's account: 'the whole organisation of the classical republics finds its faithful parallel in American Indians' (Engels, *Origins of the Family, Private Property and the State* (London: Camelot Press, 1942), 91).

[100] Colley, *Britons*, 134. But see her recent *Captives: Britain, Empire and the World, 1600–1850* (London: Jonathan Cape, 2002) for a reappraisal. On the figure of the Indian as the icon for America, see also E. McClung Fleming, 'The American Image as Indian Princess, 1765–1783', *Winturther Portfolio*, 2 (1965), 65–81, and 'From Indian Princess to Greek Goddess: The American Image, 1783–1815', *Winturther Portfolio*, 3 (1966), 37–66.

land and natural virtue ('I think I see the inhabitants of our plundered cities quitting all the elegancies of life and, possessing nothing but their freedom, taking refuge in the forest') or that James Adair deployed in his *History of the American Indians* ('The Indians have an intense affection to their country, and so have the British Americans...soon...they will be able to maintain all the invaluable blessings of freemen for themselves').[101]

Such identifications of colonial interests with symbolic Indians obviously contained their contradictions, not least the continued hostility and profound sense of racial and cultural difference that existed between America's native and colonial populations, not to mention the colonists' social status as lawyers and merchants rather than hunters and fishers. Samuel Johnson's *Taxation No Tyranny* capitalized on this in his derisive account of colonial attempts to 'speak as the naked sons of nature' while desiring full participatory status in Britain's imperial–commercial modernity. While such colonial identity claims were clearly inconsistent, they should also, as Philip Deloria's important study has shown, be read in terms of a particular cultural reality. His *Playing Indian* reveals how the white colonial political elite at the turn of the war used the figure of the Indian in its transformation of the province's popular cultural practices— black-face rituals and Tammany masquerades—into persuasive demonstrations of a distinctively American patriotism.[102]

While for those who supported the colonial cause such imaginary identity-claims may well have suggested the affirmative meanings of natural liberty, patriotic attachment, and virtuous resistance, those who felt aggrieved on Britain's behalf read the figure of the Indian from the opposite direction. Thus in *The Parricide*, the Indian–Macaulay is used to suggest the ingratitude, savagery, and violence inherent in the colonial rejection of the mother country. This rejection of imperial/filial sentiment suggests the Indian–Macaulay figure's third set of meanings: those of gender. In *The Parricide*, transatlantic opposition, national distinction, and cultural enmity are expressed in terms of the stark contrast between

[101] MOW to CM, 11 Sept. 1774, MOWP1. James Adair, *The History of the American Indians* (London: E. & C. Dilly, 1775), 427. Adair's *History* is an intriguing and little-discussed example of the links between American revolutionary republicanism, stadial social theory, and the colonial fascination with native cultures and customs.
[102] Samuel Johnson, *Taxation No Tyranny: An Answer to the Resolutions and Address of the American Congress* (London: T. Cadell, 1775). Philip Deloria, *Playing Indian* (New Haven: Yale University Press, 1998).

two female bodies. While that of Britannia is helpless, benign, and restrained, the dagger-plunging Macaulay is cruel, energetic, and Medean. National difference here *is* gender difference—it is the distance between feminine aggression and passivity, between naturalness and deviance, between violence and violation. Thus in *The Parricide* Britannia, the imperial power, seems to solicit a protective, sentimental gaze while the viewer can only recoil in horror from Indian-Macaulay's violent femininity.

The Parricide's depiction of the Atlantic conflict as the contrast between savage and sentimental femininities had become a cultural commonplace in Britain by the time independence was declared. During its early years, a particular language of violent excess and wounded sentiment came to dominate descriptions of the war in Britain. As one loyalist pamphlet put it, echoing the visual vocabulary of *The Parricide*: 'they [British radicals] bind the hands of the mother country while they plant a dagger in those of the daughter, to stab her to the heart.'[103] Moderate and loyal Britons described their sense of being betrayed and injured by those politically and nationally closest to them through images of female bellicosity and brutality, or, conversely, of feminine suffering and sorrow (Figs. 18 and 19). But why might this gendered opposition between feminine savagery and sentiment provide such a powerful and pervasive means of defining the difference between colonies and mother country?

As the important work of Jay Fliegelman has shown, 'the relationship of the American colonies to England had long been accepted by both the British government and its subjects in America as analogous to that of a child's relationship to its parent'.[104] Such filial or familial analogies did not only describe a political and commercial relationship that was recognized as one of dominance and dependency, but suggested a real division of family members, property, and economic interests across the Atlantic, as well as the new friendships and correspondences that improved travel had enabled. As one pamphleteer put the then

---

[103] James MacPherson, *The Rights of Great Britain Asserted Against the Claims of America* (London: T. Cadell, 1776), 6.

[104] Fliegelman, *Prodigals and Pilgrims: The American Revolution against Patriarchal Authority*, 93. See also Melvyn Yazawa, *From Colonies to Commonwealth: Familial Ideology and the Beginnings of the American Republic* (Baltimore: Johns Hopkins University Press, 1985), and Winthrop D. Jordan, 'Familial Politics: Thomas Paine and the Killing of the King', *Journal of the American Republic*, 60 (1973), 294–307.

Fig. 18. *The European Diligence* (1779). Engraving. Published by W. Humphrey. Reproduced by courtesy of Library of Congress Prints and Photographs, LC-USZ62-45438.

familiar formula: 'we are of the same language, the same religion, the same manners and customs, sprung from the same nation, intermixed by relation and consanguinity.'[105] This political and personal consanguinity meant that the conflict was represented from the outset as internecine, and that defining a clear sense of Anglo-American opposition might be both uncomfortable and tricky. As Edmund Burke wrote:

civil wars strike deepest of all into the manners of a people. They vitiate their politicks; they corrupt their morals; they pervert even the natural taste and relish of equity and justice. By teaching us to consider our fellow citizens in an hostile light, the whole body of our nation becomes gradually less dear to us.[106]

Such anxieties over the estrangement of, in Burke's terms, 'natural' national affection awakened correspondent fears around the threat of

[105] [Unattrib.], 'A True Briton', *Observations on American Independency* (n.p., 1779), 6.
[106] Edmund Burke, *A Letter from Edmund Burke, Esq., One of the Representatives in Parliament for the City of Bristol*, 2nd edn. (London, 1777), 20–1.

Fig. 19. *Britannia's Ruin* (1779). Engraving. Published by Mary Darly. Reproduced by courtesy of Library of Congress Prints and Photographs, LC-USZ62-58615.

the unnatural or de-natured. 'Connected as we are', wrote Abigail Adams to Catharine Macaulay, 'by one common language, by one common religion as protestants and as good and loyal subjects of the same king, it is hard to think that the three fold chord of duty, interest and filial affection may be snapped asunder'.[107] In Britain, concerns at the severing of this umbilical/imperial cord generated representations characterized, like *The Parricide*, by their contrasting gendered extremes: by savage female violence and helpless feminine violation.

In some suggestive work on the American war, Dror Wahrman notes the spate of condemnations of 'Catharine Macaulay's Amazonian fire' and the increasing importance to British culture of 'the contrast... between manly, unnatural women and properly feminine, maternal ones'.[108] It was

[107] AA to CM, n.d., 1774, in *AFC*.
[108] Dror Wahrman, 'The English Problem of Identity in the American Revolution', *American Historical Review*, 106 (2001), 1236–62 at 1252. See also Dror Wahrman, '"Percy's Prologue": From Gender Play to Gender Panic in Eighteenth Century England', *Past and Present*, 159 (1998), 156–9.

the force of this figurative contrast which, I think, often lent much of the strength to the troubled accounts of the meanings of the war in Britain in its early years. A persuasive idea of colonial ingratitude or rebellion might be expressed through the symbolic figures of women like the pro-American Catharine Macaulay acting against the 'natural' dictates of her sex by perpetrating violent intra-familial acts. Equally, the accounts of national similarity or resemblance, which were demanded to define a full sense of imperial injury, were drawn from increasingly conventional notions of gender, in which femininity was defined as necessarily private and usually maternal, neglected, violated, or grieving.

This problematic gendered distinction between savagery and sentiment is crucial to understanding the cultural reaction to the American war in Britain and its correspondent effect on the representation of Catharine Macaulay. In the following section I draw out the importance of this distinction in Britain through a reading of one extended example—a novel that importantly captures how figures of savage or sentimental femininity might become the source and focus of that anxiety with which Britain responded to the American war in its early years.

III A War of the Affections

Samuel Jackson-Pratt's *Emma Corbett* exemplifies the British representation of the war as a familial conflict characterized by its indistinct sense of opposition.[109] His novel grafts onto the familiar narrative frame of the mid-century sentimental novel (virtuous English girl loves against her unyielding parent's wishes, absconds family home, and ultimately dies) a story of the national/familial relationships and allegiances disturbed by the American war. So the reader's conventional sentimental pleasures of intimate conflict and resolution are endowed unresolved international resonance in the breakdown of the imperial family. The war has enforced arbitrary oppositions and false enmities on a once-unified Atlantic community. 'Since we are cruelly taught to make a sanguinary mark of distinction between an Englishman and an American,' the heroine's father

---

[109] Samuel Jackson-Pratt, *Emma Corbett, or, The Faithful Modern Lovers*, 3 vols. (Philadelphia: Robert Bell, 1782). The novel was extremely popular on both sides of the Atlantic in the latter years of the war. It was published in Britain under the title, *Emma Corbett, or, The Miseries of Civil War*. Dror Wahrman's 'English Problem of Identity' includes a brief discussion of the representation of deviance in the novel. I read *Emma Corbett* as more desperate and agonized than deviant.

(Corbett) remarks, 'I own myself the latter'.[110] While Corbett clearly admires the colonists' professed love of liberty, his sense of direct political sympathy throughout the novel seems rather vague. What binds him to the colonies are private rather than public 'ties the most tender and interesting'—namely, the bonds of family and property (a lucrative New England estate, the death of a spouse, and a son for whom he still grieves on American soil).[111] Equally, his proposed son-in-law (Henry Hammond's) identification as English rather than American is similarly dictated by a patriotism that is suggested to arise from a certain form of self-interest (in his case, a youthful desire for military glory). It is such private or circumstantial identifications within the imperial family that drive the lovers apart, and impels the plot inevitably towards the Atlantic theatre of war. A keen red-coated Henry leaves for America. Corbett instructs Emma to renounce her romantic attachment, exclaiming:

The rapacious Henry is gone to plunge another poignard in thy [America's] bosom! The bosom of my country—the tomb of Emma's mother and the vault of every generous affection. Nature herself lies bleeding on thy shore and there the inhuman mother has plunged the dagger with her own barbarous hand into the bowels of her child![112]

While such images were, as I have suggested, the war's metaphoric stock in trade, Corbett's outburst still seems surprising in its grim, symbolic confusion. He (father/America) sees Henry (child/Britain/imperial mother) violating America (colonial child/mother's tomb). While Henry enacts Britannia's perceived barbarism and brutality (a savage Medea slaughtering his/her own offspring), America is both murdered child and violated maternal grave. To figure the colonial conflict as a war of the affections, the novel's conventional language of sentiment morphs here into one of horror, transgression, and unnatural excess.

Associated with familial estrangement, the broken promise of conjugal affection, and later, imperial maternity, the body of Emma Corbett ultimately becomes the experiential site of the destabilizing and injurious effects of the war. Unable to deny her affection for either her parent (an American in England) or her lover (an Englishman in America), the emotionally tortured Emma demands of her father, 'shall I be unnatural in order to be filial?'[113] What follows witnesses Emma's renunciation of

[110] Jackson-Pratt, *Emma Corbett*, ii. 40.   [111] Ibid. i. 39.
[112] Ibid. ii. 39.   [113] Ibid. i. 18.

the filial in the service of what some readers may well have seen as the unnatural—that is, the rejection of her gendered and cultural (perhaps racial) character. From an identity defined wholly by its privacy, domesticity, and the cultivation of a sensibility that her friends and family recognize has dangerously self-referential tendencies, Emma instructs herself in history and surgery and absconds the parental home for America after successfully disguising herself as a man. She is captured as a prisoner of war, and later released by a magnanimous Washington, who declares, 'I am not at war with the *affections*' (the novel was written before Washington's British reputation as a man of feeling suffered following the affair of Major André).[114] In order to move through camps and lines of battle, Emma stains her skin and adopts the costume of an American Indian. She discovers Henry weakened and disillusioned by a bloody civil war, and the pair are briefly reunited and married, only to later die from poison (though the child Emma carries survives her parents).

This swift summary of the novel's third volume conveys only some of the ways in which Jackson-Pratt's sentimentality and symbolism are not just conventionally excessive (one might expect filial tension, mistaken identities, and separated lovers in any such novel of sensibility) but have an almost crazed or agonized quality. Though never condemned as deforming or corrupt, Emma's masculine and Indian disguises are certainly represented as a particular form of desperation that arises directly from the horror of intra-familial conflict. While there is something of the picaresque adventurer about Emma, the masquerade is never wholly comfortable, or indeed wholly sustained (her costumes become peculiarly ill defined). Moving beyond the bounds of sex or race affords her no enhanced agency or sense of liberation. The never-really-more-than-conventional Emma acts—and is disturbed by acting—beyond nature only because she is compelled to do so by the exigencies of the unnatural 'war of the affections' that finally claims her life.

In *Emma Corbett*, an unnatural civil war turns the imperial family against itself and destroys its daughters and sons. Corbett recognizes that his assumed patriotic character obliterated his 'natural' sentimental and paternal identity. Speaking as a sort of repentant eighteenth-century Brutus, he exclaims: 'I treated the most dutiful of children with unwonted harshness and in the patriot I extinguished the parent.'[115]

[114] Jackson-Pratt, *Emma Corbett*, iii. 15.   [115] Ibid. iii. 7.

Unnatural acts (the denial of a father's affection; a daughter's deviation from her gendered and cultural character) are seen to destroy filial attachment and familial unity, resulting only in grief and horror: 'I am childless, look what civil war has done for me.'[116] This tone of discomfited mourning is what really defines the novel and what makes it, I think, a characteristically British response to the American war. Set in 1775–6, the novel highlights the ways in which the American war was initially predominantly a source of confusion, regret, and real grief for many Britons.

A blanket unease and anxiety characterized private responses to the American war in its early years across Britain's political and religious divides. 'I have little hope of any good to the public by such a quarrel,' the Tory and Anglican Elizabeth Carter wrote to her friend Elizabeth Vesey.[117] 'I see no prospect of good,' Horace Walpole repeated time and again in his letters of the war's opening years, 'a whole continent to be re-conquered, what lives, what money to be squandered, what damages, what breaches to be repaired! And reconciliation, how to be effected?'[118] 'My heart draws many a deep sigh for the days that seem near at hand,' wrote Macaulay's Quaker friend Mrs Knowles.[119] 'Must not humanity shudder at such a war?' asked the radical dissenter Richard Price.[120] The nation seemed united in its agonized reaction to an intra-familial conflict. Catharine Macaulay was equally appalled by the British war against its colonies, but had also expressed her opposition in her 1775 *Address* in terms of the necessity of vigorous patriotic resistance to ministerial oppression. The pro-American bellicosity that a troubled, anxious Britain associated with her politics following the publication of the *Address* is visually captured in *The Parricide*. From the perspective of a nation reflecting on the meanings of a war against itself, and where political affiliations were often disguised or subsumed beneath the grief and fear such reflections prompted, Macaulay's confrontational republicanism clearly appeared deviant or unnatural. It is in this

---

[116] Jackson-Pratt, *Emma Corbett*, iii. 41.
[117] Elizabeth Carter to Elizabeth Vesey, 2 Oct. 1777, in Montagu Pennington (ed.), *A Series of Letters between Mrs Elizabeth Carter, Miss Catherine Talbot and Mrs Elizabeth Vesey*, 3 vols. (London: F. C. and J. Rivington, 1819), ii. 320.
[118] Horace Walpole to Horace Mann, 26 Dec. 1775, in *The Correspondence of Horace Walpole*, xxiv. 161.   [119] M. Knowles to CM, 27 Sept. 1774, GLC.
[120] Richard Price, *Additional Observations on the Nature and Value of Civil Liberty and the War with America* (London: T. Cadell, 1777), 71.

context that her representation as a figure of gendered and cultural deviance—a 'savage' deficient of feminine sensibility—should, then, be understood.

By 1778 representations of Macaulay were characterized not just by their deviance, but by their grotesque nature. This year saw her second marriage and the publication of her *History . . . in a Series of Letters* as well as the reinvigoration of the British opposition to North's ministry, a growing national discontent, and, later, fears of the 'other Armada'. At the moment the empire was threatened with destruction, so the nation seemed to be revelling in its own senseless folly. Catharine Macaulay—now known for her sartorial excess and her unconventional relationships as much as her pro-American radicalism—was derided as a figure of fashionable caprice and sexual perversion. In this chapter's closing sections I look at how she might be seen to embody that cultural absurdity and imperial monstrosity which by then seemed to characterize the British cultural experience of the American war.

IV Fashionable Monstrosity, 1777–1778

Stephen Conway has explored how, during the later years of the American war, 'the sense of being a beleaguered nation seems to have captured the [British] public imagination'.[121] This sense of being besieged is generally understood as symptomatic of the ways in which the war was brought much closer to home with the threat of French invasion, but it is intriguing how much Britain felt itself to be internally beleaguered and self-estranged in 1777–8. Britons expressed themselves increasingly horrified at the way the Empire appeared to be brutally devouring itself. The metaphors of imperial family conflict which characterized debate on the war in its opening years now carried for many a shocking resonance in the experience of families not only divided but destroyed in the continuing violence of the Northern campaigns. 'I have no very good public hopes, but one wishes heartily that private families may receive some account of their friends,' Elizabeth Carter wrote to Elizabeth Vesey late in 1777: 'I felt for the Miss Clerkes when I read in the papers, that General Burgoyne was going to storm a place . . . oh that they were all safe in England.' Some weeks later, Carter was expressing sympathy for the 'poor Miss Clerkes', whose brother had

---

[121] Conway, *The British Isles and the War of American Independence*, 355.

died at Saratoga: 'may God comfort all who mourn.'[122] 'Can the people of England, famed for humanity, look calmly on such a scene?' asked a moderate 'English Freeholder': 'If they can, where is their boasted humanity? Alas for my country if such is their insensibility, barbarism and impiety!'[123] 'We are Burgoyned, bamboozled, and beat,' wrote another pamphleteer, convinced of the war's grim fatuity.[124]

This shocked and despondent national mood resulted, in 1777–8, in a spate of pamphlets and poems which couple the desire for imperial conciliation with horror at the war's continued excesses. Thomas Day's bleak pro-peace poem 'The Desolation of America' (1777), for example, imagines in tones of hopeless desperation the deaths of modern Sabine women whose violent intercessions might prevent the war from degenerating into further brutality:

> Dash your tender bodies on the plain,
> Although polluted with the crimson flood,
> Of thousands slain, and wet with kindred blood—
> Meet the stern warrior in his dreadful way.[125]

Some women who travelled with their soldier-spouses and families in Canada and Upper New York had already, to the horror of loyalists and radicals alike, suffered at the hands of Day's 'stern warrior'. This was most notably the case in the shocking death of Jane McCrea, a loyalist mistakenly killed by a Wyandot Indian in the pay of Burgoyne who became the focus of an agonized sentimental reaction on both sides of the Atlantic.[126] Edmund Burke was not the only one who attributed Burgoyne's humiliating defeat at Saratoga to his reliance on the native militia thought by many Britons to embody and epitomize the war's savage excess.[127] In the now apparently irretrievable loss of its American

---

[122] Elizabeth Carter to Elizabeth Vesey, 24 Dec. 1777; 24 Jan. 1778, in Pennington (ed.), *Letters... Mrs Elizabeth Carter*, 322, 327.
[123] [Unattrib], *An English Freeholder's Address to His Countrymen* (London: G. Robinson, 1780), 15.
[124] [Unattrib.], *Opposition Mornings, with Betty's remarks* (London: J. Wilkie, 1779), 46.
[125] Thomas Day, 'The Desolation of America' (London: Kearsley, Richardson, Urquart and Flexney, 1777), 5.
[126] On McCrea, see Colley, *Captives*, 228–30, and June Namias, *White Captives: Gender and Ethnicity on the American Frontier* (Chapel Hill, NC: University of North Carolina Press, 1993).
[127] On the effects of the death of Jane McCrea and opinions on Burgoyne's use of the native Militia, see James A. Holden, 'Influence of the Death of Jane McCrea on the

colonies, the death of its own innocents, and the slaughter and defeat of its armies, Britain appeared to be killing and consuming itself.

As I suggested in my discussion of *The Parricide* and *Emma Corbett*, during the early years of the war, anxieties about the way national integrity was endangered by imperial conflict were figured through images of threats to the integrity of the feminine. By 1778 such threats appeared to have been fully realized and the Empire really appeared to many Britons to be on the brink of collapse. This shift was correspondingly reflected in changes to those sentimental or bellicose feminine figures that had become part of the defining language of the war in Britain. Thus the violated or abandoned national body of 1775 was transformed into images of monstrous maternity, women nursing dead children or consuming their own offspring. In one typical example, 'A True Briton' proposing peace and conciliation wrote in emotive terms that North's ministers 'do not consider' when formulating military policy 'how many innocent, as the infants who perish in the cold bosom of their helpless mothers, and who knew nothing, nor had any hand in the dreadful dispute, are ruined and destroyed'.[128] In Leonard Smelt's *Speech . . . at the meeting of the County of York*, North's administration is described rather more horribly as the hideous offspring of a monstrous national mother: 'Britannia, in better days the parent and the nurse of heroes, now but the putrid carcase of herself, gives birth to a nauseous brood of reptiles that owe their existence to her dissolution, that only in corruption can find their proper nourishment.'[129] Such images of maternal monstrosity did not only appear from the radical or moderate lobby against North's ministry, but also peppered the patriotic sermons of the loyal Anglican clergy. In George Ion's fast sermon, for example, Britain's spirit of internal discord and discontent is discussed in terms

---

Burgoyne Campaign', *New York State Historical Proceedings*, 12 (1913), 249–310. See also Harrison Bird, *March to Saratoga: General Burgoyne and the American Campaign, 1777* (Oxford: Oxford University Press, 1963), 78–83; Fairfax Downey, *Indian Wars of the United States Army* (New York: Doubleday, 1963), 11–19; Don Higginbotham, *The War of American Independence: Military Attitudes, Policies and Practice 1763–1789* (London: Macmillan, 1971), 191. On Burgoyne's defence, see Robert W. Jones 'Manliness and Defeat', unpublished paper, Gender and Enlightenment Colloquium, London, May 2001.

[128] 'A True Briton', *Observations on American Independency* (1779), 22.

[129] Leonard Smelt, *The Speech of Leonard Smelt Delivered by Him at the Meeting of the County of York, December 30th, 1779* (York: A. Ward, 1780), 22.

of Moses' Deuteronomy prophecy of a woman consuming her own issue. Ion also captured the sense of national unease and despair by quoting Matthew 24:19: 'woe unto them that are with child and to them that give suck in those days.'[130]

Most intriguingly, perhaps, the images of monstrous femininity engendered by the horrified reaction to the war were often mingled with condemnations of another specifically feminine or feminising monstrosity—fashion. The loyalist sermons of the late 1770s are characterized by their consternation at the era's fashionable culture. While condemnations of luxury and consumption are, of course, an expected part of the genre, such sermons are distinctive for the nature of their response to the modish spirit of the times. For the loyal Anglican clergy, the *ton* was now the focus not simply of disquiet, but of genuine horror. Anthony Temple compared fashion to a 'gangrene that pervades all ranks and ages'. 'Perhaps never was the nation in so extreme danger,' he pronounced in his *Sermon . . . for the Fast Day*:

> The united fleets of our enemies rode triumphant in our seas. Every post announced the great probability of a powerful invasion . . . Every post at the same time contained crouded advertisements of public diversions and the meetings were full and riotous and dissolute. The sense of the most alarming public danger was lost in the spirit of dissipation.[131]

Others concurred that Britain was experiencing a grotesque disjunction between a necessary national anxiety and a fatuous national dissipation. 'I know not what to say to you about public affairs,' Elizabeth Carter wrote to Elizabeth Vesey; 'we dream of wars and invasions: but it does not break our sleep. In private life people are sufficiently awake to run and fly from one fashionable folly to another till they drop into ruin.'[132] The letters of Carter and her circle in the late 1770s are distinguished by this troubled sense that the nation was sleepwalking unconcerned into its own absurd disaster. Horace Walpole similarly felt that there was something darkly bizarre about the current national temperament. 'One

---

[130] George Ion, *A Sermon Preached at Bubwith on Friday February 4th, 1780* (York: W. Blanchard, 1780), 17.
[131] Anthony Temple, *A Sermon Composed for the Fast Day, Feb 4th 1780* (York: W. Blanchard, 1780), 10.
[132] Elizabeth Carter to Elizabeth Vesey, 21 May 1778, in *Letters of Elizabeth Carter*, ii. 331.

Fig. 20. *Mr Trade and Family, or, the State of ye Nation* (1779). Engraving. Reproduced by courtesy of Library of Congress Prints and Photographs, LC-USZ62-1520.

effect the American war has not had, that it ought to have had,' he wrote to Horace Mann:

it has not brought us to our senses. Silly dissipation rather increases, and without an object. The present folly is late hours. Everybody tries to be particular by being too late; and as everybody tries it, nobody is so. It is the fashion now to go to Ranelagh two hours after it is over. You may not believe this but it is literal.[133]

As well as a time of national beleaguerment and anxiety, then, this was the era of high heads, late hours, and lost fortunes (Fig.20).[134] The satiric print culture of the late 1770s evidences how much this sense of cultural disproportion, fuelled jointly by the reaction to Britain's imperial violence and its fashionable absurdity, was figured in images of

---

[133] Horace Walpole to Horace Mann, 18 June 1777, in *Correspondence of Horace Walpole*, xxiv. 310.
[134] On the notorious spate of bankruptcies of 1778–8, see, for example, JA to JW, 16 Apr. 1777, WAP.

monstrous femininity. For many Britons in 1778, Catharine Macaulay—a woman well known for her fashionable tastes and whose sexual desires were now deemed as inflammatory as her politics—came to exemplify this new notion of the female grotesque. In the *Town and Country Magazine*'s famous caricature, for example, Macaulay's high head and extended behind are decorated with feathers, ribbons, and deflated caps of liberty. Her political and her fashionable and sexual tastes are thus deemed comparable deformities: female desire and republicanism here both signify monstrosity and excess (Fig. 21).[135]

The satiric prints produced by Matthew Darly in the 1770s capitalized on the era's notorious fashionable eccentricities and expressed their excesses as a reaction to the American war. In 1776 he had produced images of ludicrous heads adorned with fully equipped canon and camps (Figs. 22, 23, and 24). In these prints, fashionable excess is turned into the absurd commemoration of the war's military engagements. As a gibbet becomes an ornament worn by 'the rebellious daughters of America', Darly's prints suggested, for their British audience, the deforming inordinance of republican politics. As if continuing the series, the following year Darly produced an image of a high-headed Macaulay, *A Speedy & Effectual Preparation for the Next World*. This print associated her then notorious fashionability to her as notorious fear of death (Fig. 25). Her decorative plumes are those of the hearse that races across her exaggerated head, while the cosmetics and curls she adjusts in the glass cannot hide the bald reflected figure of death, who holds out to her the sands of time. The print appeared after the 'charade' of Macaulay's forty-sixth birthday, engineered by her much-derided 'absurd patron', Thomas Wilson (also depicted in Darly's print). It was for this occasion, and the publication of the reverential *Odes* that commemorated it, that Macaulay was condemned by a shocked Elizabeth Carter as 'an ideot . . . dressed out with the very rags and ribbons of vanity like a queen in a puppet show'. Darly's *Speedy & Effectual Preparation* also followed the publication of a letter from Macaulay to her then doctor and future brother-in law, the infamous quack James Graham, which commended his medical expertise and thanked him for his attempts to save her from the grave.[136]

[135] See *Town and Country Magazine*, 10 (1778), 623.
[136] The letter was included in James Graham, *A Short Inquiry into the Present State of Medical Practice* (London: F. Newberry, 1777).

Fig. 21. *The Auspicious Marriage* (1778). Engraving. Published in the *Town and Country Magazine*, 10 (1778), 623.

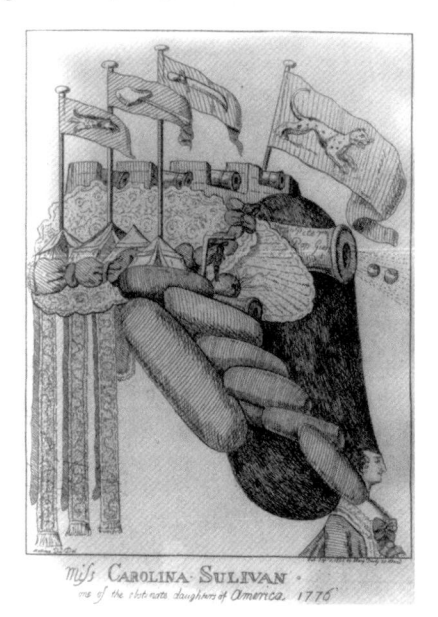

Fig. 22. Matthew Darly, *Miss Carolina Sulivan, one of the Obstinate Daughters of America* (1776). Engraving. Reproduced by courtesy of Library of Congress Prints and Photographs, LC-USZ62–5284.

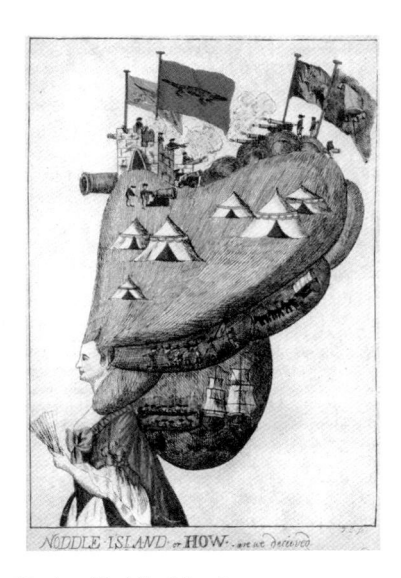

Fig. 23. Mathew Darly, *Noddle Island, or, HOW we are Deceived* (1776). Engraving. Reproduced by courtesy of Library of Congress Prints and Photographs, LC-USZ62-5323.

Fig. 24. Matthew Darly, *Bunker's Hill, or, America's Head-Dress* (1776). Engraving. Reproduced by courtesy of Library of Congress Prints and Photographs, LC-USZ62-54.

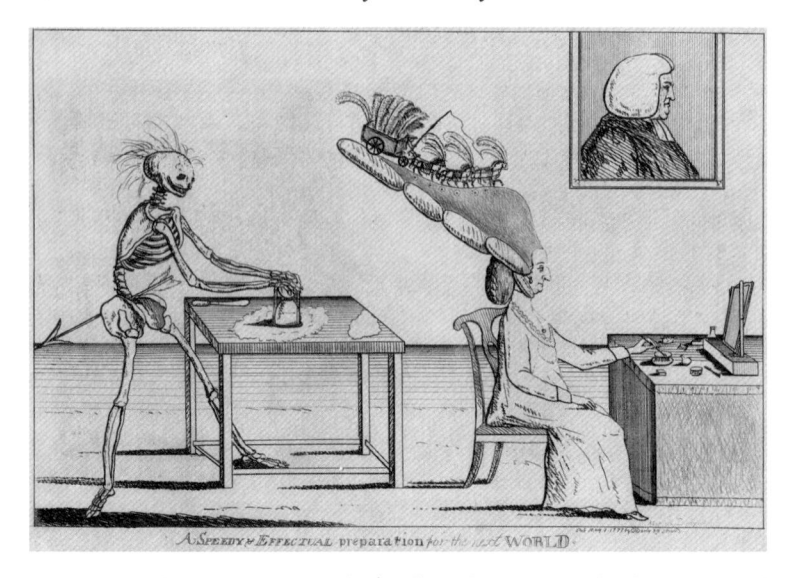

Fig. 25. Matthew Darly, *A Speedy & Effectual Preparation for the Next World* (1778). Engraving. Reproduced by courtesy of Lewis Walpole Library, LWLPR, 04194.

As previously mentioned, much of the emphasis of the widely ridiculed birthday charade was the dangerous illness Macaulay had suffered in 1777. In the third of the six odes that commemorated the celebrations, for example, the muse of history is depicted weeping at Macaulay's failing health ('ward her from the fatal blow | That bids my Catharine die!'), while in the fifth ode the spirit of King Alfred intercedes for Macaulay's recovery as an adjunct to the recovery of Britain's lost liberties ('Health to her body, vigour to her mind | With manly sense, and resolution join'd.').[137] Darly's print connects Macaulay's proximate mortality to the self-referential conceit and preposterous fashionable tastes that were for her many critics epitomized in the birthday charade, 'that puppet scene | Where open vanity moved all the wires'.[138] For the

[137] *Six Odes*, 28, 38.
[138] [Unattrib.], *The Female Historian to the Patriot Divine, or, A Modest Plea for the Rights of Widows. A Didactic Epistle* (London, n.p., 1779), 38.

era's satirists, then, the fashionable and fearful Macaulay might provide an ideal occasion for a coupling of death and affectation that was in 1777 both culturally poignant and absurd. Here she is a figure of folly and admonition, of fashionable caprice and imminent danger. Like the women in Darly's earlier satires on the war whose rifles, bayonets, and cannon were also frivolous, modish ornaments, in *A Speedy Effectual Preparation* Macaulay illustrates that grotesque incongruity between anxiety, horror, and the era's dissipation which had become, as I have suggested, such a feature of reactions to the war.

Walter Benjamin wrote that such conjunctions of fashion with death are generally characteristic of the experience of modernity: 'The modern woman who allies herself with fashion's new-ness in a struggle against natural decay... mimics the mannequin, and enters history as a dead object, a "gaily decked-out corpse".'[139] Such representations of Macaulay as a 'gaily decked-out corpse', though, should be read in terms of the ways in which a specifically feminine monstrosity, extravagance, and horror marked out British responses to the excesses of the continuing American war.

V   *The Belle Sauvage, 1778*

In Britain's popular press, Macaulay was frequently mentioned in the same breath as General John Burgoyne, whose humiliating defeat at Saratoga helped define 1778's beleaguered national mood. In February, for example, the *Morning Post* had announced that the pro-American Macaulay was to make a celebratory visit to Saratoga, with a 'partee quaree' of Thomas Wilson, Patience Wright, and James Graham, to place her minervan statue as a commemorative monument 'on the very spot where General Burgoyne piled his arms'.[140] That August, the *St James Chronicle* reported that Macaulay was, once again, dangerously ill: 'like General Burgoyne she hallooed before she was out of the wood, for all her complaints are returned as bad as ever.'[141] Macaulay's fatuous 'hallooing' at her recovered health is linked here to the histrionic proclamation Burgoyne issued before his defeat at Saratoga, which one

---

[139] Susan Buck-Morrs, *The Dialectics of Seeing: Walter Benjamin and the Arcades Project* (Cambridge, Mass.: Massachusetts Institute of Technology Press, 1989), 101.
[140] *Morning Post*, 20 Feb 1778.   [141] *St James's Chronicle*, 20 Aug. 1778.

satirist captured the sense of as follows:

> I will let loose the dogs of Hell
> Ten thousand Indians, who shall yell
> And foam and tear and grin and roar,
> And drench their moccasins in gore.[142]

There are, of course, obvious differences in representations of Burgoyne and Macaulay, but an important similarity connected them in 1778. Both figures were by then seen as representative of the nation's peculiar excesses in ways that combine notions of savage violence with fashionable eccentricity. Burgoyne was the disgraced 'military macaroni' thought to have sanctioned the savage atrocities from which Britons had recoiled in horror. Macaulay's republicanism, meanwhile, was often, as I have shown, represented in terms of its savage excess, while she herself had come to exemplify the exorbitance of the contemporary *ton*. In a year in which anxieties about impending imperial dissolution were combined with consternation at the nation's folly, Burgoyne and Macaulay seemed figures whose contrarieties were comparably symptomatic of the Zeitgeist. As representatives of fashion and of savagery, their depiction similarly amalgamated the extremes, the opposite ends, as it were, of the scale of civilization.

When William Blake annotated his copy of Joshua Reynolds's *Discourses* with the comment that 'savages are fops and fribbles more than any other men', he was expressing an eighteenth-century commonplace concerning the cultural preoccupation with adornment.[143] Just as American Indians' assumed lack of intellectual depth or comprehension was said to be encapsulated in their fascination for cosmetics and tattoos, feathers and baubles, so imperial modernity revealed its own superficiality in its commodity culture and the whimsical shifts of fashionable taste. 'We are given up to profusion, extravagance and pleasure,' Horace Walpole wrote of the British inattention to the boding Atlantic crisis in 1775; 'our young ladies are covered with more plumes than any nation that has no other covering'.[144] Walpole's description of modern women

---

[142] [Unattrib.], *On the Surrender of General John Burgoyne* (n.p., n.d. [1777?]), broadsides, New York Public Library.

[143] William Blake, 'Blake's Annotations to the Discourses', in Robert R. Wark (ed.), *Sir Joshua Reynolds' Discourses on Art* (New Haven: Yale University Press, 1988), 307.

[144] Horace Walpole to Horace Mann, 20 Mar. 1775, in *Correspondence of Horace Walpole*, xxiv. 85.

as befeathered savages not only suggests their costumes are similarly deforming or excessive, but associates the extravagant profusion of British fashionable culture with that love of pleasure and lack of forethought said to characterize 'savage' societies in the era's conjectural histories. In his *On Savages and the Mode* (1779) James Boswell summed up what had by then become a familiar cultural stereotype. Arguing that fashionable women were 'savage' in their obsession with their own desires and pleasures, their cold lack of sensibility, and, indeed, their gaudy appeal, Boswell wrote: 'Extremes will meet . . . a fine lady . . . is no better than *une belle sauvage*.'[145] Such comparisons between fashion and savagery not only captured that topsy-turvy amoral absurdity Britons thought a national characteristic in the late 1770s, but suggested the 'savagery' of the war in which they were engaged as well as the grotesque corruption of the imperial culture that had precipitated it.

Condemned and ridiculed for her extravagance, vanity, and savagery, Catharine Macaulay became in 1778 Britain's *belle sauvage*. As such, she might be read in terms of *both* of the figures in the print of *The Female Combatants* with which I began this chapter (see Fig. 15). As the historian who displayed the insensibility of a Brutus in her condemnation of Charles I and the radical who had encouraged political dissent and revolution in her *Address to the People*, Macaulay could be seen as the ungrateful Amazonian republican, violently attacking her imperial mother. On the other hand, her reputed insensibility, her vanity, and her derided fashionable caprice might equally be interpreted in terms of the deforming imperial monstrosity that the rouged and ornamental figure of Britannia represents in the print. Because Macaulay's political and gendered character had, throughout the 1770s, been associated with excesses—Judith with the severed head of Holofernes; a Boudicca, violent and triumphant; a dagger-wielding Indian; an imperious puppet-queen receiving bauble-homage from her subjects—she seemed perhaps easily appropriable to those notions of feminine monstrosity

---

[145] James Boswell, *On Savages and the Mode* [1779], in Margaret Bailey (ed.), *Boswell's Column* (London: William Kimber, 1951), 123. Another intriguing use of this stereotype occurs in Tobias Smollet's *Humphry Clinker*, where the ludicrous fashionability of Matt Bramble's ageing sister Tabitha is brought out in her admiration of the wedding costume of an Indian bride (including 'bobbins of human bone' and 'the fresh scalp of a Mohawk warrior'). Tobias Smollett, *The Expedition of Humphry Clinker* [1771] (Oxford: World's Classics, 1984), 195.

which had come to define British responses to the war. Like the fiendish, devouring Britannia of Leonard Smelt's *Speech*, Macaulay seemed a figure of unnatural alterity, a representative of the nation's grotesque estrangement from itself.

VI The Female Grotesque, 1779

At the close of the year that saw French troops in the English Channel and the publication of her controversial attack on the ministry and the war in her *History... in a Series of Letters*, Macaulay married William Graham, the younger brother of James Graham and her friend Mrs Arnold. By her critics her marriage was seen as a final symptom of her exorbitance and inadvertency. In the much-discussed satires that followed the marriage, the contrarieties that Macaulay represented as the figure of the *belle sauvage* were reinforced and extended. Often perceived in terms of the cultural extremes of savagery and civilization, she now also signified a gendered deviance thought both masculine and feminine. In the satires, Macaulay appears as a voracious seducing Eve (the embodiment of a specifically feminine rapacity) and as a military or warlike figure (whose sexual liberty and independent pursuit of desire renders her manly). Elizabeth Montagu's arch remarks capture the ways in which Macaulay's identity following her marriage was associated with a sort of dual-gendered transgression. 'Are you not shocked that Mrs Macaulay has taken Minerva from her coach and put Venus, & cupid rampant in the place of ye chaste and modest goddess?', Montagu asked Hesther Thrale early in 1779:

all this has happened from her adopting masculine opinions and masculine manners. I hate a woman's mind in men's cloaths as much as her person. I always look'd upon Mrs Macaulay as rather belonging to such lads and other boisterous rebels than as one of the gentle sex. Indeed, she was always a *strange fellow*.[146]

In seeing Macaulay in terms of Venus rather than Minerva, Montagu suggests her marriage has revealed a femininity shockingly passionate and sensual, the antithesis of that manly rational restraint that Minerva

---

[146] Elizabeth Montagu to Hesther Thrale, 'Monday 14th' [n.d. but probably Jan. 1779], Montagu correspondence, John Rylands University Library, Manchester, ENGMS551. Emphasis in original.

represented and to which Macaulay was so often compared. But, for Montagu, this Venus-like sensuality is itself symptomatic of Macaulay's masculine excess, her adoption of a public, political character that appropriately belongs to the other sex. Macaulay's republican masculinity and her feminine fashionable and sexual proclivities have here realized themselves in an inordinance that suggests the excess of masquerade or transvestism. Montagu's indictment of her as a *strange fellow* implies the deviance of a woman in man's clothing as much as the transgressive superfluity of a man in drag. This figure of cultural and sexual perversion, with her radical politics, her masculine manners, and a patriotism and publicity whose ultimate outcome is a marriage read here in terms of its sexual impropriety, is everything Montagu assumes the 'gentle sex' is not.

These now familiar images of Catharine Macaulay as a female grotesque should be read in terms of the broader shifts in notions of patriotism and gender prompted by the American war. The disproportionately nasty response to her tastes, her friends, and her husband cannot be divorced from what her politics might, at the close of the 1770s, have represented to such critics as Montagu. Writing to Thrale that she had expected Macaulay to marry 'one of ye congress, or even a distant descendent of one of ye regicides', Montagu reads the marriage as symptomatic of the political deviance of the republican who had attacked the private character of Charles I and vigorously supported the colonial cause.[147] Macaulay's public character, her republican writing, and her reputedly treacherous pro-American activities seemed inimical to Montagu's Tory politics and her sense of patriotic feeling as a British woman. As Mercy Otis Warren wrote in support of her derided friend, Macaulay had merely sought to marry 'with the same impunity as a gentleman of three score and ten might marry a damsel of fifteen'.[148] For loyalists like Montagu, though, such a desire might easily be read in terms as radical as she thought Macaulay's republican politics: as inflammatory and disruptive, as monstrous and violent.

In her engaging study, Mary Russo has argued that the radical alterity of the female grotesque always defines by default the idea of feminine

---

[147] Elizabeth Montagu to Hesther Thrale, 'Saturday Morning' [n.d., but again probably Jan. 1779], Rylands University Library.
[148] MOW to JA, 27 Apr. 1785, WAP.

acceptability and propriety.[149] Kathleen Wilson sees a newly acceptable, normative patriotic femininity emerging from the British experience of the American war:

> women's role in empire and patriotism was being presented as more beneficial if less direct... the moral standing and superiority of Englishness itself came to rest in no small part on English women's capacity for, and exhibition of, domestic virtue... Women's engagement with the processes of war, imperial expansion and national aggrandisement both reflected and shaped these concerns while also influencing their aspirations and identities in novel and unexpected ways.[150]

Such conservative notions of nationhood, which might identify the rectitude of imperial endeavour with the stable feminized space of the home, or notions of the family, domestic virtue, and private sentiment, can be seen as part of a shift in responses to the American war and images of Britishness at the turn of the 1780s. This shift is marked in the quiet, loyalist, 'spirit of unanimity' James McPherson perceived to be harmonizing and motivating the nation to its own protection and defence. It is there in that 'comfort and national pride' which Stephen Conway sees accompanying Rodney's victory at the Saints. It is there in the reinvigorated national security against the 'other Armada'; in the renewed conservative anger against the petitioning and association movements; and in the hysteria surrounding the Gordon Riots (whose violence Hannah More defined as the predictable outcome of all republican ideals of 'mad liberty').[151] It is there in the inward, sentimental turn of liberal women's writing and in Richard Samuel's 1779 celebration of Britain's blue-water nationhood through the figures of its female authors and artists, *The Nine Living Muses of Great Britain* (an image in which Catharine Macaulay appears, as I argued in an earlier chapter, rather incongruously). And it is there, too, at the turn of the

---

[149] Mary Russo, *The Female Grotesque: Risk, Excess and Modernity* (London: Routledge, 1995).

[150] Kathleen Wilson, *The Island Race: Englishness, Empire and Gender in the Eighteenth Century* (London: Routledge, 2003), 19.

[151] Hannah More, *The Slave Trade: A Poem* (London: T. Cadell, 1788), ll. 30–6. Hannah More's opinion of Macaulay was notoriously low. In 1782 she wrote that she 'did not esteem her. I knew her to be absurd, vain and affected' (Hannah More to 'Patty' More, 1782, in *The Letters of Hannah More*, ed. R. Brimley Johnson (London: John Lane, 1925), 80).

1780s in the continued condemnations of Catharine Macaulay's politics as deforming, her patriotism as savage, her sexuality as monstrous, and her femininity as grotesque.

In the introduction to the sixth volume of her *History of England from the Accession of James I* (1781), Macaulay responded to the abuse and invective with which her career had been dogged since the beginning of the American war:

> Criticisms formed with judgment and temper command attention; but when personal invective supplies the place of argument, and the reputation of authors are attacked in order to decry their writings, it is a very strong symptom in favour of those productions against which the battery of abuse is levelled; and in this case an individual, in the full enjoyment of that internal satisfaction which a faithful exertion of mental abilities affords the rational mind, must look down with contempt on the angry crowd, nor suffer their fierce and loud clamours, in any respect to divert him from pursuing the grand object of his honest ambition.[152]

Suggesting her writing and political principle emerged from a space of almost Olympian virtuous abstraction, Macaulay perhaps seemed as confident as ever, defending the rectitude of her desire for historical candour and again speaking of her authorial role in terms reminiscent of another familiar republican sacrifice: 'it would be very unbecoming the character, and contrary to the duty of an historian, to spare even the memory of a parent, if he was found defective in those patriotic virtues which eminently affect the welfare of society.'[153] Though she prided herself on her capability to sacrifice private interest to the historical public good, her British audience was, she wrote, depressingly unable to forgo its prurient interest in the personal and private. While Macaulay might proclaim republican integrity with characteristic self-assurance,

---

[152] CM, *The History of England*, vi, p. xiv. Note Macaulay's use of the masculine pronoun here in reference to herself, which I discuss as a feature of her writing in Chapter 1.

[153] Ibid. vi, p. xiii. Macaulay is clearly speaking of 'parent' in general terms (referring to Britain's national, monarchical, and political ancestry and perhaps particularly Charles I), but may also be pointing to her account of her own grandfather's (Jacob Sawbridge's) involvement in the South Sea Bubble, discussed in her *History in a Series of Letters*. Some reviewers sniped at her insertion of her own family history into national history, and criticized her attempts to vindicate his actions. See, for example, *Gentleman's Magazine* (1778), 530.

she was also clearly deeply hurt by the manner of her defamation over the past five years. She spoke in biting terms of the pain inflicted by 'those anonymous writing calculated to anguish the feeling heart... [which] inflict the poignancy of mental sufferings not only on the defamed persons, but on all those who are attached to them, either by the ties of blood or the yet stronger ties of affection'. Simultaneously representing herself as the nation's last bastion of 'masculine' political virtue and as a woman of wounded sentiment, Macaulay wrote here, as I have suggested she often wrote, in the republican characters of *both* Brutus and Cornelia.

Catharine Macaulay's remarkable *œuvre* is now finally receiving the attention that has long been its due.[154] What I have wanted to do in this chapter and the two that preceded it was to look at that *œuvre* and the woman that produced it in terms of some particular cultural conditions—both enabling and limiting—in Britain during the years which surrounded the American War of Independence. In my first two chapters I examined how Macaulay might write, and be acclaimed as writing, in both 'masculine' and 'feminine' characters, intertwining a familiar Whiggish narrative of patriotism and political virtue with the emergent languages of sentiment and sensibility. This chapter has explored how those intertwined narratives and languages came to be torn apart in Britain at the turn of the 1780s and has examined how that tearing affected the woman who was perhaps their most famous exemplar. The unpleasant denunciations of Macaulay in 1777–9 are not examples, as Cecile Mazuco-Than suggests, of some sort of blanket prejudice eighteenth-century Britain levelled at women of learning.[155] Rather, as I have argued throughout this chapter, the representations of Macaulay as savage, brutal, or grotesque should be read in terms of the very particular threat that she as a woman, a republican intellectual and a pro-American radical represented to a nation at war with itself and which often sought to resolve its troubled sense of its own identity through notions of gender difference.

On the other side of the Atlantic, Americans shared similar perceptions of troubled national and gendered identities, but saw the problem, from the other direction. While for Britons the feminized figure of

[154] See, for example, the excellent recent work of Philip Hicks, 'Catharine Macaulay's Civil War: Gender, History and Republicanism in Georgian Britain', *Journal of British Studies*, 41 (2002), 170–98.

[155] Mazuco-Than, ' "As Easy as a Chimney Pot to Blacken" '.

imperial monstrosity represented the Empire's self-estrangement, in the colonies she might denote all that republicans rejected in their goal of national independence. Equally, as ideas of women's feeling and domesticity began to bolster the self-protective nationalism of a Britain threatened by French invasion, so conservative models of female patriotism might serve a comparably nationalist function in an America imperilled and riven by war. If colonists saw Britain as an unnatural imperial mother violently slaughtering her own loyal offspring, then alternative notions of virtuous femininity might come to symbolize their resistance and reparation. When *Emma Corbett*'s 'war of the affections' was seen to destroy Anglo-American kinship, so the private attachments and sentimental patriotism of American women might suggest the viable possibility of a new national family. In the following chapter, I explore the representation of these ideas of patriotic femininity, privacy, and domesticity in the correspondence of Mercy Otis Warren and her female friends. While such models of gender and patriotic feeling might well have been conservative, so they also, I suggest, provided an opportunity for women to imagine a role for themselves in America's wartime associational political cultures and to see themselves as central to the writing of a new national public history.

4

Mercy Otis Warren's Revolutionary Letters

This chapter examines what Edith Gelles has termed the 'domestic patriotism' of wartime New England.[1] This idiom (perhaps conservative in origin yet nonetheless suggestive of women's understanding of their own political legitimacy) can be traced in the revolutionary correspondence of Mercy Otis Warren and her female friends. It has been usual to treat Warren as an eighteenth-century American exception: a woman with enough extraordinary acumen and ambition to dare to enter the 'public' sphere of print.[2] Yet here I am more interested in the literary form that made her a conventional figure among the women of her politics and position in revolutionary New England: the familiar letter. Like many other women, Warren had a network of friends and relatives with whom she regularly corresponded. Like other women too, the letter was a form in which she excelled. Because she could also turn her hand to genres uncommon among the writing of her female contemporaries, her most prolific and (I would argue) most characteristic prose has been somewhat overlooked.[3] Catharine Macaulay wrote more

---

[1] Edith Gelles, *Portia: The World of Abigail Adams* (Bloomington, Ind.: Indiana University Press, 1992), 37–57.

[2] See, for example, Joy Day Buel and Richard Buel's description of Warren as 'exceptional' in 'her attempt to produce serious literature', as opposed to 'other women of her generation', who only 'wrote and received letters' (Joy Day Buel and Richard Buel, *The Way of Duty: A Woman and her Family in Revolutionary America* (New York: Norton, 1984), p. xii).

[3] In the few critical accounts of Warren's writing, her letters usually serve as a source of biographical or background information for her plays and other writing rather than being seen as an important medium in their own right. The exception is Jeffrey Richards's useful introduction to Warren's writing, in which he dedicates a chapter to the discussion of her letters. Jeffrey Richards, *Mercy Otis Warren* (New York: Twayne, 1995).

than once of her friend's 'animated' political and personal style, and I want to begin with a letter which really captures that animation as well as suggesting the central issues I will go on to explore.[4]

This letter dates from 1774, a period that Warren later described as 'one of the most extraordinary eras in the history of man'.[5] That autumn and winter saw acts of American resistance which culminated in war the following spring. With its legislative assemblies dissolved, its political representatives disenfranchised, and order enforced under the rule of the Intolerable Acts and George III's army, the Bay colony thought of itself as reduced to the twin political extremes of anarchy and tyranny. While the continental congress at Philadelphia deliberated upon those resolutions that so impressed Catharine Macaulay, parishes across Massachusetts demonstrated against the dissolution of their political institutions and the appointment of the Mandamus councillors.[6] Troubled by these patriotic skirmishes, those who remained loyal to the Crown began to pour into Boston, fearing for their safety and seeking protection from the King's troops. One evening early in September, a rumour spread fast that Gage, under the authority of the new Intolerable Acts, had orders to arrest Massachusetts' radical leaders and deport them to England to be tried for treason. Mercy Otis Warren's husband James, who was prominent in the illegal closed-door session of the Salem Assembly at which recommendations for the new continental congress were formulated, was said to be high on the list of Gage's most wanted. Mercy Warren was then far from home at Cambridge, visiting her good friends Hannah Winthrop and her husband John, Harvard's Hollis Professor of Mathematics. As the news of Gage's orders reached the Winthrops' house, Warren felt compelled to leave to seek out her husband and travel home to her sons and farm at Plymouth. On her safe return she wrote to Hannah Winthrop:

Though I lately left my dear friends with precipitation, yet you could not but discover the reluctance with which I parted from them and the struggle in my bosom between inclination and what I then thought my duty; and when I

---

[4] See, for example, CM to MOW, 15 July 1785, WAP.
[5] MOW, *History of the Rise, Progress and Termination of the American Revolution* [1805], ed. Lester Cohen (Indianapolis: Liberty Classics, 1989), 80. All references (with continuous pagination) to this edition.
[6] On Macaulay's view of the resolutions, see, for example, CM to Mr and Mrs Northcote, 20 Jan. 1775, GLC.

arrived at my own house & found all well, my regret was greatly enhanced that I had not indulged myself a little longer in the company of those persons who stand highest both in affection & esteem—nor will you think it an unpardonable weakness if I confess my mind was not at ease till the return of the person whose safety and happiness lies nearest my heart. The evening I left you, my apprehensions were awake and prevented my lids from closing, or the feeble frame to receive any refreshment from the slumbers of the night; I arose in the morning weary and undetermined whether to proceed on my journey homewards or return again to him whom I had reason to fear was one of the devoted victims marked out by the guilty tools of administration to satiate the vengeance of disappointed tyranny; for if they should sacrifice a number of those who have boldly exerted themselves in the noble cause of freedom, they could not hope thereby to extinguish the heavenly spark; their blood, I trust, would be precious seed from whence would spring a glorious race of patriots and heroes; heroes youthful and undaunted, who in full confidence of the justice of their cause will buckle on the harness and not trusting for victory in the strength of their own sword, they will go for the relying on the God of Armies as their leader, whose right hand hath planted this vine and who I doubt not will nourish it till its branches spread from sea to sea and this western world becomes perhaps the only asylum of religion and of freedom and in her turn may boast of science and of Empire; of Empire not established in the thraldom of nations, but on a more equitable base and on such an exalted plan that while for mutual security the authority of rulers is acknowledged, they may not be prompted by ambition and avarice to infringe the natural rights of their fellow men, or debase their own species by requiring abject and unworthy submissions where there is no distinction but what arises from the weakness and imperfection of human nature, which has made it necessary to submit to some subordination. Though such a happy state, such an equal government may be looked upon by some as a utopian dream, yet it is easy for you and I to conceive of nations and states rising to the highest pitch of grandeur and glory on a more liberal and enlarged plan than would be pointed out by the cruel and arbitrary hand of the marble hearted despot. It is not at all strange that persons of equal firmness in the support of Liberty and virtue should yet vary in sentiment with regard to some particular measures and perhaps 'tis much best it should be so that every point may be more accurately discussed and that no step may be taken in this important crisis without due deliberation and the most critical survey of future consequences.[7]

The letter is quoted at length and deserves close attention for its swift shifts in tenor as well as for the ways in which Warren weaves and

[7] MOW to HW, Sept. 1774, WWC. A revised version of this letter is also found in MOWP1.

establishes her patriotic persona. The letter opens where she left the Winthrops: torn between the duties of marriage and friendship. In the assurances of her affection and the sociable pleasures of their company, there reads the reinforcement of a particular sentimental and feminine character, which is developed and extended in what follows. Warren clearly represents herself as a woman of feeling, her language turning inward to express the fearful heart, the struggling bosom, the weary body. The writing seems to emerge directly from a raw sensibility that experiences connubial anxiety and patriotic resentment as physical sensations. As unease at her husband's persecution turns to political conviction, the 'heavenly spark' seems ignited jointly by Warren's sensibility and her broader commitment to the colonial cause. Here the vocabulary moves from a sort of vacillating, bodily sentiment into one of providential certainty, as Warren shifts gear into a New England jeremiad. In her ringing celebration of the new world's Protestant elect and God's vine cultivated and defended by its determined, virtuous inheritors, Warren speaks both as a proud daughter of Old Plymouth Colony (who, like her husband, could trace her ancestry to the *Mayflower*) and as a colonial Congregationalist whose faith frequently took a millennial turn.[8] This visionary republicanism fuses in turn with classical enlightenment narrative, as Warren enlists the familiar notion of the *translatio studii* to support her patriotic prophecy. From her solid Whig background, Warren draws on that narrative of progress which suggested that, because of their unique status as refuges of political and religious liberty, the American colonies had precipitated the westward migration of empire and the Atlantic rise and progress of the arts and sciences.

Warren's robust confidence in the rectitude of America's cause, in its providential calling and its patriotic integrity, seems to dispel the wavering uncertainty of the letter's opening sentences. And yet it is precisely her sentimental and feminine character, her domestic, social, and emotive attachments, which themselves initially generate her concern for and connection to the public cause. The letter establishes a dynamic relationship between privacy and sensibility, on the one hand,

---

[8] James and Mercy Warren shared a great-great-grandfather, Edward Dotey, a founder of Plymouth Colony. On Dotey, see Jean Fritz, *Cast for a Revolution: Some American Friends and Enemies* (Boston: Houghton Mifflin, 1972), 6–7, and Rosemarie Zagarri, *A Woman's Dilemma: Mercy Otis Warren and the American Revolution* (Wheeling, Ill.: Harlan Davidson, 1995), 4–5.

and patriotism, on the other—between the faltering heart that fears for its husband and the prophetic voice that speaks for its country. The mode of address thus seems simultaneously that of intimate friend and of public orator. This mingling of registers is in turn characteristic of the radical political predictions Warren goes on to share with Hannah Winthrop, of society's 'equitable base' and freedom's 'exalted plan'.

In her *History of the Rise, Progress and Termination of the American Revolution* Warren wrote that Britain's dissolution of Massachusetts' political and juridical institutions in the autumn of 1774 meant that 'the bands of society [were] relaxed, law [was] set at defiance and government unhinged throughout the province'.[9] Massachusetts had effectively been reduced, she wrote, to a 'state of nature', in which 'the exertions of spirit awakened by the severe hand of power had led to the... levelling of all ranks'.[10] For Warren, such levelling enhanced a positive, patriotic unanimity rather than produced lawless disorder. 'It is to be ascribed to the virtue of the people', she wrote, 'that they did not feel the effects of anarchy in the extreme'.[11] The letter to Winthrop, in its breathy celebration of such obliterations of social distinction, clearly conveys Warren's conviction of the radical potential of such a return to pre-political origins, and the promise offered by the rebuilding of the political structure with the republican–democratic tools curtailed by imperial rule. This radical argument is presented quite extraordinarily as a sort of familiar aside in which the 'easiness' of Warren's shared utopia suggests the lively debates and discussions she and Hannah Winthrop clearly held about such issues.

The ease Warren associates with her own and Winthrop's patriotic imaginations calls up the particular political and social context her letter operates within. Her shifts in tone and register, her movement between the sharing of intimacies and patriotic principle, are bound up with the epistolary medium itself, which enacts and reinforces a friendship whose grounds are a well-established mutual understanding of each other's political and private characters and which is also able (as Warren stresses in the letter's closing lines) to accommodate debate and difference. Implicit in this letter is Winthrop's and Warren's awareness of the social meanings of their friendship; their assumed identities as women of sensibility,

[9] MOW, *History*, 80. [10] Ibid.
[11] Ibid. See also MOW to Hannah Lincoln, 3 Sept. 1774, MOWP2. A version of this letter is also included in MOWP1.

learning, and piety; and their position (as members of Massachusetts' old republican families) in New England's political elite. Warren's confidence in their shared sentimental and republican characters is implied by default in the contrast with the marble heart and arbitrary hand of imperial Britain. As well as serving its obvious intimate relationary function, then, this letter also constitutes an intervention, a contribution to that debate over political difference which Warren suggests will ultimately enhance American unanimity. Importantly, it is also a statement of political determination and resistance, as its movement between bodily sensibility and patriotic conviction suggests a familiar republican sublimation or absorption of the personal into a particular public cause.

As much as being a form of private address, Warren's letter is also a semi-public performance. This letter would not only have been seen by John Winthrop (who particularly enjoyed Warren's writing) but would likely have been read to and circulated among the Winthrops' family and friends in Cambridge and Boston. Warren's letters were well known for the 'animating' patriotic effect they could have on their audience.[12] Finally, beyond the semi-public sphere of the circulation and recitation of personal–political writing, Warren's letter is part of a larger body of correspondence which displays its author's awareness of a larger public in posterity. Warren and her female friends and correspondents felt, even as they were writing, that their letters constituted a documentary record of political events and American patriotic feeling at an extraordinary historical moment.

This letter, in its combination of the personal and the political, the intimate and the oratorical, speaks to the concerns I want to address here. The important work of Mary-Beth Norton, Edith Gelles, Elaine Forman Crane, Laurie Crumpacker, Carol Karlsen, Patricia Cleary, and Catherine La Courreye Blecki and Karin Wulf has established elite women's friendship networks as central to the provincial culture of the North and Middle colonies.[13] Sarah Richardson, Toby Dietz, and Clare Brandt have written persuasively, meanwhile, of the ways in which

---

[12] See, for example, HW to MOW, 4 Jan. 1773, WWC: 'Your kind favour of Nov 13. was truly animating. That noble patriotic spirit which sparkles through your agreeable letter must warm the heart that has the least sensibilities, especially must it invigorate a mind posses't of a like fellow feeling for this once happy country.'

[13] See, for example, Mary-Beth Norton, *Liberty's Daughters: The Revolutionary Experience of American Women, 1750–1800* (London: Little, Brown & co, 1980); Edith

the boundaries between public, private, and social in eighteenth-century familiar letters are 'drawn in ways oblique to our own'.[14] Here I want to suggest that, in wartime New England, women's friendships and the letters that sustained them should be thought of in terms of such an 'oblique' semi-public sphere.

Mercy Warren was at the centre of a correspondence network that connected republican women across Massachusetts. This network figured importantly in the day-to-day aspects of women's lives through the variety of emotive and material exchanges it fostered and also provided a forum for intellectual debate and the exchange of political opinion. Women's friendships, largely sustained by letter in each other's absence, engendered and maintained systems of information and ideas across Massachusetts and beyond, as they wrote, copied, transmitted, or carefully retained letters which came to play a vital role in New England's revolutionary political culture. While they thought of their

---

Gelles, *Portia*, and *Abigail Adams: A Writing Life* [1998] (London: Routledge, 2002); Elaine Forman Crane, *The Diary of Elizabeth Drinker: The Life Cycle of an Eighteenth-Century Woman* (Boston: Northeastern University Press, 1991); *The Journal of Esther Edwards Burr, 1754–1757*, ed. Laurie Crumpacker and Carol F. Karlsen (New Haven: Yale University Press, 1984); Patricia Cleary, *Elizabeth Murray: A Woman's Pursuit of Independence* (Amherst: University of Massachusetts Press, 2000); Catherine La Courreye Blecki and Karin Wulf (eds.), *Milcah Martha Moore's Book* (University of Pennsylvania Press, 1997); Alfred Young, 'The Women of Boston, "Persons of Consequence" in the Making of the American Revolution, 1765–76', in Harriet Applewhite and Darlene B. Levy (eds.), *Women and Politics in the Age of the Democratic Revolution* (Ann Arbor: University of Michigan Press, 1990), 181–226.

[14] See Sarah Richardson's excellent essay, ' "Well Neighboured Houses": The Political Networks of Elite Women, 1780–1860', in Kathryn Gleadle and Sarah Richardson (eds.), *Women in British Politics, 1760–1860: The Power of the Petticoat* (Basingstoke: Macmillan, 2000), 56–73; Toby Dietz, 'Formative Ventures: Eighteenth-Century Commercial Letters and the Articulation of Experience', in Rebecca Earle (ed.), *Epistolary Selves: Letters and Letter Writers 1600–1945* (Aldershot: Ashgate, 1999), 59–78, at 73; Clare Brandt, 'Varieties of Women's Writing', in Vivien Jones (ed.), *Women and Literature in Britain, 1700–1800* (Cambridge: Cambridge University Press, 2000), 285–306. On letters and letter-writing generally, see Keith Stewart, 'Towards Defining an Aesthetic for the Familiar Letter in Eighteenth-Century England', *Prose Studies* (1982), 179–92; Bruce Redford, *The Converse of the Pen: Acts of Intimacy in the Eighteenth-Century Familiar Letter* (Chicago: University of Chicago Press, 1986); William Merrill Decker, *Epistolary Practices: Letter Writing in America before Telecommunications* (Chapel Hill, NC: University of North Carolina Press, 1998); and, from rather different critical perspectives, Janet Altman, *Epistolarity: Approaches to a Form* (Columbus, Oh.: Ohio State University Press, 1982), and Linda S. Kauffman, *Special Delivery: Epistolary Modes in Modern Fiction* (Chicago: University of Chicago Press, 1992).

letters as patriotic acts, Warren and her friends also understood their political identities to be peculiarly domestic—to be definitively and conventionally feminine. They wrote of a privacy, founded on retirement, sentimental exchange, and familial attachment, as the source of patriotic, republican virtue. And yet, far from simply being missives from one private sphere to another, Warren's letters of this period ultimately formed the basis of the early volumes of her assured, republican *History... of the American Revolution*, whose palimpsest she was to revisit and revise over the next forty years. Mercy Warren was a well-educated, well-placed woman of Massachusetts' provincial elite. Her position and the particular circumstances of the revolutionary war meant that she and her friends experienced their domestic and political interests as peculiarly coexistent. In what follows I explore the implications of this coexistence for Warren and the women of her circle.

I The 'Yellow Parlor'

Jeffrey Richards rightly notes the deep importance Mercy Otis Warren placed on her 'female circle of correspondence'.[15] Her friends and fellow letter-writers during the 1760s and 1770s included Hannah Winthrop, Abigail Adams, Hannah Lincoln, Penny Winslow, Sarah Hesilridge, and Ellen Lothrop. These were women of notable, old Massachusetts' families, many of whom had received solid literary and historical instruction (though excluded from the classical learning and university educations their brothers received).[16] Warren and Winthrop had already

---

[15] Richards, *Mercy Otis Warren*, 14.
[16] On Warren's early life and education, see Katharine Anthony, *First Lady of the Revolution: The Life of Mercy Otis Warren* (New York: Doubleday, 1958) (a now rather dated and inaccurate account); Zagarri, *A Woman's Dilemma* (clearly the best biography of Warren to date); Maud Hutchenson, 'Mercy Otis Warren 1728–1814', *William and Mary Quarterly*, 10 (1953), 378–402; John Waters, *The Otis Family in Provincial and Revolutionary Massachusetts* (Chapel Hill, NC: University of North Carolina Press, 1968); Mary Elizabeth Regan, 'Pundit and Prophet of the Old Republic: The Life and Times of Mercy Otis Warren', Ph.D. Diss. (University of California, Berkeley, 1984); Jean Fritz, *Cast for a Revolution: Some American Friends and Enemies, 1728–1814* (Boston: Houghton Mifflin Co., 1972); Paul Engel, *Women in the American Revolution* (Chicago: Follett, 1976), 45–70. On Abigail Adams's literary interests and education, see Elaine Forman-Crane, 'Political Dialogue and the Spring of Abigail's Discontent', *William and Mary Quarterly*, 56 (1999), 745–74, and Edith Gelles's definitive work in *Portia* and *Abigail Adams*.

achieved a certain notoriety across Massachusetts Bay as women of learning and daughters of liberty, and they and their friends took a great deal of pride in their literary acumen and wide range of intellectual interests (while Warren's knowledge of classical history was widely admired, Hannah Winthrop shared her husband's interests in European philosophy and astronomy).[17] Some were childhood friends (Winthrop, Warren, and Lincoln, for example, all grew up on Cape Cod); others had grown close in later life, and all had made marriages which maintained or enhanced their position in Massachusetts' political and religious elites. Their husbands were lawyers, scholars, farmers, or churchmen: men of property and position who played prominent roles in colonial public life. Warren's husband James, for example, was a member of Plymouth's most prominent and wealthy merchant family. The sizeable fortune he inherited enabled him to become a gentleman farmer and agricultural innovator whose often-repeated desires to return to his plough were much more than the republican commonplaces of his contemporaries.[18] He was also a representative for Plymouth, and the sometime speaker of the Massachusetts Congress. The women were proud of their familial connections and heritage. Hannah Winthrop's husband, as Warren was later to write of him in her *History*, 'was lineally descended from the first governor of the Massachusetts, and inherited the virtues and talents of his great ancestor, too well known to need any encomium'.[19] As elite Whigs, Warren and her female friends felt that their husbands' economic position and ancestry meant they were especially suited to public life. They reserved a particular contempt for Massachusetts' aspirant, mercantile Tory classes, 'many of them without education', Warren wrote with characteristic republican disdain, 'some who are devoid of talents requisite for any department beyond the shop

[17] On Warren and Winthrop as 'Daughters of Liberty', see, for example, HW to MOW, 29 Apr. 1769, WWC. On Warren and Winthrop as Massachusetts' learned women, see HW to MOW, Sept. 1780, in which she reports a passage in the *Advertiser* in which they are represented as such. On Winthrop's interests in astronomy, see, for example, HW to MOW, 14 Jan. 1777. All in WWC.
[18] See, for example, MOW to AA, 6 Aug. 1779, WAP. On Mercy Warren's representation of James Warren as a farmer, see also Marianne B. Geiger, 'Catharine Sawbridge Macaulay and Mercy Otis Warren: Historians in the Transatlantic Republican Tradition', Ph.D. Diss. (New York University, 1986), 134.
[19] MOW, *History*, 73. Warren was not unequivocally admiring of the first Winthrop and, as one might expect, criticized the religious intolerance of Massachusetts' first settlers in the opening sections of her *History* (pp. 10–11).

or the counting house'.[20] Their partners' public roles lent the women of Warren's circle a certain degree of cultural prominence and also carried certain responsibilities (the wives of political representatives like Warren often fielded electors' grievances in their husbands' absence or, like Abigail Adams, managed the family estate and its tenants). It did not mean, however, that they led lives of metropolitan sociability. It was intensely important to these women that they might describe themselves in terms of a rural identity defined by its privacy and its retirement.

During the war, Warren's friends mostly lived a distance from Boston and indeed from each other, spread out among the small settlements and farms of Massachusetts. Warren divided her time between her two Plymouth residences (her village house at the north-west corner of Liberty Square, and the agricultural estate she loved on Eel river); Abigail Adams was occupied with her farm at Braintree for most of the year, while Hannah Winthrop lived across the Charles river in Cambridge. Of all Warren's friends, Winthrop had the closest access to the sources of news and information which Boston provided and was perhaps the most actively engaged with Massachusetts' burgeoning polite culture through her involvement in Harvard's social milieu. 'Her letters, we expect,' Warren wrote of Winthrop, 'will be filled by more brilliant periods, fixed near the seat of science, of politicks and polite intelligence'.[21] And yet, it was as important to Winthrop, as to all her republican female friends, to think of her domestic situation in terms of its opposition to Boston and modern metropolitan culture. 'I have not been to the capital for more than three months,' she wrote to Warren:

I suppose when I make my appearance I shall look not unlike one of the last century, at least like one unacquainted with polite life. The encreasing dissipation, the round of elegant amusements which are become the work of every evening have not those attractive charms for you and myself... What a different circle do we tread? Immured in the country and yet happy perhaps in contemplating the lives of those who walked the stage before us.[22]

In comparison with Warren and Adams, Winthrop's position could hardly be described as rural, but it is important that she might use it here to claim a virtuous immurement from modernity. While she mocks her

---

[20] MOW to HW, Aug. 1774, MOWP1.
[21] MOW to HW, 31 Jan. 1774, MOWP1.
[22] HW to MOW, 12 Apr. 1773, WWC.

lack of refinement, it is her antiquated appearance which itself connects her to the seventeenth-century New Englanders whose cultural memory she and Warren are described here as happily contemplating. There is thus the sense that the feminine pleasures of retirement are bound up with the patriotic experience of republican history written in the landscape.

Warren and her friends felt that their rural retirement gave them a particular attachment to and purchase on the landscape of New England and its meanings. Warren celebrated her distance from Boston, 'the centre of polite amusements', writing: 'I would not exchange my retired manner of life for the elegant refinements of modern dissipation'.[23] She often described her own retirement in obvious civic humanist terms as the leisured occasion for patriotic reflection and what she often called 'the pleasures of rational philosophy'. 'If you should find me sublime,' Winthrop wrote to her, 'remember I catch it from you, for I admire the thoughts your rural retirement affords you'.[24] Warren thought of herself as unambiguously connected by blood, birth, and a profound sense of place to the settlers of the old colony. Plymouth was 'the first residence of our heroic and pious ancestors', where manners still recalled 'the original freedom of our progenitors'.[25] 'Where there is most simplicity of manners,' she wrote, 'there is most felicity... uncontaminated by luxury those virtues which spring up in the soil and are most congenial to the nature of man have a chance for improvement'.[26] Her claims to an ancestral identity, rural simplicity, and attachment to the land allowed her many opportunities in the correspondence for the historical commemoration and reflection that Winthrop found so 'sublime'. In 1778, at a low point in the war for Massachusetts' old republicans, Warren invited Winthrop to visit her in Plymouth:

While the statesman is plodding for power and the courtier practising dissimulation without checks; while the rapacious are growing rich by oppression and fortune throwing her gifts into the lap of fools; I wish my philosophic friend... would spend a few days in the decayed village of Plymouth, and while we contemplate beside the broken cliffs the revolutions of states, the fall of kingdoms and the rise of Empire, we will not forget that this

[23] MOW to HW, 17 Aug., MOWP1.
[24] HW to MOW, 14 Aug. 1772, WWC.
[25] MOW to HW, 31 Jan. 1774, WWC.
[26] MOW to HW, n.d., 1774, MOWP1.

dreary shore was once the asylum of our ancestors when they fled from the oppressions of the house of Stuart.[27]

Plymouth here first signals a domestic retreat from current political disappointment, a consolatory haven marked by the passage of time and historical memory. Warren's private attachment to the landscape and her adoption of the meanings of the broken cliffs of the old colony engenders the apparent obliteration of the present and its unpleasant exigencies as she and Winthrop are pictured contemplating New England's heroic past and utopian future. Warren conjures their political imaginations to exist in a sort of prophetic, temporal continuity, in which the sweep of history connects all acts, all revolutionary instances of colonial resistance against imperial oppression, and is able to predict the happy outcome of the struggle in the inevitable rebirth of empire. For Warren and Winthrop, figures in this landscape bound to it by personal attachment and cultural memory, Plymouth's cliffs first provide the occasion for the experience of political solace before offering the hopeful opportunity of sublime historical foresight.

Philip Gould has argued that: 'The rural elite of Massachusetts deliberately cultivated their identities according to a classical-pastoral ideal of agrarian simplicity that... managed to incorporate a softened heart, refined sensibility and benevolence.'[28] Gould is writing here of those prominent, wealthy men of the early republic for whom an imaginary, unmediated pastoral identity became immensely important, but the argument is perhaps equally pertinent to the women of that class during the 1760s and 1770s. In 1766 Warren wrote 'An Invitation to Retirement' for the absent James Warren, in which she compared their happiness on the Eel river estate to the prelapsarian felicity of 'the first pair on Eden's banks'.[29] Her sense of her position as peculiarly blessed was quite unequivocal.

Warren and her friends felt that their rural retirement accorded them particular kinds of patriotic virtue and cultural authority through their

---

[27] MOW to HW, 29 May 1778, WWC.
[28] Philip Gould, *Covenant and Republic: Historical Romance and the Politics of Puritanism* (Cambridge: Cambridge University Press, 1996), 27. See also Tamara Plakins-Thornton, *Cultivating Gentlemen: The Meaning of Country Life among the Boston Elite, 1785–1860* (New Haven: Yale University Press, 1989).
[29] MOW, *'An Invitation to Retirement'* [1766]. This poem was not published in Warren's lifetime and appears in the MS of her private poems held at HL. It is reproduced in Edmund Hayes, 'The Private Poems of Mercy Otis Warren', *New England Quarterly*, 54 (1981), 206–7.

attachment to the land and its history. If they saw Massachusetts as a land of exceptionalist republican promise where God's vine had been planted for his virtuous elect, then they thought of themselves, as farmers and women of old families, as members of that elect: the protectors of that promise and the domestic cultivators of that vine. This conviction was religious and republican in equal measure.[30] Warren's circle clearly felt they had a very particular connection to God's revolutionary design for New England. 'Shan't we form hope from that divine benignity which has been so conspicuous toward New England from its earliest ages?', Hannah Winthrop asked Warren in the uneasy months before the war.[31] Her friend agreed that one's faith in and purchase on the providential plan as an inheritor of what she often called 'the sacred Plymouthean spirit' strengthened patriotic resolve. As she reassured an anxious Ellen Lothrop in 1775, 'I think we have abundant reason to acknowledge that the hand of the almighty governor of the universe has hitherto appealed on our behalf, and if he is for us, who can be against us?'[32] Warren's confidence in her position meant she might claim the language of a religious sublimity whose acme, in the poems she first circulated in her correspondence among her friends in the 1770s, is the privileged ability to see and speak for God's political plan for New England. In 'A Political Reverie' (1774), for example, the narrator/ Warren's patriotic conviction is rewarded with the sublime vision of New England's 'bright Millenial prospects' as the goddess of Liberty leads her beyond the stars to view America's rising glory:

> A bright form with soft, majestic grace,
> Beckoned me on through vast, unmeasured space;
>   .   .   .   .   .
> Beyond the height's of nature's wide expanse,
> Where moved superb the planetary dance
> Light burst on light, and suns o'er suns display'd
> The system perfect nature's God had laid.[33]

---

[30] On the interweaving of republican and religious discourses in this period, see Ruth Bloch's engaging study *Visionary Republic: Millennial Themes in American Thought, 1756–1800* (Cambridge: Cambridge University Press, 1985).
[31] HW to MOW, 27 Oct. 1774, WWC. [32] MOW to EL, n.d, 1775, MOWP1.
[33] Mercy Otis Warren, 'A Political Reverie' [1774], in Warren, *Poems Dramatic and Miscellaneous* (Boston: I. Thomas and E. T Andrews, 1790). There is perhaps something of Hannah Winthrop's influence in the astronomical language of this poem.

Warren's exclusive identification with this divinely ordained political plan is suggestive of her real political and aesthetic self-assurance.[34]

The claims of Warren and her friends to leisure, to learning, and to the land itself suggest those pre-political features of the civic humanism which was so important to the seventeenth- and eighteenth-century British–Atlantic world. Their awareness of themselves as exemplary Protestants and members of families of historical prominence, their confidence with a language of political and religious sublimity, and their antipathy to the dissipation they saw as perhaps distinctively British and certainly distinctively modern might be read in terms akin to the position of an idealized, republican masculinity familiar, say, to the detractors of Walpole's administrations. But though their contemporaries often used the familiar republican shorthand 'masculine' to describe their intellects in positive terms, these women also valued their leisure, retirement, and domesticity because they felt it defined them as uniquely and unambiguously feminine.[35] Warren and her friends often wrote of their characters as traditionally feminine, private, and sentimental, and it was this virtuous privacy that made, they thought, their patriotism so affirming and so distinctive. They described themselves as engaged in a process of sisterly sentimental exchange which married their discourse of virtuous republican retirement to the language of the heart.

It is this language that really defines the women's correspondence. Warren's circle wrote of themselves as 'sister hearts' drawn together by mutual affection and a sort of uncanny emotive association or resemblance. They congratulated each other for their retention of the 'tender impressions formed in youthful life and nourished by maturer age', and repeatedly assured each other of the sincere mutuality of their affection: 'friendship always allows a reciprocal communication', wrote Warren, 'and demands a sympathetic tear'.[36] 'You have been the object of my waking thoughts and my nightly dreams,' Winthrop wrote of Warren, 'the friend of my heart, who is engraven there as with the point of a

---

[34] Warren's use of the republican and religious 'sublime' suggests to me an aesthetic very similar to that of Anna Laetitia Barbauld—especially in her marvellous 'Summer Evening's Meditation'. Barbauld's poems were later published alongside Warren's writing in the *Boston Magazine*. See my discussion in Chapter 5.

[35] In a letter that is typical of his accounts of her, James Warren described Mercy Warren as having 'a mind possessed of a masculine genius well stocked with learning fortified by philosophy and religion' (JW to MOW, 6 June 1776, MOWP2).

[36] MOW to HW, 31 Jan. 1774, MOWP1.

diamond'.[37] Warren thought of her friendships not just as sympathetic reciprocity or exchange, but in terms of a sentimental proximity that amounted to sublimation or participation. She described herself to Winthrop as 'one who has not only long been united with you in sentiment, but from some sympathetic movement of soul, participated both your anxieties and returning joys'.[38] Similarly, she wrote of herself as bound to Ellen Lothrop by 'the engaging tie of sisterly affection', and defined their friendship as a symbiotic sentimental and patriotic experience: 'I daily regret the long absence of a person to whom I could without reserve impart my fears, my hopes, and my pleasures on such a day as this, when every mind swells with expectation and every heart expands by anticipating the most important events.'[39]

If the women wrote of themselves as sisters, this sense of friendship as familial attachment was consolidated through what one might term the imbrication of their domesticities. Though separated from each other by many miles, they thought of themselves and their families as interwoven in specific ways. As was common in New England, the women hosted or lodged each other's children for extended periods of time. Mercy Warren's sons stayed with Hannah Winthrop while they were studying at Harvard, while Abigail Adams junior came to be thought of as one of the Warrens' family through her visits to Plymouth. Such familial proximity was reinforced by the women's own personal attachments to each other's relatives and husbands. Much of their infrequent socializing before the war and their partners' absences was as couples, and, while they considered masculine and feminine roles as distinct in quite traditional terms, they clearly thought of themselves in terms of their intellectual equality and sentimental attachment not just to their own but to each other's partners. 'I often contemplate your and my happy lot in the kind disposition of providence in our dear consorts,' Winthrop wrote to Warren, 'not keeping that awful distance some persons imagine heaven destined between the social tye'.[40] Winthrop and Adams were both very fond of Warren's husband James (whom they commended for his 'expanded heart' and masculine sensibility), while Warren was equally close to John Winthrop (for whom she wrote a number of

[37] HW to MOW, Apr. 1775, WWC. [38] MOW to HW, 1 Jan. 1774, WWC.
[39] MOW to EL, n.d., 1775, MOWP1.
[40] HW to MOW, 23 June 1775, WWC.

poems).[41] Warren, of course, also held a more edgy and productive intellectual relationship with John Adams, with whom she sparred over politics and poetry during many a visit to each other's home.[42] Their families were all party to the women's correspondence, and (as later discussed) they read and wrote letters collaboratively with their husbands.

These personal interconnections were further extended by the women's mutual support through material exchanges of money and other commodities. They lent each other specie from their own small supplies (sometimes against their husbands' wishes), while their positions across the breadth of Massachusetts meant that some might have access to goods which others in the group found it difficult to acquire.[43] From coastal Plymouth, Mercy Warren was able to supply her friends with thread and medicinal herbs, as well as acting as Abigail Adams's agent in the difficult later years of the war, selling on the handkerchiefs and other small items her friend had begun to trade in.[44] At Cambridge, meanwhile, Hannah Winthrop had access to more accomplished artisans than her rural and provincial friends, whom she was able to assist with manufactured commodities. 'I have at last accomplished the making of your shoes,' she wrote to Warren, assuring her resolutely ascetic friend that the shoemaker 'was as prudent as he could have been of your trimmings'.[45] Thus in limited, but nonetheless important ways, the meanings of these women's privacy or domesticity both subsumed and mirrored those of the provincial marketplace.

---

[41] On James Warren's 'expanded heart', see HW to MOW, 17 Jan. 1780, WWC. See also Warren's patriotic poem 'To the Honourable J. Winthrop, esq' [1774], in her *Poems Dramatic and Miscellaneous* (1790).

[42] I discuss John Adams's and Mercy Warren's relationship at greater length in Chapter 6. As Warren's critics and biographers point out, in the 1770s he encouraged her in many of her writing projects, including *The Group* and *The Squabble of the Sea Nymphs*. See, for example, Zagarri, *A Woman's Dilemma*, 62–3, 72–4, and Richards, *Mercy Otis Warren*, ch.3.

[43] For example, Mercy Warren lent Penny Winslow, the wife of James Warren's arch political enemy (and relative) Ned Winslow, sums of money on a number of occasions in the 1770s. Penny Winslow was, until the enmity between their husbands became too acutely painful in the later years of the war, one of Warren's close friends and frequent visitors. On one of Penny's visits, Warren described herself and her friend affectionately to James Warren as 'a Whig and a Tory lodging in the same bed' (MOW to JW, 22 Apr. 1772, MOWP2).

[44] For an illuminating discussion of Abigail Adams as a 'modest merchant', see Gelles, *Portia*, 44.   [45] HW to MOW, 9 Jan. 1778, WWC.

The women of Mercy Warren's network never questioned the association of their femininity with the privacy they idealized and the attachments and exchanges of the domestic sphere. Such attachments—to family and ancestry, to one's sisterhood of friends, to the spaces of home, to the land and its history—were necessarily normative, conservative, and in traditional republican terms, pre-political, yet they also served as the assumed source of these women's patriotism. All the women considered themselves as sociable beings ('the highest cordial of life', Warren wrote to Adams, 'is the social intercourse of the friendly mind'), but they importantly saw the sphere of the social in terms of its extension of, rather than its opposition to, the domestic. These women thought about sociability and domesticity as one and the same thing largely because what socializing they did was conducted at each other's rural or provincial hearths. I have already noted their strong antipathy to what they described as metropolitan dissipation, and the only grand event Winthrop and Warren ever seemed to take any sort of guilty pleasure in was Harvard's commencement (as was the case with many women of her class, the young Warren had reputedly first noticed her future husband there). In contrast to Boston's modern glare, the women thought of their sociable domesticity as keeping alive the virtuous manners of the old colony. The welcome Hannah Winthrop would receive in Plymouth, Warren assured her, would always imitate the 'ancient days of simplicity and hospitality'.[46] Visits to one another's homes, and converse in person, were pleasures their letters constantly sought to imitate or capture. Warren and Ellen Lothrop usually lived in sight of one another at Plymouth, and, in the latter's absence, Warren wrote of her letters as a means of 'calling on her friend', and lighting the darkened windows of the house she could see from her own.[47] All the women's letters eulogized each other's domestic spaces, their firesides and parlours, as idealized sites of what they termed 'rational', 'reciprocal', and 'improving' converse. 'I long to make me at your social fireside... [and] listen to the refined and delightful accents of rational and unfeigned friendship,' Mercy Warren wrote to Winthrop in the tense February of 1775.[48]

[46] MOW to HW, 31 Jan. 1774, MOWP1.
[47] MOW to EL, n.d., 1775, MOWP1.
[48] MOW to HW, Febr. 1775, MOWP1.

The women thought of their domestic sociability as a distinctively national, or perhaps regional, characteristic and described their homely, rational converse in terms of its opposition to the more public salon culture their female contemporaries in France or Britain enjoyed. When Adams (the only one of the group to visit Europe) wrote to Mercy Warren from London that she 'sigh[ed], (tho not allowed) for... the friendship of my chosen few and their agreeable converse', Mercy Warren replied that she quite understood how her friend might miss 'the calm delights of quiet friendship and rational simplicity' that Massachusetts afforded:

> One who has been long acquainted with the taste of Mrs Adams; who knows her love of her country and her domestic connections; her early attachment to modes of life incompatible with the gaieties of public appearance need not apologise when she supposes her to have enjoyed more real felicity in the little yellow parlor with the companions of her youth amidst a smiling fraternal circle and a few select friends than she has yet found in the assembly, the drawing room... the coterie of the most distinguished fair, or the palace of the most magnificent court.[49]

The yellow parlour is the sign of an irrefutable attachment to a domestic sphere and a country that are represented here as one and the same. Beyond its personal resonance, the parlor calls up a singularly American cultural difference in Warren's comparison of the quiet exchanges of the fraternal circle to the extravagant glare of European publicity. The old world is all gaudy monarchical show, all servility and dependence, while the benefits of the new are suggested by Adams's domestic sociability and the equality it fosters. Warren's allusions to the self-regarding excesses of fashionable women help define by default an American femininity characterized by its virtuous simplicity and sentimental reciprocity. As an agent of rational equality and a space of sentimental, domestic, and patriotic attachments, the yellow parlor can be read here as Warren's idealized image of American republicanism itself.

---

[49] MOW to AA, 18 Sept. 1785, MOWP1. There is perhaps some of Warren's characteristically and contradictorily barbed writing in this letter—she was clearly fascinated and repelled by London as it appears in Adams's lively letters of this period. Her encomium to the yellow parlor is clearly also meant to suggest the consistency and superiority of *her* patriotic attachments in comparison to those of her now expatriated and, to some extent, already estranged friend.

II Interruptions, Reparations

Warren and her friends understood the war with Britain as a disruption of their idealized domestic sphere and its sentimental exchanges in two crucial ways. First, they wrote of themselves as, in Winthrop's words, 'afraid of the fatal interruption of each social enjoyment', as they were forced to abandon their homes and relinquish their sons and husbands to the militias or continental army.[50] Warren wrote of her patriotic fears for her country as themselves affording a 'fatal interruption' of the leisured domesticity she enjoyed. Following a sociable afternoon with her sister and niece in which they had 'regaled several times on the finest strawberries', she wrote that 'the beauties of nature and the bounties of providence nor the social intercourse of friends can I taste with unalloyed delight so long as my country is threatened with desolation and bloodshed'.[51] Second, like most of their contemporaries, Warren's circle thought of Anglo-American opposition as *itself* a war of the affections: a conflict that not only divided families into factions across the Atlantic world but was also understood as the breakdown of the sentimental, familial relationship that had formerly existed between imperial Britain and its colonial 'children'.[52] In her *History*, Warren wrote that, in the pre-revolutionary years, the idea of the imperial relationship as domestic was written in America's language and sentiments—colonists still thought of England as 'home . . . the seat of happiness, the retreat of all the felicities of the human mind . . . too intimately associated with the best feelings of the heart to renounce without pain, whether applied to the natural or the political parent'.[53]

During the war, Warren and her friends wrote that their maintenance of the rational and reciprocal friendships they idealized was an

---

[50] HW to MOW, 27 Sept. 1774, WWC.

[51] MOW to JW, 15 June 1775, MOWP2. Warren's kitchen garden was well known for its fine fruit.

[52] See my discussion of the representation of the familial relationship between Britain and America in Chapter 3 and also Jay Fliegelman's definitive study, *Prodigals and Pilgrims: The American Revolution against Patriarchal Authority* (Cambridge: Cambridge University Press, 1982). Warren's own family was divided by the war, as her loyalist cousins returned to England and settled in Sleaford in Lincolnshire. Warren was very fond of Elizabeth (Otis) Brown, her niece, despite the fact that she had, in Warren's eyes, betrayed her birthright by marrying a British officer. The two women shared a warm correspondence in Warren's later years.   [53] MOW, *History*, 166.

act both of resistance to, and of reparation of, the imperial war of the affections that threatened to divide the colonies from their domestic and imperial 'home'. When Winthrop was forced from Cambridge to the New Hampshire border during the siege of Boston (she compared her feelings leaving her home to those of Milton's Eve shut out of Paradise), she wrote to Warren that 'the sons of tyranny and lawless power have abridged us of many pleasures but they shall not deprive us of that blessed privilege of conveying our thoughts by pen and ink... or take from us the heartfelt satisfaction of mutual affection and friendly converse'.[54] 'The noise of war', she assured Warren, 'can never drown the soft alluring voice of friendship'.[55] In the letters of Warren's circle, the encroachments of the British administration and the war itself are internalized as forms of domestic estrangement, while correspondence (testimony to women's strong sentimental attachments) is seen to afford powerful patriotic consolation. For example, in a letter in which she condemned Thomas Hutchinson in characteristically virulent terms for his 'crimes too big and too far spread to expect the pardon of [his] fellow man', Warren also congratulated Winthrop and herself for the consistency and fidelity of *their* affections: 'If we may set our affection on any thing below the stars,' she wrote, 'we shall surely find indulgence for our fond attachments to friends, whose rational and reciprocal affection we have no reason to think will terminate with time'.[56]

For Warren's circle, patriotism was entirely bound up with the terms of women's sentimental friendships. Warren's and Adams's famous choice of epistolary pseudonyms is telling in this respect, suggesting beyond the familiar conventions of women's correspondence a genuine identification with those republican virtues they claimed as women, friends, and patriots.[57] Marcia and Portia were, of course, sentimental as well as patriotic Romans—women whose private characters,

---

[54] See HW to MOW, Apr. 1775, WWC. Winthrop quotes from *Paradise Lost*, bk. 10, 'O unexpected stroke, worse then of Death! / Must I leave Thee paradise? Thus leave / Thee native soile, these happie walks and shades, / Fit haunt of Gods?' (bk. 10, ll. 268–72).

[55] HW to MOW, 7 Aug. 1777, WWC.

[56] MOW to HW, 31 Jan. 1774, MOWP1.

[57] Hannah Winthrop was inclined to poke fun at such literary conceits. 'Give me leave to use the signature of Narcissa,' she wrote to 'Marcia', 'or give me one agreeable to you'. But she often called Warren 'my Philomela', in reference to her poetic talents. See HW to MOW, 5 Nov. 1775, and HW to MOW, 2 Apr. 1776, WWC.

personal attachments, and love of country were constituent parts of their exemplary femininity.[58] Such combinations of ideal feminine feeling or domesticity with republicanism certainly provided, during the years of the war, legitimating models for American women's own political involvement.[59] The letters of Warren's circle reveal an energetic engagement with public affairs and a real sense of themselves as participants in a sentimental–political network that extended beyond Massachusetts across the Atlantic.[60] They eagerly shared their thoughts on each turn of events in the colonial dispute and war and copied or passed on pamphlets, newspapers, and any intelligence they and their local communities had been party to. Winthrop shared all the news contained in the packages her husband received from his contacts in London with Warren, whom she and her friends described as notoriously 'well-versed in politics'.[61] At Braintree, Abigail Adams was often hungry for news and the 'seasoning of politicks' she enjoyed in Warren's correspondence. Complaining that letters she had recently received from Warren (then at Watertown) contained no 'publick intelligence', Adams wrote: 'I wish my friend, you would be kind enough to write me often . . . and let your letters be of the journal kind; by that means I could participate in your sentiments.'[62] As Adams felt a doubled pleasure in the sentimental and political forms of 'participation' Warren's letters might afford, so Hannah Winthrop repeatedly described her friends' political and affectionate attachments as one and the same thing. In a letter in which she denounced Massachusetts' Tories for their 'narrow hearts' and misguided loyalties, she commended republicans like herself and Warren for their sentimental and political consistency. 'Be it known unto Britain,' Winthrop wrote, 'American daughters are politicians and patriots and will aid the good work with their female efforts'.[63]

[58] Warren's 'Marcia' is usually thought to suggest the wife of Cato the younger, though, particularly given Warren's excellent knowledge of the history of Republican and Imperial Rome, she may also suggest the resolute and 'Amazonian' partner of Commodus, who successfully interceded on behalf of the Christians.

[59] See my discussion of women's history in the U.S. and classical models of patriotism in the introduction to this book.

[60] Robert Sparks, the 1978 editor of the Warren–Adams microfilm made for the MHS, averred that the letters between Mercy Otis Warren and Abigail Adams were apolitical and only 'concerned social and family matters.'

[61] HW to MOW, 2 Apr. 1776, WWC. Winthrop asked Warren in this letter for her opinion of Tom Paine's *Common Sense*.   [62] AA to MOW, 19 Oct. 1775, WAP.

[63] HW to MOW, 1 Jan. 1774, WWC.

In her *History* Warren was to define the personal letter as a particularly American sentimental exchange (proscribed, in some instances, by what she described as British inhumanity). For example, during the occupation of Charleston in 1781, according to Warren, the 'heroic' and patriotic women

> gave a glorious example of female fortitude. They submitted patiently to... hardships they had never expected; and wept in secret the miseries of their country, and their separation from their tenderest connexions with whom they were forbidden all intercourse and were not permitted the soft alleviation of the exchange of letters.[64]

Here Warren represents the alienating experience of occupation (the women are rendered, in effect, grieving strangers in their own country) as a sort of literalization of the small-scale division of their domestic spheres: a process of patriotic estrangement forbidden 'alleviation' by the letter's sentimental exchange.

For Mercy Otis Warren, letters between friends might, as it were, re-enact or repair those sentimental, social bonds which the revolutionary war threatened to destroy. She felt that American women's idealized private and domestic characters made them better patriots as well as better friends and correspondents. When, in 1774, her childhood friend Hannah Lincoln expressed disquiet at the increasingly seditious tone of Warren's letters (which were circulated among Lincoln's conservatively inclined family circle), Warren replied that it was inevitable that women became politicized when private attachments were at stake:

> As every domestic enjoyment depends on the decision of the mighty contest, who can be an unconcerned and silent spectator? Not surely the fond mother or the affectionate wife who trembles lest her dearest connections should fall the victims of lawless power or at least pour out the warm blood as a libation at the shrine of liberty, 'eer she unmolested may again erect her cheerful standard on the American shores; and painful as is this last idea, is it not less irksome than to embrace the odious alternative, and acquiesce that the chains of thraldom should be forever fixed on the descendents of a race of worthies who, to secure to them the rights of nature, rivalled the much-admired heroes of antiquity in the exercise of illustrious virtues, of fortitude, patience, and self-denial?[65]

---

[64] MOW, *History*, 449.
[65] MOW to Hannah Lincoln, 3 Sept. 1774, MOWP2. Jane Rendall and Linda Kerber both cite this passage, but do not read it in terms of Warren's strategic complexities. Jane

The moves Warren makes in this passage are similar to those of the letter with which I began: she starts with the language of the domestic affections and ends with a rousing encomium to the heroic virtues of Massachusetts' first settlers. She suggests that because of the imperial conflict's inevitable impact on domesticity, American women are simply compelled to discuss what concerns them. This is certainly a concessionary and conservative account of women's patriotism—being, as it were, forced from the domestic sphere at a moment of national exigency—but one must remember that these comments were certainly seen by, and in a sense partly addressed to, Lincoln's husband Benjamin, who found Warren's unabashed support of Massachusetts' 'refractory' classes a little hard to swallow. There is, then, perhaps something strategic about the way Warren claims disinterest for her own position through the sentimental irrefutability and universality of the figure of the wife and mother (she was to suggest her gender or her privacy made her politics morally incontrovertible many times over the next three decades).[66] And yet beyond this carefully persuasive rationale, there is also the suggestion, I think, of the desirability, the viability, and the utility of women's political interests and a real sense of the necessity of their engagement with the affairs and interests of the nation. Warren valued Lincoln's friendship and opinions and enjoyed the way their political differences lent them opportunity for spirited epistolary debate. 'I should have a very ill opinion of myself if any variation of sentiment with regard to political matters should lessen my esteem for the disinterested, undesigning and upright heart,' she wrote; 'your correspondence is to me a pleasing proof that the early attachments of youth are not obliterated from your bosom but that the sentiments of friendship...are matured by time and strengthened'.[67] For Warren, the enduring sentimental friendship and the letters which sustained it provided a setting and a medium for women's patriotic consciousness beyond their many differences.

Rendall, *The Origins of Modern Feminism: Women in Britain, France and the United States, 1780–1860* (Basingstoke: Macmillan, 1985), 35; Linda Kerber, *Women of the Republic: Intellect and Ideology in Revolutionary America* (Chapel Hill, NC: University of North Carolina Press, 1980), 84.

[66] See my discussion of this issue in Chapter 6.
[67] MOW to HL, 3 Sept. 1774, MOWP2.

By 1776 Warren was writing of women's sympathetic exchanges and their maintenance of friendships as being both supportive and representative of the national public cause. Encouraged by Abigail Adams and Ellen Lothrop, Warren wrote letters to elite women in other American states who had achieved a certain notoriety as women of learning, sensibility, and patriotism. These letters began new correspondences between the North and Middle colonies; new sentimental and republican exchanges which were to last, in some cases, for more than thirty years. Warren's friendship with Janet Livingston Montgomery, which began with a letter of sympathy on the death of her husband in the Northern campaigns, is one of the most interesting of these exchanges. This letter was copied and seen by many other elite women from New Hampshire to New York. It came to be read as an act of semi-public commemoration, an animating performance of female sensibility and republican feeling. Warren wrote to Montgomery:

it may still further brighten the clouded moment to reflect that your friends are not confined to the limits of a province, but by the happy union of the American colonies (suffering equally by the rigor of oppressions) the affections of the inhabitants are cemented and the grave of the companion of your heart will be sprinkled with the tears of thousands who revere the character of the commander at the gates of Quebec.[68]

Here cross-colonial feminine sympathy represents a bond of affectionate concord that itself defines republican America's unity of purpose. Montgomery, a grieving figure who exemplifies the equal suffering or oppressions of the colonies, clearly suggests for Warren the wounded, sentimental figure of a united America *her*self. Hannah Winthrop felt (having seen it) that Warren's and Montgomery's exchange displayed exemplary patriotism and feeling. Their letters, she wrote, 'discover[ed] hearts endowed with the most exquisite sensibility'.[69] Warren wrote of her correspondence with Montgomery as a patriotic duty recompensed by the pleasurable experience of sympathy: 'if the reward of patriotism is not to be received in another world but is to be reaped in the present state, I am sure it must consist in the sublime satisfaction of performing the social duties from a principle of disinterested benevolence.'[70] Thus

[68] MOW to Janet Montgomery, 20 Jan. 1776, MOWP1.
[69] HW to MOW, 1 May 1776, WWC.
[70] MOW to JW, Dec. 1775, MOWP2. Warren also made a copy of the letter to Montgomery for JW.

Warren and her friends wrote of women's sentimental exchanges, their experience and expression of sensibility, as alleviating the effects of the painful 'war of the affections' and themselves contributing to the patriotic cause. For these women, an associational privacy whose medium was the familiar letter and which was defined by what they described as a rational, sociable, and sentimental domesticity exemplified what was most positive and distinctive about Massachusetts' political culture during the colonial dispute and war.

III   Every Fireside was a Theatre of Politics

With the disruption of conventional channels of communication, the dispersed provincial culture of New England really relied on correspondence for the transmission of local and international news and information. During the war, the familiar letter's boundaries between private, social, and public became inescapably political. The conveyance, transmission, retention, destruction, and careful copying of letters were regarded as patriotic acts, and the homes of Mercy Warren and her circle of friends became repositories of political information and intelligence. The women came to regard their hearths, their parlours, and their letters as spaces of patriotic resistance and political debate. While it should certainly be acknowledged that it was their marriages to prominent republican men which granted them access to the public sphere by proxy, Warren and her friends also felt that they, as women and as writers, had a clearly defined role to play in an epistolary culture that had become newly and importantly politicized.

As Massachusetts' legal and political institutions were suspended in 1774, colonial political resistance to Britain was increasingly encouraged by out-of-doors epistolary exchanges. In her *History*, Warren argued that the associational epistolary culture of Massachusetts on the eve of the war demonstrated how 'a regular democracy sometimes arises from the severe encroachments of despotism'.[71] The spark of this exemplary democracy was first lit, she wrote, 'on the visit of a private friend' to her own fireside.[72] By the mid 1770s, her Plymouth home had become a notorious haven of radical political debate, and it was during a visit to the Warrens that Sam Adams agreed with them to establish the Boston

---

[71] MOW, *History*, 63.   [72] Ibid. 61.

Committee of Correspondence. Of the Committee Warren wrote:

perhaps no single step contributed so much to cement the union of the colonies and the final acquisition of independence as the establishment of committees of correspondence. This supported a chain of communication from New Hampshire to Georgia that produced unanimity and energy throughout the continent.[73]

Richard Brown has written how the BCC, and Massachusetts' associational epistolary culture more generally, 'stimulated... a shift in contemporary attitudes regarding political roles—a democratization—in which everyone was believed to have an active part in politics'.[74] Brown does not suggest that this cultural shift extended to women, but I would argue that in a particular sense this was certainly the case for those elite groups who, like Warren and her friends, clearly saw themselves as integral parts of the 'chain of communication' perceived to consolidate inter-colonial unanimity. As the BCC's circular letters began to have their desired effect in 1774, there was, then, perhaps a certain amount of personal hubris in Warren's frequent encomiums to the development of the epistolary culture she described as 'a regular democracy'.[75] 'The newly established correspondence between the several provinces', she wrote to Hannah Winthrop, 'will... communicate a laudable breathing after the original freedom of our progenitors that will spread far and wide to the confusion and terror of the abettors of despotism'.[76] All her friends knew that the BCC had arisen out of the political debate at her own fireside. Thus in terms typically partisan, Warren claimed the origins of America's republican unanimity and patriotic purpose for her own domestic sphere.[77]

It is of course important to remember that it was because Warren and her friends were married or related to radical leaders and because they shared what they described as intellectual and equitable relationships with their partners that these women had access to New England's wartime republican culture. As Edith Gelles writes of Abigail Adams,

---

[73] MOW, *History*, 61.

[74] Richard Brown, *Revolutionary Politics in Massachusetts: The Boston Committee of Correspondence and the Towns, 1772–1774* (New York: Norton, 1970), 246.

[75] MOW, *History*, 63.   [76] MOW to HW, 31 Jan. 1774, MOWP1.

[77] On the Warrens' involvement in the establishment of the BCC, see Anthony, *First Lady of the Revolution*, 77–8. See also William Gordon, *History of the Rise, Progress and Establishment of the Independence of the United States* (New York: Campbell, 1789), i. 207.

marriage might enable women to 'experien[ce] the domestic and the public spheres as a continuity'.[78] Through the political discussions that occurred in their homes and the writing and reading of letters, they came to regard themselves as participants in the debate on America's future. In the introduction to her *History*, Warren wrote that she was 'connected by nature, friendship and every social tie with many of the first patriots and most influential characters and in the habits of confidential epistolary intercourse with those employed in the highest stations'.[79] Her network of well-placed friends and correspondents meant quite simply that she had, as she put it, 'the best means of information'.[80] Warren's correspondents (and particularly John Adams before the strains in their friendship really showed) often recognized that her carefully sustained epistolary connections meant she was ideally situated to trace and record America's political transitions. 'There are few persons possessed of more facts', he flattered her, 'or who can record them in a more agreeable manner'.[81] For Hannah Winthrop, Warren's real (and, for her, highly enviable) proximity to the political public sphere meant her letters might provide her female friends with the 'animation' to steel their patriotic resolve. 'Your faith that the united efforts will be blest with success animates me,' Winthrop wrote: 'I catch a spark of that heavenly flame which invigorates your breast knowing your faith has a permanent foundation and your acquaintance with those in the cabinet must enable you to form a better judgment than those who have not those advantages.'[82] For Winthrop, Warren's patriotism was that bit more irrefutable because of her reliable, personal sources of political information.

Warren's acknowledged position at the centre of an important epistolary network was enhanced by a particularly supportive relationship with a partner who encouraged her intellectual interests and regarded her political acumen as more than a match to his own. His letters to her are unabashedly affectionate and admiring. During his absences on political

---

[78] Gelles, *Portia*, 23. As Gelles rightly notes, however, such ideals of companionship were marked by months, even years, of absence and can be read from the other direction: that is, as reinforcing prevailing eighteenth-century gender stereotypes as much as allowing women contact with political culture. See *Portia*, ch. 2, 'A Tye More Binding', 24–36.   [79] MOW, *History*, p. xli.
[80] Ibid.   [81] JA to MOW, 25 Dec. 1787, WAP.
[82] HW to MOW, 17 Aug. 1775, WWC. The emotive letters Winthrop sent to Warren during this period from Andover really convey the fear and isolation she felt in her enforced absence from Cambridge.

business in the 1770s, he was forever reminding Warren that, as a woman of letters, patriotism, and what he often termed 'rational philosophy', she too had a particular role in promoting the public good. She wrote, he told her, for 'the good of mankind, the good of your friends, for the promotion of virtue and patriotism'.[83] James Warren clearly felt his wife's literary abilities had a distinctly republican purpose in wartime America. It was through him that Warren was introduced as a correspondent to a range of political leaders, and there is no doubt that it was as the wife of one prominent republican and the sister of another that her characteristic self-assurance as a patriot and writer was derived. Yet, while Warren was undoubtedly privileged in her social position and personal relationships, she also wrote and read within a literary–epistolary context in which women's access to and participation in the political correspondence of their families and communities were entirely commonplace.

For the women of Warren's circle in the 1760s and 1770s, the reading, writing, and transmission of political letters were social and family occasions. As John Adams later wrote to Warren, in wartime New England, 'every fireside was a theatre of politics'.[84] Warren shared her correspondence with her then young family and Winthrop's older son Johnny had (as she joked) often been party to her letters: 'he desires I should beware of imparting treason to a sister heart'.[85] The very real danger of interception meant the women were often concerned for their letters' safe passage, and, at anxious times, their husbands or sons acted as the personal medium and messenger of their correspondence. 'Follow my example,' Warren wrote reassuringly to an uneasy Abigail Adams, 'and set down immediately and write, and I will ensure you a safe conveyance by a gentleman [James Warren] who I hope will call on you on Saturday'.[86] The women read their husbands' correspondence ('I have had the pleasure of seeing several of your letters,' Warren told John Adams) and, indeed, opened their letters in their absence ('I read it', a disingenuous Abigail Adams told Mercy Warren after sharing with her daughter a letter her husband had addressed to John, 'not regarding the

[83] JW to MOW, 6 Apr. 1775, MOWP2. Copy also in WAP.
[84] JA to MOW, 27 July 1807, in *Correspondence of John Adams and Mercy Warren* (Collections of the Massachusetts Historical Society, 4; Boston: MHS, 1878), 355.
[85] HW to MOW, 23 June 1775, WWC.
[86] MOW to AA, 7 Feb. 1776, WAP.

"Dear Sir").[87] Importantly, the women did not merely read their partners' political correspondence, but were also participants in it. Abigail Adams, Hannah Winthrop, and Mercy Warren all wrote letters collaboratively with their partners.

The following example of such a letter—from James Warren to John Adams written during Adams's absence at Philadelphia in 1775—suggests that culture of companionate collaboration which the women of Warren's circle certainly profited from:

> I want to see trade (if we must have it) open, and a fleet to protect it in opposition to Britain... we must have a test, that shall distinguish Whigs from Tories, etc etc. I have a thousand things to say to you; I want to see you. I want you there and I want you here. What shall I do without you and my friend [Sam] Adams at Congress? And yet you are both wanted here. I believe you must stay there; I mean, belong to that body once more.... She sits at the table with me, will have a paragraph of her own; says you 'should no longer piddle at the threshold. It is time to leap into the theatre, to unlock the bars, and open every gate that impedes the rise and growth of the American republic, and then let the giddy potentate send forth his puerile proclamations to France, to Spain and all the commercial world who may be united in building up an empire which he can't prevent.
>
> At leisure then may G——his reign review,
> And bid to empire and to crown adieu.'[88]

This letter clearly shows the Warrens' engagement as a political couple (as well as individuals with distinct literary styles) with the large questions that shook the colonies on the eve of independence. James Warren often wrote that he disliked composition and described himself (rather unfairly) as a poor correspondent. Here there is both energy and vacillation in what he writes—the desire to impart everything decisively and the inevitable inability to do so immediately.[89] Mercy Warren, who had been celebrating the prospect of independence in her letters to Catharine Macaualy since 1774, is clearly keen to interject with her brisk fantasy of the decline and fall of the British Empire and instruct John Adams to hurry up and

---

[87] MOW to JA, 5 July 1775, and AA to MOW, Nov. 1775, WAP.
[88] JW and MOW to JA, 14 Nov. 1775, WAP.
[89] When writing to her sons, Mercy Warren had to excuse her husband for his failure to add a fatherly line or two—all of them knew, as she often reminded them, that their father 'does not love the pen' (MOW to Charles Warren, 29 Dec. 1785).

hasten the inevitable. Her impatience at what she here describes as the 'piddling' of the continental Congress is itself a sign of her total immersion in Massachusetts' epistolary political culture, since 'piddling' was the shorthand of the Warren–Adams circle for John Dickinson (who they thought a too cautious man of rather meagre political virtue).[90] While this letter is certainly distinctive (in the sense that it suggests the Warrens' particular relationship and the trajectory of their politics), the culture of familial epistolary collaboration it exemplifies was entirely conventional. As I have suggested, the letters of Abigail Adams, Hannah Winthrop, and, indeed, other women of similarly prominent political families during this period reveal comparable examples of collaboration.

Companionate marriages brought these elite women, as readers and writers, into a network of political debate otherwise dominated by public men. And yet Warren's circle also understood the activities of writing and reading about politics to be something specifically and suitably feminine—something appropriately shared between female friends. In this sense it might be said that their heterosexual relationships provided the supportive backdrop for a culture of patriotic homosociality. In one example of an argument she was to repeat many times during the 1770s, Mercy Warren told Hannah Winthrop: 'it is not within the sphere of female life to be any way active in the manœuvres of state.'[91] But she followed this with the suggestion that, *because* women were excluded from the activity of public life, their leisure itself entailed a particular patriotic duty: 'might it not be deemed an omission if we make no observations?'[92] For Warren and her friends, the privacy and leisure they valued as signs of their attachment to the land and to each other became, during the war, the site of an independence or impartiality that legitimized a role for them as women, as political commentators, and as writers. This notion of women's privacy as the source of political disinterest was something James Warren often drew on in the supportive letters he wrote to Mercy Warren in his absence (suggesting writing as a cure for the melancholy from which she often suffered).[93] John Adams also made a case in these terms for women's particular patriotic independence. In a letter to Mercy Warren (composed before their political

---

[90] See, for example, JA to JW, 25 July 1775, and MOW to AA, 7 Feb. 1776, WAP.
[91] MOW to HW, 1 Jan. 1774, WWC.   [92] Ibid.
[93] See, for example, JW to MOW, 6 Apr. 1775, MOWP2.

differences erased that strain of gallant flattery with which his early writing to her was characterized) he argued that unlike men, who were all too easily distracted from the public good by personal ambition or party interests, women's private and moral characters (themselves the result of their exclusion from public life) meant their patriotism was incorruptible and incontrovertible. 'The ladies, I think, are the greatest politicians,' he wrote, 'because they consider questions more coolly than those who are heated with party zeal and inflamed with the bitter contentions of active public life'.[94] For Warren and her circle, then, those spaces of domesticity, privacy, and leisure associated with elite women might be understood as the ideal locale from which to apprehend, and write about, the public good.

In December 1774 Warren wrote to Catharine Macaulay requesting 'more of your excellent sentiments and judicious observations on the subject of the present dispute'. 'You see, Madam,' she continued:

I disregard the opinion that women make but indifferent politicians. When the observations are just and do honour to the heart and character, I think it very immaterial whether they flow from a female lip in the soft whispers of private friendship or whether thundered in the senate in the bolder language of the other sex. Nor will the one be more influential than the other on the general conduct of life or the intrigues of statesmen in the cabinet so long as private interest is the [illegible] sole star that governs mankind from the king to the cottage.[95]

Warren uses the familiar republican complaint of the prevalence of private interest to bestow a sort of back-handed authority on the political characters of Macaulay and herself. Initially, she presents the media in which women and men appropriately express their political opinions as the only, rather nugatory, difference between them—feminine whispering and masculine thunder are clearly gendered, but apparently equivalent in their significance. Yet, if private interest pervades from the king to the cottage and the senate is a space where the expression and promotion of the public good are therefore impossible, then the personal epistle, the confidential whisperings of friends, becomes the last medium in which political opinion can be truthfully and honourably expressed. The letter is a space, for Warren, of the heart's unmediated display, of an

[94] JA to MOW, 16 Apr. 1776, WAP.
[95] MOW to CM, 11 Sept. 1774, MOWP1.

intimacy that simply cannot deceive. A friendship, based on the cultivation of mutual affection and shared republican principles, supplies a sort of consolatory privilege for the deficiencies of the public sphere. Since the thunderings of the senate represent a betrayal of political rectitude, female correspondents, whose soft whisperings 'do honour to the heart and character', can seem better politicians.

IV A Republic of Letters

By opening a correspondence with Catharine Macaualay, Warren was also seeking to draw the most famously politicized woman in the Atlantic republican community into her epistolary network. That she wrote to Macaulay with such confidence and held such lively optimism about the necessity of women's engagement in the revolutionary debate between Britain and America suggest her very real conviction in the political purpose of letters and women's writing more generally. As I have argued, Warren associated herself with a domesticity and sentiment which itself shaped her republican love of country. She felt that her privacy defined, produced, and legitimated her interest in the public good. As public and private were interwoven in Warren's sense of her own patriotic character, so it was with the literary form in which she and other women predominantly wrote: the familiar letter. Rebecca Earle has rightly described letter writing and reading as, until recently, a 'communal practice' and an 'entirely social affair'.[96] As I am suggesting here, this was certainly the case for the elite women of revolutionary New England.

The letters of the women of Warren's circle were social in the sense that they had a communal audience and function beyond their immediate addressees. They were lent, copied, orated, and shared among

---

[96] Rebecca Earle, 'Letters, Writers and the Historian: Introduction,' in Earle (ed.), *Epistolary Selves*, 7. See also Joanne Freeman on 'public minded personal letters', Freeman, *Affairs of Honor: National Politics in The New Republic* (New Haven: Yale University Press, 2001), 114–16, and Decker, *Epistolary Practices*. See also Naomi Tadmor's account of the social nature of reading in the eighteenth century: ' "In the Even my Wife Read to Me": Women, Reading and Household Life in the Eighteenth Century', in James Raven, Naomi Tadmor, and Helen Small (eds.), *The Practice and Representation of Reading in England* (Cambridge: Cambridge University Press, 1996). These accounts of the culture of eighteenth-century reading and writing as social rather than private phenomena, and my discussion here, might be set against Linda Kerber's more restrictive account of the 'private'. See Kerber, *Women of the Republic: Intellect and Ideology in Revolutionary America* (New York: Norton, 1980–84).

family groups and communities. They possessed a social meaning not only in the maintenance of particular friendships, but in the exchange of opinion; the expression and acceptance of political difference; and the consolidation of women's sense of themselves as contributors to debates of local, national, and international significance. The women of Warren's circle admired each other's letters for their literary style, the particular intellectual interests they exhibited, and the exemplary republicanism or piety demonstrated in their writing. While the perusal of letters might well be a solitary occasion, they were also read aloud as rousing performances of patriotic feeling, acts of republican commemoration, or animating displays of sensibility. Letters defined the republican sense of community in provincial New England, and further afield beyond the Atlantic. Massachusetts' women and their families regularly corresponded with friends, relatives, and political associates in Britain. These letters, which took many months to arrive and which often passed through a number of willing hands before reaching their destination, had a similar social function in motivating and strengthening the political resolve of a dispersed Atlantic republican community. Letters from Warren (referred to as 'the American lady') were admired by Macaulay's Whig friends in London and clearly had an effect on the radical turn of British pro-Americanism in 1774 and 1775.[97] Equally, Catharine Macaulay's letters to James Otis, John Adams, and Mercy Warren were immediately circulated among her many New England fans (Macaulay's letters carried a real cachet).[98] Moreover, while the women of Warren's circle acknowledged the social functions their letters performed, they also came to feel they held potential as public documents. Their correspondence reveals a keen awareness of living and writing in what they frequently described as revolutionary years.[99] These

[97] As I argue in Chapter 3 of this book.
[98] See, for example, MOW to AA, 28 Jan. 1775, in *AFC*. 'Yours of Jan 3rd begins with an instance of curiosity which I am willing to cherish. Nay even to gratify provided I may be indulged in return with the sight of Mr and Mrs Adams' correspondence with the lady referred to.' The lady is clearly Macaulay, to whom Abigail Adams had written towards the end of 1774. As I argued in Chapter 3, the Dilly brothers (Macaulay's friends, publishers, and, to an extent, promoters) also copied a number of her 'private' letters for 'public' circulation among her American friends. Sarah Prince-Gill, for example, had seen Macaulay's letters to James Otis.
[99] See, for example, MOW to CM, July 1789, MOWP1. Edith Gelles notes this as an imperative to Abigail Adams's scrupulous retention and copying of letters: 'the Adamses, with their acute historical sensibilities, saved "every scrap they wrote"' (*Abigail Adams*, 5).

women knew that, as they carefully arranged and stored bundles of letters or copied their own correspondence to a journal or letter-book, they were writing not only for their own political communities but for an audience beyond their own time.[100]

To Mercy Otis Warren, this applied in a very particular sense. Her friends knew that she was planning to write a history of the colonial dispute and continuing war from the resources her own correspondence provided. 'I hope the historick page increases to a volume,' Abigail Adams wrote expectantly in November 1775.[101] By 1776 Warren was writing to Adams about her preoccupation with her writing and during the following year, Adams chided Warren for putting aside her pen at a moment when 'many memorable events which ought to be handed down to posterity will be buried in oblivion'.[102] Her friends also knew that, when their letters included one of Warren's celebrated 'characters', they were reading her history's preparatory material. 'I was charmed with three characters drawn by a most masterly pen,' John Adams wrote after receiving a letter with copies of Warren's material. 'Copley's pencil could not have touched off with more exquisite finishings the faces of those gentlemen . . . I hope posterity will see it, if they do I am sure they will admire it.'[103] Indeed, when John Adams wrote to Warren in the late 1770s and early 1780s, it was often with a view to determining the terms of his historical representation or discovering how *his* character was, as it were, shaping up.[104] Warren wrote that 'nothing depictures the

---

[100] My reading here of letters as both social and public might be read alongside and against Michael Warner's rather more narrow sense of the public in his *Letters of the Republic: Publication and the Public Sphere in Eighteenth-Century America* (Cambridge, Mass: Harvard University Press, 1990). [101] AA to MOW, Nov. 1775, WAP.
[102] MOW to AA, 17 Apr. 1776; AA to MOW, 14 Aug. 1777, in *AFC*. Rumours about the production of Warren's *History* also appeared in the Boston papers. See, for example, HW to MOW, 1 Sept. 1780, WWC: 'I was much surprised at the paragraph in the *Advertiser*. Not surprised that the lady of Gl. Warren intends to favour the world with the history of America, for I have often heard it was the expectation of those friends who knew the abilities, and were wishing for such an entertainment for the fair hand of so good a penwoman.'
[103] Possibly referring to Warren's characters of Joseph Warren and Thomas Hutchinson.
[104] See, for example, JA to JW, 9 Dec. 1780, WAP. Adams writes that he is concerned about how he will appear in the Abbé Raynal's *History of America* and closes the letter with: 'my most profound respect to Mrs Warren. I dread her history more than that of the Abbé.' This 'dread' is apparent in later letters when Adams imagines Warren's account of his character. See, for example, JA to MOW, 29 Jan. 1783, WAP: 'I shall appear

characters, the sentiments and the feelings of men more strongly than their private letters'.[105] This focus on 'private' letters as an index of sentiment and character dominated her approach to historical composition. As Warren's correspondents, her friends knew that their letters held potential as historical evidence. For example, Hannah Winthrop's now famous account of the aftermath of the British defeat at Saratoga was clearly drawn on by Warren in her *History*.[106] The same was the case with the bundles of letters and papers from London or Philadelphia that Winthrop and Abigail Adams carefully saved and sent on to Plymouth.[107] Thus, when they exchanged letters in what Warren called the 'soft whispers of private friendship', these women knew they were also observing public history as it happened and recording it for posterity.

During the 1770s and 1780s Warren was continually sorting through her correspondence and revising and reworking her letters for what she called her 'annals'. In 1785 she wrote to her son Winslow of how her time was occupied with 'letters to arrange and history to complete', and by 1789 she told Catharine Macaulay she would soon see her 'annals, in two or three volumes, if life is spared'.[108] She referred to herself as 'the writer who compiles and composes'—a phrase which really captures her working methods.[109] The history that finally emerged from Warren's letters in 1805 is a forty-year palimpsest of description and observation. Her letters to her friends were clearly the testing ground for different models of historical explanation, narrative technique, and character sketches. One sees the same phrases and paragraphs reworked, retried, discarded, and then reappearing ten years later in a letter to another

---

a domestic animal, never at home, a bashful creature, braving the fronts of the greatest ones of the earth, a timid man, venturing on a long series of the greatest dangers, an irritable fiery mortal, enduring every provocation and disgust, a delicate valetudinarian bearing the greatest hardships, an humble farmer dispising pomp, shew, power and wealth, as profuse as a prodigal and as proud as Caesar—but an honest man in all and to the death.' Joanne Freeman notes Adams's desire to control the meanings of his identity in posterity. See Freeman, *Affairs of Honor: National Politics in the New Republic* (New Haven: Yale University Press, 2001), 108–9.

[105] MOW, *History*, 388.
[106] See HW to MOW, 11 Nov. 1777, WWC. Copy also in WAP. Winthrop's vivid letters on the state of Burgoyne's captive army are often cited. See, for example, Ray Raphael, *The American Revolution: A People's History* (London: Profile Books, 2001), 124.
[107] See, for example, HW to MOW, 20 Jan. 1776, WWC.
[108] MOW to CM, July 1789, MOWP1.
[109] MOW to WW, Sept. 1785, MOWP1.

correspondent. Thus the villainous character of Thomas Hutchinson Warren wrote for Hannah Winthrop in the 1760s might re-emerge as John Hancock in Warren's later letters to Elbridge Gerry.[110] It is Warren's palimpsestic approach to her letters, which were often copied and revised, integrated, and reintegrated many times, that has made her personal archive seem confusing.[111] But this process itself also suggests the ways in which, for Warren and her friends, the boundaries between 'private' letters and 'public' history might be far more fluid and indistinct than many scholars imagine.

Warren's historical palimpsest, which began in the 'soft whispers' she shared with Catharine Macaulay and her other friends, was circulated in a number of different forms and had a range of different audiences or publics between the 1760s and its final 'publication'. Choosing just one example, this characteristic passage on the disposition of Howe's army first appeared in a letter to Macaulay in 1777:

> Not the purple of princes, nor the splendor of a diadem, can sanction the deeds of cruelty that have already been perpetrated on these Western shores; perpetrated by men whose crimes emblazoned by title will hand them down with redoubled infamy when the tragic tale shall be faithfully transmitted to generations yet unborn.... It requires the pen of a Macaulay to trace the origin and give the true colouring to the source and progress of a war kindled by avarice, whetted by ambition and blown up into a thirst of revenge by repeated disappointments...[112]

The declamatory, classical, and syntactically complex literary style that distinguishes Warren's historical writing is here clearly apparent as she acknowledges the then widespread assumption that Macaulay was gathering information with a view to writing a history of the American war.[113] Smuggled across the Atlantic at a dangerous time in the hands of

---

[110] For example, MOW to HW, Aug. 1774, MOWP1; MOW to HW, 29 May 1778, WWC; MOW to EG, 6 June 1783, MOWP1. See also my discussion of Warren's descriptions of Hancock in Chapter 5.

[111] See, for example, Geiger, 'Catharine Sawbridge Macaulay and Mercy Otis Warren', 70.   [112] MOW to CM, 1 Feb. 1777, MOWP1.

[113] Macaulay was, in a sense, writing a history of the American war in 1777, but perhaps not in the way her American correspondents expected—her take of the war was, as I argue in Chapter 3, displaced onto her account of the 1720s in her *History in a Series of Letters* (1778). She did, however, tell Warren that 'the history of your late and glorious revolution is what I should certainly undertake were I again young, yet as things are I must for many reasons decline the task' (CM to MOW, 6 Mar. 1787, WAP).

a trusted traveller, this communiqué from one political commentator to another would also have been circulated among Warren's and Macaulay's republican circles, and, by 1781, it was likely to have been among the papers of Winslow Warren which were seized upon his arrest in London on suspicion of espionage.[114] Warren regarded her lively, literary son as her ideal reader and was in the habit of copying her letters, arranging them by the moments in the revolutionary war they depicted, and then handing them over to him in large bundles.[115] For example, as he set out on one of his European trips, Warren told her son the revolutionary letters she gave him had a double function in reminding him both of his sentimental bond to his native country and of the display of her affectionate patriotic 'heart':

At the earnest request of my son I put into his hands . . . a number of letters chiefly wrote when America was verging to the crisis of civil war or plunged in its distresses. They may be an amusement in his absence from his native country, and perhaps of some use in future life; at least it will shew him the feelings of a heart warmly interested for the happiness of mankind when the writer is no more. He will take care that they are not scattered or exposed to the disadvantage of his most tender friend and affectionate mother.[116]

But the many copies Warren made of her letters to Macaulay were often to be 'exposed', by her own agency or that of others, and in London they were read by Winslow's British captors. After his release from jail Winslow wrote to Warren that Lord Hillsborough 'and others to whom my papers were consigned lavished praises on my mothers letters—said they "would do honour to the greatest writer that ever wrote" '.[117]

In later life, when her blindness necessitated the use of an amanuensis, Warren's letters to Macaulay continued to be duplicated, revised, and rearranged by other hands. A note on one manuscript copy, possibly in her eldest son James's handwriting, informs the reader that these letters

[114] For the background to WW's capture in London, see Charles Warren, 'A Young Man's Adventures in England and France during the Revolutionary War', *Proceedings of the Massachusetts Historical Society*, 65 (1932–6), 234–67. I discuss Warren's relationship with Winslow at greater length in Chapter 6.

[115] One such bundle is included in a folder of letters addressed from MOW to WW in MOWP2 entitled 'Letters Containing Many of the Most Remarkable Events for the Memorable Era of the Stamp Act, 1765, to the Commencement of Hostilities between Great Britain and the American Colonies, 1775.' Much of the raw material of Warren's *History* is here.   [116] MOW to WW, 7 Apr. 1784, MOWP1.

[117] WW to MOW, 28 Apr. 1781, Winslow Warren correspondence, MHS.

'were afterwards transcribed by the author into her annals of the American Revolution'.[118] In the 'annals' published in 1805 the passage Warren first drafted in 1777 finally reads:

> We must now pursue the progress of a war enkindled by avarice, whetted by ambition and blown up into a thirst of revenge by repeated disappointment. Not the splendor of a diadem, the purple of princes or the pride of power can ever sanction the deeds of cruelty perpetrated on the Western side of the Atlantic, and not unfrequently by men, whose crimes emblazoned by title, will enhance the infamy of their injustice and barbarism, when the tragic tale is faithfully related.[119]

The substance of the passage is the same, repunctuated and reworked into Warren's typically polished syntactical rhythms. As she draws her reader in with an inclusive 'we', Warren has, as it were, claimed for herself the historical authority imputed to Macaulay in the earlier letter. *She* is the republican faithfully relating from her own correspondence the 'tragic tale' of the 1770s and 1780s for a public of 'generations yet unborn'.

Thus the letters that enacted the exemplary sociability, sensibility, and piety Warren's circle thought characteristic of New England femininity; the letters that brought women together to share their political thoughts in the 'soft whispers of private friendship'; and that served as acts of collective patriotic resistance to the imperial 'war of the affections', also came to be integral to the writing of its history. In the opening pages of her *History* Warren wrote that her femininity itself qualified her to write the political history of her nation's first decades. She wrote of her gender in the conservative terms her contemporaries would have recognized and commended. It was her 'sympathizing heart', and her awareness that 'every domestic enjoyment depends on the unimpaired possession of civil and religious liberty', that enabled her to write.[120] Her literary interests had never, she told her audience, as she had once told Hannah Lincoln and her husband, compromised her acceptably private character ('the historian has never laid aside the tenderness of the sex or the friend') but had rather enhanced the moral imperatives of feminine sensibility ('she has endeavoured on all occasions that the strictest veracity should govern her heart and the most exact impartiality be the guide

[118] Note, MOWP1, 19.   [119] MOW, *History*, 98.   [120] Ibid., p. xlii.

of her pen').[121] Warren described her authorial position and persona as conventionally domestic, private, and sentimental. And yet, she suggested, this feminine privacy enabled that independence so necessary to the character of a historian. As a woman, Warren could claim to be dissociated from party or faction: 'I can say with an ingenious writer, "I have used my pen with the liberty of one, who neither hopes nor fears, nor has any interest in the success or failure of any party." '[122] She also suggested that, while men were too preoccupied to gain an appropriate perspective on the public good, her leisured retirement enabled her to see and write about the bigger picture: 'At a period when every manly arm was occupied and every trait of talent or activity engaged, either in the cabinet or the field . . . I have been induced to improve the leisure providence had lent.'[123] While she was 'connected by nature, friendship and every social tie with many of the first patriots', she did not participate in a 'busy and active' public life.[124] Yet precisely because of her leisured exclusion from the public sphere and her personal 'habit . . . of epistolary intercourse' with well-placed individuals, she was, she argued, ideally situated as a public historian.[125] In this 'Address to the Inhabitants of the United States', with which her history was prefaced, an assured and self-confident Warren was in effect claiming that an elite, literate woman defined by her private character, her sentimental attachments, and her patriotic feeling had the best qualifications to write the public story of revolutionary America.

As they wrote of themselves as 'patriots' or 'politicians' resisting the encroachments of corrupt, imperial Britain, the epistolary culture of revolutionary New England offered women, as Jane Rendall puts it, 'a way of uniting public and private responsibilities'.[126] Mercy Warren might well have been unusual in that she turned her talent for the epistolary into literary flair in other related genres, but her letter writing—covering such a range of social, political, and personal subjects and serving to shore up and share what she saw as a traditional New England pride in patriotic feeling—was, among the women of her rank, quite commonplace. The letters of earlier elite colonial women used female friendship as the medium for the exchange of cultural and political opinion, as Laurie

[121] MOW, *History*, p. xliii.   [122] Ibid., p. xlii.   [123] Ibid., p. xli.
[124] Ibid.   [125] Ibid.   [126] Rendall, *The Origins of Modern Feminism*, 34.

Crumpacker and Carol Karlsen have shown in their excellent edition of the journal Esther Burr wrote for Sarah Prince-Gill.[127] Letters enabled Hannah Winthrop, Abigail Adams, Ellen Lothrop, Mercy Warren, and the other women of their circle to think of themselves as such a community of 'friends of liberty': a group of republicans with a particular political purchase on the affairs of their region and nation. They saw a distinctive continuity between their private identities and the political characters they claimed as patriotic New Englanders. As women of old families, as sentimental friends, as retired yet sociable beings, and as the partners of virtuous public men, they felt that they defined the moral heart of republican Massachusetts. The epistolary culture through which they celebrated their femininity and their patriotism was clearly private in its association with domesticity, filial propinquity, and feeling, but, as it served as a forum for political debate and the discussion of difference, as it enabled the circulation of supportive information which bolstered feelings of resistance, and as it connected and consolidated dispersed wartime communities, it shared some of the most familiarly idealized aspects of the public sphere as well.

[127] *The Journal of Esther Edwards Burr, 1754–1757*, ed. Laurie Crumpacker and Carol F. Karlsen (New Haven: Yale University Press, 1984). See my discussion of Prince-Gill's and Macaulay's correspondence in this book's Introduction and Chapter 1. See also Alfred Young on the associational culture of congregationalism and how this encouraged political community among women, Alfred F. Young, 'The Women of Boston'. In an otherwise suggestive article Young, however, argues that there was little 'publicly' significant about women's (and particularly Warren's) 'private' epistolary networks and asserts that Warren 'had hardly a word to say about women' in her *History*.

5

Free and Easy:
Boston's Fashionable Dilemma

> As droll a sight as, 'ere you see
> Arose about the Sans Souci...
>
> ('Celia', *Massachusetts Centinel*, 26 January 1785)

In the early months of 1785, Catharine Macaulay and Mercy Otis Warren had a misunderstanding. Macaulay, Britain's celebrated republican historian, visiting New England to much acclaim after the close of the war, had looked forward to meeting Mercy Otis Warren. Warren, a writer well known in Boston for her patriotic plays and prolific correspondence, was equally keen to develop Macaulay's friendship. Their disagreement was difficult for both women; played out in the public eye, it became the focus of satire and conjecture. Yet, prior to this, Macaulay and Warren had corresponded with one another for over a decade. Over the course of the war between Britain and America they had maintained a close epistolary friendship based on the similarity of their political principles and their views of their own roles as women. While Warren admired Macaulay's famous *History of England* and her support of the American cause, Macaulay was clearly impressed with both Warren's writing and her republicanism. 'I suppose', wrote their mutual friend John Adams, on hearing the two women had finally met, 'that Mrs Macaulay and Mrs Warren have compared notes on the history of liberty on both sides the Atlantic'.[1] Warren and Macaulay had indeed enjoyed each other's company in the closing weeks of 1784.

[1] JA to JW, 26 Apr. 1785, WAP.

'Without exaggeration of character,' Warren had written to her son Winslow, 'she has an uncommon share of merit both as a writer and a companion'.[2] What then might have caused a breach in their friendship only two months later? The problem was neither the assumed impropriety of Macaulay's marriage to a man more than twenty years her junior, nor Warren's evident dislike of Macaulay's hosts, John Hancock and his political associates, though both were well known and both in post-war Boston perhaps equally controversial. Warren and Macaulay disagreed over the *Sans Souci* club, one of the town's principal amusements during the long winter of 1784–5.

The *Sans Souci* was the name associated with the tea assembly where it was proposed Boston's fashionable elite might meet every other week for an evening of cards, music, and dancing. The intention was to establish Boston as a centre of American metropolitan sociability. At the *Sans Souci*, the polite and aspirant of both sexes would be able to display their urbanity and taste, their accomplishments and conversation, gambling at one of the club's forty tables if they chose for no more than a small, agreed stake. Nothing quite comparable had existed in Boston before. As one writer in the *Massachusetts Centinel* put it, the *Sans Souci* was meant to be 'very useful in polishing the manners and promoting harmony and social intercourse in the town'.[3] While many Bostonians agreed, and welcomed the *Sans Souci* for the opportunities of sociable commerce it afforded, for others the very idea of a mix-sexed assembly at which gambling was legitimate and even encouraged created immense anxiety. Instead of indicating Boston's ascent to a new era of civilization and refinement, the assembly was thought by many to herald the town's cultural and moral decline. The *Sans Souci* caused a noisy hullabaloo, becoming, as it were by chance, the focus of some key political and economic debates which preoccupied Boston in its difficult post-war years. Its teacups rattled beyond the hall where they received their fortnightly outing. They rattled loudly in the pages of Boston's newspapers throughout January and February 1785. They rattled through Massachusetts and beyond, precipitating public controversy, an attack on a printer, and the publication of a notorious play. And they rattled political allegiances and personal

[2] MOW to WW, Dec. 1784, MOWP1.
[3] 'Son of Candour', *Massachusetts Centinel*, 26 Jan. 1785.

friendships, perhaps most notably that of Catharine Macaulay and Mercy Otis Warren.

The *Sans Souci* was the subject of an article by Charles Warren in 1927.[4] Since then, it has played a familiar anecdotal role in many of the now-canonical histories of the revolution and early republic.[5] Described by Gordon Wood as 'inexplicable and indeed ludicrous' to the modern eye, the nature and strength of the opposition the *Sans Souci* aroused have been dismissed as a symptom of old republicanism's near obsolescence in 1785, a pseudo-puritanical absurdity, soon to be wiped out by the Federalist era.[6] Why then revisit its story now? The *Sans Souci* remains an intriguing controversy, I think, because of what it suggests about the representation of gender, republicanism, and the relationship between both. More specifically, it is interesting to me because of the questions it raises about the ways in which women's political and intellectual identities were regarded in early republican America. The values which the *Sans Souci*'s supporters extolled as polishing, or its detractors condemned as corrupting, were by both sides described in gendered terms, and the assembly was thought of, from opposite perspectives, as a particularly feminine space. Integral to the debate over the *Sans Souci*'s rectitude or reprehensibility was a struggle over the meanings of gender. This struggle is important because it reveals some of the ways in which late-eighteenth-century women might understand or describe their relationship to cultures of leisure and pleasure, of print and politics. It is also important because it suggests how central the representation of learned, republican women—women like Catharine Macaulay and Mercy Otis Warren— were to Boston's post-war self-understanding. In what follows I trace the story of these two women's involvement with the *Sans Souci*: the story of Boston's fashionable dilemma.

I Femininity and Commerce

In November 1784 Mercy Otis Warren described Massachusetts' political and economic condition to her son Winslow, then in Lisbon.

---

[4] Charles Warren, 'Samuel Adams and the Sans Souci Club in 1785', *Proceedings of the Massachusetts Historical Society*, 60 (1927), 318–44.

[5] See, for example, Kenneth Silverman, *A Cultural History of the American Revolution* (New York: Thomas Crowell, 1976), 509–10.

[6] Gordon Wood, *The Creation of the American Republic, 1776–87* (Chapel Hill, NC: University of North Carolina Press, 1969), 422.

'Local vices are growing rampant among us', she wrote, 'and may... prove fatal to the honor and happiness of America'. Warren saw the nation's moral character being eroded by the twin evils of a public sphere dominated by a man she regarded as a corrupt demagogue and a developing, but poorly regulated and poorly defined, commercial culture. The internal politics of Massachusetts had become a mere 'burlesque on government' led by some 'very dangerous and insignificant characters'. 'Depend upon it,' she remarked gloomily to Winslow, 'nothing less than an American monarchy is in contemplation'.[7] Winslow would have known that, in her royalist burlesque, his mother was complaining of John Hancock, the State's then governor.

For Warren, a republican ever obdurate in her sense of political enmity, Hancock was personally responsible not only for the political persecution and exclusion of her family and friends from office, but for the steady corruption of Massachusetts' public life.[8] Prosperous, popular, and incredibly flamboyant, Hancock had a finger in every political and commercial pie in the state. By the 1780s he effectively controlled a network of influence and dependence that drew in wealthy Essex merchant and struggling Worcester farmer alike. To Warren and her republican circle, Hancock's toleration of the idea of an hereditary principle in office and his toadying to the wealthy Tory class (implicitly including former loyalists with claims on confiscated property) made him seem another Thomas Hutchinson. Moreover, his canny sense of his own public status and successful management by his associates enabled him, on more than one occasion, to maintain his popularity by sitting on the political fence, 'a man hid in holes and corners', as Warren's by no means objective husband James had put it.[9] No less a fault than Hancock's politics of capitulation and compromise to Warren was his personal style, which she thought of in terms of a pseudo-aristocratic prodigality and excess. Comparing him on more than one occasion to Caesar, who 'meditated triumphs over the citizens and

[7] MOW to WW, 10 Nov. 1784, MOWP1.
[8] On the Hancock/Warren factions, their opposition, and the political climate of 1780s Massachusetts generally, see, among others: James Patterson, *Political Parties in Revolutionary Massachusetts* (Madison: Wisconsin University Press, 1973); Van-Beck Hall, *Politics Without Parties: Massachusetts 1780–91* (Pittsburgh: University of Pittsburgh Press, 1972); William M. Fowler, *The Baron of Beacon Hill: A Biography of John Hancock* (Boston: Houghton Mifflin & Co., 1980).
[9] JW to Samuel Adams, 18 Aug. 1778, WAP.

trampled on the liberties of Rome' while 'scatter[ing] largesses among the people', Hancock, with his showy hospitality and calculated displays of his own benevolence, seemed the antithesis of that New England simplicity which Warren celebrated in her poems and letters.[10]

By 1784 the governor's colourful personality seemed to Warren to have tinged the whole state as the urban populace mirrored what she saw as his characteristic prioritizing of style over substance. From her house on Milton Hill, she looked down on a town she thought caught in a web of desire and gratification—a culture of appearances that disguised what was rotten at its core. As Boston's fashionable elite seemed dazzled by the new commodities that peace had brought from British markets, so they appeared in equal measure blind to the real economic problems with which the state was beset: a dearth of capital; the loss of value on land; heavy taxes; and consequent increasing debt and bankruptcy—difficulties which were affecting metropolitan merchants alongside western farmers. 'The value of real estates depreciates fast,' Warren wrote to Winslow:

> owing to the amazing scarcity of cash, which is continually transmitted to foreign markets for innumerable superfluities, nor will the influx be suspended, so long as there is any thing among us that will support the present ideas of elegance that have universally taken hold of a people whose interest is oeconomy and whose honor would be to establish a character of their own independent of the fashions or taste of foreign nations.[11]

Warren expressed her opposition to the continued British control of American commerce and by extension its character through what was becoming, in post-war Massachusetts, a familiar language of economic contamination. America's markets were dominated by British imports and its goods exported in British bottoms, and she regarded this as a clear compromise of the idea of independence. For a writer whose republicanism was built on a series of marked contrasts—American rationality

---

[10] This description of Hancock first appears in a letter to Warren's friend Hannah Winthrop, 29 May 1778, WWC. It appears in a more unequivocal and stronger form in a letter from Warren to Elbridge Gerry, 6 June 1783. C. Harvey Gardiner, *A Study in Dissent: The Warren–Gerry Correspondence, 1776–92* (Carbondale and Edwardsville: Southern Illinois University Press, 1968), 161. As I suggested in Chapter 4, Warren honed and reworked descriptions she was fond of in her letters and other writings over a number of years. She was evidently fond of this description of Hancock.
[11] MOW to WW, 10 Nov. 1784, MOWP1.

against British fantasy; national unity against cosmopolitan dissipation, and so on—Massachusetts' post-war political and economic difficulties confirmed her worst suspicion: that the conflict with Britain had 'caused a greater revolution in manners than in politics in a country long distinguished for purity of morals'.[12]

Warren was by no means alone in her indictment of Massachusetts' 'revolution in manners', nor indeed in her sense of its causes. Throughout 1784 and 1785, Boston's papers were filled with a noisy debate on the moral implications of the economic crisis. Writer after writer expressed concern that the character of the state itself was being steadily destroyed by debt, depreciation, lack of specie, and a disturbing prodigality, seen as the infectious disease of old England (or very occasionally France, depending on the writer's perspective). Perhaps expressing disquiet at Hancock's failure to intervene in the crisis effectively, one writer in the *Gentleman and Lady's Town and Country Magazine* wrote in dark terms of how the vices of showy wealth and luxury provided a 'certain index' to the 'intentions of those who preside at the helm of affairs'. The people must be watchful, the author warned, that their leaders did not become 'corruptors' spreading 'the love of luxury, effeminacy... and excit[ing] the rich to engage in ruinous expenses'.[13] Political corruption was linked for this writer to an idea of the effeminization of culture.

For other commentators, Massachusetts' economic problems might be traced directly to British attempts to regain control in America. 'Abstain from British luxury, extravagance and dissipation *or you are an* UNDONE PEOPLE!' exclaimed 'a farmer' in the *Boston Gazette*.[14] For 'an unshaken Whig' in the *Independent Chronicle*, the return of loyalists from Halifax and associated claims on confiscated estates, together with the influx of British commodities and factors and consequent scarcity of specie, were all part of the same obvious imperial design:

By the return of these outlaws and their connections from England... every species of luxury is introduced here, and every kind of gew-gaw imported into this town with a view to drain us of our circulating medium... shall we be so infatuated as to continue our commercial intercourse with that nation who

[12] MOW to WW, 28 Apr. 1783, MOWP1.
[13] *Gentleman and Lady's Town and Country Magazine* (Sept. 1784), 182.
[14] 'A farmer', *Boston Gazette and Country Journal*, 31 Jan. 1785.

endeavoured to enslave us by the sword, but not succeeding in those measures, is now endeavouring to do it by imperceptible, but more sure means?[15]

These writers express their opposition to Massachusetts' post-war commodity culture through a language of corrupt desire that seems commercial and sexual in equal measure. Their anxious accounts of possession and depletion, deluded infatuation, and America's undoing, resonate here with powerful and familiar eighteenth-century ideas of political emasculation.[16] Britain seems a colonial temptress luring America into dangerous commercial and sexual encounters: inspiring desire, draining specie, and with it national substance in exchange for her gaudy commodities. America was in danger of being enslaved anew by its enthralled attachment to British *Luxuria*. These writers' sense of national difference and commercial identity is expressed in terms their audience would have recognized as clearly gendered.

Writing on the crisis as 'Candidus', Benjamin Austin attempted to regain rhetorical control of Massachusetts' economic value. While the populace neglected cultivation in favour of fashionable adornment, luxury was fast producing 'worms and caterpillars which will ever suck the richest produce of their land and labour',[17] Austin's Old-Whig arguments were juxtaposed in the *Independent Chronicle* with an advertisement from the merchant Luke Baker, whose litany of British commodities, newly imported on *The Mermaid*, possessed a persuasive rhetoric all their own:

Superfine English broadcloths, variety modes; sattins, great variety; black and white gauzes...ladies leather gloves, hats and bonnets...silk quilted petticoats...ladies stays with busks and braces; gown trimmings, various colours...very elegant assortment of plain and needle-worked muslins of the newest taste.[18]

As a number of historians and critics have pointed out, the commodity culture of revolutionary and early republican America was understood by contemporaries, in a variety of ways, as particularly feminine or

---

[15] 'Annshaken Whig', *Independent Chronicle*, 21 Oct. 1784.
[16] See Jay Fliegelman, *Prodigals and Pilgrims: The American Revolution against Patriarchal Authority* (Cambridge: Cambridge University Press, 1982), and my discussion in Chapter 3.
[17] 'Candidus' (Benjamin Austin), *Boston Independent Chronicle and Universal Advertiser*, 27 May 1784.   [18] *Independent Chronicle*, 27 May 1784.

feminizing.[19] For political commentators in Massachusetts, gender played a key role in shaping the moral debate on the economy. It was frequently through notions of gender that writers assigned value to their economic and political views or expressed their assent or opposition to an increasingly complex and contentious culture of exchange. The poems that Mercy Otis Warren wrote before and during the war with Britain exemplify this shifting relationship between gender, commerce, and national morality. Warren's poems are full of the symbolic figures of women who are seen to maintain or damage, to purify or corrupt, America's moral/economic identity. For example, in 'To the Honorable J. Winthrop esq', a playful echo of Pope which she wrote for the 1774 non-importation agreement, Warren contrasts the anglophile Clara, who is willing to exchange American national identity for fashionable British commodities ('Though for the purchase paid her father's blood'), with the patriotic figures of 'Cornelia and Arria', who maintain national character in their refusal to consume.[20] These patriotic women, in their combination of classical restraint and modern sentiment, are seen to enact the commercial regulation of American morality.[21] In a rather different vein in 'A Political Reverie', Warren expresses a positive idea of the freedom of trade through the figure of a carefree youthful female, oppressed and distressed by commercial monopolies: 'Round all the globe she sails from sea to sea | And smiles and prospers only when she's free.'[22] But perhaps Warren's most forceful characterizations of gender and commerce arise from her frequent contrasts between the figure of Britain as a sort of ageing society beauty 'wrap't in refinements both absurd and vile' and a vaguely pastoral or picturesque image of America as a wasted, wounded, or grieving woman who rejects commercial culture and maintains national simplicity.[23] By late 1784

[19] See, for example, T. H. Breen, 'Narrative of Commercial Life: Consumption, Ideology and Community on the Eve of the American Revolution', *William and Mary Quarterly*, 50 (1993), 471–501.
[20] MOW, 'To the Honourable J. Winthrop esq.' [1774], in *Poems Dramatic and Miscellaneous* (Boston: I. Thomas and E. T. Andrews, 1790), 208–12, at 211.
[21] For further discussion of ways in which femininity might be represented as commerce's moral regulator in the late eighteenth century, see my 'A Moral Purchase: Women, Commerce, Abolition', in Elizabeth Eger *et al.* (eds.), *Women, Writing and the Public Sphere 1700–1930* (Cambridge: Cambridge University Press, 2000).
[22] MOW, 'A Political Reverie' [1774], in *Poems*, 188–94, at 194.
[23] See MOW, 'Simplicity' [1779], in *Poems*, 229–34, at 233. See also 'The Genius of America Weeping the Absurd Follies of the Day' [1778], in *Poems*, 246–52.

it seemed to republicans like Warren that this figure of American simplicity was beginning to dress and look dangerously like her corrupt British counterpart. By a host of anxious republican commentators, Boston's new fashionable culture was opposed through recourse to ideas of *Luxuria*—to specifically feminine or feminizing forms of corruption.

So in Boston in 1784, femininity and commerce were curiously imbricated. It was not simply that women did the shopping, or that the majority of the goods advertised addressed themselves to the tastes of women presumed to be aspirant and fashionable, but that, for a culture which remained characteristically republican, luxury, consumption, and commerce itself held inescapable feminine connotations. Thus when Mercy Otis Warren complained to Winslow of how 'the trivial article of *gauze*, imported in quantity, is now considered a necessary article of life among the lower class of females', she not only expressed her disquiet at the confusion of class distinctions fashion seemed to engender, but captured a traditional republican sense of the insubstantiality of consumer culture.[24] If republican commentators described the loss of specie as a process of emasculation, or condemned the women of Britain or New York for their fashionable excess, they were drawing on a discourse in which the idea of *Luxuria* was associated with figures of feminine desire and contamination. Behind the complaints of the deleterious moral effects of British gew-gaws and fashionable consumption was a set of gendered values in which femininity and corruption seemed inevitably linked.

In Massachusetts in 1784 anti-British feeling had increased with an influx of merchants, factors, and commodities, and there was a sense of republican unease surrounding Hancock's style of leadership and his apparent inability to intervene in the economic crisis. It was into this charged atmosphere that Catharine Macaulay, 'the celebrated female historian'—a republican author and notoriously fashionable woman—arrived in July, on *The Rosamond*, after nine difficult weeks at sea.[25]

I discuss Warren's representations of wounded or grieving women at greater length in Chapter 6.

[24] MOW to WW, 10 Nov. 1784, MOWP1.
[25] *Independent Chronicle*, 22 July 1784.

II Learning and the Literary Marketplace

Catharine Macaulay's public character was less the focus of celebration than derision in her native Britain by 1784. As I explored in Chapter 3, during the conflict and war with America, she opposed government policy in ways that, to the conservative and nationalistic sectors of the British populace, marked her out as a dangerous radical. Moreover, her marriage in 1778 to the young William Graham—the brother of a notorious quack doctor and a man almost half her age—caused a scandal that rocked fashionable London. In Britain her republicanism had come to be regarded as the signature of an excess both sexual and political.

How would post-war New England receive Macaulay, the writer after whom children in Providence had been named and whom Boston had fêted and sent packages of intelligence during the war?[26] Abigail Adams, for instance, was clearly shocked by Macaulay's marriage, and, following her arrival, women like Sarah Vaughan did not wish to meet her on account of William Graham, 'a living monument to her want of common understanding and delicacy'.[27] 'While her distinguished talents exhibit the sex at least on a footing of equality,' Mercy Otis Warren wrote after meeting her, 'their delicacy is hurt by her improper connection'.[28] Yet Macaulay's husband was, Warren said, 'a man of understanding and virtue'.[29] Warren repeatedly defended Macaulay's marriage, to John Adams, her sons, and other correspondents that year, in ways which suggest how problematic an issue it may have been.[30] Macaulay was also well known as a woman of some high style. In the British prints in which she was frequently satirized, she appears coiffed with the enormous wigs for which the late 1770s were notorious.[31] 'She paints', wrote Sarah Vaughan to Catherine Livingston, 'and wears plumpers in her cheeks to hide the hollowness toothlessness

---

[26] See *Newport Mercury*, 26 Jan. 1772, for the announcement that a newborn baby had been named after Macaulay.
[27] See, for example, AA to John Thaxter Braintree, 15 Feb. 1778, and AA to MOW, 10 May 1785, in *AFC*, ii. 391, vi. 140. Sarah Vaughan to Catherine Livingston, 20–26 May 1785, Ridley Papers, MHS.   [28] MOW to WW, Dec. 1784, MOWP1.
[29] MOW to WW, Dec. 1784, MOWP1.
[30] See, for example, MOW to JA, 27 Apr. 1785, MOWP1.
[31] See, for example, Matthew Darly's satiric representation of Macaulay, *A Speedy & Effectual Preparation for the Next World* (1778) (Fig. 25), in which she sports an outlandish coiffure. I discuss this print in Chapter 3.

gives'.[32] By Vaughan and others, Macaulay's fashionability and her sexuality were thought of in terms of physical deviance.

While in private some women may have regarded Macaulay's marriage as a serious impropriety, and her fashionable status as a compromise of her republican character, publicly at least she was enthusiastically received. Apart from the odd bogus anecdote in the papers, Boston seemed to welcome her visit warmly. For example, when a light-hearted yarn concerning Macaulay's confusion encountering a sequence of male visitors each disguised as Lord Chatham appeared in the *Independent Leger*, an indignant reply was immediately printed in the *Independent Chronicle*. Macaulay was a 'celebrated lady... whose literary abilities have made her name respectable throughout Europe, and whose delicacy and politeness since her arrival in this state have justly entitled her to the highest respect of its citizens'.[33] It was Macaulay's republicanism and her support of the principles of the revolution—what her contemporaries understood and described as her masculine political character—which had secured her fame in Massachusetts in the 1760s and 1770s.[34] By 1784, however, it was her delicacy and politeness—the specifically feminine qualities of a woman of learning—that marked her out for celebration in the Boston press.

In the *Gentleman and Lady's Town and Country Magazine*, shortly following Macaulay's arrival in Boston, the following stanzas 'inscribed to a celebrated female historian' appeared:

> See Learning's sun, with gradual, slow decay,
> Declining westward, leave Britannia's isle,
> To beam on Columbia's realms unfading day,
> And bless her sons with wisdom's seraph smile.
> Say, is it true? Or floats some empty shade
> Or light fantastic form before my eyes;

---

[32] Sarah Vaughan to Catherine Livingston, 20–26 May 1785, Ridley Papers, MHS.
[33] *Independent Chronicle*, 28 Oct.1784. See *Independent Leger*, 11 Oct. 1784, for the original anecdote.
[34] In England, Macaulay's role as public historian was understood as a particularly masculine one, and her writing was frequently praised for its masculine qualities—in Macaulay's own words, for 'that more than ordinary energy' that was understood 'to render a female mind...masculine' (CM, *Letters on Education with Observations on Religious and Metaphysical Subjects* (London: E. & C. Dilly, 1790), 204–5). Among many examples, see *Gentleman's Magazine*, 36 (1766), 439, for an account of Macaulay's 'masculine' republican prose. These issues are discussed at greater length in Chapter 1.

It cannot be, for Pallas, heavenly maid,
Or brighter GRAHAM gilds Columbia's skies.
She comes, she comes, see pensive Britain weep,
Her arts, her arms, adorn this infant clime
And GRAHAM, past the limits of her deep,
Reigns nature's equal on the throne of time.[35]

In this adaptation of Berkley's familiar narrative of Empire's westward course, the global transfer of cultural precedence is represented by the idea of enlightened knowledge or learning, which in turn is embodied by Macaulay/Graham in her journey from Britain to Boston.[36] Though the verse associates her with arms and Pallas, and while she might certainly be described here as an imperial figure, Macaulay/Graham is hardly masculine or republican, all floating, bright, and 'light fantastic'. 'Gilding' Columbia's skies, the function of her learning here seems perhaps purely decorative. Rather than being associated with the politics she was renowned for espousing, she here represents Boston's cultural promise of politeness and refinement as the ornamental figure of the woman of learning.

These representations of Macaulay as a woman of learning should be viewed alongside contemporary developments in Massachusetts' literary marketplace. In 1783 and 1784, Boston's first specifically literary periodicals, the *Gentleman and Lady's Town and Country Magazine* and the *Boston Magazine* were established.[37] These new periodicals addressed themselves to a mix-sexed audience—readers who were described as possessing sensibility and republican virtue in equal measure—and actively solicited the contributions of women writers.[38]

---

[35] [Unattrib.], 'Stanzas Inscribed to a Celebrated Female Historian', *Gentleman and Lady's Town and Country Magazine* (July 1784), 120. This verse appeared immediately after Macaulay's arrival in Boston.

[36] I refer to Berkley's famous *On the Planting of the Arts and Sciences in America* (1726).

[37] Many of the same group of men who established the *Boston Magazine* later went on to form the Massachusetts Historical Society in 1790. See Samuel A. Green, 'The Boston Magazine', *Proceedings of the Massachusetts Historical Society* (May 1904), 326–30.

[38] On the new magazines of the early republic, see Caroll Smith-Rosenberg, 'Dis-Covering the Subject of the "Great Constitutional Discussion", 1786–1789', *Journal of American History* (1992), 841–73; David Lundberg and Henry F. May, 'The Enlightened Reader in America', *American Quarterly*, 28 (1976), 262–93; Silverman, *A Cultural History of the American Revolution*, David Paul Nord, 'A Republican Literature: A Study of Magazine Reading and Readers in Late Eighteenth-Century New York', *American Quarterly*, 40 (1988), 442–64.

An article in February 1784 urged the *Boston Magazine*'s 'female subscribers to take up their pens' and 'urge[d] the fair sex to become candidates for literary fame'. The writing of the women of Boston and surrounding towns was characterized, the author claimed, by its 'delicacy' and 'easy flow of expression' and 'some of their letters would be sufficient to establish the reputation of the magazine'.[39] A few issues later, a letter from Mercy Otis Warren to her son Winslow, in which she produced a damning critique of Lord Chesterfield, was published in the *Boston Magazine*.

Warren's letter was already well known in Boston and was the piece upon which her post-war literary reputation was clearly established.[40] She began by criticizing Chesterfield's thoroughly unrepublican failure to defer gratification: 'When he sacrifices truth to convenience, probity to pleasure, virtue to the graces, generosity, gratitude and all the finer feelings of the soul to a momentary gratification, we cannot but pity the man.'[41] But Warren's major objection to Chesterfield's *Letters* was the attitude to women they displayed. Criticizing his account of gallantry and seduction as a remnant of the antiquated libertinism of the European old regime, Warren wrote that more equal relations between the sexes suggested a more modern ideal of polite virtue. 'I think his trite, hackneyed, vulgar observations are as much beneath the resentment of a woman of education and reflection as derogatory to the candour and generosity of a writer of his acknowledged abilities ... I ever', she concluded, 'considered human nature as the same in both sexes.'[42] Warren's letter on Chesterfield was read as a spirited defence of American education, culture, and honest sociability. In its warm reception she was praised for her 'elegance of stile ... solidity of judgement ... discernment and penetration'. She was 'a lady born and educated in this State', and the Massachusetts press clearly took pride in her learning.[43]

---

[39] *Boston Magazine*, (Feb. 1784), 52.

[40] The letter was originally written in 1779 and first printed in the *Independent Chronicle*, 18 Jan. 1781. It appeared in the June 1784 issue of the *Boston Magazine*. For further discussion of the letter's publication history, see Edmund M. Hayes's useful article, 'Mercy Otis Warren versus Lord Chesterfield, 1779', *William and Mary Quarterly*, 40 (1983), 616–21.

[41] MOW, 'A Letter from an American Lady to her Son in Europe', *Boston Magazine* (June 1784), 326.   [42] Ibid. 327.

[43] *Independent Chronicle*, 18 Jan. 1781.

While other American women were encouraged to contribute to the *Boston Magazine*, it also reprinted the work of British women in significant numbers. Many issues, for example, included a poem by Anna Laetitia Barbauld (who had many New England friends and was renowned on both sides of the Atlantic for her literary character).[44] The magazine also published Hannah More's 'Sensibility' and her 'Bas Bleu', in which she celebrated the sociable virtues of the Bluestocking Circle, and reprinted John Duncombe's 'Feminiad', a poetic catalogue of Britain's learned women from the sixteenth century through to the middle decades of the eighteenth century.[45] A number of essays on female education appeared, and the editors sought out and published a wide variety of pieces on the treatment of women in different ages and cultures.[46] Perhaps most notably on this score, the magazine reprinted, over a series of several issues in 1784 and 1785, extracts from William Alexander's *History of Women from the Earliest Antiquity to the Present Time*.[47] Alexander's text provided the clearest articulation of the by then familiar argument of a number of works of the Scottish and European Enlightenment:

The rank ... and condition, in which we find women in any country, mark out to us with the greatest precision, the exact point in the scale of civil society to which the people of such country have arrived; and were their history entirely silent on every other subject, and only mentioned the manner in which they

---

[44] For example, the *Boston Magazine* printed Barbauld's 'Mouse's Petition' in Jan. 1784, 'The Invitation' in May 1784, and her 'Ode to Spring' in Apr. 1785. Barbauld's New England friends included the members of the Vaughan family. She had written a short poem commemorating the virtues of Sarah Hallowell-Vaughan (a relative of the Sarah Vaughan who had so disliked Macaulay). The poem is reproduced in *The Poems of Anna Laetitia Barbauld*, ed. William McCarthy and Elizabeth Kraft (Athensga, Ga.: University of Georgia Press, 1994).

[45] Hannah More's '*Sensibility*' was published in the *Boston Magazine* in May 1785. John Duncombe's '*Feminiad*' was printed in stages in the *Boston Magazine in* Oct. Nov., and Dec. 1785.

[46] Among numerous examples in the *Boston Magazine*, see: 'On the Advantages Derived from the Society of Virtuous Women' (Aug. 1785), 297–301; 'Female Characters' (Oct. 1785), 363–6; 'Desultory Observations on the Education and Manners of the Female Sex' (Feb. 1786), 54–6; the unattributed 'Song to Columbia' in the Dec. 1784 issue, in which women of genius are celebrated as emblematic of American progress: 'no less shall thy fair ones to glory ascend | And Genius and Beauty in Harmony Blend.'

[47] The *Boston Magazine* began to print extracts from Alexander's *History of Women* in Dec. 1784 and completed the serialization in July 1785.

treated their women, we would, from thence, be enabled to form a tolerable judgement of the barbarity or culture of their manners.[48]

The *Boston Magazine*'s key aim—as issue after issue reminded its readers—was to position the town and, by extension, the nation firmly on the cultural map. 'At no time did literature make so rapid progress in America,' exclaimed one writer, echoing the narrative of learning's westward course; 'the torch of learning... now shines with lustre in this western hemisphere'.[49] As the torch of learning was said to move westward, literary periodicals and publications like them could be read as indicative of America's post-war civilized pre-eminence: 'how delightful the idea that America once immersed in barbarity is now distinguished by literary characters who will stand conspicuous in the list of fame,' the magazine enthused early in 1785.[50] Thus the magazines' concern with women's education and writing and their celebration of female intellectuals—represented by, for example, the figure of Mercy Otis Warren as an instance of home-grown literary talent, or that of Catharine Macaulay bearing learning from Britain to America—was quite clearly bound up with its larger project of the display of Boston's new cultural precedence and civility. As one writer in the Boston Magazine put it enthusiastically, the encouragement of women's education and the presence of women of learning in America brought 'almost endless advantages' rendering the nation 'a civilized paradise'.[51] Through the figures of women of learning, then, seen as emblems and ornaments of its own liberality and refinement, Boston, in the terms it set out for itself in the pages of its new magazines, might boost its own cultural capital and hence its claims to an enlightened civility.[52]

---

[48] William Alexander, *The History of Women from the Earliest Antiquity to the Present Time* [1779], ed. Jane Rendall, 2 vols. (Bristol: Thoemmes Press, 1995), i. 151. See Rendall's introduction for a useful discussion of the publication and reception of Alexander's work. [49] *Boston Magazine* (Jan. 1785), 38.
[50] *Boston Magazine* (Mar. 1785), 134.
[51] 'Anaximander', *Boston Magazine* (June 1785), 213–14.
[52] Another intriguing example is the *Boston Magazine*'s celebration of Mary Wilkes-Hayley (the sister of John Wilkes, the widow of one of the London Opposition's most prominent American radicals, and, of course, a good friend of Macaulay. Hayley, who had travelled to America to claim her husband's estate on Rhode Island (a situation that seemed hardly likely to endear her to New England's inhabitants), was praised for her 'liberal and beneficent spirit' as a woman of taste and learning, and her patronage of American artists. Hayley apparently later owned the Hutchinson estate at Milton where Mercy Warren then lived. See *Boston Magazine* (Feb. 1785), 64.

So, when Catharine Macaulay arrived in Boston in 1784, she found herself in a town whose cultural sense of itself might be said to be partly defined by two competing contemporary accounts of femininity. The first, integral to the republican critique of the economic crisis, associated femininity with consumption and fashionable display: with the luxurious craze for British commodities that drained specie from the populace and, with it, virtue from the state. This account linked femininity to ideas of excess, decline, and contamination. The other account, as expressed in Boston's new literary periodicals, described women's learning and their liberal education as central to the town's post-war cultural development and linked femininity to notions of progress, politeness, and civilized restraint. It was the fault-line between these two accounts that the debate on the *Sans Souci* opened up, threatening in turn the friendship of Catharine Macaulay and Mercy Otis Warren.

III Sans Souci, or, Free and Easy

News of the *Sans Souci* furore spread fast through New England in the early months of 1785. Writing from Newburyport, Warren's son George asked his mother what it was all about. Warren replied that the assembly was 'a ridiculous institution for such a country as this', which revealed how far Boston had gone in the 'contagion of fashionable amusement'. 'There is no stemming the tide,' she wrote resignedly; 'passion is stronger than the winds and more likely to overleap the foundations of reason than is the ocean to break over the mounds of nature'.[53] Letters had already begun to appear in the Boston press protesting the ways in which the town's fashionable elite found their entertainment: 'our mushroom gentry in conjunction with those from the other side of the Atlantic, introducing every species of foreign luxury', and disturbing the peace of the town 'rattling through our paved streets' in carriages after midnight.[54] Echoing Warren's feeling that in the *Sans Souci* Boston had lost its senses, 'Observer' (identified by contemporaries as Samuel Adams) wrote in the *Massachusetts Centinel*:

If there ever was a period wherein reason was bewildered and stupefied by dissipation and extravagance, it is surely the present. Did ever effeminacy with

---

[53] MOW to GW, 7 Mar. 1785, MOWP1.
[54] *Boston Gazette and Country Journal*, 24 Jan. 1785.

her languid train receive a greater welcome in society than at this day? New amusements are invented—new dissipations are introduced to lull and enervate those minds already too much softened, poisoned and contaminated by idle pleasures and foolish gratifications. We are exchanging prudence, virtue and oeconomy for those glaring spectres, luxury, prodigality and profligacy. We are prostituting all our glory as a people for new modes of pleasure, ruinous in their expenses, injurious to virtue, and totally detrimental to the well being of society.[55]

This repellent culture of novelty and dissipation was summed up for Adams in 'an assembly so totally repugnant to virtue as in its name, *Sans Souci, or, Free and Easy*'. Adams's contrast between a society of pleasurable expenditure and one of hardy thrift is quite clearly gendered. The threat posed by luxury and the *Sans Souci* is here represented by opiate figures of feminine desire, softening virtue and virility through seduction. In the letters that followed in his support, these oppositions were repeated. The dangerous appeal of the *Sans Souci* and its evenings of mix-sexed consumption and speculation was expressed in a highly sexualized language of allurement, attraction, desire, and gratification, while the authentic character of Boston from which it represented a deviation was marked by a restrained masculine simplicity.[56]

The *Sans Souci*'s fashionable subscribers immediately struck back. Adams was effectively condemning the development of Bostonian politeness and civility. His suggestion that the *Sans Souci* encouraged licentiousness and dissipation was a direct slur on the characters of the 'virtuous and irreproachable countrywomen' who attended.[57] As another writer argued in the *Independent Chronicle*, in condemning the assembly Adams was insulting 'the inoffensive and amiable sex whom the most enlightened nations have invariably regarded with tenderness and respect'.[58] Supporters and detractors both agreed that the cultural effect of the *Sans Souci* was particularly effeminate or feminizing. But they were in strong disagreement over the meanings of those effects. The difference between the two positions in the *Sans Souci* debate came to be

[55] 'Observer' (Samuel Adams?), in *Massachusetts Centinel*, 15 Jan. 1785.
[56] See, for example, [unattrib.], *Boston Gazette and Country Journal*, 24 Jan. 1785; 'Cato', *Massachusetts Centinel*, 29 Jan. 1785; 'The Censor', *Massachusetts Centinel*, 2 Feb. 1785; *Boston Gazette and Country Journal*, 28 Feb. 1785.
[57] [Unattrib.], *Massachusetts Centinel*, 19 Jan. 1785.
[58] *Independent Chronicle*, 10 Feb. 1785.

expressed as the difference between two feminine-associated ideas: between fashionable corruption, on the one hand, and civilized politeness, on the other.

A writer in the *Independent Chronicle* put the case for the defence perhaps most clearly. The *Sans Souci* was Boston's 'only school of manners'. Assemblies and entertainments like it were evidence of the 'improved taste', and the 'ease and elegant sociability', of a culture as it began to advance to the height of civilization. Without such entertainments, a visitor from Europe would 'conclude us extremely distant from civilization and refinement'. The company of women in such assemblies and the social effect of femininity were absolutely central to this civilizing process. In fact, the author argued, it was 'the progress of feminine genius which ... hath led them [cultures] from solitude and barbarism to society and civility'. In an obvious echo of William Alexander, the writer asserted: 'As nations are rough or improved, the usages of women are tender or intolerant. The more ideas refine and as they acquire a taste for what is rational they become more enamoured of feminine society, induced not by personal charms but drawn by intellectual beauty.'[59] The treatment of women as rational rather than physical creatures brought further social benefits, this writer argued, through the effects of an educated, polite femininity. The culture of civilized sociability which the *Sans Souci* exemplified and the mere presence of women of learning in it indicated just how far Boston had come: 'Amidst a multitude of instances, to cite only Madame Dacier; the Lady Montagu, and is not the celebrated Mrs Macaulay resident among us?'[60] To this writer, the figure of Catharine Macaulay summed up the positive, feminizing effects of the *Sans Souci*. Macaulay *had* actually subscribed to and attended the assembly, and the fact that she had done so meant that its supporters might regard her as its mascot. Macaulay's public patronage of the *Sans Souci* could be seen to afford it a certain degree of cultural legitimacy. To the *Sans Souci*'s champions, Catharine Macaulay seemed to seal approval on their project of polite civility.

Yet Macaulay was a republican whose politics would seem to link her much more clearly with Mercy Otis Warren and Samuel Adams than with the proto-federalist defenders of the *Sans Souci*, like the then young

---

[59] *Independent Chronicle*, 10 Feb. 1785.
[60] 'One of a Number', *Massachusetts Centinel*, 19 Jan. 1785.

and fashionable Harrison Gray Otis.[61] After all, she was a writer who in the subscription proposal she had printed in the *American Herald* the previous November had suggested that the instructive example of her *History* might help America maintain the isolationist republican virtue the revolution had secured.[62] She had also, in her *Treatise on the Immutability of Moral Truth* (1783), produced a damning indictment of luxury and commercial desire in terms the *Sans Souci*'s detractors admired. Commerce, she wrote,

> naturally tends, by affording the means of extending the gratifications of sense beyond their proper bounds, to destroy that due balance which nature has formed between corporeal appetites and mental enjoyments: it furnishes means to delude the imagination, by an endless variety of fantastic objects of happiness ... commerce has acted with a prevalence and an universality superior to every other cause in the spreading the contagion of a flagitious luxury.[63]

Mercy Otis Warren had in fact cited these very remarks approvingly in the letters she wrote to Winslow Warren in November 1784, describing Massachusetts' moral/economic crisis.[64]

For Warren, Macaulay's patronage of the *Sans Souci* and her appropriation as symbolic patron by its supporters indicated her friend's tacit approval of Boston's new fashionable consumer culture in ways entirely at odds with her republican character. 'The name of Macaulay as a subscriber to this frivolous society casts a shade on her character,' Warren wrote to George, 'at least as inconsistent. I am sorry,' she

---

[61] Otis had in fact written a number of pro-*Sans Souci* pieces in the Boston press. His aunt, Mercy Otis Warren, was well aware of this, as she wrote to George: 'It is said HGO is the author of the pieces signed Sans Souci—very severe they are... He is a youth of genius and fire, and hope he will always have self command to temper wit with discretion' (MOW to GW, 7 Mar. 1785, MOWP1). See *Massachusetts Centinel*, 19 Jan. 1785, for an attack by 'Sans Souci' on 'Observer' (Samuel Adams?).

[62] Macaulay wrote confidently that her *History of England* 'enforce[d] sentiments of public and private virtue, which exalt the dignity of the human character, and which... if steadily preserved, must render the advantages obtained by the late revolution a growing and permanent felicity' (*American Herald*, 1 Nov. 1784).

[63] CM, *A Treatise on the Immutability of Moral Truth* (London: A. Hamilton, 1783), 9.

[64] MOW to WW, 4 Dec. 1784, MOWP1. In this letter Warren quotes Macaulay as 'a celebrated theorist' who had argued that commerce 'afford[ed] the means of extending the gratifications of sense beyond their proper bounds; tends to destroy the due balance which nature has formed between corporeal appetites and mental enjoyments and furnishes means to delude the imagination by an endless variety of fantastic objects of happiness.' This letter provides a particularly intriguing account of Warren's ambivalent attitude to commerce to her merchant-adventurer son.

continued, 'that a lady of her superior talents should be concerned in such a foolish business'.[65] Indeed, it was expected by others in Boston that Macaulay would add her voice to the republican critique of the tea assembly and its deleterious moral effects. But this never happened. Macaulay did not speak out against the *Sans Souci*.

In the midst of the brouhaha, the publishers Warden and Russell announced the appearance 'on Monday morning next' of 'A new farce. SANS SOUCI, alias, Free and Easy, or, an Evening's Peep into a Polite Circle. An entire new Entertainment in Three Acts.'[66] In the play's series of short dramatic sketches, Catharine Macaulay appears erroneously as the assembly's most vocal critic. Represented by the character of 'the republican heroine', in conversation with her friend 'Mrs W—n', she condemns the prevalence of 'British gew-gaws, etiquette and parade' in Boston and speaks of the assembly as a form of fashionable corruption. 'I . . . indulged such pleasing ideas respecting this country . . . during the war', the republican heroine complains, 'that when I find those sentiments of their virtue turn out mere chimeras of my own imagination, I cannot but lament my disappointment.'[67]

The variety of meanings which Macaulay's femininity and political allegiances commanded meant that, as figure or symbol, she might be appropriated and interpreted in the *Sans Souci* controversy from opposite directions. On the one hand, her republican politics linked her to the critique of fashionable society and commodity culture that, in the wake of the crises of debt and scarce specie, damned the *Sans Souci* as evidence of *Luxuria*'s corrupt hold on the morals of Massachusetts. In many ways Macaulay *was* the 'republican heroine': the articulate critic of Britain's imperial, monarchical, and commercial character. Yet, on the other hand, her status as a woman of learning and fashion meant she might be associated with, and indeed represent, that culture of refined and enlightened civility which the defenders of the *Sans Souci* believed the assembly exemplified. Woman of fashion, woman of learning, cultural patron, and republican critic: Macaulay might in fact be all these things at once. But, in a charged debate in which far more in political and economic terms than the tea assembly itself was at stake, her

---

[65] MOW to GW, 7 Mar. 1785, MOWP1.
[66] *Massachusetts Centinel*, 15 Jan. 1785.
[67] [Unattrib.], *Sans Souci, Alias, Free and Easy: An Evening's Peep into A Polite Circle* (Boston: Warden and Russell, 1785), II. i. 11.

character was associated with a series of cultural contradictions that appeared irreconcilable.

In any case, Macaulay was evidently annoyed about her appearance as the censorious figure of the 'republican heroine' in Warden and Russell's slight farce and was by no means the only prominent figure to be so. Despite the disclaimer that its circumstances and characters were 'mostly imaginary', some patrons of the *Sans Souci* realized that they might be singled out as the brunt of its derision.[68] A night-time attack on the printers followed in an attempt to prevent its publication and discover its origin. Rumours about the farce's authorship began to circulate, and top of the list of candidates was the unlikely name of Mercy Otis Warren.[69] Warren was already well known as the author of the satiric plays and sketches she had written during the crisis and war with Britain. It perhaps seemed obvious to some Bostonians that she might be behind *Sans Souci, Alias, Free and Easy*, condemning the assembly in the voices of herself and her 'republican heroine'.[70] Warren did not, of course, write a play in which the characters of herself and Macaulay were effectively the focus of ridicule, but many patrons of the *Sans Souci* were willing to believe that she had. Among these was her friend Catharine Macaulay. 'Some ill-natured persons suggested to her [Macaulay] that your mama was the author,' Warren wrote to George with evident anger, 'but I hope I shall never write anything I should be so much ashamed to own as that little indigested farrago'.[71] Macaulay questioned Warren about the play; she indignantly refuted its authorship, and they subsequently quarrelled. Warren was hurt by their disagreement. 'She has endeavoured', Warren tersely remarked, 'to apologise to her friend.'[72] The argument also clearly had an effect on Macaulay. In a letter written

---

[68] See the advertisement in the *Massachusetts Centinel*, 15 Jan. 1785: 'The characters exhibited and the circumstances mentioned are mostly imaginary, and are intended rather to satirise the measure than to point at particular persons. However, as all publications of this nature cannot but fall in some degree on certain characters, if this should be considered as too pointed, on any individuals, the author can only plead the apology that he is sorry the portrait could not be softened down to a more agreeable likeness.'

[69] A spirited account of the assault, perpetrated by a 'Mr S⎯⎯J⎯⎯' appears in the *Massachusetts Centinel*, 19 Jan.1785. Those satirized included Perez Morton and his wife, Sarah Wentworth Morton.

[70] The play is erroneously attributed to Warren by Kenneth Silverman in his *A Cultural History of the American Revolution*, 509.

[71] MOW to GW, 7 Mar. 1785, MOWP1.   [72] Ibid.

some months later, she ribbed Warren about her 'animated severity, which I acknowledge has sometimes wounded the delicacy of your friend's [i.e. Macaulay's] sentiments'.[73]

Warren's and Macaulay's argument did not only uncover their personal differences but, to their contemporaries, exposed Massachusetts' factional differences as well. Political capital was made out of the women's disagreement, as the *Sans Souci* controversy became embroiled in the contentious debate on the state's political leadership.

IV Political Capital

John Hancock had resigned as governor on 29 January and Thomas Cushing, the 'man of little arts' whom Warren regarded as a pocket-Hancock, was put forward as his successor.[74] He was opposed in the gubernatorial campaign by James Bowdoin and Warren's husband James among others. In the public debate that followed his resignation Warren and Macaulay were regarded as being on opposite sides of the political fence. While Macaulay was seen to court the friendship of John Hancock's camp at gatherings like the *Sans Souci*, Mercy Otis Warren was increasingly seen as the spokesperson of that political faction which linked her and her husband, Sam Adams, and Benjamin Austin together in opposition to the state's wealthy and influential Tories. As the question of the election was absorbed into the *Sans Souci* controversy, it took on a more pointed and personal flavour. Articles appeared, evidently produced by Hancock's camp, suggesting that those who opposed the *Sans Souci* were the proponents of a 'silly zeal'. The stability of the state had been endangered more by the 'spirit of envy and detraction'— by the political jealousy and defamation of Hancock and his supporters, in other words—than by the 'public or private luxury' with which the *Sans Souci* had come to be associated. Mercy Otis Warren's reputed authorship of *Sans Souci* was linked to her well-known opposition to the Hancock faction.[75] By her political enemies, Warren was singled out as a woman whose oppositional politics and literary character represented a betrayal of femininity itself.

[73] CM to MOW, 15 July 1785, WAP.
[74] MOW to WW, 10 Nov. 1784, MOWP1.
[75] Warren wrote to George that she had 'been abused in one of the papers as the author of [*Sans Souci*] and several satirical pieces in the newspapers' (MOW to GW, 7 Mar. 1785, MOWP1).

Falsely naming Warren as the author of *Sans Souci* (as well as some anti-Hancock articles), Warren was attacked by 'Guess Who' in the *Boston Gazette*. 'Guess Who' argued that her writing was the product of 'disappointed ambition'. 'Is it consistent', 'Guess Who' asked, 'for this l——y thus to find fault with men and manners because the public have no better opinion of her dear g——l's [i.e. James Warren's] ability than she has?' 'Guess Who' wrote bitterly that 'every emotion of resentment' was rendered 'feelingly alive' by Warren's alleged abuse of Hancock, who was the 'most worthy of our citizens, whose steady and firm conduct have merited... the effusions of gratitude from their country'. In this extraordinary use of the language of feeling, Warren is represented as being somehow deficient in sentiment. With her 'satire and abuse' and her failure to recognize the debt of gratitude that was clearly Hancock's due, she was simply not a woman of sensibility: 'We cannot but regret the depravity of her heart.' Her writing was, according to 'Guess Who', a betrayal of the appropriate sentimental and literary characters of women:

Many of this l——dy's productions have appeared which reflect no great honor on either the goodness of her heart or the brilliancy of her pen. If instead of satirising those whom she caresses as her bosom friends, she were to follow the example of a celebrated female historian, whose talents and abilities are well known in the world of genius and literature, by copying from so perfect a pattern, she would be likely to arrive at that degree of perfection which she certainly never will attain by the composition of f–r–c–s.[76]

While Macaulay apparently displayed appropriate feminine talents and abilities (including, presumably, 'a goodness of heart'), Warren was said to have betrayed her femininity and overstepped the bounds of her gender in her alleged authorship of a farce and republican political invective. 'Let the features of your sex be traced in the compositions of your pen', 'Guess Who' advised Warren in conclusion, 'and thus shall you receive the applause which is due to *real* genius'.[77]

In The *Boston Gazette*, Warren is initially condemned for allowing her private character and family connections to enter the public sphere— because she is said to write as a wife, her politics are regarded as insufficiently objective. Yet her politics of privacy and of family are set in opposition to what is in itself a familial or private model of political

---

[76] 'Guess Who', *Boston Gazette and Country Journal*, 14 Feb. 1785.   [77] Ibid.

attachment. 'Guess Who's' account of Hancock's leadership is emotive, even physical in its trembling resentment. Hancock appears a figure of sentimental paternity, a benevolent father eliciting debts of gratitude from his electors. While his is a politics of the heart, and of feeling, Warren's heart is said to have been hardened by her politics to the extent that she seems insufficiently feminine. Her learning and her politics are represented here as a form of sexual deviance (she just cannot write like a woman) unlike Catharine Macaulay (who apparently can).

In 'Guess Who's' article, then, the figure of Hancock lays claim to the sentiment and sensibility—to the authentic politics of feeling—that Mercy Otis Warren is described as lacking. Her republicanism and literary character are here said to have rendered her unfeminine, and her departure from her sex's appropriate character is compared to the exemplary instance Catharine Macaulay apparently provides of female genius. 'Guess Who' criticizes Warren on behalf of a doubled resentment, one part of which is felt for John Hancock, Warren's *bête noire* and the sentimental figurehead of the state's political republic. The other figure of resentment is Catharine Macaulay, now thought of in terms of her difference rather than her allegiance to her republican friend: the symbolic patron of the fashionable *Sans Souci* and the mascot of Boston's polite republic of letters.

In the Boston press, then, evidently there were right and wrong kinds of learned women. While Warren's writing had been extolled by the *Boston Magazine* as evidence of the town's new civilized advancement, for the *Gazette* her literary abilities might be described as a form of gender deviance. Macaulay could equally be read from opposite directions. While some New England women privately regarded her love of fashion and her marital status as confirmation of her vitiated character, in public she was extolled as a model of feminine propriety. These contradictory representations of Macaulay's and Warren's characters reveal not only how slippery ideas of women's learned or political identities were in early republican Boston, but what prominent and persuasive functions they fulfilled. As I have suggested here, ideas of women's learning or the figures of learned women might be used to boost the town's cultural sense of itself; to support arguments for the *Sans Souci*'s respectability or to establish a clear sense of political difference between competing factions in the gubernatorial campaign. As Macaulay's and Warren's literary and political characters were pulled this way and that in the *Sans Souci* controversy, the debate became less about the women themselves than about what they might *mean*: about how political or cultural capital might be made from what they represented.

These representations, these appropriations of their characters, inevitably affected the way Macaulay and Warren related to Bostonian society, its political culture, their friendship, and their sense of themselves. The women had previously been thought of (and indeed thought of themselves) as very much alike. At the turn of the 1770s, they were frequently twinned in celebratory accounts of women's learning, patriotism, or sentiment.[78] But the debate on the *Sans Souci* had disclosed their many differences. Macaulay, a woman who in previous years had been the toast of cosmopolitan London, Bath, and Paris, evidently had no scruples about attending a small-scale assembly. But Warren, whose characteristic Old Whiggish antipathy to speculation and fashionable consumption was forever in the foreground, regarded the *Sans Souci* as a damaging example of Boston's pursuit of pleasure at the expense of its virtue. The two women had simply quarrelled about an allegation of authorship (which turned out to be false) and about what seems a small difference in perspective (the presumed levity of the *Sans Souci*). But at the heart of their argument were far larger issues: the new cultures of consumption, leisure, and pleasure; the representation of gender and commerce; the contemporary understanding of women's political and literary identities; Boston's internecine factional quarrels; its internal economy; its foreign trade; and, finally, the difficult question of what might be regarded as properly Bostonian, or indeed, as properly American.

Both Warren and Macaulay were shocked by the direction the debate had taken, by the way their political and their gendered characters had become imbricated in Boston's cultural clash over the *Sans Souci*. While Macaulay, unlike Warren, did not regard her attendance at the *Sans Souci* as a compromise of her republicanism, she certainly agreed with her friends in terms of the broad strokes of contemporary American politics. 'The Americans', she wrote to Samuel Adams a few years later, 'have a little too much of the leaven of their ancestors in them: they

---

[78] See, for example, 'The Paradise of Female Patriotism', *American Magazine*, 1 (1779), in which both Macaulay and Warren appear as patriotic exemplars.

appear to turn their views and desires more to the acquiring of gain than the enjoyment of rational liberty'.[79] For Warren, the public attacks on her literary and feminine character confirmed and compounded her profound sense of political disaffection. Later that year she began to develop those ideas of oppositional privacy, retirement, and resistance, which became so important to her later work. She wrote to her friend Elbridge Gerry that she and James Warren

> are retired from the crowd, to the calm and delightful shade of Tremont, where with little interruption but such as we choose, we can smile at the ambitious canvassing for place, contemplate the inconsistency of human nature, the frivolity of mankind, the sudden revolutions of states, which seldom better their condition by their struggles; the rise of kingdoms, the fall of empires and the convulsed state of human affairs from the death of Abel to the slaughter of many of the heroes of America.[80]

As I argue in this book's final chapter, it is this combination of the domestic and the sublime that makes Warren's voice in her later *History of the Rise, Progress and Termination of the American Revolution* so particularly distinctive.

V Femininity in the Early Republic

Women could—and did—legitimate their involvement in the early republican spheres of letters or politics, of fashion or polite society, through recourse to the different notions of femininity I have been discussing in this chapter. These ideas of gender shaped the way women related to family, work, and the marketplace; the way they thought of themselves as educated, writing, consuming, or potential political subjects. In defining their own sense of themselves as patriotic, women might draw on a republican discourse that, in its condemnation of fashionable or commercial excess as a specifically feminine corruption, seems shot through with a characteristic eighteenth-century misogyny. Or they might lay claim to a new liberal discourse of sentiment, which, even as it

---

[79] CM to Samuel Adams, 1 Mar. 1791, Samuel Adams Papers, Lennox Foundation, New York Public Library.
[80] MOW to EG, June 1785, in Gardiner, *A Study in Dissent*, 172. Note the similarities between this passage and Warren's letter to Hannah Winthrop in 1778 (which I discuss in Chapter 4) extolling the virtues of retirement beneath Plymouth's 'broken cliffs'. A version of this passage also concluded Warren's *Observations on the American Constitution*, as discussed in Chapter 6.

endowed femininity with a persuasive moral authority, by prioritizing the essentially private and domestic characters of women, in effect confirmed their continued exclusion from the political public sphere.[81]

It is in the context of these varied and sometimes contradictory representations of gender that the sentimental figures of the 'women in white' in David Waldstreicher's illuminating work might be further understood.[82] Or, equally, that we might begin to reread the conservative accounts of patriotic femininity which Rosmarie Zagarri curiously regards as enabling for Federalist women.[83] A wide range of ideas of femininity became important to America's political and literary cultures during and after the revolutionary war. These ideas supported changing ideologies of sexual, filial, or familial relations; propped up the contesting values of new political and economic discourses; and, indeed, helped define the nation's early republican sense of itself. This is why the *Sans Souci* is not just a daft controversy and why it might be important to reassess similar debates and the roles of the women involved—such as the two I have been discussing here.

In what was seen as a surprising victory (and, to Mercy Otis Warren and her republican friends, a welcome one) James Bowdoin defeated Thomas Cushing in the race for governor. Stamping his identity on the state the following June, Bowdoin issued a public proclamation 'for the encouragement of piety, virtue, education and manners, and for the suppression of vice'.[84] With its suggestion that the promotion of manners and the suppression of vice might actually be the same thing, Bowdoin's proclamation seemed to dissolve those stark moral oppositions upon which the *Sans Souci* controversy had depended.

---

[81] Sarah Knott's work has produced some intriguing readings of the relationships between sentiment and sensibility, and femininity and masculinity in revolutionary and early republican America. See her 'A Cultural History of Sensibility in the Era of the American Revolution,' Ph.D. Diss. (Oxford University, 1999).

[82] See David Waldstreicher, *In the Midst of Perpetual Fetes: The Making of American Nationalism, 1776–1830* (Chapel Hill, NC: University of North Carolina Press, 1997).

[83] See Rosmarie Zagarri's 'Gender and the First Party System', in Doron Ben Atar and Barbara B. Oberg (eds.), *Federalists Reconsidered* (Charlottesville, Va.: University Press of Virginia, 1998). Other interesting recent accounts of gender and early republican culture include Peter Messer, 'Writing Women into History: Defining Gender and Citizenship in Post-Revolutionary America', *Studies in Eighteenth-Century Culture*, 28 (1999), 341–60, and especially Joanne B. Freeman, *Affairs of Honor: National Politics in the New Republic* (New Haven: Yale University Press, 2001).

[84] See Fowler, *The Baron of Beacon Hill*, 259.

When Catherine Macaulay left for England a few weeks after Bowdoin's announcement, having failed to secure sufficient funds for the new edition of her *History of England*, which she had in part undertook her American trip to promote, her relationship with Mercy Otis Warren had been amicably restored. She wrote to Warren of her feelings on leaving America. 'Can patriotism', she enquired of her friend with no small degree of affection, 'dwell in a heart where friendship has no place?'[85] Both women had been hurt by the contradictory representations of their characters during the *Sans Souci* controversy. But, out of their renewed friendship, their shared political commitment, and their new awareness of their differences, emerged, as I shall argue, the accounts of women's intellectual and political equality which both were clearly to articulate only a few years later. Though undoubtedly a storm in a teacup, the *Sans Souci* controversy reveals some of the ways in which ideas of women's political and literary identities began to shape the cultural identity of the early republic.

[85] CM to MOW, 15 July 1785, WAP.

6

Mercy Otis Warren's Independence

On 16 November 1787 George Washington wrote to Catharine Macaulay of 'the plan of Government proposed by the Convention for the United States':

> You will very readily conceive, Madam, the difficulties which the convention had to struggle against. The various and opposite interests which were to be conciliated; the local prejudices which were to be subdued, the diversity of opinions and sentiments which were to be reconciled; and in fine, the sacrifices which were necessary to be made on all sides for the general welfare, combined to make it a work of so intricate and difficult a nature, that I think it is much to be wondered at, that any thing could have been produced with such unanimity as the constitution proposed.[1]

The heated hostilities of 1787's hot summer apparently made the final agreement that bit more marvellous. Thirteen states' niggling doubts and prickly personalities had been smoothed, assuaged, and surrendered to the nation's best interests. Washington tells Macaulay the constitution is a triumph of public spirit: the perfect abstracted unity of America's many differences.

But Macaulay was soon to receive a letter from Mercy Otis Warren which suggested quite the opposite. Her friend was deeply troubled by the divisive document that had emerged from behind Philadelphia's closed doors. For Warren, the proposed national constitution which Elbridge Gerry had refused to put his name to merely confirmed that

> the times we have lived in are not the most favourable to the noblest feelings of the soul. Old attachments have been eradicated by the diversity of political

---

[1] George Washington to CM, 16 Nov. 1787, in *The Writings of George Washington 1745–1799*, ed. (John C. Fitzpatrick, Washington: Library of Congress, 1931–44), xxix. 316–17.

opinion; animosities heightened by the severity or indiscretion of parties; new political connexions formed as it were by accident without any principle of public or private virtue for their basis.[2]

Looking west across the Atlantic, Macaulay would perceive no national harmony, no public spirit, no unity of purpose. 'We must appear to you a very divided people,' Warren concluded grimly.[3]

Mercy Otis Warren saw in the Federal convention of 1787 the final failure of the revolution. Public and private disaffection always seemed to her equivalents, and it is typical of her writing of these years that political disappointment is expressed here in terms of wounded feeling. The severance of Warren's deeply felt personal 'attachments' through separation, death, or difference was mirrored in the painful rupture she perceived between the new nation and the principles of 1775. The hopeful patriotism which defined the letters she circulated among her female friends during the 1770s seemed to hold no currency in an America of bitter antipathies and party hostilities. Her partner was utterly disillusioned with the public office that should have confirmed his gentlemanly status, her sons had failed to find their feet in an era of economic instability, and she had been abused in the Boston press for her literary presumption and supposed lack of feminine sensibility. Politically isolated in eastern Massachusetts, Warren often felt through the 1780s and 1790s like a lone voice in the Federalist wilderness.

And yet, it was during the two decades following the Federal convention that Mercy Otis Warren displayed most political and literary confidence. She wrote pamphlets, poems, plays, and history, trying out ideas and formulations in a lively correspondence. Her very distance from the political culture in which she longed to have a greater say lent her, she maintained, an enviable objectivity. Unabashed, sharp, and often funny, she frequently expressed her belief in her own intellectual equality and that of other women. Though she insisted (sometimes bitterly) on her estrangement from the political interests of a nation which, as she saw it, was hastening swiftly on towards its own imperial decline and fall, the detachment she claimed allowed her political expression greater clarity. As she frequently told Catharine Macaulay and Elbridge Gerry, if you had little to hope, there was nothing to lose.

[2] MOW to CM, 15 Dec. 1787, MOWP1.   [3] Ibid.

In her plays, history, and letters of this period, Mercy Otis Warren speaks in two discursive registers. The first is found in the grief and resentment she expressed at difficult losses doubled on a personal and public level: what she perceived as the defeat of the revolution and the public rejection of her family for the politics they continued to espouse. The other is the deft, damning, and utterly assured voice of democratic republicanism, opposing the constitution, welcoming the radical potential of the French Revolution, scorning America's first two presidents and their administrations, and expressing a guarded pleasure, as the nineteenth century turned, in Jefferson's election. Both registers are intertwined in the writing of one of America's most articulate Anti-Federalists. Both are similarly bound up with the sentimental and melancholic ideal of the Roman *Matrona* against which Warren often measured women's political resolution and latent public characters. For Warren's critics and biographers, though, her bitterness often almost erases her articulacy.[4] Here, however, I will argue that it was precisely out of deep public and private disaffection and her identification with what one might read as the normative associations of her gender that Warren's distinctive sense of her own political potential emerged.

This chapter is written in nine sections, which might be approached as one long accretive reading, or as a series of short essays. I begin by looking at Warren's cultural 'displacement' in Federalist Massachusetts, suggesting how she might have viewed familial separation, the breakdown of friendship, and political betrayal as parallel processes. The grieving *Matrona* who appears in Warren's poems, political writings, and *The Sack of Rome* afforded her, I argue in Section 5, a compelling figurative rationalization for both the history of American independence and her own experience of it. Later sections of the chapter show how Warren drew on the privacy, sensibility, and retirement she claimed as a

---

[4] See, for example, Rosemarie Zagarri, *A Woman's Dilemma: Mercy Otis Warren and the American Revolution* (Wheeling, Ill.: Harlan Davidson, 1995), particularly ch. 5, 'An Old Republican'. Zagarri's book provides a good overview of Warren's life, but really fails fully to address the strategic complexities of her writing. An excellent (and perhaps more literary) introductory account is found in Jeffrey Richards, *Mercy Otis Warren* (New York: Twayne, 1995). See also Lester Cohen's edifying article 'Mercy Otis Warren: The Politics of Language and the Aesthetics of Self', *American Quarterly*, 35 (1983), 480–98. I am indebted to Cohen's thorough and definitive work on Warren, and concur with most of what he has to say about her. Here he traces a similar development in her later writing and political articulacy, but suggests there is something 'tragic' or 'ironic' about it (at 486). I take a rather different view.

woman to lend a particular authority to her political character in her *Observations on the New Constitution and on the Federal and State Conventions* and her *History of the Rise, Progress and Termination of the American Revolution.*

I Out of Place

In 1783, in a letter she was later to rework for publication, Mercy Otis Warren wrote to Elbridge Gerry:

It is an undoubted truth that there are seasons in human affairs when genius, virtue and patriotism nod over the vices of the times, perhaps this drowsy disposition was never more remarkable than at the present period. I am at a loss whither the reigning folly is avarice, dissipation or idolatry; but when the nap is out, I hope we shall see the reanimation of patriotism take place of the apathy which has for some time hung on the lids of this people... We have set Great Britain at defiance, we have weathered the shocks of war—we have hazarded all, and waded through rivers of blood to establish the independence of America and maintain the freedom of the human mind. But alas! If we have any national character, what a heterogeneous mixture—we have a republican form of government with the principles of monarchy, the freedom of democracy with the servility of despotism, the extravagance of nobility, with the poverty of peasantry... Is not America tainted with many of the vices that stained that ancient republic [Rome]? It is easy to give a long list of the absurd follies that have crept in among us—but where are the virtues that will make a balance sufficient to support a free commonwealth?[5]

For Warren, the end of the war merely marked a stage in America's failure to fulfil its republican promise. Where she longed to perceive a determined unity of purpose, the American people appeared as supine and inattentive of their liberties, as the British did to Catharine Macaulay's eyes. For Warren, America already seemed an absurd muddle of imperial vices, a country riven by deep political and economic inequalities, which its fledgling institutions only sustained and perpetuated.

It had looked that way to her and James Warren since 1778. As the war shifted focus from New England after independence, state politics had progressively come to be dominated by merchants whose liberal and

[5] MOW to EG, 6 June 1783, in C. Harvey Gardiner, *A Study in Dissent: The Warren–Gerry Correspondence, 1776–1792* (Carbondale and Edwardsville: Southern Illinois University Press, 1968). Hereafter cited as 'Gardiner'.

commercial outlook differed widely from their own. James Warren found himself out of place in a 'house consisting of members... whose politicks are very different from mine'.[6] He was surrounded, he told John Adams, by 'men of the moderate class to which you know I never belonged'.[7] Never strenuous in their opposition to imperial Britain, such 'moderates' tolerated the return of those that many in Massachusetts still regarded as their loyalist enemies and were anxious to develop commercial policies at state and national level to protect and forward their own economic interests. These interests brought them in 1777–8 into direct conflict with James Warren (by then regarded as an obdurate old republican), who as head of the provincial congress had authored what was in effect a sumptuary law to fix the price of scarce commodities in his regulatory 'Act to Prevent Monopoly and Oppression'. 'This bill makes no small noise and difficulty here,' James Warren told Elbridge Gerry in the spring of 1777,

as it was designed to supply in some measure the want of publick virtue. When I think of it I can't help recollecting at the same time a decree I have seen read or heard of among the simple natives of some simple country to inspire courage into their inhabitants. It is however to be lamented that there should be such a venal spirit prevailing to the destruction of all patriotism... men of character... have been playing a curious game for the sake of filthy lucre, one of the blessings derived from civilization and its attendant commerce. I envy the Indians their simplicity and the Savages their barbarism. Civilization was surely the greatest curse consequent on original sin.[8]

In this passage (which is typical of Warren's political voice in this period) he clearly, and quite unambiguously, represents himself in the role of one whose duty was to preserve the integrity of the 'simple country'. He regards his bill in traditional commonwealth terms: encouraging martial virtues; arresting commercial desire; preventing the accumulation of power with that of mobile capital, and holding history at a stage before progress turned into corruption. Warren knew his particular brand of agrarian and latently democratic republicanism was deeply unpopular in a state now dominated by the political influence of wealthy eastern merchants. Indeed, despite his own family background in trade and the commission he received in 1777 from handling Gerry's shipments of

[6] JW to JA, 7 June 1778, WAP.   [7] Ibid.
[8] JW to EG, 24 Mar. 1777, in 'Gardiner'.

goods from Spain, he increasingly wrote of his patriotism as a virtue that, in its association with land and arms and opposition to empire, commerce, and modernity, rendered it equivalent to a sort of barbarism.

Warren's bill was repealed, and the following year his electors failed to return him as their representative. A piqued Mercy Warren wrote to him from Plymouth:

> one of the most subtle emissaries of Britain and the most malignant of your foes was suffered yesterday in full meeting of the town to stand up and cast the most illiberal reflections on a man whose primary object has been to rescue these people from the thraldom of a foreign yoke and to preserve their rights against the machinations of the more dangerous enemies that lurk in their own bosoms.[9]

Earlier in the 1770s Warren had perceived her husband's public status as a corollary to her own patriotic virtue. In a poem she had written for him a couple of years previously, for example ('To Fidelio, Long Absent on the Great Public Cause which Agitated all America in 1776'), she described how his 'zealous care' for the 'state . . . shook to the centre' was matched by the 'patriot zeal' she experienced in private.[10] As I argued in this book's fourth chapter, the Warrens' political relationship was as close and collaborative as it could be within the context of an equitable, affectionate, and intellectual eighteenth-century marriage. They were traditional in their commonwealth views, and for them public office found a reciprocal counterpart in the virtuous privacy that sustained it. While Warren represents her partner's exclusion from office here as Plymouth's ungrateful denial of its own best interests, it clearly also signalled her own estrangement from what her country stood for.

Through the 1780s James Warren drifted in and out of office to the margins of Massachusetts' political culture. He gained a reputation for being crabby, and uncompromising, and for turning down positions and appointments.[11] He engaged himself intermittently with his farms and Massachusetts' political affairs, 'content to move in a small sphere',

---

[9] MOW to JW, 2 June 1778, MOWP2. James Warren's enemy was Ned Winslow, whose wife, Penny, remained one of Mercy Warren's close friends.

[10] MOW, 'To Fidelio, Long Absent on the Great Cause which Agitated All America in 1776' [1776], in Warren, *Poems Dramatic and Miscellaneous* (Boston: I. Thomas and E. T. Andrews, 1790), ll. 23–5.

[11] Gardiner lists eleven appointments that James Warren rejected or resigned from between 1776 and 1787. Gardiner, *A Study in Dissent*, pp. xvii–xxiv.

while his friends took public office to the continental and international scale.[12] 'Your father is still in private life', Mercy Warren wrote to her son Winslow:

> nothing is more irksome to him than the idea of once more emerging ... to engage in the arduous attempt of saving a young republic from the consequences of their own folly and ignorance; more especially when in almost every department may be found many men unacquainted with or indifferent to the first principles of the revolution and who are ready to sacrifice the fairest advantages ever afforded for the establishment of public happiness to the narrow views which too frequently occupy the human mind and bring down the standard of the most exalted systems of policy to a level with the interests of the selfish individual.[13]

During the years of his absence from office, Mercy Warren repeatedly, perhaps insistently, represented her 'best friend ... walk[ing] towards the fertile plain, to survey the reapers, or perhaps ascend[ing] the rugged hills to view the sportive flocks' in the privacy that was the last retreat of the virtuous man.[14] And yet, however Horatian his retirement, however principled his refusals, James Warren's distance from the public sphere was never entirely easy for such a politically committed and determined couple.

The letters of the Warrens throughout the 1780s suggest how uncomfortable they both felt as old-colony republicans in a commercial culture that they saw encouraging accumulation, extortion, debt, and depreciation. As their response to the *Sans Souci* controversy showed, they profoundly disliked the material desire and display which they felt characterized Boston's new middling ranks, and there is certainly something of the indignant patrician in James Warren's complaint that 'fellows who would have cleaned my shoes five years ago are riding in chariots', while he was 'still drudging at the Navy Board for a morsel of bread'.[15] At the turn of the 1780s, the Warrens (as their contemporaries often remarked) seemed to confirm their status as one of New England's first families by adding to the extensive property they already owned around Plymouth and Maine and purchasing Thomas Hutchinson's

---

[12] JA to JW, 7 July 1775, WAP.   [13] MOW to WW, Nov. 1784, MOWP1.
[14] MOW to AA, 6 Aug. 1779, WAP.
[15] JW to JA, 13 June 1779, WAP. On the *Sans Souci* controversy, see Chapter 5 of this book.

confiscated home at Milton.[16] While moving to 'Tremont' brought James closer to the centre of state politics and suggested their sons' promising futures, the estate was an addition to their assets they could ill afford. 'I could enjoy it if it were paid for,' James Warren wrote to Winslow, 'but you know I hate to be in debt. . . . [I] should have done well enough if there had not been such a revolution in the currency; but as it is I shall be pushed and straightened but will struggle to keep it.'[17]

Though the acquisition was clearly befitting to their position as they imagined it should be in post-war Massachusetts, there was always something incongruous about the self-professedly ascetic Warrens in Hutchinson's impressive home. Mercy Warren's letters from Milton acknowledge this as she strains to appropriate the house to the picturesque aesthetic she had developed to define her privacy at Plymouth. Tremont was always for her 'this little villa' concealing itself from view beneath 'delightful shade'.[18] But such snug, diminutive terms did not disguise the visible ostentation of a hill-top house built on the grand scale. Warren's writing suggests she was never fully at her ease there, although, as she put it to her niece in the winter of 1787, she was grateful that her 'lot has always fallen in pleasant places'. But she clearly regretted the distance that separated her from both a house and a time she had loved: 'I often look back upon Plymouth, take a walk from room to room, peep through the lattices that have lighted my steps, revisit the little alcove leading to the garden, and place myself in every happy corner of a house where I have tasted so much real felicity.'[19] Warren was at the peripheries of a political culture for which she had little respect or hope,

---

[16] Their friend Elbridge Gerry performed a similar move when, after his marriage, he bought Elmwood, the confiscated estate of Thomas Oliver in Cambridge. On the purchase, see George Athan Bilias, *Elbridge Gerry: Founding Father and Republican Statesman* (New York: McGraw Hill, 1976), 135–6. On the Warrens' purchase of Milton, see Jean Fritz, *Cast for a Revolution: Some American Friends and Enemies* (Boston: Houghton Mifflin, 1972), 199–202, and Zagarri, *A Woman's Dilemma*, 130–1.

[17] JW to WW, 28 Sept. 1781, MOWP2. See also MOW to JW, 27 Jan. 1781, MOWP2, in which Warren expresses anxiety about the cost of Tremont. The house cost James Warren £3,000.

[18] See, for example, MOW to Sally Sever (later Russell), Dec. 1787, MOWP1, and MOW to EG, 6 June 1783, in 'Gardiner'.

[19] MOW to Sally Sever, Dec. 1787, MOWP1. In Warren's letters to her niece she liked to 'retrospect[s] the Plymouth fireside where Miss Sever used to set till many a midnight hour and chat away the agreeable moments with her affectionate aunt Warren' (MOW to Sally Sever, 1785, MOWP1).

and felt drawn by the purchase of Tremont to the limits of her competency. Her elegy to Plymouth's contented spaces suggests just how out of place she felt at Milton.[20]

In 1807 Mercy Warren recalled for John Adams a conversation that marked their political differences after his return from England in the late 1780s:

> Your ideas appeared to be favourable to monarchy and to an order of nobility in your own country. Mr Warren replied 'I am thankful that I am a plebeian.' You answered: 'no sir, you are one of the nobles. There has been a national aristocracy here ever since the country was settled—your family at Plymouth, Mrs Warren's at Barnstable and many others in very many places that have kept up a distinction similar to nobility.'[21]

Though 'the conversation subsided by a little mirth', the republican Warrens were, she reported, 'much hurt by the apparent change of sentiment and manner'.[22]

This conversation reaches to the heart of the contradictions that rendered James and Mercy Warren out of place in Massachusetts during the 1780s. The Warrens were utterly appalled by Adams's turn toward a conservatism they saw as complicit with hereditary honours, empire, and coercion, bound to repeat the injustice and disproportion of European monarchies in (as Mercy Warren put it) 'a government made for the enjoyment of individuals not for the ease, the benefit, the happiness of the people'.[23] Theirs was a material ideology of land, labour, and thrift rather than speculation, expenditure, and display. While their familial fortunes were rooted for generations in colonial trade, they saw themselves as farmers and associated their republicanism with the still persuasive ideal of the virtuous New England yeoman fixed in perpetuity at civilization's middle stage. With a firm emphasis on association and popular sovereignty, their politics were incipiently democratic. It was unsurprising that James Warren would identify himself as a plebeian: that he would rather be a barbarian than a stockjobber.

---

[20] On competency and its limits, see particularly the letters Warren wrote to her son George, who was reputedly overextending himself in new building projects in Maine. For example, MOW to GW, 13 Aug. 1792, MOWP1.
[21] MOW to JA, 28 July 1807, in *Correspondence of John Adams and Mercy Warren* (Collections of the Massachusetts Historical Society, 4; Boston: MHS, 1878), 361.
[22] MOW to JA, in ibid.   [23] MOW to EG, 25 Dec. 1793, MOWP1.

But Adams scored a palpable hit (and knew he did) by associating the Warrens with aristocratic distinction. They were proud of their familial heritage, their common ancestors among the old colony's first settlers, and their profound attachment to the land of New England (compounded by their proprietorship of sizeable portions of it). They now lived at showy Tremont, which, their instinctual dislike of adornment notwithstanding, they had decorated with fresh blue wallpaper sent from England.[24] Their fashionable, cosmopolitan son Winslow sojourned in Europe, had his portrait painted by John Singleton Copley, and was now using his father's reputation to secure himself the profits of the post-war Iberian trade.[25] Their republicanism perhaps seemed more patrician than plebeian, more gentleman capitalist than yeoman farmer. It was easy for the deft and spiky Adams to set his friends' politics against the expectations of their rank, to represent Anti-Federalism as a betrayal of their class. Adams was basically suggesting that the fact the Warrens *looked* like Federalists made it surprising they did not favour a politics of entitlement over one of equality.

Distanced from a public sphere (which they saw as autocratic and corrupt) marginalized by their politics (increasingly perceived as dangerously democratic), and alienated and fleeced by the very estate they had bought to confirm their status, the Warrens felt culturally displaced in their own country. These sensations were to become particularly acute during the Shays crisis and constitutional debates.

II The Golden Age of Federalism

On 24 May 1786 Abigail Adams wrote to Mercy Warren from London: 'Let not the popular torrent which at present sets against your worthy partner distress you, time will convince the world who are their approved and unshaken friends, whatever mistaken judgements they at present form.'[26] From that summer through to the spring of 1788, James Warren's reputedly radical views were to make him, to Mercy Warren's pain and chagrin, a principal target of Massachusetts Federalist 'torrent'. Throughout the 1780s both Warrens had criticized the state government's prioritizing of merchant interests over those of farmers and

---

[24] See WW to MOW, 17 Aug. 1784, MOWP2.
[25] On the Copley portrait, see MOW to WW, n.d., 1785, MOWP1.
[26] AA to MOW, 24 May 1786, *AFC*.

fisheries; bemoaned the scarcity of specie; sympathized with the predicament of impoverished debtors; and supported the people's right to freedom of assembly. While James Warren's sons and close friends were quick to join Lincoln's militia, and though he complained to John Adams of Massachusetts' 'state of anarchy bordering on civil war', to the Boston commercial elite his politics were clearly linked to those of the Shaysite rebels who shut down the western courts and stormed the Federal arsenal at Springfield.[27] Suspicions of James Warren as a covert insurgent were only compounded by his horrified reaction to the prospect of a Federal standing army being used against the rebels. To Warren, ever mistrustful of the hereditary Cincinatti, this was the chance they had been waiting for to usher in 'artificial inequality of condition' via an aristocratic order supported by an oppressive national military force.[28]

Many historians of Shays's rebellion have noted the particular tenor of the reactionary language used against the backcountry farmers.[29] As the proto-nationalist Boston elite sought to reappropriate the meanings of revolution and independence, so they projected ever more extreme fantasies of racial or cultural anarchy and excess onto the local politics of the disgruntled debtors. In a remark which is merely typical of the conservative hyperbole of 1786–7, the rebels were described as 'men who have been civilized returning to barbarism, and threatening to become fiercer than the savage children of nature'.[30] It was perhaps a simple move—and one that many Federalists were swift to make—to associate opposition politics of any hue with the prospect of a savage return to nature.[31] The connection between the threat of Shays's supposed

[27] JW to JA, 22 Oct. 1786, WAP.   [28] See JW to JA, 18 May 1787, WAP.
[29] See, for example: Robert A. East, 'The Massachusetts Conservatives in the Critical Period,' in Richard B. Morris (ed.), *The Era of the American Revolution* (New York: Columbia University Press, 1938), 359–60; Stephen E. Patterson, 'The Federalist Reaction to Shays' Rebellion', in Robert A. Gross (ed.), *In Debt to Shays: The Bicentennial of an Agrarian Rebellion* (Charlottesville, Va.: University Press of Virginia, 1993), 101–18; Michael Lienesch, 'Reinterpreting Rebellion: The Influence of Shays' Rebellion on American Political Thought', in Gross (ed.), *In Debt to Shays*, 161–82; Isaac Kramnick, 'The "Great National Discussion": The Discourse of Politics in 1787', *William and Mary Quarterly*, 45 (1988), 3–32; Caroll Smith-Rosenberg, 'Dis-Covering the Subject of the "Great Constitutional Discussion", 1786–1789', *Journal of American History* (1992), 841–73. Smith-Rosenberg's influential article describes Shays's rebels as 'a republican other' (p. 854).   [30] *American Museum*, 2 (Oct. 1787), 316.
[31] See, for example, Brutus, *Independent Chronicle*, 13 July 1786: 'Do they wish to become as HOTTENTOTS or set up a government upon the lawless sentiments of the ALGERINES?' The language of 'savagery' was typically unspecific.

barbarian invasions and opposition to the Federal constitution was perhaps most clearly and definitively made in *The Anarchiad*, the hysterical Federalist mock-epic by Barlow, Trumbull, Humphreys, and Hopkins. Here, Anti-Federal questioners of conservative national constitutional politics are described as 'traitors' sacrificing 'union'd empire' to 'jealous, local schemes'. Any prospect of debate, of opposition, is immediately shot down as the perfidy which threatens weakness and allows 'fierce bickering tribes' and 'storms of Goths' purchase on a divided nation:

> See! Proud Faction waves her flaming brand,
> And discord riots o'er the ungrateful land;
> Lo! To the North, a wild, adventurous crew,
> In desperate mobs, the savage state renew;
> Each felon chief his maddening thousands draws
> And claims bold license from the bond of laws.[32]

As historians of the Anti-Federalist movement note, many opponents of the constitution fell foul of a familiar nationalist conservative strategy of condemning all legitimate political opposition as unpatriotic or branding popular discontent an act of terrorism.[33]

---

[32] [Joel Barlow, David Humphreys, John Trumbull, Lemuel Hopkins], *The Anarchiad: A New England Poem* [1787–8], ll. 41–6. First published as: 'American Antiquities, no. X: Extract from the Anarchiad Book XXIV. The Speech of Hesper', in *The New Haven Gazette and Connecticut Magazine*, 24 May 1787.

[33] Adams described Shays's rebels as 'terrorists' to Thomas Jefferson in 1813. Cited in Lienesch, 'Reinterpreting Rebellion', 182. On the conservatism of the canonization of the 'rising glory' poets, see Cathy Davidson's excellent discussion in *The Revolution and the Word: The Rise of the Novel in America* (Oxford: Oxford University Press, 1988), ch. 9. See also Saul Cornell, *The Other Founders: Anti-Federalism and the Dissenting Tradition in America 1788–1828* (Chapel Hill, NC: University of North Carolina Press, 1999); Herbert Storing, *What the Anti-Federalists Were For: The Political Thought of the Opponents of the Constitution* (Chicago: University of Chicago Press, 1987); Paul Finckelman, 'Anti-Federalists:, The Loyal Opposition and the American Constitution', *Cornell Law Review*, 70 (1984), 182–207; Michael Lienesch, 'In Defence of the Anti-Federalists', *History of Political Thought*, 4 (1983), 65–87; Cecelia Kenyon, 'Men of Little Faith: The Anti-Federalists on the Nature of Representative Government', *William and Mary Quarterly*, 12 (1955), 3–43. On the ratification debates in Massachusetts, see Samuel Banter Harding, *The Contest over the Ratification of the Federal Constitution in the State of Massachusetts* (New York: Longman, Green and Co., 1896), and Jackson Turner Main, *The Anti-Federalists Critics of the Constitution* (Chapel Hill, NC: University of North Carolina Press, 1961), 200–9. For the impact on the Warrens' political circle, see Charles Warren, 'Elbridge Gerry, James Warren, Mercy Warren and the Ratification of the Federal Constitution in Massachusetts', *Proceedings of the Massachusetts Historical Society*, 64 (1930–2), 143–64.

James Warren was politically distanced from the incendiary Shaysistes yet certainly sympathized with their economic difficulties. To the correspondents of the rabid *Massachusetts Centinel*, these sympathies and his later reservations about the Federal constitution marked him as 'an abett[or] of anarchy and confusion'; 'It is curious to observe', one writer put it in November 1987,

> the *affected* concern of the Anti-Federalists for the constitution of this state, when it is a notorious fact that three of the principal enemies of the proposed constitution were heart and hand with the insurgents last winter.... Shall such characters compass the ignominy and destruction of America, by causing us to reject the plan of the Continental Convention?—FORBID IT HEAVEN!![34]

Anti-Federalism was clearly equivalent to insurrection.[35]

A few days later, another *Centinel* article alluded to the Warrens' home at Milton as the setting for an anarchic conspiracy to build an Anti-Federal flotilla in opposition to 'the well-built ship *Constitution*':

> The *Chuff Cutter*... is now fitting out by the Anti-Federal carpenters for a *tender* to the ship W——n, which is anchored in M——n road, laden with inflammables and other stores for the Anti-Federal fleet. This ship has been remarkable for taking large cargoes on board at every wealthy port she puts in at, and never making any remittances, so that she is now obliged to join the enemy's fleet, in hopes by the junction, she may stand a better chance to discharge her portage and bills, and other debts, without being stripped of her rigging.[36]

While the *Chuff Cutter* was the Warrens' good friend James Winthrop (with his gruff eccentricities), the tenders, cargoes, and unpaid remittances were a reference to James Warren's opposition to Massachusetts' economic policies and his family's troubled finances, reputedly crippled by the expensive 'rigging' of Tremont.

Though some correspondents protested that such intensely personal invective almost operated as a gag threatening Massachusetts' prized

---

[34] The *Centinel*'s three 'principal enemies' are probably James Warren, Elbridge Gerry, and James Winthrop.

[35] Saul Cornell mentions the *Massachusetts Centinel* as a prime arena for the articulation of his Federalist 'twist'. Cornell, *The Other Founders*, 153.

[36] 'Ship News', *Massachusetts Centinel*, 24 Nov. 1787. 'M——n' refers, of course, to Milton, where the Warrens lived. The description of Warren and Winthrop as Anti-Federal carpenters possibly relates to Winthrop's defence of the interests of local ship carpenters in his letters as 'Agrippa' that appeared in the *Massachusetts Gazette* between November 1787 and February 1788. The letters are included in the fourth volume of Herbert Storing's *Complete Anti-Federalist*.

freedom of speech, the alarmist language of barbarity, monstrosity, and disorder levelled at Warren and other Anti-Federalists became, as the new year turned, perhaps even more excessive.[37] In one crazed article, James Warren was described as a sort of gastropod, 'a finished monster of depravity' leaving behind 'the slime of defamation' in the handbills and pamphlets attributed to him.[38] Warren continued to express his opposition to the constitution until it was finally ratified, but confessed to Elbridge Gerry that he had been 'hurt by the large share of malicious slander' directed at him.[39]

Mercy Warren, who added her voice to the ratification debate in her important *Observations on the New Constitution and on the Federal and State Conventions* (of which more later), was utterly disgusted by the turn of national and state politics and deeply wounded by the public attacks on her husband. 'This year', she wrote with angry resignation to her brother Samuel Alleyne Otis of 1787, 'is certainly the golden age of Federalism'.[40] As political difference was in 1780s Massachusetts often expressed in terms of personal hostility, so Mercy Otis Warren experienced Federalism's 'golden age' as if it were a private injury. Her letters of 1786–8 are coloured by a language of public and private persecution which is an obvious and direct counterpart to the discourse of conservative reaction against which the Anti-Federal Warrens had fallen foul. Thus, when she complained of the neglect of friends, or expressed disquiet at the ill treatment of James Warren, she was also bemoaning the abandonment of old republicanism and the betrayal of the revolution. In one typically suspicious letter she told John Adams that the society of Cincinatti was ushering in a pseudo-monarchical politics of distinction and allowing

> the malignant rumour to light for a moment on one of the most decided friends to the constitution and to his country; a gentleman whose service have been distinguished; whose patriotism is unshaken and his virtues unconquerable. His fortune has been diminished, himself and his family have personally and severely

---

[37] See, for example, Benjamin Austin writing in the *Massachusetts Centinel*, 6 Dec. 1787: 'This ungenerous method of condemning characters is contrary to that candour which actuates the citizens of these states. Freedom of debate in all national questions has ever been held sacred among a free people.' See also *Massachusetts Centinel*, 1 Dec. 1787.
[38] 'Remarks ad corrigendum', *Independent Chronicle*, 3 Jan. 1788. For other attacks on James Warren, see *Massachusetts Centinel*, 23, 26, 30 Jan. 1788, and *Boston Gazette*, 21 Jan. 1788.   [39] JW to EG, 20 July 1788, in 'Gardiner'.
[40] MOW to Samuel Alleyne Otis, n.d., 1787, MOWP1.

suffered in the public cause; he is persecuted by the spirit of party and too much neglected by some who ought from particular obligations to continue his *friends*.[41]

As will be seen later in this chapter, this language of personal grievance and wounded consternation distinguishes Warren's political and historical writing from the late 1780s onwards.

Just after the election contest for Massachusetts' Lieutenant Governor in 1788, a young John Quincy Adams reported that he

> stopp'd about half an hour at Genl. Warren's. He was gone to Plymouth, but Mrs Warren was at home. The Genl's political character has undergone of late a great alteration. Among all those who were formerly his friends he is extremely unpopular; while the insurgent and Anti-Federal party (for it is but one) consider him in a manner as their head. . . . Mrs Warren complained that he had been abused shamefully and very undeservedly; but she thought me too Federal to talk freely with me.[42]

There's a sense here of Adams's warm childhood attachment to the Warrens, as well as his troubled distance from their post-war politics, which, he must insist even to his diary, are equivalent to insurgency. One sees too the characteristics that were so often attributed to the Warrens in the 1780s and 1790s: his supposed radical deviation from the political character deemed appropriate to his rank and her wronged hesitancy, her indignation. In Massachusetts' bitter proto-party feuds of the late 1780s the perceived inconsistencies of the Warrens' social position made easy political capital. They were New England's natural aristocracy protesting a new bourgeois ascendancy; impecunious debtors acting in their own self-interest; earthy, plebeian democrats in opposition to the golden *imperium*; disorderly barbarians working against the stability of modern union. Given the agrarian–classical tenor of the Warrens' republicanism and its contradictory relationship to commercial modernity, there was perhaps a certain crass logic to the Federalist attack, its blundering exorbitance notwithstanding. It was clearly hard for the Warrens to find a definitive or defendable space for their political identities in the divisive world of Federalist Massachusetts.

---

[41] MOW to JA, Sept. 1786, WAP.
[42] *The Diary of John Quincy Adams*, ed. David Grayson Auen, Robert J. Taylor, *et al.*, 2 vols. (Cambridge, Mass.: Harvard University Press, 1981), i. 413.

III Taking it Personally

John Quincy Adams was right to note that James Warren's politics had distanced him from many old friends in Massachusetts. He had even quarrelled with Sam Adams, whose vicious condemnation of the claims of the backcountry had rendered him, in Warren's words, 'the most arbitrary and despotic man in the commonwealth'.[43] In the summer of 1788 James Warren told Elbridge Gerry disconsolately, 'you are the only confidential friend I have'.[44] Throughout the 1790s Mercy Warren repeatedly remarked on 'the uncertainty of human friendships', and told her sons that they might hope for little consistency there or in the public sphere.[45] Experience had taught her, she insisted, that what she alternately termed 'dereliction' or 'versatility' was always the undoing of public men's political characters as well as their private attachments.

For the testy Warren this pertained in a very particular sense. In George Washington and John Adams she saw men she had once counted as correspondents and personal friends apparently corrupted by the rewards of office, moving away from commonwealth politics towards a conservative Federalism and acting as agents of the persecution which, among other things, had excluded her family from the public sphere. As she became increasingly dismayed at the turn of their administrations (particularly the policies of the repressive mid- to late 1790s) so she sought to define political difference in terms of the painful neglect of sentimental friendship. If republicanism was now 'thought by many', as she put it, 'to be dwindled into theory', so 'old republicans' were, she wrote to Catharine Macaulay, 'the devoted victims of vicious parties. They are neglected by their less principled but more fortunate associates—who for a time struggled with them for the security of liberty and the inherent rights of man.'[46] The unfashionable steadfastness of herself and James Warren meant, she told her friend, that they were regarded by 'the intriguers for place, titles and standing armies', simply as 'impediments in their road to ambition'.[47]

Warren thought she had seen the road to ambition corrupt the characters of the men in the nation's first office. She had met George

[43] JW to JA, 18 May 1787, WAP.   [44] JW to EG, 20 July 1788, in 'Gardiner'.
[45] MOW to JW, 14 Nov. 1792, MOWP1.
[46] MOW to CM, n.d., July 1789, MOWP1.   [47] Ibid.

Washington in the hopeful spring of 1775; kept up a friendly correspondence with him and Martha Washington (whom she obviously deeply admired) and had written a number of exuberant, in fact rather gushy encomiums to his patriotic character, which she circulated among her friends during the war.[48] She prefaced one of these with a contrast between Washington and George III, whom she of course briskly condemned and 'le[ft] to his own fate to make an observation on the more respectable character of one whose conscious worth sets him above the regalia of kings'.[49] One might only imagine how Washington's adoption of the kingly regalia of the Cincinatti and its imperial 'eagle dangling at the breast' represented to her a gross betrayal.[50] She reserved some of her most scathing remarks for him in her correspondence and *History*. He was the worst infant of the infant republic with his childlike 'fondness for nominal distinctions'.[51] She described him in an intriguingly cryptic letter to Elbridge Gerry as the 'king of hearts'—dismissing his sentimental popularity as a kind of royalist–nationalist coercion.[52] 'You will see the president's late speech in the papers,' she wrote to her son George after reading the union address of 1794:

and the servile answer of the senate. 'Self-created societies' was an unlucky phrase for him. What situation might he have been in had Americans been afraid to form themselves into conventions, committees of correspondence and such like 'self-created societies'—and in what but self and the most selfish motives originated the order of Cincinatti of which he is president?[53]

Washington's censure of democratic republican societies and his dismissal of the principle of association (always at the heart of Warren's

---

[48] In Warren's *History*, Martha Washington is described as possessing an almost magical charm and dispensing a sort of benevolent witchery: 'In this lady's character was blended that sweetness of manners that at once engaged the partiality of the stranger, soothed the sorrows of the afflicted, and relieved the anguish of poverty, even in the manner of extending her charitable hand to the sufferer' (MOW, *History*, 638).

[49] MOW to 'Madame Hancock', n.d. [Mar.–Apr.] 1775, MOWP1.

[50] MOW, *History*, 618.

[51] In her *History*, Warren described Washington as a victim of his own love of 'lustre' and the limelight. MOW, *History*, 662. See also MOW to 'the honourable——member of congress' [EG], n.d., 1796, MOWP1.

[52] MOW to 'the honourable——member of congress' [EG], n.d., 1796, MOWP1.

[53] MOW to GW, n.d. (1795?), MOWP1. Warren threw the language of Washington's famous speech back at him in her *History*'s vigorous condemnation of the Cincinatti as a 'self-created rank'. (MOW, *History*, 616). On Washington's desired prohibition of the democratic republican 'self-created societies', see also JA to AA, Jan. 1795, WAP.

politics) were her last straw. And yet she felt the cooling of the friendship of the man she still referred to in other, less frank correspondence as 'the illustrious Washington', as something like a personal affront.[54] 'I have never felt the *benign influence* of certain *idolized characters*,' Warren wrote to Elbridge Gerry, 'and we are apt to speak of our own feelings'.[55]

Warren's political and personal resentment was far more intense where John Adams was concerned. Both were always, in their own ways, temperamental, and though, the political and literary exchanges of their correspondence in the 1770s are affectionate and respectful, they clearly shared a friendship based largely on a kind of mutual infuriation. The differences in their politics (always latently there) became acutely visible during Adams's diplomatic absence in Britain, where he had declared himself, in Catharine Macaulay's words, 'a very warm Federalist'. 'You will not agree so well on public matters,' Macaulay warned Warren, clearly sympathizing with her friend's political predicament, 'as you did formerly'.[56] Warren was certainly offended at Adams's perceived neglect of her husband and his implicit acceptance of much of the scandal surrounding them in the late 1780s and at least equally incensed by his conservatism, which she read as more than merely proximate to the politics of British constitutional monarchy. 'Some men of genius,' she confided to Macaulay, 'professed republicans, who formerly shared the confidence of the people, are now become the advocates for monarchy . . . the British constitution is the idol of their warmest devotion'.[57] The terms of Warren's denunciation of Adams from the early 1790s on anticipated his representation in Bache's *Aurora* and other democratic–republican publications.[58] Her *History*'s portrait of him is certainly cruel and satiric and tinged with her own anti-British melancholia. Adams's

---

[54] See, for example, MOW to Henry Knox, 9 May 1789, WAP.
[55] MOW to EG, 25 Dec. 1793, MOWP1.
[56] CM to MOW, 26 Oct. 1788, WAP.
[57] MOW to CM, 21 May 1791, MOWP1.
[58] Adams, in fact, accused Warren of being in league with Bache and his compatriots in their famous 1807 exchange. He also suggested she was being paid to produce slander about him by the Jeffersonians. There were of course no grounds to the accusation. See, for example, JA to MOW, 11 July 1807, *Corresondence of John Adams and Mercy Warren*: 'if I were to measure out to others the treatment that has been meted to me, I could make wild work with some of your party. Shall I indulge in retaliation or not?' On Bache's *Aurora*, see Richard Rosenfeld's excellent innovative study *American Aurora: A Democratic Republican Returns* (New York: St Martins, 1997).

brusque American manners rendered him 'deficient', she wrote 'in the *je ne sais quoi* so necessary in highly polished society', but by the 1780s he had been contaminated by a sustained proximity to European courts:

> endowed with a comprehensive genius, well acquainted with the history of men and nations, and having long appeared to be actuated by the principles of integrity, by a zeal for the rights of men and an honest indignation at the ideas of despotism, it was viewed as a kind of political phenomenon when discovered that Mr Adams' former opinions were beclouded by a partiality for monarchy.[59]

One could hardly miss the barbed suggestion that Adams's formerly professed republican character was merely a mask or deception, nor perhaps the inference that she, the historian, retains the qualities that he appears to have mislaid.[60]

In 1789 Warren had written to Adams noting what she perceived as a troubling diminution of the friendship that had formerly existed between their two families. 'The sensibility of my feeling heart', she told him of the struggles of the past few years, 'has been awakened on many trying occasions'.[61] Adams replied that his heart had been equally 'hurt . . . intimately' by the fact that 'General Warren did differ . . . from all his friends and did countenance measures that appear to me, as they did to those friends, extremely pernicious'.[62] For Warren this set the seal on their differences. As Adams took up the vice-presidency on what she saw as an impertinently Federalist ticket, the language of sentimental abandonment became her principal register in reference to him.[63] 'Though the vice president of the United States and his lady may have forgotten Mrs Warren,' she wrote, including a copy of her recently published *Poems, Dramatic and Miscellaneous*, 'yet her former friend Mr Adams will accept a small volume from the hand of their sincere and

---

[59] MOW, *History*, 676. For Warren, the republican Franklin had been 'contaminated' too, but by the sexual excess she associated with European courts, rather than their models of government.

[60] See also ibid. 70, where Warren suggests the errors of her favourite villain Thomas Hutchinson are 'much more excusable than any who may deviate from their principles and professions of republicanism who have not been biased by the patronage of kings'.

[61] MOW to JA, 7 May 1789, WAP.   [62] JA to MOW, 29 May 1789, WAP.

[63] To a greater or lesser extent, this is the case with any of Warren's letters to or about John Adams from the late 1780s onwards. On their relationship, see Zagarri, *A Woman's Dilemma*, 149–55; Fritz, *Cast for a Revolution*, 303–7; and from another perspective David McCullough, *John Adams* (New York: Simon & Schuster, 2001), 594–6.

very humble servant'.[64] As Adams seemed to acknowledge in his swift repost to this message, Warren was depicting the very nature of his public office as a betrayal of the sentimental republican character he had once shared in revolutionary friendship with the Warrens and which was also celebrated in the poems the volume contained.[65] While Warren repeatedly charged Adams with neglect and disregard, she quite self-consciously and insistently represented each subsequent exchange with him as an additional wound to *her* painfully constant sensibility. In 1791 Warren received an unsealed letter from 'the vice president', which for her clearly illustrated a shift in their once close and confidential friendship, 'irreconcilable with former sentiment'. 'Delicate friendship, conscious of its own disinterested attachment, is easily wounded,' she told Adams.[66] However negligent he might be of his revolutionary circle in Massachusetts; however he might turn from the politics that once defined them all, she could 'never tax myself... with... the want of voluntary attention... toward a friend'.[67]

Warren thought of Adams as one of her best readers and also knew just how capable he was of being riled by her prickliness (if he had ever heard her express any sort of assent to a monarchical element in the constitution, she told him, 'it must have been with some additional stroke that rendered it a sarcasm').[68] As my readings of their exchanges are suggesting, there is certainly a carefully considered element to Warren's use of a language of feeling that would seem irrefutable, unassailable. Adams certainly could not counter Warren's self-representation as a woman of wounded sensibility. And, yet, there is still something there beyond the strategic. As I have argued elsewhere in this book,

---

[64] MOW to JA, 24 Sept. 1790, WAP. Warren's relationship with Abigail Adams had also cooled, and, in the fractious political climate, she came to regard her too with some suspicion. See, for example, MOW to GW, Nov. 1796, MOWP1: 'We lately had a visit of three or four days from the vice president's lady; it was unexpected—and whither friendly, political or accidental I know not, but she appeared very *clever*.'

[65] See JA to MOW, 26 Dec. 1790, WAP: 'I am ignorant, madam, of any foundation you may have for the distinction you make between the vice president and Mr Adams, or for an insinuation that either may have forgotten Mrs Warren, since Mrs Warren is certainly indebted to the Vice president and Mr Adams in partnership for the last letter.'

[66] MOW to JA, 14 Jan. 1791, WAP.   [67] MOW to JA, 14 Jan. 1791, WAP.

[68] MOW to JA, 28 July 1807, in 'Correspondence of John Adams and Mercy Warren'. Warren clearly took a great deal of pride in her facility for sarcasm and also considered Adams's sarcastic wit one of his laudable qualities. See MOW, *History*, 563.

sentimentality was an indissoluble part of the republicanism that was Warren's lingua franca. For her, there really *was* an undoubted connection between Adams's break with old republicanism and his breach of private attachment: between his rise to power and public fame and the diminution of private friendship. John Adams's significance to Warren was, then, both material and symbolic. She was dismayed by his conservative tendencies; held him in some sense responsible for her family's failure to be appropriately rewarded for their patriotic efforts; and experienced *her* loss of personal solidarity as equivalent to republicanism's loss of *him*. In her *History* he served as her principal exemplar of what time, power, and human 'versatility' might do to the virtuous integrity of the new republic. He was one source of the wounded sentiment that lent her such an authoritative language to express her political disaffection.

IV Out of Time

As biographies of Warren and her circle have detailed, her experience of the last two decades of the eighteenth century was deeply affected by absence and bereavement.[69] The sad loss of three of her five sons, all young adults at the times of their deaths, was undoubtedly decisive to the shift that I am arguing marks her writing over the course of this period. In the late 1780s and 1790s Warren frequently made reference to her personal grief and political estrangement in the same breath. She also claimed, in the prefatory 'address' to her *History*, that her loss had coloured the narrative's composition and defined her identity as an author ('the shaft flew thrice, and thrice my peace was slain').[70]

During the war, in their childhoods and adolescence, Warren's sons were certainly central to her patriotic self-representation. In the face of potential opposition from her more conventional friends and their wary husbands, she often argued away the dangerous independence of her political character by invoking the then familiar wisdom of the important moral role of mothers in the education of patriotic sons. To her pregnant relatives and young friends she wrote formal letters of advice which suggested, in effect, women's public role by proxy. 'We lessen the dignity of our own sex', Warren told Sally Sever, Elizabeth

---

[69] See Zagarri, *A Woman's Dilemma*, 127–8; Fritz, *Cast for a Revolution*, 267–71.
[70] MOW, *History*, p. xlii.

Brown, and other women,

when we accede to the opinion that our conduct individually is of little consequence to the world. The first rudiments of education are implanted by the feminine hand and the early traits are seldom wholly eradicated from the bosom of those who must tread the public stage and regulate both the religious and political affairs of human life.[71]

Women also 'regulate' the public sphere, Warren suggested in an argument familiar to the mid- to late century, through the moral and private influence of intellectual maternity. In the 1760s and 1770s, then, Warren perhaps seemed the archetype of Linda Kerber's 'republican mother'.[72] Consider the group portrait she painted for James Warren, then engaged by the revolutionary public sphere, in 1776:

little George is standing in the corner at my elbow with his usual gravity. ...Henry is reading [illegible] and Charles on the other side of the table studying the *History of England*; Winslow is in your usual chair before the fire engaged with Plutarch's *Lives*... your eldest son is on a visit to his grandfather. May they all improve this opportunity in a manner worthy of the sons of a father engaged in the grand system of American politics.[73]

---

[71] MOW to Sally Sever (later Russell), 2 May 1784; Warren also sent this letter to 'a very young lady' according to the *Letterbook*, with a copy of Hesther Chapone's *Letters on the Improvement of the Mind*. Warren had quite enjoyed Chapone but preferred the poetry of Phillis Wheatley, which she read around the same time.

[72] I discuss these issues at greater length in the Introduction to this book, but see Linda Kerber, *Women of the Republic: Intellect and Ideology in Revolutionary America* (Chapel Hill, NC: University of North Carolina Press, 1980); Mary-Beth Norton, *Liberty's Daughters: The Revolutionary Experience of American Women, 1759–1800* (New York: Norton, 1980); Jane Rendall, *The Origins of Modern Feminism: Women in Britain, France and the United States, 1780–1860* (Basingstoke: Macmillan, 1985), ch. 2; Ruth Bloch, 'Linda Kerber's Republican Mother', in Lucy Maddox (ed.), *Locating American Studies: The Evolution of a Discipline* (Baltimore: Johns Hopkins University Press, 1999) and 'Gender and the Public/Private Dichotomy in American Revolutionary Thought', in *Gender and Morality in Anglo-American Culture, 1650–1800* (Berkeley and Los Angeles: University of California Press, 2003); Margaret Nash, 'Re-Thinking Republican Motherhood', *Journal of the Early Republic*, 17 (1997), 171–91; Rosemarie Zagarri, 'Morals, Manners and the Republican Mother', *American Quarterly*, 44 (1992), 192–215; Norma Basch, *Framing American Divorce: From the Revolutionary Generation to the Victorians* (Berkeley and Los Angles: University of California Press, 1999); Jan Lewis, 'The Republican Wife: Virtue and Seduction in the Early Republic', *William and Mary Quarterly*, 44 (1987), 689–721; Smith-Rosenberg, 'Dis-Covering the Subject of the "Great Constitutional Discussion"'; Kerber's response to Lewis's article and re-evaluation of republican motherhood, 'The Paradox of Women's Citizenship in the Early Republic: The Case of *Martin vs Massachusetts*, 1805', *American Historical Review*, 97 (1992), 349–78.

[73] MOW to JW, Feb. 1776, MOWP2.

This is typical of the fearful-hopeful wartime Warren who enjoyed her Plymouth domesticity and saw her own and James Warren's patriotism in terms of complementary public and private roles. But there is still something quite remarkable in the unequivocally ideal nature of her sentimental tableau: the sons reading Plutarch and Catharine Macaulay's *History* like the good republicans they promise to be and she proud to steel the resolve of her absent husband with a depiction of patriotic maternity.

Warren clearly saw in her sons the political future of an independent America. But by the 1780s, as America seemed to her to lose its determined unity of purpose, so her own maternal role was perhaps less easily appropriable to a notion of patriotic identity. During the war, her eldest son James began to show symptoms of mental illness apparently similar to those of his uncle and namesake and, in 1781, he was lamed at sea while serving on the *Alliance*. The pious, thoughtful, and ailing Charles had finally left home only to die from his recurrent tubercular illnesses en route to Lisbon in 1786. In 1791 Winslow, the 'son inexpressibly dear', bought himself out of debt and prison by engaging as an officer in the US Army's second regiment.[74] He was killed in St Clair's disastrous expedition against the Miami Indians just five months after signing up. The youngest son George, who was making a go of farming and local politics alone in remote Maine, died suddenly, far away from his shocked family, as the nineteenth century turned. By 1790 Warren was also describing her fourth son Henry, his cheerful disposition notwithstanding, as 'the child of disappointment'.[75] Under the cloud of his family's politics, Henry found it difficult to establish himself in a public position in Massachusetts and was continually passed over, his mother wrote indignantly, in favour of men with 'no claim of merit except the ignorant servility of a dupe to the new government'.[76]

Always intensely proud and determined in her familial roles as in her politics, Warren regarded her sons' difficult futures and fates as intimately bound up with the troubled fortunes of the new nation. For a disaffected Anti-Federalist, ever making connections between public and private 'dereliction', this link was not merely incidental. If Warren's broken friendship with John Adams had taken on a symbolic

[74] See MOW to WW, n.d., 1785, MOWP1.
[75] MOW to WW, 25 Apr. 1790, MOWP2.   [76] Ibid.

sentimental meaning, then her sons for her were powerful symbols too—and particularly urbane, capricious Winslow. To Warren he had seemed the most intellectually promising of her children. Much of what she wrote in the 1780s was produced with him in mind: her critique of Chesterfield's *Letters* and the *Ladies of Castile* were for him; he was her *History*'s first reader and critic, and she granted him the copyright of her *Poems Dramatic and Miscellaneous*.[77] Winslow was clearly Warren's intellectual confidante. He had more than a taste for the classical and conjectural history enjoyed by his mother; disputed with her about the merits of Gibbon and Adam Ferguson; sent her newspapers and pamphlets for use in her *History*; flirted (to her concern) with deism; and, like her, wrote an excellent letter. But he rejected a Harvard education in favour of European travel and a life in trade. In Paris he gained a reputation for gaming; his post-war commercial ventures foundered; he failed to secure the diplomatic appointment he thought his rightful due; and by the mid-1780s he had enmeshed himself in debts spanning two continents.[78]

Winslow continually defied Warren's high expectations of him. And what was wrong with Winslow—his ostentation, inattention, selfishness, pretence—was also, for Warren, what was wrong with Federalist America. His chosen path as a modern merchant-adventurer was clearly anathema to her republican sensibilities. She was even more appalled at his position in an army she thought a potential threat to national liberty, now flexing its imperial muscle against the mid-west's Miami Indians. Following news of his military appointment, she wrote and told him what she thought of Edmund Burke's *Reflections* and Catharine Macaulay's *Observations*, which she had recently read. Perhaps the new Winslow, she wrote icily, would not concur with her opinion of these two responses to the French Revolution as troublingly reactionary and laudably republican respectively: 'it is possible a young officer of a *standing army* may view things in a different light than what he did when he was a warm advocate for the establishment of a free government.'[79]

---

[77] This significant bequest ('the only thing I can properly call my own') reveals, as I mentioned in this book's Introduction, Warren's evident awareness of the benefits of literary property to women. MOW to WW, 10 June 1791. See also Zagarri, *A Woman's Dilemma*, 126.
[78] On Winslow's troubled career, see Fritz, *Cast for a Revolution*, 236–43, 262–8.
[79] MOW to WW, 25 Apr. 1790, MOWP2.

Warren was 'exceedingly pained at the new stile of life you have adopted'.[80] Her son's professional choices clearly represented a betrayal of his familial politics.

On 29 November 1784 Warren wrote to Winslow that she now took little pleasure in the natural scenery of Tremont. Though 'Nature has ornamented this place with a liberal hand ... but with me the enjoyment is marred by the absence of my children'.[81] Five days later she continued the same letter with an attempt to account for what really spoiled Tremont's prospect for her:

Alone in the green parlor in view of the western hill tops and all the delightful imagery that a fine sunshine throws on the variegated prospect, I sit down to finish a letter begun several days since. I view the beauties of nature which cheer the soul and the bounties of providence which gladden the grateful heart—here a philosophic mind may contemplate with a kind of rapture the universal benevolence that has created so many avenues of pleasure and scattered bounties with such an equal hand over a world deformed only by moral turpitude. It is the perversion of reason, a corruption of taste, and the cravings of artificial necessity which causes the restless pursuit of objects which can seldom be obtained without hazard, fatigue and pain, and which often wear out the man before he is ready for enjoyment.[82]

Warren clearly felt Winslow's failure to settle at Milton and, by extension, in Massachusetts as a personal snub. Here she connects his absence, and particularly his choice of an itinerant life in international commerce, to her failure to feel Tremont's scenery as she ought. She strives to make her own and Winslow's native landscape reflect a desired experience of the philosophic and religious sublime: Massachusetts' variegated prospect should suggest its own sufficiency, and what the horizon promises should be an unnecessary distraction. As the view is marred by absence and disappointment (what the 'philosophic mind' *may* feel), so providential equality is disrupted by modern humanity's desire and ambition. Commercial exchange—the 'restless pursuit of objects' prompted by 'artificial necessity'—deforms nature, ushering in disproportion, inequality, and the dictates of taste. Winslow, moving like commercial desire itself across continents and seas, embodies all Warren's concern at

[80] MOW to WW, 19 Apr. 1791, MOWP1.
[81] MOW to WW, 29 Nov. 1784, MOWP1.   [82] Ibid.

what the mobility of property might do to modern America. By the end of the passage, her failure to enjoy the landscape she sees disrupted by commercial progress has become *his*. Winslow, the representative of commerce and modernity, seems exhausted, as it were, by his own restlessness.

'We are born', Warren continued her letter, 'in that period of time when the enlightened world by a kind of universal consent have agreed to the exchange of commodities'. 'Yet,' she wrote,

> I begin to think the patriarchal life was better adapted to the happiness of man than the high stages of civilisation which require such resources for the supply of a refined and elegant taste. Would not a little hermitage on one hill, a spot on the declivity of another, and the whole family of brethren placed on the winding stream in the same vista or its vicinity conduce more to the real happiness of human life than all the golden treasures that the distant world can pour in to the lap of luxury when embittered by the absence of those we most tenderly love? What then you ask would become of ambition, and where the bold exertions that open an intercourse around the globe? I would not check its rational sallies nor damp the ardour of enterprise—yet my own wishes are diminished when I retrospect that stage of simplicity when it was convenient for one of a family to remove his tent, it was reputable for the whole herd to accompany him to seek some more eligible spot.[83]

For Warren, the patriarchal life clearly represents the more moral as well as less mobile economic option. Her wistful encomium to the virtues of a society where production and exchange have not moved beyond herding or tilling is as much about the pain of ceding private attachment as it is about defying the narrative of civil, commercial progress. What is of course most telling about the patriarchal life for her is that the ardour of enterprise has not yet destroyed familial love. Here affectionate exchanges outweigh those of commerce, the appeal of the homely winding stream is greater than seas that promise imperial gold. As patriotic and filial affection are inseparable in Warren's 'stage of simplicity', so the familial separations and commercial dissipation she has found painfully characteristic of America's modern stage seem part of the same thing. Warren's fantasy of the patriarchal life allows her provisionally to contain Winslow's modern mobility or, at the very least, to picture (as she moves her tent towards the end of the passage) the

[83] MOW to WW, 29 Nov. 1784, MOWP1.

possibility of a viable proximity to him. In the despondence of her 'retrospection' is written her awareness of its temporary nature: Warren knows that history always changes the good life into something else, knows the simple country is subject to the jagged time of rise and fall. She acknowledges the movement of modernity, the push of desire and ambition that here, in the person of Winslow, turns the wheels of time inexorably onward. And yet she describes herself—and perhaps time too—'diminished' by the contemplation of the idealized social paradigm she still somehow insists is outside history, beyond change. Warren's imaginary patriarchal life enables her to stop history, to step outside it, to envisage a retreat from the disappointment that the chaotic Winslow and America's post-war political and economic muddle represented to her.

This letter is (for me at least) one of the most intriguing examples of how Mercy Warren often read her sons' lives (and indeed later their distressing deaths) into the way history had failed America, or, conversely, read that history back into her sons. Indeed, she often said she was writing her own *History* to remind her sons of the revolutionary times into which they were born.[84] Her later letters continually make connections between her maternal feeling and her sensations of political or national betrayal. In the 1770s and early 1780s she still described her private attachment to her sons as, to some extent, explaining her attachment to public matters. For example, after offering her views on the barbary pirate debate to Charles (then at sea and potentially threatened) she wrote:

> I wish I felt less personally interested in this new scene of distress that threatens my country, but I cannot, as many others do, look coldly on while the nations are negotiating their political systems and adjusting the boundaries of rapine and violence: my stake is too great—my feelings too much alive.[85]

Warren's sons—her emotive stake, her patriotic investment—are here still closely bound up with her political ideals. But, as she grew increasingly disillusioned with and disconnected from Federalist America; as

---

[84] In the introduction to her *History*, Warren claimed that she had begun writing it 'with a view to transmitting it to the rising youth of my country, some of them in infancy, others in the European world [clearly Winslow], while the most interesting events lowered over their native land' (MOW, *History*, p. xlii).
[85] MOW to Charles Warren, 5 Nov. 1785, MOWP1.

she felt progressively distanced and painfully separated from her sons; then so too her republican understanding of the connection between maternal and political identities underwent a drastic change. The figure of the abandoned or grieving *Matrona* provided for Warren a compelling sentimental rationalization of what history had done to America.

V Edoxia

In her hopeful poems and letters of the 1770s, Mercy Warren used the figures of Roman matrons to suggest the strength of women's love of country and America's republican virtue. Warren's identification of classical women as positive models of patriotic feeling is clearly behind her own and Abigail Adams's choice of epistolary pseudonyms, as well as the 'good Cornelias' and ... Arrias' fair' of 'To the Honourable J. Winthrop esq' who preserve America's integrity in their refusal to consume the commercial ephemera of corrupt, imperial Britain.[86] In Warren's poems (and indeed in her letters, as I argued in Chapter 4) republican women attain a sort of public status through the political and moral regulation of the private sphere from which national virtue is seen to arise. From 1778—the year Warren identified as the origin of the new republic's decline and fall—there is a shift in her iconic females from figures that suggest collective resolution to those whose function is more clearly that of admonition or reproach.

In 1778, for example, Warren published a poem in the *Boston Gazette* which she entitled 'The Genius of America Weeping the Absurd Follies of the Day'. 'This piece was written', she later put it, 'when a most remarkable depravity of manners pervaded the cities of the United States in consequence of a state of war; a relaxation of government; the sudden acquisition of fortune; a depreciating currency and a new intercourse with foreign nations'.[87] All the deficiencies of new nationhood ('public faith and private justice dead | And patriot zeal by patriots betrayed') are gathered into the grieving figure of Columbia's 'weeping genius', who presents America with history's 'blacken'd scroll'.[88] Shortly afterwards,

---

[86] MOW, 'To the Honourable J. Winthrop esq.' [1774], in *Poems Dramatic and Miscellaneous*, ll. 65, 141–5. See my discussion of these figures in Chapter 5.

[87] The poem was published in the *Boston Gazette and Country Journal* on 5 Oct. 1778. The note was added by Warren to its reprinting in her *Poems Dramatic and Miscellaneous*.

[88] 'The Genius of America Weeping the Absurd Follies of the Day' [1778], in *Poems Dramatic and Miscellaneous*, ll. 105–6.

Warren wrote 'Simplicity', in which she gave the 'weeping genius' figure another try, this time as Britannia. Simplicity finds embodiment in an imaginary gothic landscape: 'The cloud cap't hills, the echoing woods and dales, | Where pious druids dressed the hallowed vales.'[89] But modernity has taken Britannia from the woods and left her exposed and defenceless on time's margin:

> When taste's improved by luxury high wrought,
> And fancy craves what nature never taught;
> Affronted virtue mounts her native skies,
> And freedom's genius lifts her bloated eyes;
> As late I saw, in sable vestments stand,
> The weeping fair, on Britain's naked strand.[90]

Mercy Warren and Catharine Macaulay both clearly identified with the melancholy and sentimental figure of the grieving *Matrona* and found her a persuasive analogue of their desired characters as admonitory republican historians. As I have argued, the vocabulary of their friendship was one that blended privacy and patriotism, fusing the language of feeling with that of women's public characters. If they wrote to each other, as Mercy Warren said, as 'politicians', then they also thought of themselves as sharing what she described as their common 'experience [of] the anxieties of maternal care'.[91] Like amity and conjugal affection, then, a sentimental notion of maternity afforded one source of that legitimating continuity they saw between the private and the public which enabled Macaulay and Warren to think of themselves together as political writers and historians, as women with a visible civic role. In this book's second chapter, I discussed Macaulay's popular representation 'in the character of a Roman Matron lamenting the lost liberties of Rome' and how she sometimes referred to the American colonies as if they were her children. By 1785 Macaulay was still mingling the personal with the national in a rather different way when she told Warren that the 'calls of maternal affection' obliged her to return to England.[92] The letters of both women make their sentimental and maternal characters key to the

---

[89] MOW, 'Simplicity' [1779], in ibid. ll. 151–2.   [90] Ibid. ll. 145–50.
[91] MOW to CM, 4 Dec. 1774, and Oct. 1786, MOWP1.
[92] See my discussion of Macaulay's representation as a Roman matron in Chapter 2. CM to MOW, July 1785, WAP. In her letters to Warren, Macaulay often mentions her daughter, Catharine Sophia.

depiction of a shared political conviction and republican attachment. There was, then, a certain obvious logic to the way in which, during the late 1780s, Mercy Warren's political disenchantment shifted focus from Britannia's and Columbia's generic 'weeping genius', and found expression in the imagined figure of her tearful friend. 'Do you remember', she asked Macaulay in 1789,

> the pleasant morning when you came out from Boston and breakfasted with me at Milton? All nature looked gay and peace pervaded the land; you was delighted with the cheerful faces and independent countenances you met on your way; but I recollect you observed you could scarcely forbear weeping over my country when you surveyed its present happiness and at the same time saw a disposition in many to trifle away its advantages so recently and so dearly purchased. If you was here now, dear Madam, perhaps the tear would be indulged.[93]

Both the writer and her subject are weeping here (Warren's sorrow is simply displaced in her confirmation that her friend has grounds for tears). Macaulay and herself, women of patriotism and learning, are figures of reproach for what Warren saw as the Federalist failure of Atlantic republicanism: *Matronas* who find the public sphere a source of sentimental pain or who might read back into their experience of private disappointment a language of political betrayal.

From 1778 on, Mercy Warren had, as I have been suggesting, many sources of public and private disillusion. The political rejection of the partner she felt to be the model of the ideal public man and his vilification as an insurgent; her sensations of being misplaced in the province to which she felt a strong patriotic attachment; the 'versatility' of personal friends only mirrored by the 'dereliction' of the public sphere; the ascendance of a political ideology she thought characterized by its excesses and inequalities; the dearth and extortion of New England's post-war economy; and the anxieties of her maternal role, which she saw as peculiarly bound up with the disappointments of 'the golden age of Federalism'. During this period, her affirmative patriotic women are replaced by the melancholy and admonitory figure of the grieving *Matrona*, with whom she evidently identified. I want to conclude this section with a reading of some passages from her *Sack of Rome*, her letters, and *Observations on the New Constitution and on*

[93] MOW to CM, 4 July 1789, MOWP1.

the Federal and State Conventions, which show how clearly this was the case.

Warren's *Sack of Rome*, which she composed during 1787, might be read as putting an Anti-Federalist spin on the subject matter of the rabid *Anarchiad*. It was certainly no coincidence that her drama was set in an imperial Rome 'torn' from within by 'furious factions' and threatened from without by a brooding Vandal invasion. Warren took her subject from the part of Gibbon's *Decline and Fall* when, as she put it, 'the character of man was sunk to the lowest stage of depravity'.[94] One might easily read into Gibbon's chapters 35 and 36 Massachusetts' affluent merchant class and oppressed agrarian debtors:

> oeconomy was neglected in proportion as it became necessary; and the injustice of the rich shifted the unequal burden from themselves to the people, whom they defrauded of the indulgencies that might sometimes have alleviated their miseries [and] compelled the subjects of Valentinian to prefer the more simple tyranny of the barbarians, to fly to the woods and mountains.[95]

If one was in any doubt as to the contemporary resonance of what she described as the 'theatrical instruction' with which she 'threw a mite into the scale of virtue', Warren's 'preface' expressed her concern at the formulation of 'absurd systems of policy which have frequently corrupted, distracted and ruined the best constituted republics'.[96]

Warren's representation of the Empress Edoxia, said to have invited Genseric to overthrow the faithless Valentinian, is not unequivocally positive—after all, she is motivated, Warren says, by 'revenge and indiscretion' and is also the victim of what is described as 'an uninformed Christianity'—but she does get all the best lines.[97] The wronged

---

[94] MOW, *The Sack of Rome* [1787], in *Poems Dramatic and Miscellaneous*, 'To the Public', 9. On Warren's dramatic writing, see: Zoe Detsi, 'The Metaphors of Freedom: Republican Rhetoric and Gender Ideology in Mercy Otis Warren's Romantic Tragedies, *The Sack of Rome* and *The Ladies of Castile*', *American Drama*, 8 (1998), 1–25; Cheryl Oreovicz, 'Heroic Drama for an Uncertain Age: The Plays of Mercy Warren', in Kathryn Z. Derounian-Stodola (ed.), *Early American Literature and Culture: Essays Honoring Harrison T. Meserole* (Newark: Del. University of Delaware Press, 1992), 192–210; Mary Schofield, 'The Happy Revolution: Colonial Women and the Eighteenth-Century Theater', in June Schlueter (ed.), *Modern American Drama: The Female Canon* (Rutherford: Fairleigh Dickinson University Press, 1990), 29–37. See also Richards, *Mercy Otis Warren*, 114–120.

[95] Edward Gibbon, *The Decline and Fall of the Roman Empire*, 4 vols. (Halifax: William Milner, 1812), ii. 382.

[96] MOW, *The Sack of Rome*, 'To the Public', 12.   [97] Ibid. 9–10.

Edoxia is still inspired by the memory of the patriots who once died to save the commonwealth but can no longer locate her own patriotic virtue in a Rome unworthy of it: 'I have no country | What's life or empire or the world to me?'[98] Many of Edoxia's speeches are marked by her melancholic conviction of Rome's irrevocable and necessary fall. Thus Gaudentius's youthful patriotic feeling merely illustrates virtue's 'last remains': 'like a glow worm in a stormy night | It twinkles but to shew the sable hue | By nature worn through all the midnight gloom'.[99] The possibility of privacy and retirement is Edoxia's only consolation in a world of disappointment. She wishes:

> to be left retir'd
> To weep awhile the destiny of Rome;
> To pour the balm of pity on the breast
> Of virgin sorrow—to lift the drooping head
> Of undissembled grief—hung like the lily
> O'er the wasted vale—when the rough surge's
> Roaring deluge sweeps down all around,
> Except the naked bloom—propless and weak
> And quivering on the marge of the next tide—
> Whose watery wave may wash the broken fragment
> From its native soil . . .[100]

Maternal Edoxia turns from her failed civic hopes to afford sympathetic comfort to her daughters, grieving lilies denied their patriotic roots, their love of country.

Edoxia's own alienated patriotism is expressed in terms of a particular landscape and another analogy of natural fragmentation:

> Oh! Could I hide in some dark hermitage,
> Beneath some hollow, dismal broken cliff,
> I'd weep folorn the miseries of Rome
> Till time's last billow broke and left me quiet
> On the naked strand.[101]

Edoxia's broken cliffs and excluded retreat in which she mourns the lost republic not only recall the descriptions of Columbia and Britannia

---

[98] MOW, The Sack of Rome, iv. ii. 45–6. See also Edoxia's encomium to the 'shades' of Rome's patriotic heroes, iv. iii. 86–8. [99] Ibid. IV. v. 147–50.
[100] Ibid. v. ii. 9–20.   [101] Ibid. v. ii. 9–15.

in Warren's earlier poems but also appeared in her letters and other writings in reference to her *own* sensations of patriotic estrangement. After James Warren's failure in the election of 1778, for example, she invited her friend Hannah Winthrop to Plymouth to 'contemplate besides the broken cliffs the revolutions of states, the fall of kingdoms and the rise of Empire'.[102] There is no weeping here, and in 1778 the sublime cliffside retreat still provided Warren with some hope, some patriotic inspiration: 'we will not forget that this dreary shore was once the asylum of our ancestors when they fled from the oppressions of the house of Stuart'.[103] By the late 1780s, though, Warren had few political hopes for a Federalist America, and the contemplative retreat consequently becomes more isolated, more portentous, but perhaps that bit more sublime. Compare the lines which concluded her *Observations on the New Constitution and on the Federal and State Conventions*:

While the statesman is plodding for power and the courtier practising the arts of dissimulation without check—while the rapacious are growing rich by oppression and fortune throwing her gifts into the lap of fools, let the sublimer characters, the philosophic lovers of freedom who have wept over her exit, retire to the calm shades of contemplation, there they may look down with pity on the inconsistency of human nature, the revolutions of states, the rise of kingdoms, and the fall of empires.[104]

Warren recalls weeping over freedom's exit here, but the occasion seems to be one after grief has passed. The philosopher has ascended the cliff and surveys the political prospect with a kind of melancholy detachment. Distance and estrangement also afford immunity: the very remoteness of the disaffection from its source itself enables resolution, intervention. Warren often imagines herself in this authoritative position in the 1780s and 1790s. And it is the particular gendered connotations of this position that, I think, define the mordant confidence of her later writing.

---

[102] MOW to HW, 29 May 1778, WWC.
[103] MOW to HW, 29 May 1778, WWC. For further discussion of the 'sublime' aspects of this letter, see my account of it in Chapter 4.
[104] Mercy Otis Warren, *Observations on the New Constitution and on the Federal and State Conventions by a Columbian Patriot* [1788], in Storing, *The Complete Anti-Federalist*, iv. 286.

VI Republican Sensibility

As the attentions of America turned towards peace in 1783, Mercy Warren suggested to John Adams what differentiated their patriotic roles:

and do you think now, sir, to retire to sit down quietly and enjoy the sweets of domestic life? No. Never, till weary nature diminishes your capacity for acting in the sphere of dignified difficulty. You was not made for the purpose of resting in the cool sequestered shade of life. It is yours to tread the bold and craggy path of politics, to counteract the intrigues of statesmen and princes, to settle the boundaries of nations and mark the line of empire. And what is more difficult to achieve, to convince mankind that probity is the surest road to virtue.[105]

There is a familiar gendered symbolism to Adams's craggy path and Warren's sequestered shade. The public sphere is all virile agitation while the space of domestic virtue (from which she produces one of her last encomiums to his patriotic character) affords its own, quieter rewards. While Warren is clearly writing to Adams's expectations here, she certainly manages to maintain her friendly congratulation, her faith in *one* man's dignity and probity. But there is still a certain something that reads almost like an insult in the 'No' that refuses to grant Adams any rest. He seems doomed to monitor other men's corruption and police the line of empire until weary nature lets him go. The stress on the difficulty of this task itself suggests Warren's gloomy suspicion that maintaining public virtue may now be impossible in post-war America. While Adams's active patriotism appears threatened by erosion in the very sphere that confirms his public character, the stillness and distance of Warren's retirement suggest she might perhaps have got the better deal.

Just a few years later, Warren may well have seen John Adams among those she now classed 'pretended patriots' threatening to 'dupe... the whole continent... out of their liberties'.[106] He was certainly a target of her lament to Elbridge Gerry that 'there are a few whom I love with the most ardent affection; there are a few others still living who I once thought the most valuable of friends. Ah! How have I been deceived!'[107]

---

[105] MOW to JA, 4 May 1783, WAP.
[106] MOW to Samuel Alleyne Otis, n.d., 1787, MOWP1.
[107] MOW to 'the honourable——member of congress' [EG], n.d., 179, MOWP1.

For Warren, Adams's patriotic character had been irretrievably corrupted by the public sphere itself: by the pseudo-monarchical gloss of new conservative national institutions and a politics she thought distinguished more by show than by substance.[108] If the rewards of office had, to Warren's mind, damaged John Adams's republican virtue, then her privacy meant that she remained thankfully beyond reproach.

In letters between James and Mercy Warren, their privacy and retirement always suggest the unquestionable rectitude of their republican politics. 'I feel the highest pleasure from the knowledge of our integrity', Warren wrote to her husband as he left the public stage in 1778.[109] The couple's very distance from the public sphere meant they might, as she put it, 'taste the pleasures of private friendship with accumulated delight'.[110] 'Politics I hear little of and care less about', he wrote to her from New York: 'we have suffered too much by our attentions to the public weal ever again to be ... interrupted by public injustice, private vexations or ... the manoeuvres of politicians'.[111] Their virtuous suffering in the public cause had, both Warrens often wrote, lent their retirement a detachment that itself increased its stock of virtue. Yet, despite professions of indifference, the couple's political interests never waned, and, indeed, their letters constantly make this sort of feigned disavowal the disingenuous motif of an assumed objectivity. If privacy excluded you from the public sphere, wrote Mercy Warren to her eldest son, it also rendered you immune to the painful effects of its corruption:

I do not know how it is but I somehow or other feel superior to these things and look with the most perfect indifference on the versatility of man and the ingratitude of my fellow beings. We have already suffered too much from that source to be ruffled or disappointed at any thing more that can be done by the unjust prejudices of half thinking or designing politicians and their *partisans*.[112]

---

[108] Warren suggested in her *History* that Adams's 'lapse from former republican principles' had eroded his public virtue, yet his private character remained thoroughly uncorrupted: 'it is with more pleasure the writer records, that notwithstanding any mistakes or changes in political opinion, or errors in public conduct, Mr Adams, in private life supported an unimpeachable character' (MOW, *History*, 676–7).
[109] MOW to JW, 2 June 1778, MOWP1.
[110] MOW to JA, n.d. ('when Vice President of the United States'), MOWP1.
[111] JW to MOW, Apr. 1790, MOWP2.
[112] MOW to JW, 14 Nov. 1792, MOWP1.

Warren often spoke of political exclusion and disaffection as a marital or family experience. It is clearly important here that she is at the centre of her family's political persecution, that she is able to speak for it and, by so doing, can confirm *her* sense of hurt rejection and the virtuous superiority of her privacy. Disaffected privacy allows her to surmount the play of differences in a political sphere she represents as the contingent realm of profession and of party. But, as well as identifying with a characteristically classical–republican (and perhaps most usually masculine) position of elevated objectivity, she also assumes a sentimental authority in her emotive opposition to human versatility and ingratitude. Sentimental and republican registers operate in tandem, then, as Warren's often-adopted persona as the woman of injured feeling appears to corroborate and bear out her professed political indifference.

In this letter (only one of very many in which she makes similar moves) Warren uses the familiar associations of that sphere of affective sentiment and feeling (which late-eighteenth-century America described as particularly feminine) to define the parameters of an affirmative republican voice. As I argued earlier, James Warren thought of himself in traditional Commonwealth terms as a public man, and his privacy was always slightly difficult for Mercy Warren to represent. While there is something troubled about her partner's silence and wounded sensibility in Warren's later writing, her account of the personal and political benefits of her retirement became concurrently more self-confident. It is, I think, the normative associations of her gender that gave her the advantage in representing her distance from the public sphere in consistently positive terms. While she might claim her own exclusion from the public exempted her from party conflict and potential corruption, so she could also suggest that sentiment or feeling lent her politics a quality of irrefutability. And the new authority of Warren's privacy was clearly related to a domestic space and landscape in which she felt at greater ease.

'You will direct to me in future at Plymouth', Warren instructed Catharine Macaulay,

where we are again happily fixed, I believe for the remainder of life. For though the pleasant mount where you visited us has many charms in the soft season of the year, yet view it through all its changes, I think Plymouth by far the most eligible residence. I wish I could flatter myself with the idea of once seeing my friend here, I am sure she would enjoy her visit in a higher degree than she did at

Milton. I have always felt more happy in this place where I have a little social circle around me than I did in my residence nearer the capital. Indeed, I think we should both enjoy a felicity unknown to the interested and unfeeling part of mankind if we could spend a few days together in the pleasant little village of Plymouth beneath the shade of retirement and philosophical contemplation.[113]

While Milton has a temporary quality, a mutability that Warren infers is symptomatic of its proximity to fashionable, mercantile Boston, Plymouth is described in terms of a rural permanence and felicity set beyond seasonal change. Retirement here affords a perfect combination of sociable domesticity and sublime reflection: the size of the little circle is far too small to herald modish dissipation but large enough to temper the potentially anti-social tendencies of philosophic contemplation.[114] Warren's snipe at the interested and unfeeling contains her indictment of a public sphere where the betrayal of social attachment and the abandonment of republican principle had become, for her, mutually symptomatic. Plymouth's virtuous retirement affords its own rewards beyond the selfish gratification of private ambition in the public sphere. As Warren imagines herself and Macaulay happy in their disaffected privacy, she represents the virtue now sadly forsaken by faithless public men being rediscovered in the sharing of social affection and political reflection between true republican friends.

In her *History*, Warren described how public, patriotic virtue had, in the years following the war, been eroded by a selfishness she described as both savage and modern. 'Valor', she wrote,

is an instinct that appears among savages as a dictate of nature planted for self-defence; but patriotism, on the diffusive principles of general benevolence, is the child of society. This virtue, with the fair accomplishments of science, gradually grows and increases with civilization until refinement is wrought to a height that poisons and corrupts the heart. This appears when the accumulation of wealth is rapid and the gratifications of appetite become easy; the seeds of benevolence are then destroyed and the man reverts back to selfish barbarism and feels no check to his boundless ambition.[115]

This is perhaps a familiar enough narrative, but it is the sheer speed of its stages and transitions that here seems most startling. Warren's

[113] MOW to CM, 21 May 1791, MOWP1. The Warrens had sold Tremont and returned to Plymouth in 1788. Macaulay sadly died before this letter arrived in England.
[114] My account of Warren's retirement here owes much to conversations with Emma Major.   [115] MOW, *History*, 85.

breakneck version of history and modernity seems to allow the exercise of virtue very little space. Her account of the squeezing-out of diffusive patriotism from both ends of the scale of civilization chimes interestingly with William Robertson's account of savagery in his earlier *History of America*. Robertson argued that a 'savage' love of country was an extension of self-love and the sense of independence. Here, the process of patriotic identification was a question of associating the interest of one's country with one's own rather than the other way round—a process that depended on the total absence of sensibility and sociability. 'The heart of a savage', Robertson wrote, was 'only capable of forming connections which are little diffused. There is little correspondence or exchange of those good offices which strengthen attachment, mollify the heart and sweeten the intercourse of life'.[116] As a consequence of their highly limited 'correspondence', Robertson argued that savage societies lacked sexual appetite, familial or filial affection, and, therefore, were utterly unsentimental. 'Among them', he wrote, 'the pride of independence produces almost the same effects with interestedness in a more advanced state of society. It renders everyone a man to himself and renders the gratifications of his own wishes the measure and end of conduct'.[117] As the independence of Robertson's savage is based upon a form of self-love that precludes the sociable exchange of affections, so the effects of modern civilized advancement are also, he says, found in an atomized insensibility. At both ends of the scale individual desire or ambition erases communal sentiment thereby destroying patriotic sociability. And this (echoing Robertson's language of 'diffusion') is precisely the circular narrative of societal development to which Warren, in her *History*, attributed the decline of patriotic feeling in post-war America.

Patriotic feeling is squashed, she says in the passage above, under the pressure of a selfishness which the progress of refinement rather encourages than prevents. The ambition that might, in another (perhaps more Spartan) civic humanist register, lead virtuous men to compete as equals in the public sphere is, in Warren's state of civilized modernity,

[116] William Robertson, *The History of America* (Dublin: Price, Whitestone *et al.*, 1778), 159–60. Given Warren's liking for Scottish Enlightenment works, particularly histories, and her ready supply of books from England, it is highly likely that she would have come across Robertson's *History*.
[117] Robertson, *The History of America*, 158.

merely the agent of the heart's corruption.[118] For her, patriotism, the 'child of society', appears to exist only in a tentatively held middle ground between savage independence and the insensibility of refined modernity.[119] There is, then, perhaps something of the sentimental ideal of Warren's 'patriarchal life' here: patriotism is best found in the limited sociability of a middle stage where the exchange of affection and benevolence has not been distracted by the alternate gratifications of commercial desire. This sentimental patriotic space, sandwiched somewhere between savagery and modernity, suggests the very benefits Warren saw in her own rural retirement at Plymouth. It is also a space she associated with the sort of private feeling thought the appropriate possession of women.

VII An Immutable Attachment

In July 1789 Mercy Warren told Catharine Macaulay just how much she 'esteemed' and 'valued' the affection of 'a friend whom neither time nor distance nor the accidents of life will lead me to view with an indifferent eye'. But, she wrote,

> though we may feel an immutable attachment, yet we live in an age of revolution when not only the most extraordinary political events are exhibited, but the most sudden reverse of private friendships and a dereliction of former attachments at once surprises and wounds the heart disposed to cultivate the social and benevolent affections to the last moment of existence.[120]

Warren characteristically links private dereliction to political caprice. While the age of revolution merely confirms the insensibility of the public sphere, women's friendship is the source of something more enduring: 'thus from the instability of the human character I have been led to expect every thing and to fear nothing beneath the supreme being. Why should we, if we feel a firmness of mind that renders us independent of... political change?'[121] Macaulay's and Warren's fearless 'immutable attachment' here becomes the basis of a political identity

---

[118] Warren found the idea of Sparta quite appealing on these very grounds. In her *History*, James Otis's patriotic virtues are described as Spartan. MOW, *History*, 49.
[119] Warren continually made this point in her *History*, See, for example, MOW, *History*, 677, on the effects of modern party prejudice.
[120] MOW to CM, July 1789, MOWP1.   [121] Ibid.

that is not liable to corruption because it is so successfully preserved and protected by sentimental sociability. Their mutual affection and disaffection, their shared experience of Atlantic dereliction, have, by the end of the passage, granted them an indisputable independence. Women friends and (in Warren's words) 'politicians', she and Macaulay are said to possess a steadfastness set beyond the temporary temporality of modern politicking. This republican firmness is perhaps even associated here with the permanence of the providential power which lends them resolution.[122] If Warren connected herself and Macaulay to a political independence that seems here both admonitory and visionary, then there was no surprise that she concluded her letter by sharing with her friend a claim to the character of a republican historian. 'Are you, madam,' she asked Macaulay, 'writing the history of American affairs for the last twenty years as is reported?'[123] Warren probably already suspected there was not much substance to the then often-repeated rumour and followed her enquiry by putting her own name to the history of America's revolution, independence, and Federalist decline and fall: 'You shall have the annals in two or three volumes collected, if life is spared, by your friend and humble servant M. Warren'. Macaulay, who by the turn of that decade was describing her 'historical laurels' as 'waning', was more than happy for Warren to adopt them. 'I look with impatience', she encouraged her friend, 'for yr history of the American Revolution because I expect it will be the most authentic account of that grand event with sagacious reflections on the subject of genuine liberty'.[124] Macaulay clearly understood how Warren's feelings of political marginality in the new United States would make her *History* particularly distinctive.

From the later 1780s onwards, Warren's letters and other writings are dominated by her profound sense of her difference from, and disenchantment with, a public political culture she now despised and the men who engaged in it. She often expressed this sense of difference in terms of a disavowal or refusal which suggests a civic-humanist notion of retirement. 'Why do my friends call me out on politics?', she wrote in

[122] See MOW to CM, 4 Dec. 1774.   [123] MOW to CM, July 1789, MOWP1.
[124] MOW to CM, July 1789, MOWP1. CM to MOW, n.d., 1788, GLC. See Devoney Looser, ' "Those Historical Laurels which Once Graced My Brow are Now in their Wane": Catharine Macaulay's Last Years and Legacy', *Studies in Romanticism*, 42 (2003), 203–25.

typical mock-angry terms to Elbridge Gerry. 'I wish to leave the bustle, the altercation, the intrigues of designing men and the pantomimes that dance in shoals about the stage to the wisdom and sagacity of a few'. 'Perhaps,' she concluded darkly, 'they may keep the bark from sinking'.[125] The exasperated language here might well be that of a refusal of a political appointment or a disillusioned withdrawal from public office. Warren often wrote, in the late 1780s and 1790s, with this tone of disgusted retrospection that also managed to suggest that her unquestionably virtuous and enviable privacy was the enforced condition of the way history had failed both herself and her country. Most intriguingly, these repeated disavowals and stresses on the value of the private come at the point in her career when she was most vocal, most politically articulate. In her letters and later in her *History*, 'immutable' affection (such as that which she and Macaulay shared) and public disaffection form the basis of a privacy which is the qualifying condition of her politics. Warren repeatedly used the language of wounded sensibility and private disavowal effectively to legitimate her political interventions.

I now want to quote one of Warren's letters which makes this point very clearly. The letter is from Warren to Sam Adams in answer to his request that she add her voice to the debate on America's constitutional future. It is worth quoting in full:

Dear Sir,

Your message was faithfully delivered by your friend. When the balance of oppression hung heavily over this land, it was the indispensable duty of every one to cast but a single mite into the opposite scale. At the request of yourself and some others of your patriotic associates, I then hazarded to the public eye several political pieces which at that time were thought to have some merit. The great struggle is over, independence is gained, but the origin of the dispute and the defenders of the freedom of their country are few of them known—and the prize thought by many not worth the conflict. I have lived long enough to see so much of the baseness and ingratitude of mankind towards some who have given the best of their lives to the public that it is a matter of perfect indifference to me whither my family and friends are depressed by the institution of a new order of nobility or by the shameful dereliction of the principles of old republican veterans; by a combination of professional characters; by the Cincinatti in military habiliments; or by the neglect, inattention or desertion of former friends. I therefore think best for me to continue a silent spectator of the

[125] MOW to 'the honourable——member of congress' [EG], n.d., 1796, MOWP1.

encroachments of bold ambition; while a gentleman whose political consideration is unsupported, even by some of those patriots from who he has the highest claim and who all acknowledge his merits.

I would not look ahead or even dream of the manoeuvres of politicians or the intrigues of statesmen—sensible that neither the sleeping or the waking reveries of the muses can be influential in any degree amidst the bustle for place and distinction, for fortune and rank, that has at this period almost wholly eradicated the nobler feelings of the soul.

I love my country. I revere the few virtuous and uniform characters that yet adorn it and equally despise the servility and duplicity of others. But though sensibility may be wounded by the delinquency of private *friendship*, the patriotic feelings which once animated my pen are not less hurt by seeing the advantages which America had obtained by the blood of her sons wantonly sported away by luxury and inattention, by imbecility and ambition. Yet while my family and connexions *whom you sir very well know* seem to be forgotten and my *husband* in private life, I think the quiet contemplation of the instability of human affairs, the fickleness of popular opinion, the dignity of independence, the weakness of adulation, and the beauty of virtue is the most becoming line of conduct for your friend and humble servant, M. Warren.[126]

This is a riveting letter, and a very rude one too. Sam Adams may escape association with Warren's despised 'new order', but she is certainly representing him as guilty of inattention and a certain 'delinquency'. Warren again connects herself to stillness and spectatorship, setting her position of observant immobility against the corrupting bustle of the public sphere. All the elements of that disenchantment I have been suggesting as characteristic of her later writing are here: the deep sense of familial injury; the attack on a politics of duplicity and display; the deleterious effect of personal ambition on revolutionary principles; the link between public and private dereliction; and the indissolubility of her patriotic feeling and her wounded sensibility. Adams could be left in no doubt as to what really animated Warren's political pen. On a first reading, her identity here seems entirely dependent on the treatment of James Warren, but this is rather missing the point of her sneaky political self-determination. She certainly expresses a connubial resentment that was (for her) undoubtedly genuine, but it is also, in terms of what this letter is really doing, clearly and self-consciously strategic. The wife of

---

[126] MOW to Sam Adams, 26 Feb. 1786, MOWP1. The date of this letter, as with many reworked and retranscribed letters in the Warren papers, is possibly incorrect.

the injured and rejected public man, she tells Adams, cannot and will not speak out. Observing a companionate virtuous silence is, of course, she says, the most becoming line of womanly conduct. There can be no doubt that Warren is deftly exploiting all the conventional wisdom on feminine propriety here in order to reinforce the sense of her own unassailable privacy and sensibility—*her* righteous, moral, domestic character. Adams is left accused of neglect and importunacy while she claims a gendered high ground. Indeed, her professions of feminine silence belie the vigorous political noise that she is already making in a letter which she knows will be read by others than the man she is presently insulting. And, of course, they also belie in advance the even louder noise she was about to make in the constitutional debate under the name of 'a Columbian patriot'.

VIII A Columbian Patriot

'Does anything yet transpire from the *conclave*?' a sceptical Mercy Warren asked Elbridge Gerry of the Federal convention in 1787:

> Or is all yet locked up in silence and secrecy? Be it so: yet some of us have lived long enough not to expect every thing great, good and excellent from so imperfect a creature as man, therefore can patiently wait till the best systems the wisest of them can devise are sufficiently ripened for the vulgar eye; my own opticks will never again be deceived by the false glossery of pretended statesmen and superficial politicians, therefore shall not be disappointed either at the mouse or the mountain that this long labour may produce.[127]

Warren (always fond of using her own troubled eyesight in a figurative relation to her political vision) here sees herself, with the rest of America, in collective political exclusion.[128] She is positioned with the 'vulgar eye' that the closed doors of Philadelphia seem to pronounce unqualified to scrutinize the operations of government. But even the vulgar eye can claim, she says, a leisurely detachment to the labours of pretended

---

[127] MOW to EG, n.d. [summer], 1787. MOWP1.
[128] Instances of Warren's metaphoric use of her own sight are numerous, but see, for example, MOW to GW, 10 Oct. 1793, MOWP1: 'It is my opinion that a disclosure of the intrigues and designs of a powerful class will be more generally laid open in future than they have been in times past. The weakness of my opticks, I mean literally not politically, must prevent me saying more by candlelight, but it does not require the meridian sun to see that some of the great political projects are mere matter of moonshine and only held up as a tub for the people to gaze at till they lose sight of more important objects.'

statesmen. Typically for the Anti-Federal Warren, retirement on the debarred margins of political culture grants its own calm authority.

As I have been suggesting, it was during the debate on the national constitution that Warren's distinctively assured political voice really emerged. In a letter she must have felt compelled to write to Catharine Macaulay just three days after the constitutional proposals were published, she said she was afraid that their adoption would 'distort the fairest features in the political face of America'. 'We have struggled for liberty and made costly sacrifices at her shrine,' she told her friend, 'and there are still many among us who revere her name too much to relinquish beyond a certain medium, the rights of man for the dignity of government'.[129] The first effect of the proposed constitution was, she said, a sort of aghast silence. 'Almost every one whom I have yet seen reads with attention, folds the page with solemnity and silently [illegible] his own opinion within his own head as if afraid of interrupting the calm expectation that has pervaded all ranks for several months past'.[130] As Warren reworked this passage for her *History*, this silence suggested profound political disappointment:

Many of the intelligent yeomanry and of the great bulk of independent landholders, who had tasted the sweets of mediocrity, equality, and liberty, read every unconditional ratification of the new system in silent anguish, folded the solemn page with a sigh, and wept over the manes of the native sons of America who had sold their lives to leave the legacy of freedom to their children.[131]

It was clearly important to the elite republican Warren to claim that Anti-Federalists' attachment to the land or revolution principles were at one with their social rank and intellectual respectability, for, as previously discussed, it had become very easy to dismiss political opposition in Massachusetts as insurgency.[132] Here she uses an image of wounded

[129] MOW to CM, 28 Sept. and 15 Dec. 1787, MOWP1.
[130] MOW to CM, 28 Sept. 1787, MOWP1. [131] MOW, *History*, 661.
[132] See Saul Cornell's ground-breaking discussions of the differences of plebeian, middling, and elite Anti-Federalism in his *The Other Founders*, part 1, particularly 80–120. See also Lienesch, 'Reinterpreting Rebellion', 181–2 (who regards Warren's elite Anti-Federalism as something like class treachery); MOW, *History*, 651–6; see also ibid. 658: 'these objections were not the result of ignorance; they were made by men of the first abilities in every state . . . apprehensive of being precipitated, without due consideration into the adoption of a system that might bind them and their posterity in the chains of despotism.' Warren clearly uses the rhetoric of the revolutionary spirit of 1775 here to legitimate Anti-Federalism.

sentiment to reinforce perceptions of the integrity of her position. Those grieving for America's lost liberties are melancholic yeomen, she insists, not belligerent rebels. The reputability, rank, and status of Anti-Federalism are confirmed for Warren by a mournful sincerity of feeling which itself seems to grant the political rectitude the Federal constitution apparently betrays.

Just before she published her *Observations on the New Constitution and on the Federal and State Conventions*, a self-satisfied Warren told Catharine Macaulay:

> If you wish to know more of the present ideas of your friend and the consequences apprehended from the hasty adoption of the new form of government, I will whisper you—you may find them at large in the subjoined manuscripts I now enclose, with a pamphlet entitled the Columbian Patriot by the same hand.[133]

'Whisper' was Warren's and Macaulay's shorthand for the political mandate of their friendship. Some years earlier, for example, Warren had told Macaulay how the 'soft whispers of private friendship' might make women superior 'politicians' in a world where the masculine public sphere was regretfully characterized by ambition and caprice.[134] Warren's whispers, then, disclosed the political voice of the Columbian Patriot. The state conventions were now, she wrote, threatening the 'adoption of a mode of government that militates with . . . all ideas of republicanism and the equal rights of men':

> literary talents may be prostituted and the powers of genius debased to subserve the purposes of ambition or avarice; but the feelings of the heart will dictate the language of truth, and the simplicity of her accents will proclaim the infamy of those, who betray the rights of the people, under the specious, and popular pretence of *justice, consolidation,* and *dignity*.[135]

Warren's pamphlet (which one venerable constitutional historian musingly described as 'very readable' before wrongly attributing it to Elbridge Gerry) sets out eighteen objections to the constitution, including a closely argued polemic for a bill of rights.[136] The *Observations*

[133] MOW to CM, 15 Dec. 1787, MOWP1.
[134] MOW to CM, 4 Dec. 1774, MOWP1. See my reading of this letter in Chapter 4.
[135] MOW, *Observations*, 282.
[136] Harding, *The Contest over the Ratification of the Federal Constitution in the State of Massachusetts*, 19. For a summary of Warren's arguments in her *Observations*, see also

is distinguished by that deep suspicion of a pseudo-aristocratic abuse of power which Herbert Storing finds so characteristic of Massachusetts' Anti-Federalism and a very distinctive language of wounded feeling and sensibility.[137] The political style echoes the rousing revolutionary jeremiads of Warren's letters of the mid-1770s as well as Catharine Macaulay's introduction to her *History*, accusing her fellow-citizens of a dangerous inattention to their liberties while claiming Liberty's 'animation' for herself:[138]

> Animated with the firmest zeal for the interest of this country, the peace and union of the American states, and the freedom and happiness of a people who have made the most costly sacrifices in the cause of liberty—who have braved the power of Britain, weathered the convulsions of war, and waded through the blood of friends and foes to establish their independence, and to support the freedom of the human mind; I cannot silently witness this degradation without calling on them, before they are compelled to blush at their own servitude, and to turn back their languid eyes on their lost liberties—to consider, that the character of nations generally changes at the moment of revolution—and when patriotism is discountenanced and public virtue becomes the ridicule of the sycophant—when every man out of liberality, firmness and penetration, who cannot lick the hand stretched out to oppress, is deemed an enemy to the State—then is the gulf of despotism set open, and the grades to slavery, though rapid, are scarce perceptible—the genius drags heavily its iron chain—science is neglected, and real merit flies to the shades for security from reproach—the mind becomes enervated and the national character sinks to a kind of apathy with only energy sufficient to curse the beast that gave it milk... [139]

Warren's account of her contemporaries' dumb Federalist distraction and her own political assiduity recalls some passages on the benefits of sensibility in her letters to her sons.

Raymond Pollin and Constance Pollin, 'Mercy Otis Warren: Patriot Founding Mother', *Daughters of the American Revolution Magazine*, 123 (1989), 104–5, 150–1. See also Zagarri, *A Woman's Dilemma*, 122–3, and Richards, *Mercy Otis Warren*, 121–4. It proved effective for the Anti-Federal opposition in New York before that state moved towards ratification, with a large print run as a pamphlet and serialized publication in the *New York Journal*. The serialization began on 2 Apr. 1788. New York ratified (with objections) on 26 July.

[137] See Storing, *The Complete Anti-Federalist*, iv. 3.
[138] See my reading of Macaulay's appropriation of the language of liberty in the introduction to her *History* in Chapter 2 of this book.
[139] MOW, *Observations*, 272.

'Where there is much sensibility,' Warren told George in 1785, 'the mind lies open to a thousand avenues of pain'. Such unguarded personalities inevitably suffered injuries of feeling, Warren said, but also possessed an energy that suggested to her what it really meant to be human: 'thus framed the agent has a more arduous work—and perhaps a higher reward ... than the ox who treads the glade, returns to his fodder and reposes in the stall of his sordid master'.[140] In her *Observations*, Warren applies the same vocabulary of bovine insensibility to her contemporaries' failure to beware their liberties as they ought. While those who complacently accept the constitutional proposals are described as enervated oxen who might later curse their own dependency, she takes possession of a republican sensibility whose heightened sensitivity grants a kind of political ability to scrutinize, question, and provide a critique of government.

In her *History*, Warren repeated this account of Anti-Federalism as a politics of sensibility. The constitution, 'doubtful in its origin and dangerous in its aspect', appeared 'very alarming to the feelings of men, who were *tremblingly alive* to the smallest encroachment of rights and privileges'.[141] Anti-Federalism seems here a sort of sensitive mimosa instinctually recoiling from constitutional contact.[142] The political energy, the admonitory assurance, of Warren's *Observations*, were thus bound up with (as she put it to George) 'that susceptibility ... the parental, the filial and the family affections ... the social and benevolent feelings' she associated with sensibility.[143] Her denomination of herself as the 'Columbian Patriot' constituted a strong claim to the sort of political identity she clearly wished for but found wanting in the 'critical period'.

[140] MOW to GW, 4 July 1785, MOWP1.
[141] MOW, *History*, 663. Emphasis in orignal.
[142] The mimosa, or 'sensitive plant', was, of course, a common eighteenth-century analogy for the effects of sensibility. An excellent introductory account to the language of sensibility in the period can be found in Markman Ellis's first chapter of his *The Politics of Sensibility: Race, Gender and Commerce in the Sentimental Novel* (Cambridge: Cambridge University Press, 1998). See also: Janet Todd, *Sensibility: An Introduction* (London: Methuen, 1986); Syndey McMillan Conger (ed.), *Sensibility in Transformation: Creative Resistance to Sentiment from the Augustans to the Romantics* (London: Associated University Presses, 1990); G. J. Barker Benfield, *The Culture of Sensibility Sex and Society in Eighteenth-Century Britain* (Chicago: University of Chicago Press, 1992). On sensibility in early republican America, see the exciting work of Sarah Knox, 'A Cultural History of Sensibility in the Era of the American Revolution', Ph.D. Diss (Oxford University, 1999). [143] MOW to GW, 4 July 1785, MOWP1.

Mercy Warren's later political and historical writing made the 'philosophy' and contemplative disaffection she said distinguished her own retirement; the sociability and feeling she associated with friendship and family; and the sentiment and sensibility deemed to characterize the private characters of women, the qualifying conditions of a politics she thought truly republican. Forever obdurate in her sense of ideological difference, Warren set what she stood for in opposition to a masculine public, political culture whose hallmarks are always overweening ambition, inevitable duplicity, and empty display. Because her gender supposedly distanced her from the nation's new contentious party prejudices; because her privacy and retirement excluded her from the public sphere; because, as a woman, she could claim a sort of moral indifference, even superiority, to the petty hustle and bustle of modern politicking, she might claim a political character that was untainted, authentic, and somehow said to be beyond reproach.

Thus Warren used the displacement and exclusion she experienced in the golden age of Federalism as her passport to political and literary participation in the debate on the nation's future. For her, sentimental disaffection enabled political intervention: the authenticity of the private feeling itself intimated the indisputable nature of the public voice. In her *History* she found many ways of suggesting this. She might, for example, draw attention to her gender and the qualities of moral incontrovertibility associated with it ('the historian has never laid aside the tenderness of the sex or the friend').[144] Or she might divide her authorial and sentimental personae to suggest an unquestionable objectivity ('the heart of the annalist may sometimes be hurt by political deviations which the pen of the historian is obliged to record').[145] Or, indeed, she might speak the language of the heart through an abstracted masculine pronoun ('truth is most likely to be exhibited ... when the feelings of the heart can be expressed without suffering itself to be disguised by the prejudices of the man').[146] Warren found that the normative associations and traditional expectations her era identified with her gender (which she, as many other women, knew to limit her potential) nonetheless afforded, in a whole variety of ways, legitimation for her political character and her public role as a writer. I now want to move towards a conclusion with a

[144] MOW, *History*, p. xliii.   [145] Ibid. 675.   [146] Ibid. 4.

brief reading of the language of republican 'boundaries' in Warren's *History*, suggesting one of the ways she used her own gendered and sentimental identity in conjunction with the public authority she claimed as America's historian.

IX Setting Boundaries

Many readings of Warren's *History* point out its isolationist tendencies.[147] This is not just a feature of her discussions of foreign policy (though of course she has much to say about what she sees as the damaging effects of European goods and treaties).[148] Rather, it proceeds from her traditionally republican concern with what time and empire might do to national integrity, as well as from her recurrent and related preoccupation with the human cost of westward expansion. Warren had been expressing unease that America, like the classical republics before it, was doomed to lose itself in the control of its provinces for over twenty years. This concern realizes itself in the *History*'s dominating language of limits and boundaries, which, threadlike, ties her narrative of the seventeenth and eighteenth centuries together. 'Boundless' is a word that Warren uses in the *History* in relation to the geography of the United States, but it is also consistently associated with the private desires and personal ambitions she is convinced have hastened the republic on towards irrevocable decline. In terms of national geography, her often-expressed anxieties about 'a country almost without bounds' echo that peculiar horror that earlier British texts associated with the idea of America, which, in the rapidity of its population growth and its apparently interminable territory, seems troublingly able to expand perpetually

---

[147] See, for example, Zagarri, *A Woman's Dilemma*, 144–5; Richards, *Mercy Otis Warren*, 142. General discussions of Warren's *History* include Lester Cohen, *The Revolutionary Histories: Contemporary Narratives of the American Revolution* (Ithaca, NY: Cornell University Press, 1980); Lester Cohen, 'Explaining the Revolution: Ideology and Ethics in Mercy Otis Warren's Historical Theory', *William and Mary Quarterly*, 37 (1980), 200–18; Alma Lurtz, 'Early American Women Historians', *Boston Public Library Quarterly*, 8 (1956), 85–99; Merle Curtis, *Human Nature in American Historical Thought* (Columbia: University of Missouri Press, 1968); Lawrence J. Friedman and Arthur Schaffer, 'Mercy Otis Warren and the Politics of Historical Nationalism', *New England Quarterly*, 48 (1975), 194–215; Arthur H. Schaffer, *The Politics of History: Writing the History of the American Revolution 1783–1815* (Chicago: Precedent, 1975). Friedman and Schaffer's is a rather bald and un-nuanced approach.
[148] See, for example, MOW, *History*, 650, and, on Jay's Treaty, 668–9.

through space and time.[149] Warren's other use of 'boundless' suggests the worrying energy she associates with commercial and imperial desire ('forever kindling a fire and collecting fuel to keep the flame alive that consumes one half of the globe') and the youthful ambition that is often, for her, embodied in the dangerous and shadowy figure of Alexander Hamilton: 'Americans had nurtured sons of boundless ambition... in the yet simple bosom of their country.'[150] Warren's *History* is preoccupied with the sheer haste of American modernity (always 'increasing astonishingly... improving rapidly'), and written into this preoccupation is the underlying fear that its decline and fall will be equally speedy.[151] Her narrative constantly strives to find ways of reining in America (described as a reckless Hamiltonian youth who has too 'rapidly passed through the grades of youth and puberty') in both historical time and geographic space.[152]

Warren's desire to rein in and police America's 'boundaries of nature' in the *History* held a particular resonance for her in the terrible moral implications of the *imperium*'s westward push. Her concerns with land proprietorship and colonial–native conflict are at the centre of her critique of modern America. It says something about the particular cast of her political disposition that her only consolation in Winslow's army appointment—amidst all her disgust at his mission's objective and her often-expressed fears for his life—was the thought that he might be able to provide her with useful information about native society and manners.[153] It was something she clearly saw at the heart of her historical project. 'You cannot wonder,' she told Winslow (who was by then used

---

[149] MOW, *History*, 698. Completely different instances of this language of horror in reference to America's size and speed are found in texts as diverse as James Thomson's *Seasons* [1744], William Robertson's *History of America* [1778], and Samuel Johnson's *Taxation no Tyranny!* [1775]. [150] MOW, *History*, 645, 618.
[151] Ibid. 669.
[152] Ibid. 600; see also 639. Descriptions of America as an unruly child or youth pepper Warren's writing from the 1780s and 1790s. See, for example, the following from her observations: 'America has in many instances resembled the conduct of a restless, vigorous, luxurious youth, prematurely emancipated from the authority of a parent, but without the experience necessary to act with dignity or discretion' (MOW, *Observations*, 285).
[153] Warren clearly really *knew* what Winslow's mission was likely to involve but in her letters has almost managed to convince herself that he is not destined for 'the dreadful work' of 'invest[ing] villages', but rather might simply be able to provide her with useful sociological information about different tribes. MOW to WW, June 1791, MOWP1.

to providing his mother with texts and commentary for her 'annals'), 'if I wish to *monopolise* your information relative to the manners, country, characters, religion and government of the different tribes of savages'.[154] 'I correct, revise, and write a little history,' she told him as he marched westward with St Clair, 'and sometimes look forward with pleasing expectations of making additions from your journals and observations.'[155] There is certainly a persuasive reading of Warren's interest in 'savage' manners as one white woman's anthropological fantasy.[156] Yet she was also someone who had in her youth experienced first-hand the inflammatory issue of native proprietorship, and who, as an adult, repeatedly expressed interest in Indian culture.[157] The figures of Indians in her *History* are perhaps always symbolic in ways that suggest their author's contradictory racial and cultural preconceptions. While certainly the focus of an urgent political and moral concern, this itself is bound up with the very particular tenor of her republicanism.

For Warren this concern derived from the perennial civic-humanist dilemma of how to set a boundary to contain republican virtue before time and space might turn it into imperial corruption. So after her account of the 'sublime and astonishing' Great Lakes, she writes: 'happy it might have been for the Atlantic states had they been contented within these boundaries of nature' instead of 'attempting to wrest from the natives a vast extent of territory which it is very improbable they [i.e. the US] will be long able to govern'.[158] The unbounded West haunts Warren's *History* as the metaphoric ground for the relentless narrative of a modernity impelled ever onward by an expansionist and destructive political–economic desire. The narrative always culminates with colonial–native conflict, symptomatic of that violent imperial cruelty which, for her, has set the seal on the republic's inevitable destruction. Warren's doubled fear of the 'boundless' thus feeds itself in her *History* on these

---

[154] MOW to WW, n.d. but early Sept., 1791.
[155] MOW to WW, 16 Sept. 1791. Warren quoted from Winslow's letters to her in 1791 on the manners of the captured Indians at Fort Washington, in her *History*, 286.
[156] For example, Warren's desire for cultural exchange to replace war with American Indians includes the inevitable missionary opportunities. See MOW, *History*, 284. Jeffrey Richards rightly notes Warren's 'horror' of and 'fascination' for the wilderness. Richards, *Mercy Otis Warren*, 141.
[157] See my discussion of these issues in the Introduction to this book. On Warren's critique of Washington's Indian policies, see, for example, MOW to 'the honourable —— member of congress' [EG], n.d., 1795, MOWP1.   [158] MOW, *History*, 186.

powerful and deeply disturbing images of disaster. On a number of occasions, she describes her 'compassionate heart' being 'wounded' in an agonized present or imaginary future coloured by the 'cruel warfare and bloodshed' which devastate America's 'original proprietors'.[159] One of the most startling instances of this is the following:

> It might have been happy for the United States, and happier for the individual 'who weeps alone its lot of woe' if, instead of extending their views over the boundless desert, a *Chinese Wall* had been stretched along the Appalachian ridges that might have kept the nation within the boundaries of nature. This would have prevented the incalculable loss of life and property and have checked the lust of territory, wealth and that ambition which has poured out streams of innocent blood on the forlorn mountains.[160]

The United States' overextended views here provide a contrast to the virtuously bounded perspective of Warren's Western Indians, who are less the generic 'savages' that certainly appear elsewhere in her *History* than they are the pseudo-republican possessors of the 'natural' patriotism she sees forsaken by an administration driven by the imperatives of a brutal imperialism ('their [Indians'] strenuous efforts to retain the boundaries assigned them by nature and providence are viewed . . . as a sanction to . . . rapacity and a warrant from heaven to exterminate the helpless race').[161] The Appalachians' convenient providential boundary bolsters Warren's separatist notion of the natural, which might well rein in Americans' destructive modern energies, but which also, of course, keeps Indians out. The blurring of that natural–national border is marked, as it is so often in Warren's *History*, by the blood with which land is always (in her terms) 'purchased' and which here also suggests her own political–sentimental purchase on the land.[162] Warren draws attention at the beginning of the passage to the ways in which the horror of exceeding nature's limits is doubled on a national and a personal scale. She enters her own narrative as a figure in grief who not only mourns the

---

[159] MOW, *History*, 579, 282.   [160] Ibid., 634.   [161] Ibid., 284.
[162] The purchase of land with blood is one of Warren's favourite pseudo-puritan tropes. Examples of it are found throughout her letters, poems, and *History*. One typical instance is found in this account of the revolutionary fervour of 1775: 'the people of the country were not deficient in point of courage but . . . stood charged for a resistance, that might smite the sceptre'd hand, whenever it should be stretched forth to arrest by force the inheritance purchased by the blood of ancestors, whose self-denying virtues had rivalled the admired heroes of Antiquity' (MOW, *History*, 93).

loss of native life and property to the lust of wealth and territory, but who has lost a son to imperial ambition as well.[163] Warren thus shores up the desire to set a boundary around modern America's disturbing boundlessness with the image of feminine bereavement she clearly identifies as herself.

There is certainly something disturbing in Warren's willingness to write herself and Winslow back into the political language of her *History* (which, of course, she might elsewhere claim was written from a position of disinterested 'philosophic' exteriority). But it also shows just how compelling she felt the normative associations of her gender might be in that context. Here a femininity identified with its utterly conventional meanings of nature, sentiment, family, blood, and privacy stands as a metonym for what was, effectively, Warren's democratic–republican critique of the violent expansionist policies of America's first administrations. In her prefatory address to her *History* and, indeed, in its title, Warren associated the 'biographical' elements of the publication with its 'political' and 'moral' dimensions.[164] Warren's family history and what she describes in her preface as her 'pierced' or 'wounded' sensibility are by no means repeatedly mentioned in the narrative, but quietly underlie the national story told through each of her three volumes, emerging with a jolt at contentious moments like that quoted above.[165] While she might not want to claim the distress and disaffection she has experienced in America's first twenty years of independence as particularly exemplary, perhaps she does, as she appears here in her own narrative mourning the lost sons of the lost republic, want to suggest it is somehow typical. The language of abandonment and anger in Warren's historical account of the 1780s and 1790s was, after all, part of what John Adams found most annoying about it. Warren said her *History* drew the narrative of the revolution's 'termination'. Here that end is found in

---

[163] In her accounts of native–colonial conflict, Warren often describes Indians as property-holders in terms perhaps comparable with her own colonial republican agrarian-farmers. There are a number of moments in her *History* when this emphasis implies a citizenship qualification as well as a nominal equality. See, for example, her account of the burning of Indian farmlands and orchards (MOW, *History*, 282).
[164] The full title being: *The History of the Rise, Progress and Termination of the American Revolution Interspersed with Biographical, Political and Moral Observations*. I also discuss Warren's account of her biographical 'connection' to the 'characters active in the great scenes that produced the revolution and obtained independence for their country' (*History*, p. xliii) in Chapter 4.   [165] MOW, *History*, p. xlii.

two images: the first is the Chinese wall (the ultimately impregnable border in a fantasy of borders) and the other is the grief that is situated at the private margins of American boundlessness. Grief sets a wished-for limit, a boundary around that boundlessness, suggesting the awful personal and cultural resonances of the 'termination' of the revolution's narrative in bereavement.

The conventional meanings of her gender allowed Warren to authorize, defend, and shore up her political and historical articulacy. As I suggested in my reading of her letter to Sam Adams and her *Observations*, the traditional associations of femininity often enabled her to write with her sharp Gibbonian style and ambitious narrative sweep. Here in her *History*, as so often in her later writing, Warren linked political disaffection on the national scale to the singular, sentimental, and what she certainly saw as the indubitable figure of grieving maternity. Federalist America had, for her, betrayed 'republican motherhood'.[166]

There are many other ways, I want to suggest in conclusion, of reading the symbolic and sentimental uses to which Warren put her political disaffection and her gender in her *History* and later writings. I might, for example, have looked at how her association with what she describes as the 'common eye' (which is, in her *History*, most usually weeping) allows her to claim a certain exteriority as a female republican historian to what she represents as a masculine–professional division of labour or learning.[167] Or I could have examined, as Nina Baym has done in some excellent essays, the positive representation of the characters of women of sensibility in her *History*.[168] There are many other important arguments to be made about the ways in which Warren's gender and her particularly classical republicanism affected her self-representation, or

[166] My reading here might be read alongside and against Linda Kerber's account of republican femininity in a rather narrow high Federalist context or Rosemarie Zagarri's discussion of the way the conservative politics of Federalism were particularly enabling for women. See Rosemarie Zagarri, 'Gender and the First Party System', in Doron Ben Atar and Barbara B. Oberg (eds.), *Federalists Reconsidered* (Charlottesville,Va.: University Press of Virginia, 1998), and Linda Kerber, 'The Paradox of Women's Citizenship in the Early Republic: The Case of *Martin vs Massachusetts*, 1805', *American Historical Review*, 97 (1992), 349–78.   [167] See, for example, MOW, *History*, 650.
[168] Nina Baym, 'Between Enlightenment and Victorian: Toward a Narrative of American Women Writers Writing History', *Critical Inquiry*, 18/1 (1991), 22–41, and 'Mercy Otis Warren's Gendered Melodrama of Revolution', *South Atlantic Quarterly*, 90 (1991), 531–54.

inflected her sense of cultural and political difference. She was a contradictory and slippery writer who, as any other author, changed her meaning and mode of address depending on the moment or to whom she was speaking. She might describe, for example, 'philosophy' or 'patriotism' as inherently 'masculine' even as she claimed both as a woman and a writer. She could, as I have suggested, write about American Indians as 'savages', fixed perpetually in a generic state of nature, and then in the next breath go on to discuss the distinctive culture and traditions of native societies which were not, as she well knew, 'savage' at all.[169] Warren was terribly elitist, a patrician New Englander who might describe her husband's electors as the victims of 'vulgar' enthusiasm, or be sniffy about 'shop' men being elevated to govern the nation.[170] Yet she professed a democratic politics of association, parity, and popular sovereignty and, like her husband, thought of herself as a radical plebeian at heart. She had a range of particularly complex accounts of her maternal role, which she often wrote of in terms of weakness and dependency, as well as something that lent her and other women political resolution.[171] Far from being (as they are sometimes represented) minor variants on a monotonous theme, Warren's many accounts of her republicanism are knotty and contradictory.[172] As is the case with most of her contemporaries, addressing a range of correspondents and audiences, the strategic inconsistencies of her writing and the arguments she was capable of making are what make her politics so intriguing. Yet there was one issue that she was never in her later years

[169] Compare, for example, Warren's discussion of the Muskinghums (*History*, 282, 285) with that of the 'savages' (*History*, 85).

[170] See, for example, MOW, *History*, 664, where Warren regrets the prominence of a 'class of men' taken 'from the shop or the more simple occupations of life to command armies and to negotiate with foreign nations'. She holds them responsible for the American fascination with 'ostentation' and 'titles'. Yet she was, as I suggest in my Introduction, from a 'shoppy' family herself.

[171] Instances of this are numerous, but see, for example, MOW to GW, Feb. 1792, MOWP2: 'I dare not disclose the feelings of my soul for fear of *womanish weakness*, maternal anxiety and the creation of apprehensions and dangers that had only an imaginary existence.'

[172] In otherwise excellent work on Warren, Lester Cohen argues that 'the language of republicanism is so consistent and insistent throughout her writings that one discovers in them only one voice, one persona'. Warren, I am suggesting, had many literary personae and was often self-contradictory, as, indeed inevitably, was the republicanism she espoused. Cohen, 'Mercy Otis Warren: The Politics of Language and the Aesthetics of Self', 485.

equivocal about, and that was her strong sense of women's intellectual equality.[173]

Mercy Warren and Catharine Macaulay congratulated themselves on the sexual parity their learning and political acumen confirmed. Warren described Macaulay to her son George (whom, like her other children, she encouraged to read a range of literary and political texts by women) as 'not just an ornament to her own sex but a rival or equal to yours'.[174] She told Winslow in an admonitory letter that she 'had ever considered human nature to be the same in both sexes'.[175] And she and James Warren often expressed an affectionate hubris in the intellectual, political, and literary abilities of 'a wife equal to any man'.[176] In the introduction to her *History* Warren described herself as possessing 'a mind that had not yielded to the assertion that all political attentions lay out of the road of female life'.[177] Out of the normative associations of gender, then, might arise a sense of political legitimacy.

[173] As Lester Cohen correctly points out. Cohen, 'Mercy Otis Warren: The Politics of Language and the Aesthetics of Self', 494.

[174] MOW to GW, n.d., 1794, MOWP1.

[175] Warren's letter to Winslow on Chesterfield was written in 1779 and published in the Boston *Independent Chronicle*, 18 Jan. 1781. See my discussion of the letter in Chapter 5 and also Edmund M. Hayes's useful annotated reprinting of it, 'Mercy Otis Warren versus Lord Chesterfield, 1779', *William and Mary Quarterly*, 40 (1983), 616–21.   [176] JW to MOW, Apr. 1790, MOWP2.

[177] MOW, *History*, p. xli.

Conclusion

Public Voices

'If an interview with my friend before the race of mortality is closed, must not take place,' Mercy Warren wrote to Catharine Macaulay in 1791, 'yet let the interchange of letters be frequent while ability is lent to grasp the pen'.[1] Macaulay died at home in Berkshire before she could respond to Warren's last, warm request to continue their epistolary association—her death bringing to an end one of the revolutionary era's most significant political friendships. Yet, during the 1790s, Macaulay's republican voice continued to be heard across the Atlantic through Warren's republication of her response to Edmund Burke's *Reflections on the Revolution in France*: a pamphlet which, as Warren wrote in her introduction to the Boston edition, 'will doubtless gratify every American who has not lost sight of those principles that actuated, and the perseverance that effected, the independence of America'.[2] The shared republican voice of their friendship was also articulated in Warren's later *History* (in which Macaulay is frequently and approvingly cited) as well as in Macaulay's *Letters on Education* (which makes reference to Warren's important influence). At the close of the century, these important works reveal the emergence of that language of political entitlement which became so familiar to the feminism of the century that followed. As I have shown, Warren's *History* made a point of arguing that women made ideal political writers and it was Macaulay's *Letters* which effectively began that crucial British debate on women's civil rights in which another female republican—Mary Wollstonecraft—was to figure so significantly. In the year prior to her death, Macaulay

---

[1] MOW to CM, 21 May 1791, MOWP1.
[2] MOW, 'Introduction', to CM, *Observations on the Reflections of the Right Honourable Edmund Burke on the Revolution in France in a Letter to the Right Honourable Earl of Stanhope*, 2nd edn. (Boston: I. Thomas and E. T. Andrews, 1791), 1.

closed a literary career which, since the later 1770s, had been arraigned by particularly nasty accounts of her gender and sexuality, by concluding, in characteristically categorical terms, that there was 'no characteristic difference in sex'.[3]

In this book I have explored how Mercy Warren and Catharine Macaulay saw their republicanism and their femininity, their politics and their gender, as importantly connected and have suggested how various national and international Anglo-American contexts might have altered cultural perceptions of that connection. I looked at how their learning could seem emblematic of the civility that defined ideas of cultural ascendancy and imperial blue water or, conversely, how at other political moments the insistently civic emphases of their republicanism meant that they might be identified with an impassivity set in opposition to the properly 'feminine' feeling of women of a more liberal patriotic hue. Catharine Macaulay and Mercy Warren could be represented as bellicose Minervas or as weeping, bereaved Marias; as sentimental Clarissas taking a stand against parental–political tyranny or as aggressive Medeas striking an unnatural blow at the heart of the imperial or federal family. The radical edge of their republicanism in the debates over the American war and the constitutional formation of the United States also meant that their conservative or federalist opponents might associate them with an insubordination thought equivalent to a sort of gender deviance.

In turn, I argued that Warren and Macaulay might find familiar (even stereotypical) eighteenth-century notions of gender difference to provide useful tropes to bolster and legitimate the political characters they claimed. During the American war, for example, they might sometimes see the painful effects of transatlantic conflict encapsulated in the figures of themselves as women of wounded feeling. And yet they could also often describe their strength of thought or resolution as inherently and laudably 'manly'. On occasion, Warren and Macaulay defended the rectitude of their position by associating it with a feminine sensibility or instinct both represented as irrefutable. Or they might present themselves as female figures of rational exhortation, themselves increasing the nation's stock of virtue. One strand of argument that has run throughout this book has looked at how different ideas of the private and the social,

[3] CM, *Letters on Education with Observations on Religious and Metaphysical Subjects* (London: E. & C. Dilly, 1790), 203.

the domestic and the sentimental, might allow these women to link their experience of their gender—their understanding of their position as women—to a political discourse whose primary values remained public and civic in ways that it is sometimes assumed would logically alienate them.[4] I have also argued that it could be precisely when republicanism seemed most fruitless; when independent civic virtue seemed most lost in a debased public sphere; and when the political ideals with which they identified seemed those which were most distant, or most excluded, from national concerns that Macaulay and Warren felt most able to develop their now familiarly confident public voices. Thus at moments of political disaffection and through identification with some traditional meanings of their gender, Macaulay and Warren might come to be most articulate in their political self-determination.

There have been a number of accounts of Warren and Macaulay that have stressed the (erroneous) assumption that that they had disappointingly little to say about (and to) women. For example, Rosemary Zagarri has argued that Warren's politics effectively prevented her from being interested in the condition of her sex ('Warren's republican sentiments diverted her from considering a broader role for women').[5] For Zagarri and others, the problem seems to be that gender appears to be so often incidental to Macaulay's and Warren's general political concerns: a premiss which apparently admits the conclusion that the republican discourse of political equality somehow distracted or 'diverted' them from articulating a discourse of sexual equality properly coherently. Such a reading implies that Macaulay and Warren were able to separate their gender from their politics. Given that they lived and wrote in an era when ideas of gender difference permeated most cultural debates and

---

[4] See my discussion of John Pocock's account of Macaulay and Warren in this book's Introduction.

[5] Rosemarie Zagarri, 'Gender and the First Party System', in Doron Ben Atar and Barbara B. Oberg (eds.), *Federalists Reconsidered* (Charlottesville, Va.: University Press of Virginia, 1998), 130. Under 'Warren, Mercy Otis' in the index of Rosemarie Zagarri's biography is included 'unwillingness to argue for general reform of woman's role' (Zagarri, *A Woman's Dilemma: Mercy Otis Warren and the American Revolution* (Wheeling, Ill.: Harlan Davidson, 1995), p. 186). Among other examples, after discussing Warren's and Macaulay's friendship, Alfred Young also finds that Warren had 'hardly a word to say about women' (Alfred F. Young, 'The Women of Boston, "Persons of Consequence" in the Making of the American Revolution, 1765–76', in Harriet Applewhite and Darlene B. Levy (eds.), *Women and Politics in the Age of the Democratic Revolution* (Ann Arbor: University of Michigan Press, 1990), 212).

when national and political values might be negotiated by its means, I think that the opposite is the case. Moreover, I would argue that an awareness of the political and economic status of women and a questioning of the discourses that perpetuated their exclusion underwrite much of what Macaulay and Warren produced in the 1760s and 1770s. How else are we to read Macaulay's argument for women's autonomous annuities and the provision for the education of daughters in her utopian *Sketch of a Democratical Form of Government* (1766)? Or the way in which Mercy Warren makes domestic violence the synecdoche of political and imperial oppression in *The Group* (1774)? Macaulay's and Warren's accounts of gender difference and sexual inequality inflect their republicanism in ways that do not always seem fully enunciated or wholly coherent in a manner easily appropriable to the concerns of some modern feminisms, but that, I would argue, are what make them so interesting and so significant. It was not by chance that Warren was so adamant about women's intellectual equality in her later years or that Macaulay articulated a recognizable language of women's citizenship and rights in her *Letters on Education*.

Thus this book has emphasized the importance of the many oblique, normative, or apparently concessionary accounts of their gender to Warren's and Macaulay's articulation of a politics we might certainly want to see in feminist terms. In 1787 Mercy Warren told her brother Samuel Alleyne Otis of her 'horror' at the plans for the new national constitution ('I think America has a set of as deep politicians manoeuvring in her bosom as any country can produce'). The purpose of this letter was to give her brother the news of an addition to his family. Warren had been attending his wife, whom she left 'well in bed' and

delivered of a girl who bids fair to be as beautiful as her sisters—Poor girl—it is said the sex are doomed to slavery, but I hope it will be not her hard fortune to be doubly so by marrying a slave. It appears to me the present generation are fast verging to that disgraceful state ... this shews itself in their readiness to adopt the novelties of system makers—whither they are forging fetters in the furnace of a single despot or whither they will be the still more absurd fabrication of an aristocratic *junto*.[6]

Warren doubles a language of slavery here in ways that would soon be familiar to readers of Mary Wollstonecraft. But how are we to read her

[6] MOW to Samuel Alleyne Otis, n.d., 1787, MOWP1.

representation of the relationship between political and sexual oppression? Does her niece simply provide a conceit through which Warren might more fully express her political opposition to the Federalist ascendancy to her absent (and politically active) brother? Does her 'it is said,' constitute an implicit disavowal of, or dissociation from, the familiar idea of the 'slavery' of 'the sex'? Or perhaps the simple connection of the sex—of women collectively—to an idea of political alienation represents an important statement in itself.

We might begin to read these questions in the context of Jurgen Habermas's influential formulation of the doubling of the private sphere: 'The doubling of the private sphere on the higher plane of the intimate sphere furnished the foundation for an identification of these two roles under the common title of the "private"; ultimately, the political self-understanding of the bourgeois public originated there as well'.[7] Warren's letter to Samuel Alleyne Otis brings into view what her culture deemed most private (women's bodies; the intimate, domestic sphere; the scene of childbirth) and links that doubly excluded privacy to the critique of political relations in the public sphere.[8] There is an outward movement of association between the subjugation of her niece as a dependant within marriage to the disenfranchisement of her future husband by a political system which Warren perceived as pseudo-aristocratic and inimical to the republican ideal of independence. Thus her letter provides a critique of marriage and sexual inequality only inasmuch as it bemoans the devaluing of fraternal political equality into relations of power and dependency. But it does furnish an occasion to imagine those two things as a continuity and thereby to identify the doubly privatized married women of the rising generation with a certain political and potentially public 'self-understanding'.

[7] Jurgen Habermas, *The Structural Transformation of the Public Sphere: An Inquiry into a Category of Bourgeois Society [1966],* trans. Thomas Burger (Cambridge: Polity Press, 1989), 28–9. See Nancy Fraser's important critique of Habermas's model of the private, 'What's Critical about Critical theory?', in Johanna Meehan (ed.), *Feminists Read Habermas* (London: Routledge, 1995) 21–55, and Seyla Benhabib, 'Models of Public Space: Hannah Arendt, the Liberal Tradition and Jurgen Habermas' [1989], in Joan B. Landes (ed.), *Feminism: The Public and the Private* (Oxford: Oxford University Press, 1998), 65–99.
[8] See also Carole Pateman, *The Disorder of Women: Democracy, Feminism and Political Theory* (Oxford: Blackwell, 1989), and Carole Pateman, 'The Fraternal Social Contract', in John Keane (ed.), *Civil Society and the State: New European Perspectives* (London: Verso, 1988), 101–29.

The later writing of Warren and Macaulay afforded many occasions in which such connections between women's sexual and political identities were pictured. In particular, Macaulay's *Letters on Education* (which Warren and Mary Wollstonecraft both deeply admired) suggest the emergence and the importance of a collective public voice for women. Macaulay argued for the politicization of marital relations: 'with a total and absolute exclusion of every political right to the sex in general, married women, whose situation demand a particular indulgence, have hardly a civil right to save them from the grossest injuries.'[9] As Macaulay described courtship and marriage as a dynamic of authority and enslavement, of empire and dependency, she echoed the language of those aristocratic political relations she had spent her lifetime publicly criticizing: 'when the sex have been taught wisdom by education, they will be glad to give up indirect influence for rational privileges; and the precarious sovereignty of an hour... for those established rights, which... may afford protection to the whole sex.'[10] For Macaulay, the education of women in the republicanism she espoused promised a moment in which they might imagine themselves as intellectual and political subjects rather than as beings wholly defined by their gender. Warren, who famously considered 'human nature the same in both sexes', applauded the sexual politics of Macaulay's *Letters on Education*. She described her friend's publication as 'a masterly performance', and insisted her sons read it.[11] In her will, her personal bequest to her granddaughter and namesake, Marcia Warren, was the copy of the *Letters* Macaulay had sent her. Mercy Warren and Catharine Macaulay established the concerns of gender as central to the politics of the revolutionary Atlantic.

[9] CM, *Letters on Education*, 210. [10] Ibid. 215.
[11] MOW to GW, n.d., 1794, MOWP1. MOW, *Independent Chronicle*, 18 Jan. 1781.

Index

A Speedy and Effectual Preparation for the Next World (print) 167–8, 229
Adair, James 154
Adams, Abigail ('Nabby') 194
Adams, Abigail
  correspondence with CM 132
  friendship with MOW 187–97, 257
  on MOW's *History* 213
  relationship with JA 205–6
  trade during the American War of Independence 195
  trip to London 197–8
Adams, John Quincy 262
Adams, John
  on the characters of the Warrens 255–7
  correspondence with CM 7, 10
  disputes and friendship with MOW 195, 207–8, 265–8, 281
  as a Federalist 265
  on feminine political character 210
  on MOW's and CM's friendship 13, 220
  on MOW's *History* 206, 213, 300
  relationship with AA 205–6
Adams, Samuel 126, 236
  MOW's letter to 288–9
Agrippina 116–17
Alexander, William 233–4, 237
Alfred 170
Almon, John 8, 54
Amazon, CM as 41, 151; *see also* Indian
Anarchiad, the 259–60
André, Major John 160
Andrew, Donna 90
Annual Register, The (London), *Proposal for a Female Ministry* 79
Anti-Federalism 249–303
Arendt, Hannah 23–4
  The Human Condition 109
  Rahel Varnhagen 24
Aristocratic women, CM on 100
Arnold, Mrs (Macaulay's sister-in-law) 85, 138

Association Movement 129, 143–4
Atkinson, Richard 94
Austin, Benjamin 226

Bailyn, Bernard 54
Bankruptcy 166
Bannet, Eve Tavor 8
Barbarism 101
  and Shays' Rebellion 256–9, 262, 278
  See also Savagery
Barbauld, Anna Laetitia 81, 193, 233
  Of Inconsistency in our Expectations 102–3
  A Summer Evening's Meditation 193
Barnstable 4–5
Baron, Richard 60
Basire, James 65
Bath 146
Baym, Nina 301
BCC (Boston Committee of Correspondence) 22, 129, 204–6
Benjamin, Walter 171
Bereavement, MOW's experience of 268, 300–1
Bill of Rights, MOW argues for 292
Birthday party, CM's forty-sixth 80–1, 140–1, 167, 170
Blake, William 172
Bloch, Ruth 27
Bluestockings
  CM and 74–86, 174–5
  in early Republican magazines 233
  Enlightenment and nationalistic views of 76–86
  recent critical accounts of 24–6
Bookbinding and designing 55
Boston Magazine 231–4
Boston 29, 189–90
Boswell, James 173
Boudicca 150, 173
Bowdoin, James 12, 126, 139, 241, 246
Brewer, John 54, 78

Index

Britannia
  MOW on 276
  representations of 122–4, 152–7, 164, 173–4
British Musuem 94
Brown, Elizabeth 268
Brown, John, *Estimate of the Manners and Principles of the Times* 44, 105
Brown, Richard 9, 129
Brownlow Street Lying-in Hospital 90–1
Brutus, Marcus Junius
  CM and 49–50, 211
  Libertas print 61–71
Buchan, Lord (John Erskine), friendship with CM 129, 140
Buel, Richard and Joy Day Buel 180
Burgh, James 18, 35, 98
  Political Disquisitions 135
Burgoyne, John 138, 162–3, 171–2
Burke, Edmund 149, 156, 163
  and CM 49, 108–9, 117
  Reflections on the Revolution in France 15, 271
  Thoughts on the Causes of the Present Discontents 39–46
  Treatise on the Sublime and Beautiful 87
Burney, Frances 87
Burr, Esther Edwards 219

Caesar, Julius 61, 223
Cambridge (Massachusetts) 57, 181, 189
Cards, playing at 85, 221; *see also* gambling
Carter, Elizabeth 79, 93, 161, 163, 165, 167
  on *The Nine Living Muses of Great Britain* 77
Cartwright, John 48
Catholic Relief Act 146
Catholicism 105, 146
Cato's Letters 50
Charles I 127–8, 148–9
Charleston, N.C. 201
Chatham, Lord (William Pitt) 6, 47, 65, 230
Chesterfield, Lord (Philip Dormer Stanhope), MOW's critique of 232

Church of England
  and Charles I 127
  CM and 18
Cincinatti, society of 258, 261, 264, 288
Cipriani, Giovani Battista 61–4
Citizenship 20–3, 135–46; *see also* patriotism
Civic virtue, notions of 90–3, 105–9, 113–20
Civilization
  CM on 101–2
  MOW on 284–6
Class
  CM on 98–9
  MOW on 188, 257, 302
Classical republicanism, *see* Republicanism
Cohen, Lester 31, 296
Colley, Linda 30, 151
Commerce
  CM on 238
  and femininity 226–8
  and learning 101–4
  MOW on 195, 238
  in post-war Massachusetts 222–9
Conquest 134
Conversation 19, 68, 84, 106
Conway, Stephen 162
Cooper, William 42
Copley, John Singleton 213
Copyright
  debate on 100–1
  women and literary property 17–18
Cornelia 109–21
Cornell, Saul 291
Corruption (political) 46–54, 281–7
Cosmetics 123, 229
Crumpacker, Laurie 219
Cushing, Thomas 241, 246

Dacier, Anne Lefèvre 73–5, 237
Darly, Matthew 167–8
Day, Thomas 163
Death, CM's fears of 140–1, 167–8
Deloria, Philip 154
Demosthenes 85
Dickinson, John 112–13, 126, 209
Dilly, Edward and Charles 8, 86
Dissipation 165–71; *see also* fashion

Domesticity 90–1, 118, 187–211, 281, 287–90
Duncombe, John, *The Feminiad* 38, 233

Earle, Rebecca 211
Elections
  American 241, 246, 250, 262, 280
  British 42, 48–50, 53, 55–6
Edoxia 275–80
Eel River, Plymouth (Massachusetts) 189, 191
Effeminacy 41–54, 67–68; *see also* Masculinity
Eger, Elizabeth 78
Eleutheria 150
Elizabeth I 80
Empire
  Britain and 162–79, 198–200
  CM on 134–8
  MOW on 297–300
  the United States and 271, 273, 298
  westward course of 18, 231
Engels, Frederick 153
Enlightenment
  debate on savagery and republicanism 152–3
  on women 75, 233–4
  history 285
Espionage
  fears of 139
  Winslow Warren and 216

Family, ideas of 125, 155–62, 176, 199–204, 273–4
Fashion
  in post-war Massachussetts 226–8
  and savagery 171–4
  and war 165–8
  See also Catharine Macaulay
Fast sermons 164
Federal Convention 249, 290
Federalism 249–303
Feeling, *see* sentiment and sensibility
Female Combatants, The (print) 123–4
Female grotesque 174–9
Ferguson, Adam 152, 271
Figurines, Derby porcelain 82, 93–7
Fliegelman, Jay 125, 155, 198
France
  CM's trip to 138–40

Intervention in War of Independence 146
Franklin, Benjamin 139, 266
Freeman, Joanne 214
Freud, Sigmund 151
Friendship 1–3, 9–20, 180–219, 286–90
Fritz, Jean 183, 187

Gambling 271
Geiger, Marianne 147
Gelles, Edith 181, 185, 205–6
Gentleman and Ladies' Town and Country Magazine, The (Boston) 231–4
Gentleman's Magazine, The (London) 12, 148
George III 12, 151, 208
Gerry, Elbridge 215, 251
Gibbon, Edward 19, 271, 278
Gill, Sarah Prince- *see* Prince-Gill, Sarah
Glorious Revolution (1688) 45
Gordon Riots 146, 176
Gordon, William 12, 139
Gould, Eliga 51
Gould, Philip 191
Graham, James 167
Graham, William 162, 169, 174–5, 229
Grand Tour, the 105
Greece
  Athenians 22, 118
  language 104–5
  Spartans 80–1, 153
  virtues of 113
  See also Republicanism
Griffith, Ralph 104
Guest, Harriet 25, 93, 147

Habermas, Jurgen 23, 100–1, 308
Hamilton, Alexander 297
Hamilton, Gavin 115–16
Hancock, John 215, 223–5, 241–3
Harvard University 5, 189, 196
Hastings, Warren, trial of 14
Hay, Carla 147
Hays, Mary, *Female Biography* 5–6, 18, 85, 115, 140–1
Health, and CM 138, 140–1, 143, 170–1
Hicks, Philip 27–8, 212

… Index

Hill, Bridget 16, 98, 112, 144
History, see stadial history; see also Macaulay, Catharine, and Warren, Mercy Otis
Hollis, Thomas 8, 54–71
Hollis, Timothy 56, 85
Holofernes 149
Houghton Library, Thomas Hollis and 57, 61–2, 65
Howard, Stephen 92
Hume, David 40, 127
  on Charles I 148–50
  on scholarship 95, 98
Hutchinson, Thomas 6, 130, 199, 213, 215, 223, 254

Ignorance 106–8
Imperialism, see empire
Indians
  Indenture of 4–5
  CM represented as 152, 173
  Miami 270–1
  MOW on 154, 298–9
  Muskingham 302
  as symbol for American colonies 122–3, 153–4
  Wampanoag 5
  Wyandot 163
Intolerable Acts, CM on 132–8

Jefferson, Thomas 6
Jeremiad, MOW and 183
Johnson, Samuel 35, 58, 154
Judith 149, 173

Karlsen, Carol 219
Kauffman, Angelica
  Cornelia, Mother of the Gracchi Displaying her Children as Her Treasures 111
  and *The Nine Living Muses* 78
Kerber, Linda 26–7, 202
Knott, Sarah 19, 246
Knowles, Mrs, friend of CM 114, 137, 161
Kucich, Greg 120

Landscape, MOW and 272, 276, 279–80

Latin
  CM and 104
  MOW and 5
Learning
  and commerce 103
  women and 70–1
  See also Latin
Letters
  and collaboration 209
  and history 213–18
  and transatlantic circulation 129–30, 212–13
  and women 2–17; 181–219
  See also Macaulay, Catharine and Warren, Mercy Otis
Lewis, Jan 26
Liberty, femininity and 70
Lincoln, Benjamin 202
Lincoln, Hannah 201–2
Lindsey, Theophilus 18, 109
Literary property *see* copyright
Livingston, Catherine (Kitty) 229
Livingston, William 41, 127, 147
Lofft, Capel 143
London Magazine, The 90–1
London
  AA's visit to 197
  City of 4
  Whig and radical opposition of 35–72
Looser, Devoney 24
Lothrop, Ellen 195–6
Loyalism
  in Britain 12, 165, 176
  in America 181, 223–5
Luxury 57, 165, 225–38
Lyttleton, George 61, 88–9

Macaulay, Catharine
  on the American Constitution 15
  on the American War 132–47
  and the bluestocking circle 25, 76–87, 174–5
  as Brutus 61–72, 147–52
  on Charles I 127–8, 149–50
  class position 18
  correspondence with American republicans 125–32
  as a correspondent 10–11, 129–30, 48–50, 212

Index

early life 3–6
on the early Romans 102, 150
on Edmund Burke 108–9, 271
on education 101–9
family connections 5, 35, 177
fashion and 113, 167–71, 229
her feminism 99, 120–1, 309
friendship with MOW 1–20, 131–4, 210–11, 221–47, 276–7, 286–7; with Sarah Prince-Gill 29–30, 128–9; with Thomas Hollis 39, 59–67; with other women 114, 137, 138, 212
health 138–43, 170–1
involvement in British extra-parliamentary opposition 34–54
learning and 73–121, 230–1
on Liberty 34–5, 107
marriage to George Macaulay 6–7, 61, 88–93; to William Graham 162, 169, 174–5, 229
on parliamentary corruption 46–9
portraits of 61–7, 77, 82, 87–9, 93–7, 151–3, 167–8
on post-war America 244
recent critical interpretations of 23–5, 146–7
religion 18–19
representation as grotesque 167–78; as masculine 37–43, 59–72; as an MP 42–3; as savage 152–8; as sentimental 89, 112–20
as a Roman matron 109–21, 276–7
self-representation 34–40, 107
sense of professionalism 93–101
trip to the United States 228–47; to France 138–40
An Address to the People on the Present Important Crisis of Affairs (1774–5 and 1779) 132–8; Works: *The History of England from the Accession of James I to that of the Brunswick Line* (1763–83) 93–100, 127–8, 177 and throughout; *The History of England from the Revolution to the Present time in a Series of Letters* (1778) 141–6; *Letters on Education* (1790) 99, 106, 109, 309; *Loose Remarks . . . on Hobbes* with *A Sketch of A Democratical Form of Government in a Letter to Signor Paoli* (1767 and 1769) 84, 99; *A Modest Plea for the Property of Copyright* (1774) 100–1; *Observations on the Reflections of the Right. Hon. Edmund Burke* (1790) 15, 271; *Observations on Thoughts on the Cause of the Present Discontents* (1770) 39, 46, 108–9; *A Treatise on the Immutability of Moral Truth* (1783) 268
Macaulay, Catharine Sophia (CM's daughter) 105, 145, 276
Macaulay, George
and Brownlow Street Hospital 90
and relationship with CM 6–7, 61, 88–93
Major, Emma 24, 84, 284
Marchant, Henry 47, 85, 126
Marcia (MOW's pseudonym) 199
Marriage
CM's first marriage 88–93, 117; second marriage 171–5, 229
in general 7, 195, 308–9
MOW's marriage 206–9, 253–6
Masculinity, women's claims to 21, 193, 295, 302; *see also* effeminacy, privacy
Mashpee 4–5
Massachusetts 1774–5 10, 1777–8 250, 1780s 221–68
Maternity 91, 145, 159–64, 269, 276–7; *see also* Republican mother
Matrona, see Roman Matron
Mayflower, the 183
Mayhew, Elizabeth 58, 70–1
Mayhew, Jonathan 127–8
McCrea, Jane 163
Medicine 90–1, 140
Mellor, Anne 23–4
Middlesex, debate on parliamentary seat of 43
Millar, John 153
Milton Hill (Boston) 116, 224, 254–5, 272
Milton, John 41, 199
Minerva 151, 174
Miniatures 116–17
Modernity, MOW on 273–4, 284–5
Monarchism 14, 105, 261, 267, 282
Monstrosity, and war 164–5

Montagu, Elizabeth
  MOW and 25
  and *The Nine Living Muses of Great Britain* 79
  views of CM 174–5
Montgomery, Janet Livingston 203
Monthly Review, The (London), on CM's *History* 75–5, 88–9, 149
Moore, J. F, statue of Macaulay 69, 151
More, Hannah 76, 233
Morton, Sarah Wentworth 240
Murray, Judith Sargent 16

Nationalism, and conservatism 80, 176; *see also* loyalism, patriotism
Nationality, women and ideas of 25–6; *see also* patriotism
Neville, Sylas 85, 104
New Hampshire 199
Nine Living Muses of Great Britain, The 77–80, 175
North, Frederick, Lord, administration of 141–6, 162–4
Northern Campaigns 162
Norton, Mary-Beth 26
Nuneham, Lord 39

Olantigh, Kent 5
Olson, Alison Gilbert 8
Otis, Harrison Gray 238
Otis, James 29, 41, 126, 147
Otis, John 3
Otis, Samuel Alleyne 261, 307

Paine, Thomas 19
Paoli, Pascale 84
Parliament 35
  House of Commons 55–6
  House of Lords 41
  Party (political)
  in post-war Massachusetts 223
  and women 107–8, 210–11, 218
Patriotism
  American 180–219
  British 35–53, 63–72
  loyalist 176
  MOW's critique of 284–5
  'savage' 149, 174–6

women and 109–21, 174, 275–80, 174
See also, Republicanism, Roman matron
Patterson, James 223
Philadelphia 248, 290
Pine, Robert Edge, portraits of CM 66, 94
Plutarch's *Lives* 109
Plymouth (Massachusetts) 7, 189–91, 196, 255
Pocock, John 20–3, 102
Pointon, Marcia 78, 117
Politeness 79–86
Portia (AA's pseudonym) 199
Pratt, Samuel Jackson, *Emma Corbett, or, the Miseries of Civil War* 158–60
Price, Richard 139, 161
Priestley, Joseph 19
Prince, Thomas, *History of New England* 128
Prince-Gill, Sarah 29–30, 60, 113–14, 128–9, 212, 219
Prisoners of war, treatment of 101, 139
Privacy
  and femininity 91, 117–20, 183–218
  and masculinity 43–59
  See also domesticity
Public office 38–9, 45–55
Public sphere
  American 180–219
  British 52–9, 67–8, 101, 108, 120
  women and 23–31, 219
  See also Arendt, Civic virtue, Habermas, patriotism
Professionalism
  women writers and 18
  CM and 93–101
Publishers
  American 239–40
  British 8, 54, 63, 100
Pulteney, William 6, 47

Quebec Act, CM on 132–8
Quebec, siege of 203
Quincy, Edmund 57
Quincy, Josiah 8, 85, 126, 132–3

Rack, Edmund 80, 150
Raynal, Abbé, *History of America* 213–14
Read, Catherine 28, 79; 87–8; 109–21
Reading, women and 5, 211
Regicide 128, 149, 175; *see also* Charles I
Religion
  CM and 18, 86,106
  MOW and 18–19, 192–3
Rendall, Jane 26, 75, 116, 202, 218
Republican mother 26–7, 269–70
Republicanism
  in America 180–219
  in Britain 35–175
  classical 6, 20–3, 107, 111
  and feminism 22–3
  See also, Greece, Romans, patriotism
Retirement 189–91, 245, 283–4, 287–8
Reynolds, Joshua, *Discourses* 172
Richards, Jeffrey 3, 187
Richardson, Samuel 53, 105
Richardson, Sarah 186
Robertson, William (historian) 153, 284–5
Robertson, William (poet) 150
Rockingham Whigs 143
Roman Matron 27–8
  CM as 109–21
  MOW on 275–80
Romans
  CM on 101, 150, 153
  Gibbon on 278
  MOW on 279–80
  See also Republicanism
Rosamond, the 228
Rousseau, Jean-Jacques 107, 153
Rush, Benjamin 84, 126
Russell, Jonathan 5
Russo, Mary 175–6
Ryland, John Collett 48, 141

Sainsbury, John 143
Saint Clair, William 270
Saint Stephen, Walbrook, Church of 140
Samuel, Richard 77–9, 175
Sans Souci (club), debate on 220–47
Sans Souci, alias, Free and Easy (play) 240–1
Saratoga, Battle of 138, 171, 214; *see also* Burgoyne, John

Savagery
  CM and 151
  and republicanism 151–4
  MOW on 284–5, 298
Sawbridge, Jacob 4, 177
Sawbridge, John (CM's brother) 34, 129
Sawbridge, John (CM's father) 5
Sayre, Stephen 11, 126, 151
Schnorrenberg, Barbara Brandon 46
Scott, Mary, *The Female Advocate* 76
Scott, Sarah 53
Sennet, Richard 37
Sentiment and sensibility 19–20
  CM and 113–15
  CM described as lacking 148
  MOW and 193–4
  MOW on 294
Sever, Sally 16, 268
Seward, Thomas 38
Sexuality, female 88, 173–5
Shays' Rebellion 257–60
Shoes, MOW's 195
Silk 113–14
Sisterhood
  CM on 25, 85
  MOW and 193–207
Slavery
  and British political culture 38, 134
  and Warren household 4
  MOW's account of the slavery of women 307–9
Sleaford, Lincolnshire 198
Smith, Adam 103, 153
Smith, Paul Hunter 134
Smollet, Tobias, *The Expedition of Humphry Clinker* 53, 173
Sophronia, *see* Prince-Gill, Sarah
South Church, Boston 8, 130
South Sea bubble 4, 177
Sparta 19
  virtues of 80–1, 152
SSBR (Society for the Supporters of the Bill of Rights) 18, 129
Stadial history 113, 153, 284–5, 301–2; *see also* Enlightenment
Staves, Susan 46, 145
Stiles, Ezra 126, 138
Stockton, Samuel 126
Storing, Herbert 293
Sublime, MOW and 280

Talbot, Catherine 93
Taylor, Barbara 22
Tears, over fate of Charles I 148–9; over future of America 276–7, 301
Than, Cecile Mazuco 178
The Parricide (print) 151–4
Thomson, James 45
Thrale, Hesther 174–5
Toplady, Augustus 18
Town and Country Magazine 167–8

United States
CM on constitution of 15
MOW on constitution of 261, 280, 290–7
MOW on geography of 296–7
representation as an Indian 122–3, 153–4
representation as a woman 227–8

Vaughan, Sarah 229
Venus 174–5
Vesey, Elizabeth 84, 165
Virtue, *see* civic virtue, patriotism
Vision, MOW on 290–1, 301

Wahrman, Dror 30, 157
Waldstreicher, David 246
Walpole, Horace 58, 161, 165, 172
Walpole, Robert 43, 193
War, American War of Independence
in America 180–219
in Britain 122–79
Warner, Michael 213
Warren, Charles 269–70, 274
Warren, George 269–70
Warren, Henry 269–70
Warren, James 195
on barbarism 252
family background 188, 252
and farming 188, 253
as father 269
Federalist defamation of 258–61
friendship with Elbridge Gerry 263
with John Adams 208, 266
and letter writing 208
participant in state election for governor 241
on the purchase of Milton Hill 255
relationship with MOW 6–7, 188, 205–9, 253–4
retreat from public life 253
Warren, James (son of MOW) 216, 270
Warren, Joseph 213
Warren, Mercy Otis
on the American Constitution 261, 280, 290–7
on American expansionism 298–301
her Anti-Federalism 249–303
class position and social status 18, 188, 256–7, 302
defends CM's second marriage 229
early life and education 3–5
family connections 3–10
her feminism 210–11, 301–3, 304–9
friendship with AA 187–97; with CM 1–20, 210–11, 131–4, 210–11, 221–47, 276–7, 286–7; with EG 251–65; with Hannah Lincoln 197–98, 201–2; with Hannah Winthrop 181–212; with Janet Livingston Montgomery 203–4; with JA; with other women 16, 187, 192, 196
on George Washington 263–5
on Indians 298–302
as a learned woman 188, 232
letters 180–219; and her *History* 211–19
marriage to James Warren 6–7, 188, 205–9, 253–4
on Martha Washington 264
on masculine political ambition 263–4
on her maternal role 270–9, 300–2
on modernity and patriotism 284–5
on the New England landscape 190–3, 272–3
on the patriarchal life 273–4
on privacy and domesticity 187–211, 281, 287–90
and religion 19, 183, 192
on retirement 189–91, 245, 283–4, 287–88
as a Roman Matron 275–81
on the Sans Souci club 235, 240
on sentiment and sensibility 183, 193–5, 203, 293–5

on women as politicians 210
Works (*see also* letters): *The History of the Rise, Progress and Termination of the American Revolution* (1805) 211–19, 264–75, 285–303; *An Invitation to Retirement* (private poems) 191; *Observations on the New Constitution and on the Federal and State Conventions* (1788) 261, 280, 292–4; *Poems, Dramatic and Miscellaneous* (1790) 15, including: 'To Fidelio, Long Absent on the Great Cause that Agitated all America' 253, 'The Group' 8, 307, 'To the Honorable J. Winthrop esq.' 227, 275, 'The Ladies of Castille' 271, 'A Political Reverie' 192, 'The Sack of Rome' 277–9
Warren, Winslow 216, 222, 269–74, 297–300
Washington, George 126, 160
  to CM 249
  MOW's critique of 264–5
Washington, Martha 264
Wheatley, Phillis 75, 269
Whiggism
  American 180–219
  British 35–72
Wigs 123, 167–70
Wilkes, John 67, 111–12, 149, 151, 234
Wilkes-Hayley, Mary 234
William III 142
Wilson, Kathleen 30, 51
  on female patriotism 176
  on Whig masculinity 67–8
Wilson, Thomas 18, 68, 145
Winslow, Ned 253
Winslow, Penny 187, 195
Winthrop, Hannah 181–212
Winthrop, James 260
Winthrop, John 181, 185, 195
Wiseman, Sue 212
Withey, Lynne 46
Wollstonecraft, Mary 15, 305, 309
Wood, Gordon 222
Wright, Patience 68, 139
Wyvill, Christopher 144,

Yearsely, Ann 75
Yorkshire Association 144–5
Young, Alfred 219

Zagarri, Rosemarie 16, 26 246, 250, 306